SELECTED NEWSPAPER COLUMNS OF

IAN BOXILL

1993-2000

Compiled and Edited by David Eric King
with Delroy Chevers *and* Deborah Fletcher

Arawak publications
Kingston • Jamaica

ISBN 978 976 8282 47 7

25 24 23 4 3 2 1

Arawak publications gratefully acknowledges *The Daily Gleaner Jamaica* for its support in this re-presentation of the best articles written by Dr Ian Boxill over a period of seven years (March 1993 to August 2000) on the Opinion Page of the *Gleaner* in Jamaica. Some spelling and punctuation have been adjusted, and obvious errors have been corrected.

National Library of Jamaica Cataloguing in Publication Data
for this title is available at the NLJ

Paperback ISBN: 978 976 8282 47 7

This edition licensed by special permission of Arawak publications,

Resource Publications
An Imprint of Wipf and Stock Publishers
199 W. 8th Ave., Suite 3
Eugene, OR 97401

www.wipfandstock.com

PAPERBACK ISBN: 978-1-6667-6477-2
EBOOK ISBN 978-1-6667-6479-6

Cover and text design by A.Lewinson-Morgan
Composition by A.Prescod-Jemmott

Set in Chaparall Pro 11/14pt with Economica and Fertigo Pro

Printed in Jamaica & in the United States of America

Table of Contents

Table of Contents

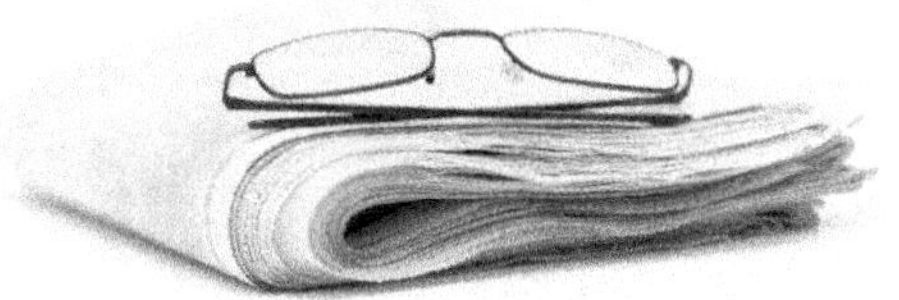

Editor's Preface

In February 1963, the late Dr Eric Williams, at the time the Prime Minister of Trinidad and Tobago and Pro-Chancellor of the University of the West Indies, in delivering the main address to the graduating class at Mona, identified "three particular responsibilities" which he said had now fallen on the shoulders of those who were graduating. Their first responsibility, he told them, would be to their alma mater – The University of the West Indies; the second would be to the West Indian community in general; and the third to themselves. Elaborating further on that third responsibility, Dr Williams pointed to "two powerful obligations" which the graduates seated before him had to themselves: "The first one," he said, "is to defend the national independence at all times. The second is just as important; it is your duty to cultivate **the habit** of reading."

Some members of the listening audience registered surprise when this second obligation was named, not so much because Dr Williams had placed the cultivation of the habit of reading on an equal level of importance as the defence of one's national independence, but more because he seemed to think it necessary to offer such a seemingly mundane piece of advice to university students at such a special moment in their lives. Surely, many in the audience might have thought at the time that one could safely assume that students matriculating into a university would all be proficient readers, let alone students graduating from one! And surely, also, one could safely assume that students graduating from a university would all be, ipso facto, not only proficient readers, but habitual ones as well!

The distinction between reading as a capacity (proficiency) and reading as a tendency, or habit, is an important one, as most teachers of reading know from bitter experience. The verb "to read", used narrowly, refers merely to the process of decoding the meaning of a message presented in writing; in this sense, it represents a capacity. But, in addition, the word may be used more broadly to refer to the habit, or disposition, developed over many years, of obtaining information from written sources. In this sense it represents a tendency. And, indeed, only some persons who acquire the capacity to read ever go on to develop a tendency so to do. Dr Williams continued as follows:

> Ladies and Gentlemen, your graduation does not represent the end of your association with the world of books and ideas. I think I can say, without exaggeration or being offensive, that I can testify personally to the fact it is **not** impossible for you to do your work, whatever it is that you are called upon to do for the society,

and to read at the same time, and to write – and by reading I do not mean reading around your particular subject or the responsibility that you have in the society.

This book, *Finding Common Ground: Selected Newspaper Columns of Ian Boxill, 1993-2000,* literally re-presents the best articles written by Ian Boxill over a period of seven years (March 1993 to August 2000) on the opinion page of the *Daily Gleaner* in Jamaica. The book seeks – more so than the individual articles themselves, which were written with the general public in mind – to help graduates across the Caribbean region fulfil that obligation, spoken of by Dr Williams some fifty-eight years ago, to become habitual readers (and writers). The hope is that they will not only read on matters relating to their own training and work, but also on issues of interest and concern to society in general and to the world today. In particular, the book also targets pre-university and first-year university students – especially those enrolled in degrees that involve basic or advanced expository or argumentative writing. In addition, it lends itself to 6th form students, those in community colleges, teacher-training colleges and other tertiary level institutions, who are learning to formulate and express a personal but informed opinion, in speech or writing, on topical events.

Putting this book together was challenging, given the difficulty the editors had in selecting from among the 300 articles written by Ian Boxill. Next in order of difficulty was the task of dividing the selected articles into subsections, and placing these subsections in some logical sequence. The selection of articles to be republished was primarily carried out by Eric King who was also instrumental in their classification and their sequencing. Finally, an introduction to each subsection was written using the identified themes. A reference list, a glossary and an index have been included to guide readers.

Acknowledgements

This book is largely the result of the hard work, tenacity and meticulousness of a perspicacious Eric King, who first conceptualised this publication over two decades ago. Unfortunately the publication was delayed for a number of years and, following his retirement as a Lecturer in English from The University of the West Indies, Mona, Deborah Fletcher and Delroy Chevers were brought on board to see the project through to completion. Special thanks are extended to Rachael Mair-Boxill and Colin Gilespie for their editorial assistance, and to Dale Webber for his unstinting support for this project.

The Editors recognize the hard work of Ms Adukae McLeod, Ms Marjorie Segree and Ms Sheree Rhoden, all of whom have worked tirelessly to assist with locating many of the articles used in this book. To the members of our respective families who have provided encouragement and support, we express our gratitude. To the scholars who reviewed the content, we acknowledge our indebtedness.

About the Author

Professor Ian Boxill currently serves as Deputy Principal of The University of the West Indies, Mona Campus. Prior to that he was Dean of the Faculty of Social Sciences, Director of the Centre for Tourism and Policy Research, and Head of the Department of Sociology, Psychology and Social Work in that faculty. In addition to his teaching and research duties as a university lecturer, Ian Boxill wrote a regular weekly column in *The Gleaner* so as to "add his voice" to the public discussion of the social, economic, and political events that were taking place at that time.

That voice is a distinctive one. Ian Boxill's job as an academic gives him the opportunity to read extensively, to attend conferences both at home and abroad, and at times to obtain actual work experience in the relevant subject areas – for example, he has worked with the Caribbean Community and Common Market (CARICOM) on some aspects of the CARICOM Single Market and Economy (CSME), formerly known as the Caribbean Single Market and Economy. This has allowed him to keep abreast of the latest thinking and information on the issues he has written about in his newspaper columns. Second, while writing these articles, Ian Boxill was heavily engaged in research and specialized in teaching research methods, and as a result he was frequently in a position to supply his readers with relevant findings from recent research done in Jamaica, findings that are not readily available elsewhere.

Ian Boxill's voice is unique, because it would seem to speak for ordinary people about the everyday problems they face, such as paying bills, taking the bus, and the lack of common courtesy and humanity with which the general public tends to be treated in Jamaica. His voice resonates because of his own lived experiences. He tells us his mother operated a small retail business (see "Theories and reality", December 21, 1993). His grandfather, he tells us also, took part in the riots of the 1930s – presumably the trade union riots. These twin bits of information about his family background may help to explain why, even in his analyses of the Jamaican economy, Ian Boxill is concerned not simply with facts and figures, but with the human beings who are involved, with their emotions, and why. When discussing the need to bring about change in society, he sees the problem not primarily from the point of view of management but mainly from the point of view of ordinary people. "When we talk about increasing productivity," he reminds us, "we are talking, fundamentally, about changing worker attitude and behaviour. For a group, or a firm or a nation to perform at its best, the people must feel that they have common interests [and] a stake in whatever they are doing. They must feel respected" (see "Compete with whom?" May 12, 1993).

Given his job in academia, and his own specialty, Boxill is understandably very sensitive to charges that there is a shortage of creative scholarship among intellectuals; and that this lack of creativity is in part responsible for the melancholy which now grips [Jamaican] society. He rejects both charges, seeking through his articles to introduce his readers to some of the "creative" thinking and research being done by academics in the Caribbean and abroad, and suggesting, at the same time, that Jamaica's current melancholia has more to do with the mindset of an earlier generation of Caribbean intellectuals who have confused "correctness" with "creativeness" of thought (and expression), than with an absence of scholarship.

Consequently, Boxill identifies himself not with the colonial generation, but with the postcolonial scholars who, he says, "are asking different questions.... Their plot, syntax, metaphors and points of reference are intrinsically different, but they are their own" ("The hero and the crowd", op. cit.). For example, Boxill does not strive for absolute truth or absolute objectivity in his articles. He has no trust in such things. And his approach to a subject matter is not academic, in the sense of being "abstract, unpractical, theoretical, cold, merely logical, conventional, or overformal" (*COD*). It is, as he puts it, his own. In fact, it is precisely the first three characteristics listed above – "abstractness", in the sense of neglect of the concrete realities of day-to-day life in Jamaica; a "lack of practicality", that is, a lack of applicability to Jamaica's situation; and being "theoretical", that is, being overly dependent on textbook knowledge or on foreign models based on assumptions which have not been examined – which Boxill has critiqued. Boxill regards those characteristics as the most serious weaknesses in the analyses offered by some of the "experts" who regularly appear as guests on popular radio talk shows, and by some advisers on, and formulators of government policies. As far as "being cold, merely logical (or cerebral), and being conventional or overformal" in style, Boxill's articles are the direct opposite.

Finally, Boxill's articles highlight the fact that Caribbean intellectuals have an obligation to "engage the society in dialogue about itself and with itself" ("The intellectual and society", October 6, 1993). Boxill does not claim to have all the answers. Some of his views – about the structure of Jamaican society in particular – are controversial, and the reader may not always agree with his conclusions.

About the Editors

David Eric King taught Use of English at The University of the West Indies, Mona for three decades before retiring from the Department of Language, Linguistics and Philosophy in 2002. A graduate of the UWI, Mona in the 1950s, he remains highly respected by both his former students and peers as a teacher and scholar of English. An active member of the Methodist Church he became a fully accredited local preacher in 1997 and in 2022 was recognised for his contribution to the Providence Methodist Church.

Delroy Chevers is a Senior Lecturer of Operations Management and Information Systems at the University of the West Indies, Mona. He is the Associate Dean of Graduate Studies and Research in the Faculty of Social Sciences. He holds a PhD in Information Systems from the University of the West Indies. His research interests are software process improvement (SPI), information systems quality and success, project management and operations sustainability.

Deborah Fletcher holds a Master of Public Administration with a focus on Global e-Policy and e-Governance, a Master of Science in Sociology and a Bachelor of Science in Social Policy and Development. Prior to joining the University of Global Health Equity (UGHE) as Safeguarding Manager she worked in planning and institutional research with The University of the West Indies, Mona, and in community development with the Social Development Commission of Jamaica.

Her research interests span the fields of gender studies, information and communication technology, tourism and development, and labour and employment studies. The author of a number of scholarly articles and reports, her most recent publication is the book entitled, *Yes!! God Still Answers Prayers*.

Organization

The articles in the book are grouped into seven sections under the following broad subject headings, which vary in size:

- I • The Role of the Intellectual In Society: Thoughts on Struggle, Creativity and Progress
- II • Africa, Asia and Our Caribbean Heritage: Our Roots and Cultural Forms
- III • Jamaican Society: Crime, Violence and Social Structure
- IV • Economic Development in Jamaica and the Caribbean
- V • Jamaica and Caribbean Regional Integration
- VI • Asia and the Pacific: Through Caribbean Eyes
- VII • Exploring Writing Styles

Section I contains one chapter with seven articles outlining the role that intellectuals ought to play in their society. One aspect of this role is to educate the public on matters of public interest. One article in this section is a "lecture" on the opinion poll, which has become a very popular tool for discovering what the public thinks about important issues. Other articles in this section introduce the reader to some central themes that keep recurring in the book.

The sixteen articles in **Section II** are further subdivided into chapters – Chapter 2: *Historical Roots;* Chapter 3: *Mental Attitudes;* and Chapter 4: *Caribbean Cultural Forms*. Chapter 2 provides information about the historical, ethnic, economic, and trading links that existed between Africa and Asia, long before Europeans set foot on those continents. Chapter 3 explores widely the subconsciously held attitudes towards race, colour and the concept of beauty in the Caribbean. Finally, Chapter 4 investigates attitudes to indigenous cultural expressions like calypso, reggae and dancehall.

Section III, which contains 43 articles and five chapters, is understandably one of the longer sections in the book as these articles were written for a Jamaican newspaper and primarily for Jamaican readers. Chapter 5 covers articles that discuss community violence in Jamaica and its relationship to poverty, class, and politics. The articles in Chapter 6 explore collectively the lack of respect for leadership and authority, as is routinely demonstrated by the average Jamaican, the chapter also seeks to examine the rationale for the frequent unrest and blockage of public roadways. Chapter 7 examines issues in public education such as the poor performance of Jamaican students in the Common Entrance Exam (which has since been twice replaced with the Grade Six Achievement Test, GSAT, and now the Primary Exit Profile, PEP) and the possible effect it has had on social class division in the society. **The chapter also seeks to identify the level of the education system that is most in need of government assistance and intervention.** Chapter 8 deals with the changing attitudes towards sex and gender in Jamaica. This section ends at chapter 9, which outlines the extent to which values and attitudes are changing in the wider society.

Section IV is the only section that is further divided into three subsections. This section covers matters relating to economic development and contains a total of 27 articles. **Subsection A**, titled Economic Development in Jamaica, consists of two chapters, **Subsection B**, titled Economic Development in Jamaica and the Caribbean, carries three chapters, and the **final subsection** which has a single chapter looks at international development and structural adjustment.

The first chapter in **Subsection A**, Chapter 10, looks at the matter of regional trade and development and the extent to which it impacts a nation's ability to function in the global marketplace. The chapter goes on to explore the factors which affect productivity within the region. Factors such as literacy and work ethics are said to have a huge impact on productivity levels, as well as on how customer service is delivered. Chapter 11 highlights the extent to which development agencies such as the International Monetary Fund (IMF) and the World Bank lend themselves to the transformation of fiscal and social conditions in developing countries.

Subsection B looks at the broader areas of development models, globalization, as well as matters relating to tourism. In Chapter 12, models of development are presented from the perspective of a social scientist, reflecting the experience of locals, as well as those of persons beyond the shores of the Caribbean. Chapter 13 looks at issues relating to globalization and development. Chapter 14 reviews the extent to which crime impacts development, and in particular the development of the tourism industry.

The **final subsection** addresses matters relating to international development and structural adjustment. The sole chapter in this section addresses the vexed issue of structural adjustment and its link with the free-market policies of the World Bank and the IMF. The debate in the public media on Jamaica's developmental problems, the day-to-day realities of living and working in Jamaica, and strategies one considers when exploring matters of interest are also covered in this section.

In **Section V**, the reader will find articles about Caribbean regional integration and the contribution each country makes towards this end. Chapter 16 places emphasis on reporting on cross-regional initiatives using the media. In addition, the chapter looks at the extent to which the media is being used to educate the wider Caribbean citizenry about the importance of regional integration, policies relating to Caribbean integration, and the importance of working together towards achieving shared economic goals. Chapter 17 looks at the extent to which our association with countries of the developed world, and in some cases the developing world, influences foreign policies. The chapter also explores the importance of having a regional vision and using that vision to guide decision-making at the regional and international level. The chapter also touches on China's increased visibility in the globe, and in particular how it has been influencing countries of the Caribbean region. Chapter 18 provides an examination of the benefits of having the Organization of Eastern Caribbean States, Caribbean

Community and Common Market and the Caribbean (now CARICOM) Single Market and Economy. The basic thesis in this section is that Jamaica did, and does, benefit more than most other Caribbean states from inter-regional trade. The section strengthens the need for greater regional integration noting that it would assist rather than hamper the region's efforts to compete in the North American and global market places. It is felt that the Jamaican public needs to be educated much more on this subject through the public media and in academic fora.

Section VI, the penultimate section of the book, details research conducted by Boxill while he was working at the University of Waikato, Hamilton, New Zealand, on a postdoctoral fellowship. Emphasis is placed on the comparative development experiences of the Caribbean, Asia and the Pacific.

Section VII, the final section of the book, ties it all together by exploring three of the writing techniques used to engage with the *Gleaner* audience. The three writing styles covered in this section are expository writing, descriptive writing and narrative.

Finally, it should be noted that the articles within each section and subsection are arranged chronologically by date of publication in the *Gleaner*. The articles selected for this book would have met one or more of the following criteria:

1 to present and discuss an opposing viewpoint of the author's own premise;
2 to provide background or historical information;
3 to examine underlying assumptions, or in some other way deepen public understanding of a controversial issue;
4 to clarify or refine a key word or concept;
5 to provide rich, up-to-date supporting data in the form of tables, charts or diagrams;
6 to provide reading references, or findings from recent unpublished research or from recently held academic conferences.

Abbreviations

ACS	Association of Caribbean States
ASEAN	Association of Southeast Asian Nations
BBC	British Broadcasting Cooperation
BWIA	British West Indian Airways
CARICOM	Caribbean Community and Common Market
CEE	Common Entrance Exam
CHOGM	Commonwealth Heads of Government Meeting
COD	*Concise Oxford Dictionary*
CSME	CARICOM Single Market and Economy
EAC	Electoral Advisory Committee
ECCB	Eastern Caribbean Central Bank
EIA	Environmental Impact Assessment
EU	European Union
FINSAC	Financial Sector Adjustment Company
FLP	Fiji Labour Party
GATT	General Agreement on Tariffs and Trade
GCC	Fijian Great Council of Chiefs
GCT	General Consumption Tax
GDP	Gross Domestic Product
GNP	Gross National Product
GSAT	Grade Six Achievement Test
HOGC	Heads of Governments Conference
IBM	International Business Machines Cooperation
IMF	International Monetary Fund
JCC	Jamaica Chamber of Commerce
JLP	Jamaica Labour Party
JOS	Jamaica Omnibus Service
LAFTA	Latin American Free Trade Area
LDCs	Less Developed Countries
LIAT	Leeward Islands Air Transport Services
MDCs	More Developed Countries
MFN	Most-Favoured-Nation
MTV	Music Television
NAFTA	North America Free Trade Agreement
NBC	National Broadcasting Company
NIC	Newly Industrialized Country/Countries
NJM	New Jewel Movement
NRCA	Natural Resources Conservation Authority
NWC	National Water Commission
OAU	Organisation of African Unity
OECD	Organization for Economic Cooperation and Development
OECS	Organization of Eastern Caribbean States
PAYE	Pay As You Earn
PAYF	Pay As You Feel
PEP	Primary Exit Profile
PNP	People's National Party
PRA	Gouganchille Revolutionary Army
PSOJ	Private Sector Organization of Jamaica
RPF	Rwandan Patriotic Front
SVT	Soqosoqo ni Vakavulewa ni Taukei
ToJ	Telecommunications of Jamaica
UN	United Nations
UNICEF	United Nations Children's Fund
USP	University of South Pacific
USSR	Union of Soviet Socialist Republics
UWI	The University of the West Indies
VoA	Voice of America
WTO	World Trade Organisation

SECTION I

The role of the intellectual in society: Thoughts on struggle, creativity and progress

Chapter 1 Society and Struggle

- The intellectual and society
- The hero and the crowd
- Struggle, creativity, and progress
- Polls and public opinion
- Crisis in Western politics
- When everything is everything
- Finding common ground

Introduction

Intellectuals are known to awaken the society through their forward-thinking approaches. They usually speculate and reflect upon the fundamental problems of their society in their quest to produce ideas, rally the masses, and contribute to the advancement of knowledge and the clarification of issues of all kinds. Their interventions in topical issues usually induce change. The articles in this section explore how intellectuals impact all areas of society in order to produce public good. A closer look at their role across societies suggests that they function as advisors, policy makers and change agents. The first article **"The intellectual and society"** looks at the role intellectuals play across societies, noting their original role as being a part of the existing status quo, and their later shift into becoming more involved in all areas of the society, yet maintaining their independence.

The second article **"The hero and the crowd"** looks at creativity among intellectuals in the society. In other words, the article looks at the extent to which intellectuals within the region are conceiving of and producing new expressions and ideas to solve the complex challenges facing their societies. It assesses the role of the intellectual in the political landscape. The article **"Struggle, creativity and progress"** looks at the extent to which institutions of the past have stymied progress, and the role creativity plays in assuring that the masses of our societies band together and redefine their situation in order to benefit from the changes taking place with the political process. **"Polls and public opinion"** explores how intellectuals have been using research to gauge how members of the population feel about a particular issue. The limitations associated with opinion polling is also explored, as well as the issue of agenda setting. **"When everything is everything"** considers the significance of understanding both the context and also the importance of lived experiences in order to give deeper meanings to nuances in society. Finally, **"Finding common ground"** looks at society's failure to buy into the view that all ideas can contend. The article explores the need to find common ground to solve the multiplicity of problems in society, noting the need for appropriate avenues through which individuals with contending views can express themselves without being stigmatized.

The intellectual and society

(WEDNESDAY, OCTOBER 6, 1993)

Recently someone asked me about the role of the intellectual in the society. The person asked why is it that intellectuals seem so critical of so many things in society, yet they do not get involved. I thought this was an interesting question, never mind that this question is asked daily on radio talk show programmes.

It should be noted that historically there has always been a debate about the role of the intellectual in the society. Should the intellectual follow the status quo or be critical of it? Should the intellectual participate in the political life of his society or should he stand outside and watch? These are questions which have challenged the minds of intellectuals since time immemorial.

In many societies of the past, it was the norm for intellectuals to be a part of the status quo, and it was even expected that they would participate in the political life of their societies. Further, in many of these societies, there was no division between the temporal and spiritual; and/or the state had a monopoly of power.

In the modern era, it is really only in mass democracies where intellectuals lead a relatively separated life from the state that they are free to be openly critical of society and engage in unhindered intellectual activities. Indeed, if one looks at theocracies such as Saudi Arabi or Iran, it will be observed that the academics are closely linked to the state. Therefore, and very often, intellectual activity is either stifled or skewed. Also, in communist countries, many universities were turned into agents of the state. Until recently, China and the former Soviet Union had abolished disciplines such as sociology in universities because they were seen as threats to the status quo and various other communist ideals.

From a historical standpoint, two activities were partially responsible for the relative independence of intellectual pursuits within society in the West. First, there was the Protestant Reformation, German Protestant theologian Martin Luther sparked a public controversy when, in 1517, his "95 Theses" questioned the relationship between the priest, God and man. Luther was a professor of scripture at the University of Wittenberg and also an Augustinian friar. It was Luther's questioning of the status quo (that under Catholicism man had to go through a priest in order to reach God) that, in large part, gave rise to the revolt within the Catholic Church and eventually the split between the Protestants and Catholics. This activity laid the foundation for the separation of reason from religion.

Split

The second event was the split between the state and the church, ushered in during Oliver Cromwell's rule of England following the execution of Charles I. This separation opened up the way for mass democracy, and took away the almost sacred powers of the monarchy. These two events have paved the way for open and unencumbered critical thinking.

There are some who argue that intellectuals should not participate in political life since this activity will compromise scientific and artistic objectivity. German social scientist Max Weber was faced with such a conflict: he wanted to pursue both politics and science as vocations. Our own C. L. R. James also faced this dilemma, that of intellectual and politician. The lives of James and Weber are interesting, since both failed in politics but were giants as intellectuals.

Their personally conflicting roles as politicians and intellectuals raise the question: to what extent can a person whose life revolves around questioning reality be engaged in activities which might be compromised because of his critical approach and intellectual perspective? There is no easy or straightforward answer to this question.

To be sure, the activity of thinking critically and experimentally (as a vocation) often leads one to attack the status quo. This critical view of reality can sometimes conflict with decisions which may be politically brilliant, but intellectually lacklustre. It is perhaps, for this reason, why many very good intellectuals do not make very good politicians. They may be uncomfortable with the inherent conflict between political expediency and intellectual credibility.

Karl Marx argued that all intellectual activity is by definition political, and therefore not to act in the name of objective intellectual truth is to be hypocritical. It would have been interesting to see how he would have fared as a politician.

Indeed, it was left up to Lenin and later Stalin who, in their roles as politicians, contradicted many of the apparently intellectually sound ideas of communism in order to govern. Lenin's famous piece "The Differentiation of the Russian Peasantry" was in my view a rather creative way of justifying a socialist revolution in Russia, since Russia's feudal state was perhaps the one country in Europe least ready for the socialist revolution, along Marxist lines.

Small developing countries, faced with a shortage of highly educated or trained people, often look to intellectuals to get involved in political life. In many cases this involvement may be good for the society; in others such activity may compromise the pursuit of "truth". Clearly, there is no right or wrong answer to whether an intellectual should pursue a political career. What is important is that there is a critical mass outside the political arena who can engage society in dialogue, about itself and with itself. This, in order to fashion options for change and progress. Peace!

The hero and the crowd

(TUESDAY, NOVEMBER 23, 1993)

It is not uncommon to hear the older commentators lamenting the shortage of creative scholarship from our country's intellectuals. This lack of creativity, they claim, is in part responsible for the melancholy which now grips our society. Even if there is truth to this claim, this situation is neither unique to this era, nor unique to Jamaica.

I also think that it is an oversimplification of the current situation to suggest that much thorough creative thinking is not being done, or that the lack thereof is the cause of this melancholia. It would appear that part of this cry for penetrating intellectual thought is also a reflection of the inability of those who were the products of the colonial era to come to terms with the changes in our society, and to accept that the seeds of destruction which they sowed are now being reaped by the current generation. Those who now chastise must realise that their ideas laid the foundation for the type of society we now have.

Extreme behaviour

We live in a society in which people seem capable of dealing only in extremes. There is a tendency to believe that there are always right and wrong answers. Everything must be polarized; thus, colonialism was either good or bad, the '70s were either good or bad, the government is either bad or good. Such a society is a breeding ground for grandstanders and front stage actors. It is an environment which is highly tolerant of people who feel they always have the right answers; and if perchance they do not, then no one else is capable of finding their "truth". Notice how tolerant we are of intolerance?

Now these learned people went to the right schools, which means they had a good colonial education, studying Greek and Roman history and mythology, Julius Caesar and the likes (appropriately). These so aptly schooled people go to great lengths in the media to scold their "inferiors" for using a "z" instead of an "S", while ignoring the content of the ten-page article which contains this omnipotent "z". Not to be neglected is their compulsive desire to speak the right English, to ask the right questions, to posit the right arguments and to do everything right – even when they give us wrong results. Still, some of these people continue to harp on the value of a British education over an American one, when the British are themselves abandoning their own system in favour of a modified American model, in the hope of obtaining more Nobel prizes, or stopping the haemorrhaging of European and Asian students to American universities.

Why struggle?

It is common to hear some of these people speak so fondly of the colonial days that I sometimes wonder why my grandfather took part in the 1930s riots, or why in the colonized world people struggled for independence from the British. Perhaps the entire colonized world comprised fools, like my grandfather, who wanted to take control of their own destiny.

But there is a paradox in much of what these people claim. These people, these colonial people, are the ones who now castigate their peers – the very ones who grew up in the same colonial boat and who had the same colonial education – for messing up the country. They are aware of the fact that tribal violence has its roots in colonial politics. They also know that the politicians most skilled in the politics of division and patronage were those who represented the cream of the colonial education. The colonial masters taught them two important things: how to speak correctly and how to make persuasive arguments, no matter how vacuous. This too, unfortunately, they often confuse with creative thinking.

Collective thinking

Many of the colonial people have sought to dismiss the 1970s as the lost decade. Few Jamaicans now want to identify with this era. In many cases this is understandable, for this was a period in which many mistakes were made, and many people suffered. But the 1970s were also, for many, a period when people dared to hope and to dream collectively. Above all, it was a time when people dared to ask the "wrong" questions and confront their own humanity. There is so much bitterness about the 1970s because there was so much hope. The glorious days of colonialism did not deliver the masses of people from poverty and starvation. The 1970s brought the hope that there had to be a better way – a way to be achieved collectively. Humans are not zombies; they have other needs and dreams which are not reflected in the GDP or per capita income figures.

Transformation

Our region is going through a great transformation. The postcolonial generation is asking different questions, or should I say the "wrong" questions? Their plot, syntax, metaphors and points of reference are intrinsically different, but they are their own. People who did not have the benefit of the colonial education, which the privileged few who got it seem to reify, have invented their own forms of expression.

Our people are trying to confront the betrayed dreams of the 1970s, and the unfulfilled promises of the 1980s. They no longer trust the wisdom of those schooled in a good colonial education or its equivalent. They see little difference between those so schooled who opposed colonialism and those who are more enthusiastic about its virtues. The days of the "hero and the crowd" are slowly drawing to a close. The 1970s opened up the consciousness of our people and took us out of our kumbla. So, they may not know much about Roman history, but they know that no one has a monopoly on the truth, not even those who ask the "right" questions and have the "right" answers. Meanwhile, the struggle continues. Peace, every time!

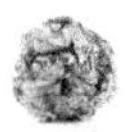

Struggle, creativity and progress

(TUESDAY, APRIL 26, 1994)

Those of us who got the opportunity to watch Brian Lara break Sir Garfield Sobers' 36-year-old test cricket record could not help swelling with pride as our sense of "West Indianness" was fed by his masterful strokes. The most exciting thing about Lara's innings was not that he broke the record, but rather the confidence with which he accomplished this feat.

Note, however, that although Lara is an orthodox batsman, he is not in the tradition of the English cricketer who tends to be more defensive. You see, even though Lara's strokes seem to fit neatly into the textbooks, they are nonetheless characterized by a spontaneous, vivacious and perilous temperament which the textbooks warn against. I agree fully with those who argue that Lara's batting style is in the tradition of Gary Sobers'. This to my mind is not accidental, for the greatness of Lara is part of that larger West Indian genius which blooms when liberated. C.L.R. James, one of the region's foremost intellectuals, in writing about Lara's predecessor, said, "Garfield Sobers... is a West Indian cricketer, not merely a cricketer from the West Indies. He is the most typical West Indian cricketer that is possible to imagine. All geniuses are merely people who carry to an extreme definitive the characteristics of a unit of civilization to which they belong and the special act or function which the possessor practises...." James notes further: "When Sobers was appointed captain of the West Indies, he was the first genuine native son to hold this position – born in the West Indies, educated in the West Indies, learning the foundations of his cricket in the West Indies without the benefit of a secondary education or British university". The point of James' observation is that while Sobers was playing a British sport, his sense of being a West Indian formed the basis for his interpretation of his game. Sobers, Richards and Lara provide, arguably, the most vivid examples of a West Indian sports aesthetic. The issue is, to my mind, fundamentally about struggle, creativity and the progress of a people. For cricket typifies the struggles faced by the people, our people. Most of the people of this region have for the last four hundred years sought to come to terms with who they are, while at the same trying to build institutions which they can call their own.

Rhythms

Like the African Americans who have taken the piano rhythms of Europe and have transformed them into ragtime, jazz and blues, we have taken the Catholic tradition of carnival and turned it into a celebration which has no equal in other parts of the world. Also, we have taken the sound of the bass guitar and created the intoxicating music of reggae.

The recurring but conflated motif in the works of our most outstanding artistes and intellectuals centres on struggle, redefinition and creativity: without this process, we are merely imitators, not innovators. Struggle is the mother of creativity – although that struggle can also sometimes lead to destruction. However, the creativity of the people in this diaspora is born out of a desire to create meaning from institutions which have not always favoured our progress or reflected our world view. In instances where we have succeeded, we have readily embraced these new institutions as our own. Therefore, cricket has captured our imagination like no other colonial institution because it is the one institution which has allowed us to beat the colonizer at his own game, and we enjoy this. But we are also good cricketers, and we know it. Despite its British origins, even our staunchest anti-colonialists have never argued that cricket is not ours, but as worthy legatees we have redefined this game, and now we can see ourselves in the players. Now all of this begs the question: why can't we transfer our success in cricket to the political and economic ovals?

Struggle

I do not believe that our political institutions have been characterized by the same type of struggle which has historically existed in cricket. That is to say, the ordinary citizen has not, in my opinion, had the same opportunity to participate in the redefining of our political institutions, in the same way that he did with cricket and with our music. Consequently, our political and economic systems are not the products of struggle and redefinition by our people. In fact, they are stagnant adaptations of colonial models which have historically excluded the masses from the redefining process.

The same level of civility which exists in some sports is virtually non-existent in the political and economic arenas. After independence, the countries in this region were handed political systems, and with the possible exception of the abortive attempts of Grenada and Jamaica, our nations have never seriously struggled with the questions of representation and relevance in the same way that the Americans and South Africans have.

The debates about a new constitution in South Africa perhaps display the clearest sign of the relationship between struggle, creativity and progress. Unlike other African countries, the unique feature of the South African constitution is that it has a bill of rights and many other provisions, which could only have emerged after attempts by contending parties to ensure that no one is marginalized by the changes taking place within the political process. This has not been the case in the West Indies. Our people have been kept out, or have kept themselves out, of the process of political institution building.

Vacuum

Therefore, the vacuum in leadership and the corresponding lack of vision which we feel in Jamaica are in part the result of (self-) exclusion. Good leadership and vision are the spawn of a people who believe that there is something worth fighting for, something worth defending. Like our leaders, too many of us no longer feel that there is something to defend, something to struggle for. Peace!

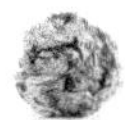

Polls and public opinion

(TUESDAY, MARCH 14, 1995)

Public opinion polls have now become an integral part of our everyday political discourse. Carl Stone, who legitimised public opinion polling in Jamaica, had some initial difficulty in trying to convince the public of their validity and usefulness. Fortunately, times have changed, and we now use polls to give us some ideas about how the public feels about a wide range of issues.

This trend towards capturing the views of members of the public is a good thing, but it is also important that we become fully aware of the limitations associated with this opinion- measuring tool.

One problem associated with political polls is methodology. A poll is a survey conducted on a representative subset or part of a population. Therefore, this subset is supposed to reflect the thinking of the wider population. The members of this subset are often selected by complex sampling methods, which will allow the pollsters to construct an appropriate margin of error, which in turn is arrived at with the aid of standard statistical formulas. Thus, in order not to affect the validity of polls, one must ensure that they are representative of the population and are of an adequate sample size.

However, there are other more serious problems associated with surveys, which can make the estimation of a margin of error, if based simply on the size of the sample, problematic. For example, a simple problem such as the interviewee misunderstanding a question, may lead to the introduction of numerous additional errors, thus reducing the validity of the findings.

You see, if a poll is to be regarded as national, it should capture and represent the opinions of a wide cross-section of the population. Hence, pollsters should always provide their readers with a description of their sampling procedure, and the number of persons interviewed should be large enough to allow the samples/subset to look/resemble the population/whole. It is also suggested that pollsters who do not have an intimate understanding of the dynamics of the local political landscape should always strive to use large samples that is 1,000 or more persons. Note well, from a statistical point of view, a national sample of 500 can have a margin of error of plus or minus 4 per cent. However, in reality the vagaries of research may introduce many more errors into one's findings, consequently widening the "true" margin of error.

Even if we are to accept that the sampling procedure is good, the manner in which questions are asked could lead to results which are not valid; even the best pollster can fall into the trap of asking questions which sometimes lead to biased results. Studies of polls undertaken by leading American polling organizations show that small changes to the wording of questions often lead to very different or conflicting results. As an example, we will examine the same question asked in two different ways: (1) "Should divorce in this country be easier or more difficult to obtain than now?" (2) "Should divorce in this country be easier to obtain, more difficult to obtain, or stay as it is now?" These two versions of the same question were used in separate surveys among the same population, using similar sample sizes, but they produced two different sets of results.

Another hotly debated aspect of polls is their ability to predict. There is no doubt that polls given similar circumstances and conducted repeatedly can enable the researcher to predict an outcome. This does not mean that the prediction will be always correct. But if we isolate and establish some patterns in political attitudes over a given period of time, we would be able to use these patterns to predict an outcome – given one's understanding of the political landscape is also reliable. Further, if we assume that there is some degree of regularity to human behaviour, a very reasonable assumption, then there is no reason why we cannot predict that behaviour with some degree of accuracy.

Admittedly, prediction can sometimes be a very hazardous exercise, especially if the results of one's polls prove to be inaccurate.

Even if the results of the polls are accurate, there are other problems which might be the source of serious concern.

How people feel

Let me elaborate. Polls tend to capture how people feel at a given point in time and, by extension, there is no way of knowing how they will feel at a later date unless another poll is conducted. So, given the dynamics of human attitude and behaviour, it is reasonable to believe that people will change their points of view several times about a single issue.

They may change their opinions because of the availability of new information. And, interestingly, the more complex the issue, the more undecided humans tend to be. However, as the situation begins to unravel, we might begin to take clearer positions.

Perhaps the most controversial question about public opinion polling is drawing inferences from the results. The reason for this is that many analysts have argued that it is not clear whether polls reflect what people actually feel or whether they reflect the influence of powerful interest groups on the population. In most modern societies, the most important sources of influence for the adult population are their peers and the media.

Setting the agenda

In Jamaica, the plethora of radio talk shows often sets the agenda for discussion while articulating the points of view of the hosts of these programmes.

In societies where information on several public issues is often restricted to those who have connections with the powerful, that which sometimes passes for objective analysis is often no more than a thinly veiled attempt by those who have access to this information to achieve some personal end. Therefore, what the public may perceive as facts may in fact be quite incorrect.

Social scientists know from research that public opinion can be affected by having a respected and authoritative figure repeat information to the public. Clear examples of this were seen during the recent health care bill debate in the United States, where those persons who opposed health care reform articulated their position in the media via sundry influential persons.

Scare tactics

Additionally, the use of scare tactics through the appeal to core American values, such as freedom and responsibility, helped to hammer home the point. We must also remember that Hitler used a variety of methods in order to cement public opinion around his cause. He manipulated the fear, insecurities and latent prejudices of the Germans, thus enabling him to fight against the Jews.

Now, this is not to say that all public opinion is formed through the manipulation of information by interest groups, since public opinion can also be formed as a result of people's own daily experiences.

Personal agendas

Furthermore, many of us can disentangle the personal agenda of a talk show host or journalist from the larger issue which affects the country.

Nonetheless, the following are some questions which will assist you in evaluating a poll:

1. Who was interviewed?
2. How large was the sample?
3. What were the questions asked, and in what order?
4. How were the interviews conducted?
5. When were the interviews conducted?
6. Who sponsored the poll and why?

Public opinion polls are fraught with many dangers and shortcomings. However, this does not mean that they are not useful. They give us an understanding of how the general population feels about an issue at a particular point in time, and how people feel at a given time may be the result of a variety of factors not the least of which being how the poll was conducted.

If we understand these influences and seek to examine this opinion-measuring tool within this context, we can continue to glean useful insights into public opinion and perhaps even advance the democratic process. Peace!

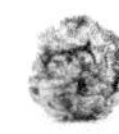

Crisis in Western politics

(TUESDAY, OCTOBER 31, 1995)

In 1992, Francis Fukuyama published a book called *The End of History and the Last Man*, in which he celebrated the victory of Western liberalism over communism and extolled the virtues of Western capitalist development. In his view, the end of communism had signalled the end of history and the ushering in of an age in which liberal capitalist development had now become universal.

It was as though he was saying that liberal capitalist development was natural to human existence. In other words, liberal democracy's apparent universality represents the triumph of individual "freedom" of nature over the nurturing artificiality of communism/socialism.

Feasibility

But to what extent is Western liberal capitalist society the ultimate stage of human political progress? Can we truly argue that the moral imperative of western democracy, within a capitalist framework, has been and will be able to sustain itself?

Three weeks ago, the BBC aired a documentary on its world service in which it looked at politics in Europe. Never, argued the presenter, has Europe witnessed such widespread accusations of corruption against leading politicians.

In Italy, the former prime minister is accused of collaborating with the Mafia during his term in office. In Belgium, the prime minister is under investigation for allegedly bribing tax officials. In Spain, the prime minister is being accused of having knowledge of, and probably aiding, death squads in carrying out executions. In France, the prime minister is accused of using public funds to renovate his house while he was deputy mayor of Paris. In Sweden, the man who appeared most likely to become the country's next prime minister has had to withdraw from the electoral race due to allegations of corruption. In Britain, a Member of Parliament resigned after being accused of taking a bribe for answering certain questions in Parliament, and recently, the secretary general of the North Atlantic Treaty Organization (NATO) resigned amidst charges of corruption. Sadly, the list goes on.

European experience

Right across Europe, fewer people are voting, more so-called fringe political parties are being formed, and the electorate is becoming more demanding and less tolerant of politicians who are accused of corruption, or of not acting in the interest of the people. One observer of the European political scene argued that people have become so disillusioned that many of the accusations made against some of the politicians are petty and oftentimes not supported by fact.

What is it that explains this apparent political malady in Europe and, increasingly, in other parts of the world? To the more than superficial observer, it would seem that communism concealed many of the cracks which existed in the liberal democratic tradition. While in office, many Western politicians, including those in the Caribbean, were able to cover up their muddy tracks by painting a rather diabolical portrait of communism.

Respectable politicians and their dutiful bureaucrats went to bed with weapons manufacturers, industrialists, and other political leaders of questionable intent, ostensibly to safeguard democracy.

Indeed, the same process which shielded, and eventually exposed, the contradictions of communism has now become anathema to liberal democracy in the West. That is to say, whereas the presence of liberal democratic states demonstrating multinational cooperation provided an easy excuse for rationalizing, temporarily, the incompetence, corruption, oppression and inefficiency of many communist states, the end of communism is now exposing the numerous inadequacies of the liberal democratic tradition within capitalist society.

The end of communism led to a more pragmatic form of governance in the West, and also reduced the necessity for the state to articulate a clear ideology of progress. Now, with no clear ideological enemy and the re-emergence of the rugged individualism associated with burgeoning global capitalism, the moral dimension of the political landscape has changed in a way which is perhaps comparable to the period prior to the Renaissance in Europe.

The strengths and weaknesses of communism and/or socialism were their religion-like appeal; socialist leaders always articulated a clear and consistent vision. It was this clear and oftentimes simplistic vision which stimulated a counter vision from liberal democratic regimes.

Intellectual crisis

The absence of a viable alternative philosophy the liberal capitalist development reflects in many ways, a crisis in intellectual thought – the "poverty" of the global intelligentsia, if you will, and not the "end of history" as Fukuyama would have us believe. For it is the intelligentsia who usually constructs philosophical notions of progress, which are then packaged by politicians, journalists, talk show hosts and writers of fiction to entice, or shop to, the masses.

New political systems and ideas are invariably the products of moral chaos in the society. These new ideas are often fuelled by the notion that human existence transcends the material realm, that there must be something more to life (whatever it is) than an existential reality, and it is our duty as human beings to find it.

Regrettably, the great tragedy of Western liberal democracy operating within a global capitalist framework is that it has stifled the collective conscience among human beings and reduced the complexity of human existence to market relations.

Of course, we cannot deny the importance of the market to our existence. However, it is the vulgarity of the market within the international relations system that seems to pose a greater threat to political stability and ecological progress at the present time.

Never before in our history has a spectre of globalization – epitomised by the General Agreement on Tariffs and Trade (GATT), the internet and Coca-Cola – resulted in such illusions of freedom for the human spirit only to imprison it, at the same time, by notions of freedom and equality that are unattainable, while the spirit is further neutered by the market.

It is therefore not surprising that even in cases of increasing economic fortunes, as in the case of the USA, there is greater pessimism and cynicism about politics and politicians. In addition, in a number of developing countries, like Jamaica, politics seem to be either trapped in a state of inertia or bordering on chaos.

This is because liberal democrats see that the idea of operating within an inherently exploitative capitalist world economy promises much more than it is able to deliver. With the "end of ideology", "humanist politics", it seems, is denigrated as a soft option, the chimera of the idealist.

Under this new dispensation, politicians seem unable to articulate a clear and compelling vision, as there is no clear moral or philosophical anchor from which to launch their rhetoric. The result is uncertainty among politicians and fear and cynicism among the public.

Reactions

As a defence mechanism, the older generations predictably resurrect visions of the "good old days", including colonialism, fascism, and for some even slavery, for anything is better than now. Others suggest systemic change is an alternative which is more difficult than it sounds. Human beings are resistant to change, and most change results in winners and losers.

Many of the well-known scientists such as Newton and Copernicus, great moral philosophers such as Confucius and Khaldun, and modern-day thinkers such as Garvey and Malcolm X saw the enduring connection between material progress and moral development. Communism was able to link the two, albeit at the level of rhetoric. Communism, however, committed the fatal error of reducing human existence to economic relations. Ultimately, it failed.

Like communism, liberal democratic regimes in so called developed capitalist societies, and in semi-feudal ones such as Jamaica, are fast losing their moral imperative. When this happens, their legitimacy is brought into question on.

The real crisis of the future will be in finding a viable alternative. Peace!

When everything is everything

(TUESDAY, NOVEMBER 12, 1996)

If a little knowledge is dangerous, where is the man who has so much as to be out of danger? — THOMAS H. HUXLEY

Recently, I reviewed a book, *The Black Diaspora*, authored by the South African activist and scholar Ronald Segal. While it is an interesting collection of essays on the Caribbean and the Americas, I could not identify with the manner in which he discusses the situation in some of the islands in which I either lived or spent extended periods over the years. Clearly, much of his work is based on what he read or what was told to him, for the experiential factor seemed quite limited.

Yet Segal's views will have greater sway in the academy than yours or mine, though we have lived a variety of these Caribbean experiences. For our lived "facts" will not be seen to be as objective as Segal's representations, since he is "removed" from the environment and thus his "objectivity" in capturing somebody else's reality is more reliable. You see, scientists (social and physical) pride themselves in being objective. Regrettably, social scientists, particularly economists, are often quick to argue that, fundamentally, all societies are the same. Hence, the notion that one has to have a particular understanding of a society, if one is to work at or in the formulation of policy for that society, is seen as not relevant or necessary. My view is that whether societies are fundamentally the same is neither here nor there, since it all depends on what we mean by "fundamentally the same". The fact is that I could easily have said, and with much justification, that all societies are different.

In case you may be wondering where I am going with this line of reasoning, it is in response to what appears to be a growing mood in our society with respect to the scant regard for history, and for its context and role, in either policy-making or commentary, or in the process of development in our society. As such, there are those who comment on the mistakes made by both the People's National Party (PNP) and the Jamaica Labour Party (JLP) governments over the past two decades without trying to understand the various factors which created or accompanied their policies during the period. Likewise, there seems to be little respect for the views of people who were part of the policy-making machinery during the period.

And so, I often hear people dismiss CARICOM and the West Indies Federation experience as useless without even having the slightest understanding of the evolution or function of these attempts at development. There are also those who would now want to dismiss the work of people like George Beckford and Norman Girvan, some of the region's leading thinkers, because their work is perceived as being irrelevant, or inconsistent with current global economic ideological fads. However, by so doing, there is hardly any attempt to contextualize their work, or to ask whether they have advanced our understanding of our economies and ourselves. But, ultimately, this is what is important, not if they won the Nobel Memorial Prize in economics.

You see, as I move around, I sense an extreme rationalism emerging across our society, particularly in policy-making and academic circles. I also sense this emergence in discussions about manufacturing and productivity where attempts are made to compare Jamaica with, say, Korea and the USA, irrespective of location within the world economy. In discussions about development, reference is commonly made to the experiences of the Asian Tigers as an example of what we should be able to do, without reflecting on the context of their development. And I often get the impression that many of our people feel that what is good for the USA is also good for Jamaica. There is nothing wrong with comparison; what is problematic is when we mistake abstraction for reality, when everything becomes everything.

It would seem that we have begun to believe all of the hype about globalization, which basically says that we are all the same. But such a view ignores the fact that there is something unique about our reality and our experiences. Indeed, in the early colonial period, the British sent out anthropologists to study various societies in great detail so that they could maintain control over them. And for all their talk of a global village, American policymakers ensure that they have experts on hand to study, in detail, aspects of various societies across the world, which will ultimately be used to their advantage. In their opinion, an understanding of these societies allows them to craft internal and external policy decisions favourable to their purposes.

Against this background, one of the most humbling experiences which I had was in visiting the Pacific region, and in realising that, with all of my training in the social sciences, it was difficult to get a handle on the functioning of these societies simply by reading the literature and talking to experts. Consequently, on my visit to Fiji, I had to question much of what I had read and was told about this society. Rational analysis based on reading and talking to experts can only tell us so much about a society; much of what makes a society can sometimes only be understood through direct interaction.

We commentators, analysts and policymakers do ourselves an injustice if we sit down and simply rationalize human behaviour without the privilege of experience. Concomitantly, we do our own people a disservice when we attempt to judge yesterday by simply looking at what obtains today. The notion that "everything is everything" may be indeed be an unfortunate metaphor. Peace!

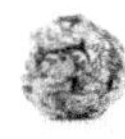

Finding common ground

(TUESDAY, APRIL 14, 1998)

Courses in relation to the financial sector and socialism are taught at The University of the West Indies; therefore, those who oppose these ideas, including those of Professor Grassl will be victimized. I had never associated this sort of distortion of facts, illogical reasoning, and confusion of ideas with the likes of Delroy Chuck. But to be fair, let me address Chuck's views, instead of his motives, about which I know nothing. I will not deal with the Grassl issue, as I am sure the authorities that Chuck accuses of victimization are quite capable of defending their decisions.

Now, Mr Chuck is correct in his view that Russian-type socialism is dead. However, it seems unfathomable that he would equate the present PNP government policies with that type of socialism. To argue that government "bail-out" of the financial sector is tantamount to controlling the commanding heights of the economy, and therefore a return to socialism, is either the height of naivety or an attempt at distortion. To be sure, a dispassionate examination of the PNP rhetoric and policy of the 1990s (see, for example, the various World Bank reports) reflects important departures from the 1970s. Indeed, to argue that the PNP's policies are socialist seems to suggest a greater level of consistency of both policy and ideology in the way the government is handling the economy than actually exists.

But how many of us have seriously interrogated this so-called socialism of the 1970s? Researchers who have done so are quite convinced that beyond the rhetoric of socialism from this period, the empirical reality of the government policy across the region shows that both Barbados, and Trinidad and Tobago were "more socialist" than Jamaica during the 1970s.

Legislations

Furthermore, on the basis of government involvement in the economy and the nature of its social legislation, Barbados today can easily be described as the most socialist country in the Caribbean. Barbados has always pursued a social democratic tradition à la the Nordic countries, rather than adhere to the Spencerian notions of development held by the USA. To quote noted political scientist Neville Duncan, "Ironically, Barbados has manifested more features of welfare socialism than Jamaica, Grenada, Guyana, and Trinidad and Tobago ever did. Like Trinidad and Tobago, Barbados never gave what it was doing a socialist label, and so neither attracted the venomous opprobrium that the other countries received from the USA...". Chuck and many others would do well to rise above the skewed rhetoric of radio and newspaper commentaries, and study the development experience of other countries.

Equally, it is also true that the socialist ideas which found strong renaissance in Jamaica during the 1960s and 1970s also struck a chord across the world. Despite his many failings at home, one reason for Michael Manley's enormous popularity outside of Jamaica had to do with his great ability to articulate sentiments which were shared by large numbers of people, from Africa to Latin America, and beyond. Contrary to what Chuck and others would have us believe, the aberrations of the '70s were not those developing countries which supported some form of socialist development during this time, but rather those which did not.

Another of Chuck's views, which I must address, is his characterization of UWI [social science] lecturers as socialist. This is perplexing, as I am sure he is aware that most of the leading socialist thinkers of the 1970s era from UWI have now openly joined the chorus of neoliberal thinkers. Based on my own experience, academics that we would normally refer to as socialist are now a rare breed on the UWI campus.

Perhaps Chuck's problem may be related to ignorance, or perhaps faulty reasoning, as I cannot speak to his motives. For instance, it is twisted logic to imply that because many people thought a certain way in the past means they will continue to do so in the present. What Chuck does not realise is that the UWI has seen a turnover in staff since the 1970s. Most of the new staff received their postgraduate education (and ideas about progress) in the USA during or after the fall of communism. Whatever the implications, Chuck will do well to note that the UWI of the '70s is certainly not the UWI of the '90s. It is also true that the UWI's teaching and research are influenced by a currency of international ideas; in many departments, such ideas have gone beyond the facile notions of capitalism and socialism, and take us into discourses such as postmodernism, and post-structuralism.

Now, there are two points which I do not want misunderstood. First, I am not saying that all is fine and dandy at the UWI. In my opinion, the UWI must earnestly engage in the type of self-examination and renewal similar to what other serious universities around the world have done. The institution also needs to be more efficient and transparent.

Second, I am certainly not suggesting that education in the USA is somehow superior to other places, nor do I feel that it is necessary or desirable to have only neoliberal thinkers around us. Rather, it is time we realise that so called free-market capitalism and socialism are ideas about human progress, which were created by human beings. Elements of these ideas exist in all societies. Both sets of ideas contain desirable as well as undesirable elements. Jamaicans now need to decide which elements are most useful for us – this is the common ground which I speak about.

On a related matter, Mr Chuck would do well to remember that tyranny is tyranny, whether it comes from the so-called left or right. We often hear about the attempt of the so-called left to suppress the ideas of the so-called right. But over the past five years, I have witnessed a rise in the passion with which people preach sermons about the virtues of the market, and an almost religious condemnation of others who do not share the same conviction. This is not at all good for the development of ideas, to which Mr Chuck refers.

I believe that the ideas of academics, in particular, should be subject to scrutiny and criticism by the public. However, the continued venomous attack on academics, based on a complete disrespect for fair and truthful representation of what takes place at the UWI, is a type of tyranny that the society can do without.

Freedom

Universities should be given the type of freedom that allows people to be socialists, capitalists, anarchists, and the like. The day that this freedom is taken from me, I will leave the UWI, Mona, for an environment which allows me to think and, also, be wrong. Indeed, in a small developing country with one or two universities, this freedom to think seems almost impossible because of the need to make one's ideas immediately relevant and to produce the correct solutions. But ideas are not right or wrong in an absolute sense. It is the context of their application which determines whether they are correct, or not.

In regard to Chuck's critique of the presence of socialist ideas at the UWI, he should take note that the largest and most prestigious universities across the world have significant members of their faculties who are socialists, neoliberals, anarchists, and so on. For many years, socialism has been part of the Western intellectual tradition. The appeal of socialism, in its myriad forms, will not die because of the collapse of communism or any other "ism". The idea associated with the different types of "socialism" predates Marx and Lenin. Marx and Lenin represent a particular type of socialism. As long as the ideal of achieving human equality exists, then socialist ideas and ideals will find resonance in the academic world, and in the society at large. Woe betide the day when public pressure forces university academics to abandon ideas simply because they are no longer popular.

My fear is that the socialist proselytizing of the 1970s has now been exchanged for the neoliberal proselytizing of the 1990s. In other words, we have gone from saying that the state is a saviour to arguing that it is the villain. We are a society that fails to see shades of grey; everything must be either black or white. Such a society will always be haven to demigods, soothsayers and megalomaniacs. We might do well to remember that explanations do not necessarily mean that solutions are simple, as some would have us believe.

What Jamaica needs now, more than anything, are ways of finding common ground to solve pressing social and economic problems. There is a great deal of intellectual dishonesty among the "chattering classes" in this country, as people who have the facility to bring about change seem more interested in gaining personal benefits and popularity, rather than promoting impartial discourses aimed at creating solutions. If talented people like Delroy Chuck and others who self-righteously clamour for change wish to succeed in their efforts, then they should begin by taking a look in the mirror. Peace!

SECTION II

Africa, Asia and Our Caribbean Heritage: Our Roots and Cultural Forms

Introduction

Section II contains 16 articles, and has been subdivided into three chapters.

Chapter 2: Historical Roots and the Impact of Europe supplies information about the ethnic, cultural and trading links that existed between Africa and Asia before the arrival of Europeans. It examines the role that European (and other) nations, the United Nations, and the international press play in the politics and geopolitics of Africa. This chapter begins with a segment sub-headed **"Defining race"** taken from a larger article entitled **"Decolonization in reverse"**. The segment highlights the origins of the terms "black" (negro) and "white" (Caucasian) as racial groups. Another group of articles in the chapter focuses the reader's attention on the many tragic conflicts that have occurred, and are occurring, on the African continent, in Ethiopia, Liberia, Somalia, Sudan, Angola, Rwanda and other countries. The articles criticize the international (and Jamaican) news media for ethnic and cultural bias and/or for shallow reporting. They provide readers with historical background to these conflicts and discuss the impact of Europe on the origins and perpetuation of these conflicts. These articles written almost three decades ago are still arguably are still arguably the best introduction available to the Jamaican newspaper-reading public concerning the tragic events now taking place in Africa. The segment was written in response to a reader's request for information about the origins of the terms "black" (negro) and "white" (Caucasian) as racial groups. It reveals some little-known facts about the term "negro" and its first use.

Chapter 3: Mental Attitudes identifies and analyses inherited beliefs that influence the images and attitudes we have of and towards ourselves.

Chapter 4: Caribbean Cultural Forms looks at carnival, calypso and dancehall within the context of the Jamaican society and by extension the wider Caribbean. Emphasis is placed on the role of culture within the society, especially within this age of world culture, where the artistic products of one culture have become the possession of all cultures. The article points members of the black community to the importance of utilizing the products of their own mass culture to their own economic advantage, noting that failure to do so may benefit others.

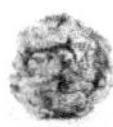

Chapter 2 ◉ Historical Roots and the Impact of Europe

Defining race (excerpt from "Decolonization in reverse")

(TUESDAY, JUNE 15, 1993)

There is much to ponder about the appointment of the new governor of the Bank of Jamaica (BoJ) – much to ponder, not because he is a Canadian, but because the state of the country's affairs has reached the stage where there is need for someone like Mr Bussières (i.e., someone who was sent in to "rescue" the Zambian economy) to sit in such an esteemed office.

The question this appointment begs is: was there no one in Jamaica or in CARICOM who was capable of doing the job? We have been told that Mr Bussières has a wealth of experience in central banking. In other words, technically, he is a competent person. But we have a number of eminently qualified economists in Jamaica and in CARICOM who also have a wealth of experience and whose technical competence (especially with respect to the region with which they are most familiar) is second to none anywhere.

If, therefore, we accept that it is Mr Bussières' technical skills we are after, in a region where there is no shortage of such skills, this begs the question, why him? What was so appealing about Mr Bussières to the government? What are the implications of such an appointment? Since I am unsure about the motives of the government, what I prefer to do is suggest some implications of the appointment; people may then wish to draw their own conclusions about motives. Now follow me closely.

Not long ago, when there were disturbances in the region, the colonial powers would send in commissions of inquiry. These commissions were sent in fully convinced that the colonial subjects were incapable of governing themselves. In times of political upheaval, the colonial masters would change governors, or even political systems, as was demonstrated when the Old Representative System was changed to the Crown Colony Government. Indeed, much of this behaviour still continues, albeit in more inconspicuous forms. Arguably the recent use of Scotland Yard police in Trinidad and Tobago to investigate a seemingly corrupt police force might be considered a new form of this"colonial guidance".

Colonial tradition

The appointment of Mr Bussières, it seems to me, vividly exemplifies this new colonial tradition. In this case, it is not the colonial power which is responsible for ensuring "discipline" and a "well managed" government, but the former colony itself which decides to be supervised by someone it deems more capable. This situation is the result of a relationship between the multilateral funding agencies and regional governments in which our countries have virtually surrendered their sovereignty to the wisdom of structural adjustment programmes.

William Demas and many others have argued that one of the reasons why governments have failed to support a Caribbean court of appeal is because of a lack of self-confidence. I believe the problem is much worse. The governments of the region lack the political courage to do such. They lack the courage, because they have always relied on the Privy Council or some other enlightened body to make very serious decisions, and because they have very little confidence in their own competence. Their very own performance in office has convinced them of their ineptitude.

The people do not clamour for change, because they themselves are aware of this softness of competence among our leaders. Leaning on Britain, the USA, Canada or an international expert is the easy way to confront the serious problem of governance. It is also an easy way to gain respect in the eyes of the international community, since they respect their experts more than ours. Unfortunately, most of our leaders also seem to feel the same way. In fact, one of the major problems with the regional integration movement has to do with the fact that our leaders themselves do not have confidence in their ability to unite the region and challenge the world.

In many ways Jamaica (and perhaps, also, others in CARICOM) is no different from Somalia or Cambodia. While the US and UN run elections in these countries, the IMF and World Bank run the economies in ours. While factional and tribal wars continue to afflict these countries, partisan politics continue to divide our society and claim numerous casualties. While civil war and tribal differences have intensified the problem of poverty and famine in these countries, patronage, classism and structural adjustment have resulted in inner-city degeneration and a country with more than 50 per cent of the population in poverty. Unlike Somalia, we will not be bombed to smithereens by the trigger-happy US and UN forces, but we will continue to reel in agony from the IMF medicine.

In many ways, Mr Bussières represents the commander who has come to return order and stability to the economy. As in Cambodia (and to a lesser extent in Somalia), his arrival has been sanctioned by segments of the economic and political elite because of possible external implications. Just as in Somalia, the problem with the BoJ is political and administrative rather than technical. Therefore, to justify Mr Bussières' appointment on purely technical grounds will solve nothing.

Defining race

One reader wants to know the origins of the terms "black" (negro) and "white" (Caucasian) as racial groups. He also wants to know whether the categories are also a way of "pigeonholing" people.

Surprisingly, for such a commonly used word, the origin of the term "race" is unclear. Race comes via French from the Italian *razza*; however, the antecedents of *razza* are obscure. A race is a biological category composed of men and women who share biologically transmitted traits that are defined as being socially significant. Current scientific evidence suggests that there is nothing such as, or even near, a pure race, as all humans are biological mixtures and have evolved from a single species out of East Africa.

In reality, the concept of race is very problematic, as the classifications of Caucasoid, Mongoloid and Negroid are not biological classifications, but arbitrary terms used by Europeans to conveniently divide up the world. It is impossible to classify races biologically, given the wide degree of variations in features and physiological systems among people who ostensibly belong to the same race. The classification of races is therefore a political activity, and not a scientific one. For instance, the term negro was first used to describe South Indians before it was applied to people of African descent. The term "African" is not based on a biological classification but means people from the land of Carthage. Etymologically speaking, "Ethiopian" is a more appropriate word to describe African people. The term Ethiopian (*Aithiopian*), literally meaning "burnt face", was used by the Greeks to describe African peoples. Similarly, the term Caucasian refers to people from the Caucasus, a place in Europe. The term Mongoloid comes from Mongol, which refers to a ruler of India.

As you can see, the concept of race is a socially constructed one and cannot be supported convincingly by biological evidence. The unfortunate use of the term as it is being used today must be located in the work of German scholars, particularly among anthropologists such as Meiners and J. F. Blumenbach, a professor of natural history at Göttingen. These scholars, during the 18th century, out of the blue, invented a theory of racial hierarchy in which they placed Caucasians (blue-eyed blonds) at the top and negroes at the bottom. It was this theory which the Nazis later used to oppress the Jews and justify a Germanic superior race. (Ironically, in the past the Germanic tribes were discriminated against by other Europeans.)

The Göttingen classification, although racist, contradictory and totally nonsensical, is still used today. What is interesting about this classification is that whenever African people were associated with an outstanding civilization, these people were either placed in some other category, or their civilization was seen as a result of miscegenation. Indians were considered to be Caucasians because the Germans wanted to locate the origins of humanity in the Asian subcontinent and not Africa. Such is the stupidity of the education which was fed to the world through colonialism. The American Anthropological Association recently acknowledged that the concept of race is very problematic and has dispensed with it as a biological category. Unfortunately, many of us continue to use this classification.

The African-Asian link

(TUESDAY, AUGUST 10, 1993)

Some weeks ago, in response to a reader, I wrote an article in which I examined the origins of racial categories. Now the same reader wants to find out about the origins of the terms "black" and "white" as they apply to people.

Now the word "white" goes back to Indo-European *Kwitnos* or *Kwidnos*, which was formed from the same base that produced the Sanskrit word *Sveta* (white) and the Russian word *Svet* (light). On the other hand, the word "black" comes via the Latin word *Niger*. To denigrate people, or to "blacken" them, comes from the Latin word for denigrate, a compound verb formed from the intensive prefix *de* and *niger*. It is out of this adjective that we get the Italian *Nero*, the French *noir*, the Spanish *negro* and English *nigger*. The word "negro" was originally a defamatory term used by Europeans to describe dark-skinned people (of both African and early Asia). By the way, this is a clear example of the way in which the uncritical acceptance of European languages, which reflect the prejudices of those societies, can contribute to the continued denigration of black people. But that's another story.

Unfortunately

I am unable to say precisely when the terms black and white were applied to distinct racial groups. My feeling is that the way in which we use black and white to represent people today is a fairly recent phenomenon, that is, since European colonialism.

The reader also wants to know about the South Indians whom I referred to as Negros. The remainder of this article looks at this issue. Part of the problem of Third World development is that our societies have been forced to construct reality with Europe at the centre. In schools across the region, history refers to European history, or history since slavery. Yet, European civilization is comparatively recent, compared with that of Africa and Asia. For us to understand ourselves better, therefore, we have to demystify the past by looking at relations between different parts of the world without placing Europe at the centre.

Civilization

It is now accepted by most anthropologists that human civilization began in Africa and spread to the Indian sub-continent through Arabia and the coastlands of Iran and Baluchistan. The descendants of these early inhabitants of India, most of them resembling Ethiopians, are known as Negritos. Small pockets of these people can be found among the Kadar and Rajamal Hill cultures in eastern Bahir and the Andomons.

Now when most people talk about South Indians, they often refer to the Dravidians, the most populous group in the region. However, anthro-photojournalist John Chandler identifies roughly six groups who inhabit the region. Three of these six ethnic groups include the Ethiopian Blacks, known as Negritos, and the Proto-Australoid (both black groups); the Dravidians (mixture of Black/Mongoloid and Black/Caucasoid); and the paleo-Mediterranean (a mixture of Black and Mongoloid people). Most of the East Indians of the Caribbean appear to be descendants of the Dravidians and the Paleo-Mediterranean people of Kannada, Tamil and Malayan regions.

Reconstruct

In attempting to reconstruct Africa's link with India, many anthropologists and historians have argued that the earliest founders of the Indus Valley civilization were of the Negrito and the Proto-Australoid groups. They built the great urban centres of Mohenjo-Daro and Harappa. This view contradicts the one articulated by many European and later Indian scholars (most of whom were influenced by European scholarship) that India's earliest inhabitants (the Negritos) contributed nothing to this great culture. Evidence of the Black (African and Proto-Australian) influence is reflected in much of the art of the era. Chandler also points to the possibility of cotton, first cultivated in Africa, being introduced to the Indus Valley by Negritos between 10,000 and 6,000 BC. Indeed, the sculpture representing Vishnu (from the 6th century AD), one of the major icons of Hinduism, is considered by many historians of India to be Negrito art.

I am not suggesting that the Indus Valley civilization owes its greatness only to the contribution of the original inhabitants of India. Indeed, the records show that the so-called Aryans contributed much, even after they destroyed Mohenjo-Daro, probably around 1,500 BC. The point being made here is that somehow in the reconstruction of history, the contribution of Blacks (both from Africa and Australia), those who first inhabited India, was overlooked.

But the link between Asia and Africa does not stop with India. China has had contact with Africa long before the Europeans sailed the East African coast and plundered it. Much of this contact is documented in a recent book by Phillip Snow, *The Star Raft: China's Encounter with Africa*. This book documents commercial trade between Africans and the Chinese, and the participation of Africans in China's dynastic wars. African soldiers were later used successfully by the Portuguese to challenge China for parts of East Asia. The book also documents the contribution of Africans to rulers. Chinese dragon dances and the exchange of contacts between East African and Chinese. It draws primarily on the writings of Chinese scholars, thus painting the relationship from the Chinese perspective.

More research is being done on the trading links stretching from Ethiopia to Sri Lanka to Indonesia, which were destroyed with the coming of the Europeans to Africa.

The historical link between Asia and Africa has been destroyed and then reconstructed by European scholarship. The stereotypes which Asians have of Africans, and Africans have of Asians are partly based on this reconstruction and an almost incomprehensible ignorance of each other – a situation which should not have arisen. The sooner we learn that Europe is not the centre of the universe, the sooner we may be able to free ourselves from mental underdevelopment. Peace!

Punting with the land of Punt

(TUESDAY, OCTOBER 12, 1993)

People around the world have been treated to stark images of Somalia. Also, we have been exposed to a barrage of talk by various American media about the US role there, in Ethiopia and Liberia, and across other African countries. Somalia has been treated as a basket case, a country with desperate people led by a crazy warlord. There are several questions which can be asked about the US and UN involvement in Somalia.

However, the one which interests me most is: why get involved in Somalia when there are more destructive and brutal wars in Sudan, Angola, Liberia and Rwanda?It is estimated that hundreds are being killed daily in Angola. In Sudan, the Black Sudanese are being overrun by Muslim fundamentalists of Arab stock, who control the north. The result is mass starvation and near genocide. Yet we see, no reports of this in the media.

By the way, Jamaica Broadcasting Corporation (JBC) and CVM Television Limited (CVM), it appears, are contented with showing the bombings in Bosnia and the occasional report on South Africa. It is as if our local news people are slaves to the American media. Consequently, they do not ferret out information for themselves. Is it not possible for the JBC and CVM news teams to find alternative means of obtaining news about the world? At present they are simply catching a few canned reports from the US-based Cable News Network (CNN) out of the skies. Are we that uncreative? Or is it that we lack the rigour with which to pursue, assess and analyze world affairs?

One possible interest in Somalia by the Americans has to do with the possibilities for oil exploration. Additionally, there is the geopolitical problem of the security of the troublesome Horn of Africa and its environs, which is convenient for those people preoccupied with the threat of Islamic fundamentalism. Pardon my cynicism, but I cannot help noticing the hypocrisy of the US and the UN when they talk about humanitarian mission, while they fly over mass destruction in other parts of Africa.

Compare the American coverage of the conflict in Somalia with their coverage of the depravation and turmoil in Iraq. There is one big difference between the Somalian and the Iraqi conflicts. In the case of Iraq, the American and European press went out of their way to show that, in spite of Saddam's intransigence, Iraq was a civilized country – the land of the glorious Mesopotamia which they say gave birth to western civilization. Note the opposite approach with Somalia – here they portrayed a desperately poor land, occupied by Blacks and off-Blacks in a state of nature, led by a two-bit warlord who can hardly balance his pants on his shrinking hips. Sounds familiar?

Real estate

The truth of the matter is that Somalia is not some old piece of "negro" real estate chalked up by colonial conquistadors. It has a long and golden history, being the centre of the fabled land of Punt. Punt was the ancient Egyptian name for the southern coast of the Red Sea and the adjacent coasts of the Gulf of Aden, corresponding to today's coastal Ethiopia and Djibouti. Greek historian Herodotus made countless references to the glory of Punt in his *Histories* in the 5th Century BC. In fact, the records show that such was the homage bestowed on this "Divine Land" that Queen Hatshepsut of Egypt (1503-1482 BC), after journeying to Punt, had the details of this most momentous occasion inscribed on the walls of her temple at Davral-Bahri.

Somalia has the distinction of being one of the few African countries which share a common language (Somali), a common religion (Islam) and a common culture (comprised of certain indigenous African and Semitic practices). This does not mean that kinship affiliations are non-existent, as the current conflict dramatizes.

Contemporary Somalia is the product of the 1960s. Between 1960 and 1969, it was ruled by the democratically elected government of President Shermarke, leader of the Somali Youth League (SYL). In 1969, the year of the last so-called democratic election, the SYL is said to have engaged in the most unsavoury of election practices, strong-arm tactics not excluded – indeed a sad commentary on African politics.

Somalia entered another conundrum when military leader Mohamed Siad Barre of the Supreme Revolutionary Council took over, following the assassination of Sharmarke in 1969. Public bliss for the changing guard was halted abruptly when they saw the signs of tyranny in their new soldier. Barre banned political parties, and he engaged in authoritarian rule. His regime tinkered with socialism, and it got the support of the Union of Soviet Socialist Republics (USSR). This relationship changed, however, and the USSR gave up on Somalia. Barre then reluctantly embraced the US during the early 1980s. This new development led to a crushing IMF programme which further alienated an already disturbed population. Barre was overthrown on January 27, 1991. This paved the way for the rise to power of an inconsequential motel owner, Ali Mahdi Muhammad, as president of Somalia. This leader of the United Somali Congress has to this date been unable to win legitimacy from the people, or maintain control of a country which has descended into chaos.

There are a number of clan leaders in Somalia, of whom General Aidid is only one. Why the US has decided to go after Aidid while ignoring the others is a question begging to be answered. The build-up of US troops in Somalia will inevitably lead to a social transformation of that country in terms of its culture, economy and confidence. This is something which deserves an in-depth examination, something the Hollywood-style reporters at CNN or CBS are not interested in, or is it that not even they are entirely competent to take on this task?

Cool Runnings and labels

(TUESDAY, OCTOBER 19, 1993)

The film *Cool Runnings* will probably go down in history as a Walt Disney classic. If it does, it will not be because it focused on the hitherto obscure sport of bobsledding, nor even because of the unlikely performance of a group of boys from a tropical paradise somewhere close to problem-plagued Haiti and stubborn Cuba. It will become a classic because *Cool Runnings* is a simple film. It is free from the romantic heroism of some demigod, and uncluttered by a barrage of the blazing guns which seem ever-present in today's action movies. It is a film about courage, conviction and pride. It is a film about pursuing a dream, in the face of great odds, with pride and dignity. This film shows that it takes hard work and discipline to accomplish dreams, and that even in the face of hardships one does not have to fall prey to deceit and corruption – habits which appear only too commonplace in today's society. In a sense, it is a film which restores confidence in human beings and speaks to values which we too often feel can only be found in some sacred character.

Very timely

Again, the showing of this film is very timely, and with Jamaica's rapidly deteriorating image abroad and at home, this positive turn of events is welcome. *Cool Runnings* is a breath of fresh air for many people who are demotivated as a result of the severe economic burdens, and the corruption which exist at all levels of the society, which seems to be the norm rather than the exception. Therefore, it is important that we welcome this reprieve from an environment which is increasingly becoming difficult. Interestingly, it is often through sports and the arts that we are reminded of our talent and potential. Consequently, it ought to be very fitting that the best of our artistes and sportspersons become our role models. Or it is through competitive sports that we witness the true relationship between discipline and vision, and how they work together to achieve one goal? Competitive sports have allowed us to see the rewards of vision, planning, discipline and persistence. Might I say, it is this vision, planning, discipline and persistence which allowed Merlene Ottey to reach her goal and win a gold medal. If only for this reason, she deserves to be honoured like others who have triumphed against the odds.

Let us celebrate

This is not to say that ordinary people do not struggle against the odds; indeed, the record shows that ordinary people do this daily. However, it is important that we celebrate with those who represent us, especially those who do it with dignity, so that it will encourage more of us to strive to do likewise.

Cool Runnings will make profits for its producers because of its theme and its rare ability to cut across cultures without being offensive. This is not to say it was perfect; indeed, a few stereotypes persisted. But, what the heck? It is a vast improvement over many others made about the tropics which I have seen.

Of course, some of it is fiction, but people often find it difficult to distinguish between good fiction and "real life". Thus, this film will probably do more for the sport of bobsledding than all the Olympic advertisements combined over the years. Also, it will serve to re-establish Jamaica, a small country, in the minds of the ordinary person, internationally. I am reminded by this film that it is the ordinary, talented, disciplined and dignified visionaries in our midst who possess the greatest potential for taking this country and this region into the twenty-first century; and we must never lose sight of this fact. Importantly, we can do this without being relegated to the position of poor dependent Third World nation. There is much that we the people and our leaders of this land and this region can learn from *Cool Runnings*.

Labelling people

A reader who has been following my writings on race and ethnicity wants to know how I feel about replacing racial categories with more "relevant nomenclature". To quote him:

> Rather than add more descriptions like Afro-American and Afro-Jamaican, why not subtract a few? Why not just do away with the terms "black" and "white" as they refer to people, and thereby force persons to use more unique terms to describe people? How do people that share the same skin colour and who all live in the same district describe each other? They go perhaps for the gender, height, width and maybe even the persons' professions.

To answer the reader, I have no problem with using such a system of referring to people. As I have stated in previous columns, there is no scientific justification for racial classifications. They are the inventions of people with small minds and sinister intentions. However, I do not think that simply changing classifications of people will solve problem. You see, the problem with dividing up people is not so much one of the classifications, in and of themselves. Rather, the problem is in the power relations which led to these classifications in the first place. The current racial classifications are not based on biology. African or

Caucasian do not refer to biological structures, but to geographical areas. But they eventually came to be associated with certain types of people in a hierarchical structure. Therefore, the problem is not simply the labelling, but also who does the labelling, and for what purpose.

It is quite possible that under the scheme which the reader proposes, stereotypes may develop based on height, gender and weight (and some of these do already exist). The stereotypes associated with being Jew and Muslim are not race-based, but yet they are at the root of the most serious conflicts in the world.

All labels are based on some type of classification which, by the way, are not always self-evident. I would agree with the reader that some classifications are more useful and indeed more appropriate than others; but then, this again depends on who is doing the classification. Therefore, the basis and motivation for any such 'classifications should be given careful thought before we become engaged in the labelling and classifying of human beings. Peace!

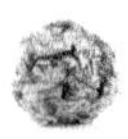

The tragedy of Africa

(WEDNESDAY, OCTOBER 27, 1993)

There is no other region in the world which is currently suffering from such social, economic and political dislocation as sub-Saharan Africa is now experiencing. Africa has the slowest growing economies; some of the most unstable political systems; the most vicious civil wars; and the continent is now being ravaged by the spread of the deadly disease AIDS. The Sahel, comprised of Senegal, Mauritania, Mali, Niger, and Chad, loses vegetation daily. The cradle of civilization is in the grip of an ecological disaster. In the midst of this calamity preside elites who siphon off the surplus and engage in repressive actions of baffling proportions. Take Angola, where hundreds die daily, victims of a crude and almost inhuman band of so-called liberators, the National Union for the Total Independence of Angola (UNITA)! Angola, Mozambique and Ethiopia have the unflattering distinction of having some of the world's most protracted civil wars. Then, there is Rwanda, a small, poor country where, as a result of war, the rare mountain gorillas might very well become an endangered species. Recently, the Republic of Burundi, located next to Rwanda and problem-plagued Zaire (modern-day Republic of Congo), fell victim to a gang of rebels who executed their president and imposed tyranny on their people. The situation in Burundi is bound to lead to more ethnic rivalry between the three major ethnic groups – the Hutu/Bahutu, the Tutsi and the Twa.

Julius Nyerere

Indeed, only Tanzania has been able to escape this ethnic calamity because of the progressive ideas of Julius Nyerere, who incidentally is unprecedented in contemporary Africa, having voluntarily demitted office as that country's president. Tanzania, a virtual UN protectorate, remains a basket case with a per capita income of approximately US$160, smaller than the US$370 of Haiti, the poorest country in the Western Hemisphere.

Cynics and racists will argue that this situation is an indication of Africans' own inability to govern themselves. However, this claim can be easily disposed of if we point to the history of Africa right up to European conquest. This period of history will provide us with the existence of strong and rich states governed by effective political systems. From west to east to south, African nations have traditionally had very effective systems of social organization. As far back as the Nile civilizations, which stretched from Uganda to upper Egypt, black Africans have been effective rulers; they were not different from other groups of people elsewhere in the civilized world.

By the way, recently there was an interesting discussion on the *Breakfast Club* in which one of the hosts sought to separate Egypt from Africa. There is enough historical evidence which now acknowledges that ancient Egypt was indeed part of "Black" Africa, and though the later Egyptians came in different colours by way of miscegenation and the settlement of Semitics and Europeans, this does not deny the link. To ask how Egyptians viewed black Africans is like asking how Kingstonians view Montegonians.

Colonial escapade

A major part of the problem regarding development in Africa results from the colonial escapade in which the continent was chopped up and different ethnic groups thrown together in artificial areas called nation states. An analogy would be the joining of some parts of France with parts of Britain, while joining the other parts of France and Britain with the Netherlands.

This creation of artificial boundaries was compounded by putting people with different cultures, experiences, and family ties together with the ultimate expectation that they would immediately sing in unison "We are the World". This has never happened in other parts of the world – not without serious conflict. Of course, an important reason for breaking up former states in the first place was to weaken the opposition. In Africa, the notion of the nation state is still in the process of evolution, at a time when it is under attack elsewhere in the world.

The other factor is that, as Africa diminished in importance as a consequence of the raping of its resources, and more recently with the end of the Cold War, there is very little interest in helping the region to survive. Between 1950 and 1967, US financial aid to Africa was about the same as that given to South Korea during the same period. Countries like Ethiopia, Sudan, Mozambique and Tanzania allowed themselves to be used as pawns during the Cold War. The US poured money into the coffers of Jonas Savimbi and his fight against the ANC and the Popular Movement for the Liberation of Angola (MPLA), both supported by the then USSR. The US knew that Savimbi was a criminal, but their interest was always geopolitical, not humanitarian. These policies are consistent with ideas of US Senator Jesse Helms, who opposes Aristide's return to Haiti. Helms, a known racist, is, along with the CIA, desperately trying to demonize Jean-Bertrand Aristide. Helms is trying to continue one of the hopeless policies of George Bush, which is to block democracy in Haiti because of their discomfort with Aristide's independence of thought.

Leadership quality

But there is one other factor which will determine whether or not Africa will make it out of its present conundrum. It is, of course, the quality of its leadership. The continent is presently haunted by the practice of authoritarianism, corruption and militarism. In many countries, corruption, incompetence and the virtual absence of civil society have led to the decay of physical infrastructure and institutions.

Not long ago, oil-rich Nigeria was importing fuel because of problems it had in maintaining one of its refineries. Mineral-rich Angola is in a hopeless state, and along with Mozambique has more amputees per capita than any other country in the world. Somalia's political system has collapsed, and Kenya's pretence of a democracy is ailing from the scourge of political corruption and government incompetence. Uganda, once regarded as Africa's breadbasket, is now faced with an influx of refugees from the Sudan – a country which is bent on destroying its Christian population in the name of Islamic fundamentalism.

Like us in the Caribbean, many African leaders seem to have a fascination with grand meaningless monuments. Some time ago, President Félix Houphouët-Boigny of Côte d'Ivoire built a monstrosity of a church to impress the Pope, in a country where only 12 per cent of the population is Catholic. (In the Caribbean, our equal is the fascination with large, empty central banks.)

The prognosis indicates no immediate reprieve for the African people from visionless leadership, intense economic hardships and continued tribal war.Ironically, South Africa seems to hold the greatest hope for the region's rejuvenation. Surprised? Peace!

The retreat to ethnicity

(TUESDAY, MAY 10, 1994)

Today, many Jamaicans will be celebrating the swearing-in of Nelson Mandela as president of South Africa. Many wait anxiously to see whether the grand old man will be able to steer the country away from the ethnic and political strife which has characterized that society and continent. Meanwhile, farther north, the United Nations battles one of the greatest human tragedies of the twentieth century: the ethno-political war between the Hutu and Tutsi peoples of Rwanda. In the meantime, the international community comes face-to-face with the tragedies of Mozambique, Angola and Ethiopia – three countries which were locked in some of the longest civil wars in recent history. In Kenya, President Daniel arap Moi presides over a country in virtual turmoil. Many human rights groups accuse his regime of engaging in acts of ethnic cleansing. Presumably, these acts are aimed at stifling the opponents of his ruling Kenyan African National Union. And not far away, in the Arabian Peninsula, the country of Yemen is embroiled in conflict between the north and the south of the country. And though this conflict is not purely ethnic, when placed in a historical context the ethnic concerns become apparent.

Tribal chiefs

Many hundreds of years ago, North Yemen or Yemen Arab Republic (former capital, Sanaa) was divided from South Yemen or People's Democratic Republic of Yemen (former capital, Aden) into two separate entities. At various periods in history, both South and North Yemen were ruled by indigenous tribal chiefs, or by invaders such as the Egyptians, Persians, Ottoman Turks and, more recently, the British. The British attempted a federation of Northern and Southern Yemen in 1963, but following their withdrawal in 1967, the South again separated from the North. Nevertheless, in 1990, as a result of the dissolution of the Soviet Union, both Yemens formed a single country. Therefore, the present North-South conflict is not an arbitrary occurrence.

Perhaps the most publicized area of ethnic conflict

is in the former Yugoslavia where Croatians, Serbs and Muslims are engaged in a fierce civil war. This war erupted after the break-up of Yugoslavia. It is perhaps of some importance to note that what was once Yugoslavia was really an amalgamation of the former kingdoms of Serbia and Croatia. The name Yugoslavia was adopted in 1929 to replace Serbian and Croatian Nationalism.

Not so long ago, following the fall of the Eastern Bloc, many people hoped for a world relatively free of the kinds of wars we have today. However, the fall of communism has allowed us to see the fissures, ethnic and political, which were present in many nations during the Cold War. As illustrated by the events in Somalia, USSR, Yugoslavia, Angola, Ethiopia, Sudan, and now Yemen, the Cold War was partially responsible for an artificial peace within these countries. In many cases, the Soviets and the Americans supported opposing groups who built large militaries, but when the Soviets and Americans withdrew from these countries, the guns were turned inward, the divisions gaped and the conflicts escalated, as in the cases of Angola and the Sudan.

Ethnic conflicts

Without doubt, Africa is the continent with the greatest concentration of ethnic conflicts. To appreciate why this is so, it is necessary to understand the historical evolution of today's African nation-states. Unlike much of Asia and Europe, the present-day African nations were configured by colonial rulers. The word "nation" etymologically refers to a breed or stock. It has also been used to refer to a species or race. Over the years, the term has come to refer to an organized territorial unit. If one used the literal meaning of nation, perhaps only Ethiopia, Somalia and Eritrea would qualify as nations in Sub-Saharan Africa – and even these countries have been reorganized because of European invasion and occupation. The others are largely creations of European colonialists. The borders created by the colonialists separated people from their own ethnic groups, as in the case of Senegal, and forced hitherto warring groups into single units. While some countries, like Tanzania, have been able to contain their ethnic conflict, others have not been so lucky. A look at the map of Africa between 750 BC and 1901 AD shows an Africa much different from the one we see and know today. And yet, in a sense the countries of Africa are still in the process of constructing their nations, and the resolution of ethnic differences appears to be the teething pains in this process.

Armed attack

One of the fundamental causes of ethnic conflict is inequality among specific ethnic groups. Recently, this was vividly demonstrated by the uprising of the Zapatista rebels in Chiapas, Mexico. These people are marginalized from the economy and the politics of their land, and so they launched an armed attack against the government. Thus, we can safely say that the struggle for power and for survival are usually key components in the ethnic conflicts across the world.

There are parallels between ethnic conflict in other parts of the world and what happens in Jamaica. Our political system with two opposing political parties is, in main ways, organized along the same lines as are many ethnic groups. Our partisan division and the fervour with which we defend our respective stances – especially in the inner-city areas – parallel the division and stances of the Serbs and Muslims in Bosnia. In both societies, people suffer and are killed because of whom they identify with. During the 1980 election, we had a murder rate of 43 per 100,000, and elements of the PNP and JLP were engaged in what could be called a civil war, which consequently can be seen as a small-scale attempt at ethnic cleansing. This country is susceptible, given the level of marginalization of our people from the economic and political systems. Many areas in our country are vulnerable to further manipulation, and this can have the same consequences as ethnic wars. Jamaica, as a country, is certainly not a Bosnia, nor is it a Rwanda. However, if history is anything to go by, we should never say never. Peace!

Rwanda: Another view

(TUESDAY, AUGUST 02, 1994)

In general, the media have been treating the crisis in Rwanda as senseless tribal conflict. However, to its credit, the Jamaican radio station KLAS' morning show *The Breakfast Club* did an analysis of the conflict and has attempted to move the discussion beyond the traditional prejudicial accounts of non-Western conflicts usually given by the Western media.

To be sure, the Western media, in their analysis of ethnic conflicts across Eastern Europe, have been much more willing to consider the impact of political and economic factors than simply to blame centuries-old ethnic loyalties, as they have shamelessly done in Africa.

This ethnocentric perspective of conflicts in Africa is, in part, responsible for this seemingly cavalier attitude of the world community to what is one of the most serious human tragedies of the 20th century – a human tragedy for which some Western nations must bear some of the responsibility, given their alleged complicity in the events leading up to this crisis.

In examining the Rwanda crisis, Africa-based Syracuse University political scientist professor Horace Campbell makes the point that one cannot fully understand the present political conflict in Rwanda unless one has an appreciation of the colonial history of the country, and of its struggle to overcome the dictatorial regime of former president Juvénal Habyarimana and his National Revolutionary Movement for Development and Democracy (MRND).

African writer Dixon Kamukama, in examining the roots of the Rwanda conflict, points to the fact that while the conflict between the Tutsis and the Hutus predates the Western colonization of Africa, the differences between the two groups have been manipulated by the Belgians and, later, the French in order to maintain their control over the territory.

Consequently, the Tutsis were used by the Belgians to control the majority Hutu population. Ironically, according to Campbell, it was a Tutsi who led the campaign against European colonization.

Conflict

In 1959, the Catholic Church and the colonial administration mobilized the poor Hutu peasants against the nationalists who were mainly Tutsis; tens of thousands died in that conflict. In 1962, Rwanda became independent under Hutu leadership. In 1973, Juvénal Habyarimana took power by a coup and killed most of the ministers and prominent leaders of the government.

Following an agreement in 1974, his regime was supported first by the Belgians, and later the French, both of whom provided military troops and military assistance to his government.

In 1990, the Rwandese Patriotic Front (RPF),

comprising mainly Tutsi refugees, launched a guerrilla war against the government from their base in Uganda. France responded by deploying more troops and by providing additional military assistance to the president, under the guise of protecting French citizens.

The armed struggle and the refugee problem which started in the 1950s were beginning to have their impact on the neighbouring countries of Eastern Central Africa. The attempt by the Organisation of African Unity (OAU) to solve the problem led to a meeting in Arusha, Tanzania, where the MRND agreed to form a coalition government with four other opposition parties, inclusive of the RPF. This coalition government was to hold power for one year, after which elections were to be held.

According to Campbell, this agreement was rejected by MRND hardliners. Subsequently, both the government and its allies began to form militias which proceeded to unleash violence against opposition politicians and the Tutsi population.

Unfortunately, another round of negotiations did not take place between the opposition and the government until August 1993, at which time the MRND signed a peace treaty with the opposition parties, including the RPF. The treaty called for power-sharing and it also established a timetable for a return to democracy in Rwanda.

It should be noted that during the 1992 Arusha negotiation the OAU, along with the UN, which had originally commended the OAU for its mediating efforts, deployed troops along the Rwanda-Uganda border to monitor the ceasefire. UN resolution 868 called for an embargo on the shipping of arms to either side involved in the conflict.

Notwithstanding these negotiations, the violence against the opposition persisted, since the French continued to supply military assistance to the government, and arms were received from Egypt, Zaire and South Africa.

Professor Campbell also argues that between September and December of 1993, some members of the Rwandan government, along with several radio stations, called on the people to carry out massacres against the opposition and the Tutsis.

Further, between September and December when the transitional government was supposed to take over, there were meetings taking place at which plans were charted to destroy the opposition. The government then distributed guns to two militia groups and to the youth arms of the dominant political groups of the country.

Attack

Interestingly, on April 6, 1994, on their return from meeting to discuss the implementation of the Arusha initiative, the presidents of Burundi and Rwanda perished in a plane crash. Although the government has claimed that the RPF shot down the plane, there are also allegations that this was a planned attack by government hardliners, with the help of the French. Campbell also states that a number of newspapers in Europe have linked French rockets and French parachuters to the plane crash.

The subsequent massacre began with a killing of the Hutus who supported the peace process. And the fact that the UN forces withdrew from Rwanda at precisely the time that they were needed did not help, but escalated the desperate situation.

The recent decision by the RPF, who now control the country, to oppose the so-called humanitarian intervention of the French was premised on experiences wherein the French military previously supported the government hardliners and opposed the RPF.

Mind you, this humanitarian intervention was coming from a country which had been accused of sheltering some of the leaders of the massacre and of providing a safe haven for an alternative to the RPF-dominated government. Instead, the RPF called for a truce comprising the OAU and the immediate withdrawal of the French from their country. In an attempt to bolster France's image and to legitimize its involvement in the crisis, French President François Mitterrand visited South Africa to gain the support of Nelson Mandela.

However, prior to Mr Mitterrand's requests, Mr Mandela preempted him by stating that no one nation should try to solve the situation in Rwanda. Mr Mandela has promised humanitarian aid and armoured personnel carriers, but he has refused to provide the military personnel requested by Mitterrand.

When the full story of Rwanda is written, it will be quite different from what we now read and hear in the media.

Clearly, the Rwandans themselves must assume responsibility for the tragedy. But despite this, we cannot ignore the role played by the Western nations in creating and accommodating this human tragedy.

To dismiss this crisis as purely tribal would be a mistake. Jamaica could do well to heed the voice coming from Rwanda and the other strife-torn countries across the world, for where there is no justice there can be no peace. Peace!

The growth of Islam (excerpt)

(TUESDAY, APRIL 04, 1995)

Last week, former heavyweight boxer "Iron" Mike Tyson walked out of prison after serving a sentence for rape. Shielding him from a battery of reporters and curious onlookers was a paramilitary-style group of Muslim brothers. A few days later Tyson delivered a statement to the media, at the end of which he wished the audience, "May Allah be with you." From the looks of things, it seems that Tyson has become a member of the Nation of Islam. If this is so, then Mike is a prized convert for the Nation of Islam, just as Muhammad Ali was during the 1960s. For one, Tyson has a high public profile, and despite all else is still admired by many black Americans. Importantly, however, is the perception that Tyson might have undergone a character transformation, not unlike the change evident among many black Americans who have served time in prison and who later join the Muslim movement.

Indeed, in his autobiography, Malcolm X states that it was the Nation of Islam which saved him and many other Blacks who fell prey to an environment of drugs, crime, and negativism. It is this ability to reform persons whom society has given up on which make Islam a most potent force for change in the United States. At the same time, it has emerged as the most attractive religion for people of African descent in the US. But this burgeoning religion is creating fear among many Americans who see it as a potential threat to the Western oriented style of Christianity, which is increasingly having little success in attracting young black men to its ideals.

To be sure, one may argue that this interest in Islam is not confined to Black Americans, since at present

Islam is the fastest growing religion in the world. However, it seems to have a special appeal for many people of African descent – particularly on the American continent. One obvious reason, of course, is that Islam as practised by most black Americans incorporates a vision of the Black person which is positive. Second, and a point often overlooked, is that there is an abundance of evidence which shows that large numbers of African slaves who were brought to the US and the Caribbean were Muslims.

In fact, prior to the coming of Europeans to Africa, many communities in Africa practised Islam for hundreds of years; for instance, the city of Timbuktu in Mali was once regarded as a leading intellectual centre for Islamic scholars circa 1400-1600. Therefore, Afro-American Muslims could very well claim that the conversion to Islam is part of the process of recapturing their heritage.

So, the Black Muslims' creation of a brand of Islam which puts at its core the struggles and interests of the black person is indeed no different from what has been done in the formation of new, or factions of, religions all over the world. Incidentally, Islam evolved from Judaism and Christianity in Saudi Arabia. Therefore, it is not accidental that much of the Islamic teachings revolve around Arab culture, aesthetics, and ideals, and has as its reference point the Old Testament. And, like Rastafari which also evolved out of Christianity, the Black Muslim movement speaks directly to the experiences of the people of the African diaspora.

When the Chinese borrowed Buddhism from India and Nepal, they made drawings and representations of the Buddha in the image of the Chinese people. The same is true of Western Europeans whose paintings of Jesus Christ are a far cry from the early representations of him found in other non-Western societies. An exhibition in the American Museum of Natural History shows that the pictorial representation of Jesus Christ depends on the society doing the depicting and also the particular period during which these etchings are done. You see, what is clear about religions is that they all have cultural interpretations of doctrines, and they also reflect a positive image of those who created the religion.

Although some of the ideological tenets of the Nation of Islam have in the past been condemned as anti-Semitic, attempts have been made to focus more on self-reliance, while developing self-respect, economic independence and honour among its followers.

The emphasis on discipline, hard work, honour and economic self-reliance is perhaps the most positive aspect of the movement. In order to solidify the pillars on which this religion is built, the Nation of Islam has its own schools and businesses, and its members do not depend on the government for welfare benefits.

Despite the accusations of anti-Semitism and authoritarianism, the conversion of Mike Tyson could be that one little thing which this organization needs to further fuel its revival – after all, it seemed to have been able to calm and convert the young and the restless. The Black Muslims in the US can safely say that they now have added legitimacy, and this by expansion should serve as impetus to the already burgeoning world religion of Islam.

Independent thinking: Part 1 (only)

(TUESDAY, FEBRUARY 25, 1997)

I have often wondered, like so many other people, why a country made up of ninety-five per cent Black people has to put aside a month (the shortest in the year) to celebrate "black history". Clearly, I can understand why this is done in the United States; it is a country where minority groups are constantly seeking to assert their worth in an inherently racist society. However, in Jamaica where the "black" aesthetic and discourse constantly dominate, setting aside a month to focus on black history is not as necessary for us as it is for Americans. In fact, what we should aim for is the celebration of black history all year round, rather than just for one month.

But, given that our thinking in almost every sphere of life seems completely dictated by what Americans do, then black history month, like Kwanzaa and all the other American inventions, will be mimicked by us in its totality. Indeed, it is not so much that there is something wrong with these American creations, it is just that they seem to be imported without context. Regrettably, this principle of always aping the Americans is seen in our discussion of economic matters, sports and politics; in short, if it works for the Americans, it will work for us.

Now, having decided to adopt Black History Month, the activities of the month seem to celebrate only the achievements of Black American entertainers, sports persons and civil rights leaders such as Marcus Garvey, and a few African leaders and civilizations. In light of this, most Jamaicans are not aware of the fact that there are Black people who live, contribute, or have done something useful in other parts of the world – namely countries other than the US, South Africa and Jamaica. In the same breath, few Jamaicans have ever heard about C.L.R. James, arguably Trinidad and the Caribbean's finest thinker; or even leaders such as George Padmore; writers such as Aimé Césaire; and a whole host of other outstanding writers, thinkers and innovators from Latin America, the Caribbean, Europe and Asia. Therefore, the process and practice of celebrating Black History Month, as is, is one of miseducation.

Furthermore, the constant fixation of condensing black history to only the struggle against European oppression does little for the very concept of black history. For, while we cannot ignore the impact of slavery on Black people, we must always remember that Black people have been interacting with other cultures and peoples, not as slaves or as "black" people, but as human beings, for thousands of years prior to their enslavement by Europeans. Put another way, Africans have always had contact with Asians, Amerindians, and other civilisations, and even to this day they still do. This, therefore, is why I detest being defined simply by what has happened to our people during the past five hundred years.

The media, to their credit, have tried to increase public education on the history of Africa, but it is still presented as though these civilizations existed outside of a larger world, or that their only point of reference was Europe. Nevertheless, if we are to understand the totality of our experiences, then we as African peoples have to capture the multi-dimensional nature of our experiences. If we are to survive the Middle Passage, then our horizon of knowledge must transcend the Middle Passage. In other words, since Africa and the diaspora existed before the European slavery machinery, then to understand ourselves we need to gasp the simple fact that life did not always revolve around Europe, the Europeans or slavery.

But moving beyond the Middle Passage does not mean that you simply reify the past. A true movement beyond the Middle Passage means that, as we celebrate "black" achievements, we must be compelled to do so critically. For African leaders, like leaders in every civilization on earth, did not always work towards the upliftment of their people. In this sense, Black History Month is as much about Black people, as it is about other (non-Black) people. Fundamentally, it is the history of human beings.

CARICOM meeting

Congratulations to JBC for broadcasting live the opening ceremony of the CARICOM intersessional meeting. When CVM Television first started, the news had a good regional and international focus. With the passage of time, however, the management has decided to take the easy way out and like JBC TV, has decided to import packaged news from the United States. Except for local news, there is little on both JBC and CVM which I cannot get on CNN or NBC. Alas, the radio stations, like JBC's Radio Jamaica (RJR), have good local news segments, and thus there is no reason to watch either JBC or CVM's nightly news.

But, back to the coverage of the CARICOM summit. One of the things we learnt from the broadcast is that, in spite its own limitations, CARICOM is growing, in membership and scope. It would now seem that, given the powerful political and economic alliances occurring across the world, it makes sense for small states, like ours, to pool resources and deal with this world in a more unified manner. Indeed, I believe that one day we will have leaders who will be honest enough to admit that Alexander Bustamante's, and to a lesser extent Eric Williams', roles in the break-up of the West Indies Federation, was one of the greatest developmental errors committed against the people of this region.

You see, politicians love to talk about sovereignty, patriotism and national pride, but they are often unwilling to give up power to achieve these nice sounding ideals. Beautiful flags and anthems, although important, are not enough to run a nation. Peace!

Chapter 3 Mental Attitudes

- Beauty and the beast
- A short note on bleaching: Part 1 (only)

Introduction

Articles in Chapter 3 explore the fact that the concept of beauty is somewhat distorted. It is emphasised that, though Jamaica and countries of the Caribbean are home to predominantly black populations, the concept of beauty held within the population is denoted by persons with very "light complexion" who appear to have "mixed" features. To cement this view, the author looks at the percentage of individuals with mixed features who have been chosen to represent Jamaica at beauty contests. The author suggests that society's concept of beauty helps to determine and reflect how people see each other and how they feel about themselves. In addition, issues relating to race relations and politics are explored in this chapter. The author highlights the fact that people tend to choose their political representatives because they can identify with them in respect of their values, backgrounds and experiences.

Beauty and the beast

(WEDNESDAY, APRIL 28, 1993)

A few months ago, I was leisurely walking downtown when I overheard a little girl say to her mother, "Mom, look. She look just like Tanya; Tanya could be a beauty queen." Looking quite pleased (Tanya must have been a relative), Mom replied, "Yes, Tanya hair is long like hers, and she got nice brown skin, too." For the next five minutes, the mother and child stared at the photograph of Miss Jamaica in the shop window and continued to comment on the virtues of having features similar to those in a photograph which had very little resemblance to them.

I shrugged at the event, because I am neither a follower nor admirer of beauty shows. But, two weeks ago another event occurred, which propelled me into action. Among a group of high school girls, one girl was made the laughing stock by companions for remarking that she could be Miss Jamaica. Needless to say, this was based on what she looked like. Realizing the implications of such behaviours, I decided to devote an entire week researching the phenomenon of beauty queens in Jamaica.

Lest I am accused of having nothing better to do, let me say that one should not take the issue of beauty contests lightly. Like it or not, beauty contests are national events. These events reflect an aspect of our society, that aesthetic part of us. Beauty contests help to determine and reflect how we see each other and how we feel about ourselves. It is for this reason that I find it most curious that, from 1955 to the present, almost 70 per cent of the persons chosen to be Miss Jamaica have been of very light complexion and appear to have what some called "mixed" features. To put it bluntly, they do not in many fundamental ways resemble the vast majority of Jamaicans.

Festival queens

On the other hand, the festival queens tend to look more like the majority of Jamaicans. One interesting characteristic about the Festival Queen competition is that the criteria for winning have more to do with the person's abilities rather than some dubious notion of beauty. This is a positive step. Unfortunately, the festival queens receive fewer prizes and less support than those in the Miss Jamaica competition. This low-key event contrasts sharply with the glitter of Miss Jamaica, which is conducted along the lines of similar events in Europe, the USA, and their satellites. It is only in predominantly black countries outside of Africa, except for South Africa, that the majority of national beauty queens do not look like the majority of the people. Something is wrong, according to the laws of probability.

Let me get a bit defensive here. I am not saying that because a contestant does not resemble the majority of the population, then she should not represent her country. Second, I do not want to engage in the stereotyping of African peoples (or any other set of people for that matter). African peoples come in various shades, shapes and sizes. Anthropologists have recently rejected the term race as a biological category because races vary more among themselves than among others. African peoples have posed the most difficulty for biologists and geneticists to classify because they are so diverse. This variation can be found from the San Bushmen, who are almost yellow in complexion with slanted eyes, to the pygmies of Central Africa who are genetically closer to aboriginal inhabitants of South Asia and the Pacific. But, although race is a socially constructed category, it has meaning for people in their everyday lives. It is in this context that definitions of beauty must be treated seriously.

The society

The fact that the majority of the Miss Jamaica winners do not resemble the average Jamaican speaks vividly about how the society views itself. Of course, someone may argue that the choices of Miss Jamaica are not necessarily popular ones, and therefore distort the reality. I do not know this for sure. I am not sure that West Indians of African descent have truly accepted ourselves for who we are.

I have found from research that Caribbean people of African descent tend to define themselves as mixed, even if they do not possess one ounce of so-called mixed blood. What is interesting, however, is that people of other races tend to emphasize their "racial purity" rather than their mixture. A recent survey (non-probability) conducted in a number of high schools by a student at The UWI showed that students tended to define themselves as "brown" even when they were very dark-skinned. In general, the students tended to avoid describing themselves as black. For people of African descent, it would appear that being "mixed" represents an ideal – almost like having the best of both worlds. A mixed (black) person can take refuge in knowing that (s)he is black, but also "better" than black, as manifested in the regularity with which they beam with pride as they announce some obscure French or Irish ancestry. It does not matter if that great-great-great-granduncle was a murderer and a rapist; the fact is that he was Swedish. Now, here is a basis for pride. This type of feeling is one which the psychiatrist and philosopher Frantz Fanon of Martinique, and others have addressed in their discourses about the psychological state of people who have been taught to hate themselves.

The fact that even Black beauty queens try their best to look as "European" (or even Indian and Chinese) as possible suggests that our concept of beauty is still not a function of the "man in the mirror". As a result, we have a large segment of our population who have to constantly contend with their looks, because they are a far cry from an ideal which is paraded in front of them yearly. African American author Toni Morrison captures this tragedy in one of her prize-winning novels *The Bluest Eye*.

Culture

In my view, there is nothing called universal beauty (not yet, at least). Because different cultures have different emphases; what is beautiful for one may be ugly for another. Last year, a rap song called "Baby Got Back", which made number one on the Billboard charts, was at the centre of debate across America. This song challenged the conventional view of beauty by celebrating the larger bottoms of Black women and rejecting the Cosmopolitan magazine type beauty. For a long time, Black women in the USA were made to feel ashamed of their bottoms. (Although if one saw Jessica Rabbit in the movie *Who Framed Roger Rabbit*, one would think otherwise). The fact that "Baby Got Back" made number one on the Billboard charts suggests to me that the celebration struck a chord somewhere and things may never be the same for America.

Anytime non-Europeans enter a predominantly white Miss Universe contest, the standards by which they will be judged will invariably be European. Likewise, if a European woman enters a beauty contest which is judged by non-European standards, then she will be disadvantaged. This is a fact of life. Miss Black America was a response to the fact that Black women could never, until recently, become a Miss America. The irony is that most of the Black Americans entering these contests tended to look very much like White Americans. To win a beauty competition like Miss Universe, non-Whites have two choices: be as "white" as possible, or be very exotic to the extent that it stands out. Both types of behaviour should not be encouraged, as they force people to become something other than normal. Why should an African or Asian woman be considered exotic when the vast majority of the women in the world resemble them? I do not believe African or Asian women should humiliate themselves by entering this so-called Miss Universe. What is beautiful is not self-evident. Beauty is socially constructed. Perhaps it may be good for us to remember how much beauty is found in the beast.

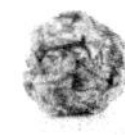

A short note on bleaching: Part 1 (only)

(TUESDAY, OCTOBER 07, 1997)

The problem of bleaching is again being examined by physicians and pharmacists. Bleaching the skin has now become a serious public health issue. I am not surprised. For years, this issue has been a "hot" topic for many of us conducting research in the social sciences. One of the problems which we face in our society is a seeming insistence on the primacy of "mixed" heritages combined with the superficial celebration of our "Africanness" through the use of numerous symbols and a great deal of rhetoric. I often get the impression that many of us who openly "celebrate" our Africanness do it out of a sense of duty and/or insecurity. This may be, in part, a function of the fact that for most of us, throughout our lives, we are bombarded with images of beauty and worth which do not reflect us or our experiences. Certainly, we have come a very long way in setting our own standards of beauty; however, society's perception of beauty is still moulded by Euro-American ideals.

Some years ago, a few of my students at The UWI conducted a study on perceptions of beauty in two large high schools. The results illustrated that girls considered a lighter complexion and an "oval-shaped" face (whatever that is) to be the most beautiful features. However, boys tended to show a preference for the curvaceous body shapes, long straight hair and "soft" skin. Again, these findings are not surprising, given that the standards of beauty in our society are often determined by middle- and upper-class people, most of whom are not themselves of "dark" complexion.

I find it amazing that Jamaican representatives in international beauty contests do not resemble 90 per cent of our population. Contradictory to what the organizers may claim, local beauty pageants are consciously biased in favour of lighter-skinned women with phenotypes that vary significantly from those of the majority of Jamaicans. In this regard, organizers and uncritical supporters of these pageants unwittingly contribute to the bleaching problem which currently haunts our society.

The message and the messenger

One of the enduring features of human society seems to be the role that celebrity and authority play in setting agendas, or bringing public attention to issues which affect us. A number of charities and organizations across the world rely on celebrities to plead their case for financial assistance. Most of these celebrities are from the arts or sports.

Diana, Princess of Wales, for example, used her star status to raise consciousness about landmines and to raise funds for AIDS and other forms of medical research. Another example of the impact of celebrity or perceived authority is the recent attention paid to the comments of US Ambassador to Jamaica, J. Gary Cooper, about the state of the country's environment. Yet, the very same issues raised by the ambassador have been explored by numerous persons and groups throughout the society for years, and they have received little or no response from the media. The fact is that we have had serious environmental problems related to water quality and deforestation for years. The Natural Resources Conservation Authority (NRCA) is not to be envied, for it is faced with the difficult task of dealing with what seems to be an impeding environmental catastrophe in our society.

Unfortunately, many in the media seem to take issues seriously only if a "celebrity" is involved, when we are threatened, or when the messenger is not "one of us". Too frequently, journalists in their reporting fail to distinguish between the message and the messenger. Regrettably, interesting stories are ignored in favour of banal statements from politicians or celebrity figures. Peace

Chapter 4 Caribbean Cultural Forms

- Carnival, soca and the Jamaican middle class
- Economics and cultural dispossession
- Jamaica and world culture
- Business and the hip-hop generation
- Carnival: The alternative
- Roots of our music

Introduction

Chapter 4 details different aspects of Caribbean culture. Emphasis is placed on Caribbean music and its influence and appeal. The author explains that the genre of music may appeal to different segments of the population depending on the country. The chapter looks at the extent to which dancehall music appeals to the masses as opposed to the middle and upper classes. The appeal of carnival is also discussed. In fact, the chapter explores the extent to which carnival is used as a metaphor for a larger process of cultural dispossession, something which has plagued the African experience since the days of slavery. The author also seizes the opportunity to criticize the elite for what he describes as the double standards and hypocrisy that underlie the debate on values and attitudes in Jamaican society. Finally, the author makes a rallying cry for members of the region to move beyond being creators of culture, and learn to market our culture, or others will do it for us while we complain.

Carnival, soca and the Jamaican middle class

(WEDNESDAY, APRIL 14, 1993)

Carnival is perhaps the only time when the Jamaican upper and middle classes get to let go of their pretentious social disposition, openly that is. It is a time when they unlock the spontaneity and creativity that is associated with the masses they look down on. But, more importantly, it is a time when they can do all of this and not be tarnished by the social mores associated with the masses. After jumping in the streets, they brush off the sweat and dirt and speed away in their air-conditioned cars to the heights, hills and terraces which dot the sad landscape of urban poverty around Kingston.

Jamaica has one of the most unique carnivals I have ever seen. Unlike the Trinidad and Tobago carnival (from which aspects were borrowed, lock, stock and barrel), it is a festival with no connection to the lives of the masses of the people; not yet, at least. Carnival in the eastern and southern Caribbean countries has a history which is strongly linked to the lives of the masses. In Trinidad and Tobago, carnival has its roots in the French culture. However, it was taken over by descendants of slaves and made into what it is today. Thus, the Trinidad carnival is fundamentally of an Afro-Caribbean orientation. Carnival in Trinidad and Tobago reflects the expressions of the masses of the people. It is not reserved for a privileged few. Furthermore, carnival is not just about jumping in the streets; it is about creativity, through music and more. In the rest of the region, carnival (and Crop Over in Barbados) have gained their legitimacy through people participation and creative adaptation. The activities associated with these festivals include arts and craft, song competitions, and a whole host of other events which require people to do more than just "lift yuh foot an wine". In all of these countries, carnival is about the lives and culture of the masses.

African origins

In Jamaica, carnival is really a way for the middle and upper classes to separate themselves from the people and "bend down and touch their toes" without feeling ashamed. It is a time when many (including the so-called "brownings") seek to touch base with their often-denied African origins in the same way the proper British tourist limbos with the natives while escaping to one of the well-known tourist hideouts somewhere along the fabled north coast. The Jamaican middle and upper classes have rejected dancehall music because it is associated with the masses. Ironically, they have embraced soca (and calypso for those few who are concerned with the lyrics) which is the creation of the masses of the other Caribbean countries. It reminds me of the White middle class in the US rejecting the rap music of the urban ghettos (only because of its origins) while clinging to the rhythms and lyrics of Aswad, Bob Marley and Peter Tosh.

In both cases, both groups reject the grass roots music of their society, while adopting the music of another society because it serves to separate them from the rest of the ordinary masses at home. But when they do accept the cultural creations of their own people (they have to accept somebody's, for they themselves do not create much), they often make it into something different by giving it new labels, like when the American intellectuals and yuppies hijacked jazz and made it avant-garde to keep away the very people who created it. Unfortunately, the Jamaican middle and upper classes in their endless search for difference and deference have embraced carnival in its most elementary and amorphous form.

But this will change. I have no doubt that the masses of the people will take over carnival and add some creativity to it. The masses are the most creative among us; they have to be in order to survive. While the middle and upper classes can institutionalize carnival, the ordinary people are the only ones who can make it truly Jamaican. Already, we see the creativity of the masses in the crossover between soca and dancehall music.

It is good that we in Jamaica are taking part in an activity which is shared by all of the other English-speaking Caribbean countries. It is good when we in the region share more of our culture. For years, other Caribbean countries have been listening to Jamaican reggae. Let us all share in the fruits of the people who have created these many facets of Caribbean culture – the ordinary people, the masses. Many loves!

Economics and cultural dispossession

(WEDNESDAY, JUNE 02, 1993)

Some weeks ago, I wrote an article on carnival in Jamaica criticizing its narrow middle- and upper-class orientation. As a result, I received a number of letters from readers. Some agreed with my argument, while others were obviously very angry (to put it euphemistically) with what they perceived to be an attempt to "deny the right of the people of the upper class from listening to whatever music they choose". I want to make it clear that I have no such lofty ambitions. Suffice it to say, I shall continue to stand firmly by my article.

Perhaps one of the most interesting letters I received came from a Trinidadian colleague of mine, Deryck Brown, a very talented political scientist who is a researcher at the Institute of Social and Economic Research at The UWI, St. Augustine, Trinidad and Tobago. Brown's letter is worth quoting at length. He writes:

"Just a short note to comment on your article in *The Gleaner* (14th April 1993) entitled 'Carnival, Soca and the Jamaican Middle Class'. You are correct in arguing that the T&T [sic] Carnival, in spite of its French roots in the masked balls (from where, incidentally, the term 'playing mas' comes), is a celebration born of the Afro-Trinidadian masses. The historical record shows that black slaves and ex-slaves were physically brutalized for carrying on carnival festivities in the 19th century.

Festivity

You will observe that carnival is really a Roman Catholic festivity. As such, it is present in those former colonial territories which had strong Roman Catholic influences, including Brazil and New Orleans. And, like everything else that is associated with the Roman Catholic Church, carnival has a high degree of hypocrisy built into it.

What you may perhaps find interesting – and it is certainly something which I think deserves some careful attention – is the class nature of carnival even here in Trinidad. For it is my feeling that, in Trinidad, the masses are actually being marginalised from that which was born of masses. Carnival in Trinidad is fast becoming the preserve of the high coloured white and brown (red) elites. Pure economics have conspired to exclude the black man from all but possibly the consumption of rum while chipping down the road behind the steel band. Even Indians – the holders of real wealth in the country – have become heavily involved, parading their own bands on the two days of Carnival. Prices of costumes, of entrance to fetes and pre-carnival shows like the calypso tents and [Steelband] Panorama, even of alcohol, are keeping black people on the periphery of carnival. J'ouvert (the opening Monday) is perhaps the only avenue open for masses to become participants in the annual festivities, no doubt because the costumes are not elaborate and include such things as mud, tar and old clothes.

Essentially, what I am trying to say is that carnival in T&T is fast becoming a middle-class thing, just like it is in Jamaica. The masses are at risk of losing their festivity. I would therefore be very surprised if a reverse trend is expected in Jamaica as you are trying to suggest."

Middle class

Brown is therefore pessimistic about carnival in Jamaica, for he sees it as remaining firmly among the middle (and upper) classes. I am an optimist, for I strongly believe the masses will take it over one day.

It is also clear from Brown's letter that the basis for the class character of carnival in Jamaica and Trinidad is rooted fundamentally in economics. However, in Jamaica the situation may be complicated due to the fact that there appears to be a feeling among certain groups that carnival should remain largely a middle/upper class event. I wish them luck.

But what is being raised here is not simply a matter of carnival as a festivity. Carnival is really a metaphor for a large process of cultural dispossession, something which has plagued the African experience since the days of slavery. The fact of the matter is that economic dispossession often leads to cultural dispossession (even though cultural invention has arisen from this dispossession). Take for example rock 'n' roll which is now considered to be an art form of European-Americans, and from which, unfortunately, many African-American disassociate themselves. This musical art form emerged from the rhythm and blues of Black America. In fact, if you study the history of rock 'n' roll, you will find that conservative Whites called it the music of the devil: an attempt to corrupt White people through the culture of the Blacks. There was mass demonstration against this black music, and one white businessman was even imprisoned by the US government for recording this music. However, the economic benefactors of this music have been the very people who condemned it initially. Blacks who were not allowed to record in the 1950s and 1960s were forced to allow White Americans and Europeans to record their music. The Beatles was one group which benefited immensely from this discrimination. By the way, if you look at the Grammy Awards, virtually all black artistes are put into the rhythm and blues category, no matter how much hard rock they sing (presumably, blacks cannot play rock 'n' roll music anymore). Blacks have allowed Whites once again to pigeonhole them in categories which are most ridiculous.

But even in the music which they dominated, rhythm and blues, Blacks have not reaped the economic benefits. Only a few years ago, blues singer Bonnie Raitt had to set up the Rhythm and Blues Foundation to help support Black artistes who made so much for the white recording companies, the US government and the tourist industry, but little for themselves. What these examples point to is the necessity for Black people to recognize the imperative of controlling their economic destiny. I hope the inventors of the steel pan are taking note.

Perhaps nowhere is this issue of cultural dispossession and economic self-reliance more intimately intertwined than in the current struggle among the African and diaspora intellectuals to reclaim their history. I have heard people suggest that this issue of history is not important. I saw some intellectual on JBC Television decrying its importance. (All I have to say to him is: ha!) I will take up this issue in a later article. Right now, I cannot be bothered with those who do not see the link between the past and the present. A way of seeing is also a way of not seeing.

Last week, a young man called a talk show and argued that the Nubians were a Caucasian people. Armed with his dusty 1950s encyclopaedia, he argued forcefully that it is wrong to characterize the Nubians as black (based on the logic of his reference text, I guess that I could classify my mother as a Martian, or my father a Scandinavian). Fortunately, the young man was asked by the host Leahcim Semaj to critically examine the political context of his statement. I do not think that he will suck up information from such learned sources with such enthusiasm again. Others among us are not that lucky. Many among us, thanks to German and British scholarships of the 18th and 19th centuries, still hold on to the view that the Egyptians were some strange race of people who happened on the African continent by some inexplicable process. By the way,

Orlando Patterson, Jamaican historian and sociologist, tells us that there is too much concern with Egypt by Black scholars (I guess this is what Harvard can do to you). Why not tell white Americans that there is too much concern among them with Henry VIII and his wives, or the Japanese-Americans they are too concerned with the Meiji Restoration?

Let me tell Orlando a story. When I was working on my doctoral dissertation at a US university, I wrote a little paragraph criticizing the geographical characterization of African by an anthropologist. I quoted from the works of Martin Bernal (Bernal has been recognized for his famous piece of work on the link between European and African civilization). One of my dissertation committee members, who also happened to have been trained at Harvard, wrote a most scathing critique of my paragraph and, of course, Bernal, for he was more concerned with Bernal than with me. When I confronted this very learned professor, he apologized for getting carried away by his emotions and accepted that my comments were reasonable, but I should make them carefully (meaning, try not to say what I mean). In view of the fact that I was interested in getting my PhD, not in history or anthropology but in sociology, I made my point but much more subtly (and this was difficult, for I am not a terribly subtle person). By the way, this professor was of Greek ancestry. Bernal was the one who attacked the view that the Greeks were the founders of civilization and suggested the Greeks learned much from Africa. This view was heretical, since Black people have produced nothing of significance.

It is interesting to note that Western (and Eastern) scholarship accepts the contribution of Asia, the Middle East, and the Americas to world civilization. Africa is the only part of the "puzzle" which they have the most problems with. Part of the reason is that Blacks still do not control the means of communication and intellectual production. More than 90 per cent of the books about us are written by people other than us. Tell me, can a dog see through the eyes of a cat, particularly when they are constantly at odds with each other? Black people cannot expect other people to write their history objectively. In fact, there is nothing called objectivity in its absolute sense. We fool ourselves if we believe that history is simply about facts. History is not simply a recollection of the past, but it is also about discussing that past. At the risk of offending historians, I would like to say that history is partly a self-serving enterprise; it is about myths and all types of therapies to give people a sense of meaning. Study European or Asian history and you will realise that part of the historian's work has been to give meaning to his/her own reality and sometimes to revel in it.

Cultural expression

Let me make it clear that I do not believe that cultural expression is the preserve of any one group of people. For me, curry and roti are as much a part of my culture as are festival and the Bogle. Carnival does not belong to any one group, neither does reggae, rap, calypso or cricket. Human creativity belongs to all humans who can benefit from it. Since we do not exist in isolation, we all borrow from each other. Aspects of even the most authentic cultural practice can be traced to other people or societies. We are both more different and alike than we realize.

My attempt here is to suggest that if we Black people do not get our economic act together, then we run the risk of being marginalized from the very fruits of our own creativity. It is useless to blame others for that, for it is within the right of other people to use (appropriately) the creations of other people, just as we have the right to use those of others. It is imperative for us to recognize that economic clout makes words speak louder. Reality is something which is constantly constructed. Only if you have the power are you able to massively construct this reality. If African Americans owned the recording studios, they would have been able to benefit from rock 'n' roll. If Black people owned large publishing houses, intellectuals would have been in a better position to reconstruct and articulate history from our perspective. I say, seek ye first the economic kingdom and then it will be easier to deal with carnival or the Greeks. Ride Natty, ride.

Jamaica and world culture

(TUESDAY, AUGUST 24, 1993)

Two years ago, a few of my American friends invited me to listen to a reggae band at a small night club in Colorado. I immediately agreed because I was longing to hear some genuine Caribbean accents and culture. On my arrival at the night club, I sat in great anticipation. For some time, my excited eyes surveyed the quaint little stage for these Caribbean people, until they were lured by five white American Rastafarians shouting praises to the Most High, Jah Rastafari.

Draped in red, gold and green, this dreadlocked group of four men and one woman proceeded to give a most spectacular performance. Halfway through their performance, I totally forgot that they were Americans, as they communicated with the audience in a Jamaican accent that could easily be mistaken for an original. I thought to myself, in the middle of a "reclaimed" desert thousands of miles from the Caribbean, here was a case of cultural penetration by a society which is too small to appear on the world maps of political analysts across American universities.

Lest you shrug at the foregoing as some insignificant occurrence, let us put it in context. Jamaica is 10,991 square kilometres (about half the size of Wales) with a population which is not even half of New York's. It has a gross domestic product of about US$3,800 million, which is small even by the standards of developing countries. In UN parlance, Jamaica is what one would call a micro-state. Yet this small size belies the cultural influence of the country on the world. Jamaica has given the world the newest world religion, Rastafari. Although overlooked by encyclopaedias, no one knows for sure how many Rastafarians there are in the world. Yet we know that there are Rastafarians, followers and believers, in virtually all corners of the globe. I do not think that Rastafarians, or Jamaicans in general, are aware of the magnitude of Rastafari's contribution to human philosophy and theology. Interestingly, the majority of the scholars who research Rastafari philosophy are non-Jamaicans.

World music

At this moment, the number one song on the Billboard charts is a reggae song, sung by a British pop group. Reggae is no longer Jamaican music; it is world music. There are reggae festivals all over the world; in many cases, most of the participants have never travelled to Jamaica. Jamaicans are no longer the only major authoritative articulators of reggae. Like jazz and quaint, reggae is international. What reggae and Rastafarians have done to promote Jamaica as a tourist destination the Tourist Board could never do on its own.

There is another interesting development about the Jamaican culture – its cuisine. From Washington D.C. to New York, from London to Paris, Jamaican cuisine is enticing people. Jamaica is the only country in the English-speaking Caribbean that has a cuisine which is being marketed internationally. In fact, Jamaican restaurants now compete with Vietnamese, Thai, Indian, Mexican, Ethiopian and others in the developing world for a place in the international cuisine market.

There can be no doubt that Jamaica has over the years internationalized its culture. It has given the world art, cuisine and religious philosophy. For sceptics, I challenge them to look at the records of great civilizations of the world and see what their contributions to the world were.

Of course, what I have just described is a process, and Jamaica is only in the beginning stages. Unfortunately, the economic situation and political leadership of the society have failed to rise to the occasion. The contribution of Jamaica to world civilization has been the contribution of the masses of people, not the government nor the elite. In these most difficult times, it is the masses who must now take control over their lives economically and politically, as they have done in other spheres of life.

Fathers Incorporated

The work of Fathers Incorporated is one example in which ordinary people have begun to take control over their lives. Fathers Incorporated is an organization which seeks to encourage men to bring out the more positive side of masculinity. It seeks to encourage men to take responsibility for their actions and become partners with women in raising children and constructing a new and more humane society. Last weekend, the organization, in association with UNICEF and The UWI, sponsored a conference on crime and violence.

Unlike other conferences, where people sit and listen to experts, this one enlisted the full participation of those people who were most affected by crime and violence. The event was refreshing, as people were not constrained by nice-sounding titles and other authority images, which often lead to deference and stifle frank discussion. This was the first conference that I have attended in which the participants were always on time and never slept after lunch. Conference participants seemed very concerned about what they could do themselves, rather than relying on government for assistance. It is this self-reliance and discipline that need to be encouraged among all sections of the society.

I would like to conclude by thanking all those readers who have taken the time to drop me a line or call me on the telephone to discuss my articles. I am truly amazed at the public response to my columns. I thank you for your very constructive comments and your words of encouragement. You, readers, are my inspiration. One love.

Business and the hip-hop generation

(TUESDAY, NOVEMBER 30, 1993)

As technological changes shrink the world, a strong global popular culture is emerging. What was once urban black (rap/hip-hop) and suburban white American (rock) culture is now being embraced by youth worldwide through the satellite and fibre-optic networks which crisscross the globe. At the forefront of this global culture stand American rap, Americanized dancehall (with the Bogle and butterfly dances), and rock music, along with the now trendy baggy wear of urban Black America.

Youth in Japan pay large sums of cash to change their hairstyles into the pseudo-dreadlocks copied by African Americans from Jamaican Rastafarians. It is no longer a novelty to hear rap and dancehall music in Portuguese (from Brazil), Arabic, Japanese or Hindi. If part of the world is withdrawing into ethnic chauvinism, another part is embracing the apparent postmodern American-inspired cultural revolution.

Phenomenal

Indeed, so phenomenal is this cultural transformation that a group of young entrepreneurs became extremely wealthy by selling clothing – popularized by the young duo Kriss-Kross – all over the world.

In the US, television networks which at first resisted this seemingly pugnacious youth culture are now beginning to see potential profits. In every part of the world, there are large and prosperous youth populations. On the cutting edge of this change among television networks is Music Television (MTV), which hooks into 211 million households worldwide. MTV has successfully marketed the urban/suburban or rap rock American culture to teenagers and other young adults across the globe. Their entertainment line-up includes the world's most famous singers Michael Jackson and Madonna. It was MTV which began to canvass the idea of Michael Jackson as the "King of Pop". Their cleverly made advertisements and music videos worked well to successfully convince the American public, and the world, that Michael Jackson is the King of Pop (not that they had much convincing to do).

Considerable income

Developments in communications technology have meant that entertainment networks such as MTV have been able to make considerable income from marketing American (and Jamaican) popular culture to the largest segment of the global market – the youth. MTV has been able to develop affiliates across the world to spread the messages and ideas of the hip-hop generation. For instance, there is MTV Brazil and MTV Asia; the latter is based in Hong Kong and broadcasts to both West and East Asia. It is indeed a conduit for American popular culture. However, some of the programming is devoted to serious youth discussions. Issues such as the environment, sex, politics, sexually transmitted diseases, and homosexuality are openly discussed, which did not happen hitherto. This new situation has led to the emergence of cultural universals which have a strong American orientation.

Global cultures

Now there are two interesting features associated with this process of cultural globalization. First, two regions, sub-Saharan Africa and to a lesser extent the Caribbean, are on the periphery of this process. It appears that many of the large entertainment firms believe that, with the exception of South Africa, sub-Saharan Africa does not have a large enough middle class to merit the type of investment found in

Asia and Latin America. Ironically, as globalization intensifies, much of sub-Saharan Africa is becoming marginalized. The formation of major global trading blocs and the revolutions in microchip and fibre-optic technology have electively removed parts of the continent from the mainstream of international economics. This situation will worsen unless there is a radical change in the destructive nature of African politics.

Investment rebuffed

In our region, it would appear that small size, coupled with declining economic fortunes, has worked to rebuff serious investment from the global entertainment industry in our region.

The second point is related to the fact that as globalization intensifies certain issues have begun to assume universal importance for business. One such issue, which business people associated with the entertainment industry have been especially crafty in handling, is ethnic and racial conflict. The recently held Miss World pageant is an excellent example of such creative business practices. The organizers took advantage of the location, South Africa, to show how cross-cultural their pageants were. For good measure, they had an unusually large number of non-White judges, but more importantly the message from the organizers was one of unity, peace and togetherness. The problem here is that in practice not much will be done afterwards; in fact, much will be forgotten once the splendid speeches have been delivered and the noble pledges made. Beauty pageants, like other forms of global entertainment, depend on an increasingly diverse audience for financial success. Therefore, it is in the interest of the organizers to speak the politically correct language to maintain the confidence of global viewership and make a profit.

The lesson in all of this for us in the Caribbean is that it is not enough to be simply creators of culture. We must learn to market our culture or others will do it for us while we complain. Why is it that our entrepreneurs will sell Michael Jordan t-shirts, and not any with Viv Richards or Brian Lara. Quite recently, Richie Richardson started to market his hats; perhaps this captain is about to captain a new industry. Peace!

Carnival: The alternative

(TUESDAY, APRIL 12, 1994)

Not so long ago, our country was embroiled in a debate about values and attitudes, and many public commentators launched scathing attacks on dancehall music and the so-called vulgarity which supposedly characterizes its culture. For the critics, not only is the music slack and disgusting, but they also feel it lacks creativity. Come to think of it, this criticism has been made of every musical form created by people of African descent in the Western Hemisphere. But, while I do not find everything about the dancehall culture pleasing, I question the sincerity of some of these criticisms. Their sincerity is even more questionable in view of what happens during our annual carnival celebrations.

Last week, in the calypso tent at Cinema 2, Jamaicans were treated to some fantastic performances by calypsonians from Barbados and Trinidad and Tobago, but throughout the show, performers and one emcee in particular, continuously focused on sex. This was done no less explicitly than that which is done and heard at Reggae Sunsplash or any other mass reggae show in this country. But, alas, it was done, much to the delight and sometimes embarrassment of the crowd.

Intriguing

However, there was something very intriguing about these events. How does one explain the perpetual complaints on the radio against the airing of General Degree's "Pianist" – a very creative and amusing song – while at the same time there is praise for a similar song "For Cane" by Gypsy the calypsonian? Further, how does one explain the castigation of the apparently over-sexual movements of dancehall dance when performed by dark-skinned women from the inner city, while there is celebration by a largely middle-class, middle-aged group of the virtually naked so-called Dancehall Queen, Carlene, as she "wines" down to the ground with the Mighty Sparrow? Why is wining to calypso music innocent fun, but vulgar when it is done to dancehall music? An immediate response to the foregoing is the double standards of our society. You see, the so-called higher classes determine what is acceptable and what is not. And, of course, part of the acceptability of Carlene by the middle class has to do with her skin colour and the fact that radio programmes like *The Breakfast Club* have unwittingly legitimized her to their large middle-class audience. However, I want to pursue the explanation from another angle and argue that the differences in treatment between dancehall music and calypso are not just due to differences in social class, but also in generations.

Female audience

Demographically, carnival in Jamaica attracts a larger female audience. Calypso in Trinidad no longer attracts the type of youth audience it did in the past, for it is losing the young people to dancehall music. Also, carnival in Trinidad and Tobago attracts a largely female, adult, middle-class audience, while the reggae shows attract a largely male, young, working class crowd. Increasingly though, Reggae shows, like rap shows in the United States of America, are beginning to attract the young middle-class meals.

Dancehall music has captured the imagination of Caribbean youth in a way that calypso never did. It has done this in the same way that rap has captivated the Black American youth who hitherto doted on rhythm and blues. Consequently, the most popular calypso songs in the Caribbean are those which have crossed over to the Jamaican dancehall genre.

We seem to be moving into an era in which young people are seeking forms of expression which are different from those associated with traditional calypso, reggae and R&B. There is something more blunt and focused about dancehall and rap, which is not found in the subtlety of either the Mighty Sparrow's music or Marvin Gaye's sexually suggestive songs. In short, the music of today's youth has little time for subtleties. Interestingly, research has shown that the greater the societal turmoil and freer the environment, the more candid the musical expression. Therefore, as young males become more marginalized economically, as is the case throughout the Caribbean and the US, then the bluntness of dancehall lyrics or rap will become more appealing to them. Of course, this phenomenon is no different from the era of the 1960s when the youth embraced the then harsh sounds of rock 'n' roll and reggae music – musical expressions criticized by the elite at the time.

Sexual ideas

Now, when our young people listen to some types of calypso, they are aware that the songs express the same sexual ideas which they hear in rap and dancehall music, only that the use of language is different. When young and poor people see teachers, politicians, bank managers, physicians, lawyers, university lecturers, and the likes, wining and jamming along the streets in Half Way Tree, they realise that they are no different from them. What offends them is that these same half-naked women and men who are gyrating as if it were their last day on earth will on the following day condemn the slow tantalizing hip movements associated with dancehall music. Our young people are fully aware of the hypocrisy of our society.

When young, especially poor, people look at carnival parades here in Jamaica, they see another, just another, dancehall scene. They also know that carnival is the only occasion on which they see the elite and older people honestly expressing themselves. For, on these occasions, these people move their hips with meaning, without having to hide and without the cover of darkness. Poor young men see women – who probably would not normally look at them twice because of their station in life – do things which are normally reserved for the likes of people like them. Thus, for many young, poor people, carnival in Jamaica is simply an alternative dancehall, one that for the time being many prefer to observe. The same thing happens to them when they are in their dancehall. Peace!

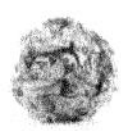

Roots of our music

(TUESDAY, APRIL 08, 1997)

Well, another carnival has come and gone and the controversy relating to its relevance to our society continues. You see, some of our opinion leaders still maintain that the "foreign" and "decadent" nature of the revelry and the associated calypso music is not good for our society, particularly at a time when our country is losing its moral centre. Now, while I believe that there is little local creativity associated with the Jamaican carnival, neither the music nor the revelry is as foreign as they may appear to be. For the problem is not so much with the carnival, but rather with the way in which the organizers of the event have mimicked Trinidadians, often without context.

Vernacular

One of the problems which we have in this region is that we suffer from ignorance about ourselves, more so about our cultures. For instance, we often hear how unique an individual country's vernacular is. The following anecdote illustrates this nonsense notion and its consequences. Some years ago, a St Lucian political leader castigated St Lucian youth for importing "foreign" dancehall music from Jamaica. Of course, the youth ignored him, having found little difficulty in identifying with the structure, rhythm and idiom of the art form. Surely, there are differences in certain expressions and rhythms across countries; however, underlying these seemingly idiosyncratic music forms and languages of this part of world are aspects of West African culture, which all the countries of our community share. As one calypsonian put it, most of our ancestors came on the "same trip and ship" and experienced the same Middle Passage.

This brings us more precisely to calypso; we often hear that calypso is a Trinidadian art form; this is only half of the truth. Calypso is more accurately an art form of the Caribbean which owes its development primarily to the efforts of the Trinidadians. Since, long before the era of rocksteady and ska, Jamaicans, like other Caribbean people, sang forms of calypso music, even though these music styles might have been called by other names, for example, mento.

Calypso music, to be sure, has its roots in the West African praise songs and songs of derision. Some writers argue that, for instance, Nigerian *jùjú* and *fújì* music styles have a strong resemblance to early calypso, and that the word "calypso" is thought to be a corruption of the Hausa term "kaiso". More interesting, though, is the root of the art from within the region itself. Early calypso music developed from the cross-fertilization of music from among some of the Caribbean countries, including St Vincent, Guadeloupe, Grenada, Barbados, Carriacou, Dominica and St Lucia. And, as people travelled around the region, they took the music of their countries with them.

Close proximity

In Trinidad, this migrant music was embraced and became part of the calypso idiom. Here, it should be noted that the French Caribbean islands also had a great deal of influence on the early calypso. As such, Grenada, an island settled by both the French and the British and located in close proximity to Trinidad, had considerable impact on the music. So much so, that many of Trinidad's outstanding calypsonians were born in, or have strong connections with Grenada. The Mighty Sparrow, for instance, was born in Grenada. Note well, however, that the Spanish influence that is so often celebrated in this type of music came at a much later date.

Consequently, the emerging picture is that of a music which owes its existence both to its West African past and also to the intermingling of the cultural expressions from the various Caribbean countries. In light of this, early calypso should be more accurately viewed as a regional music rather than the preserve of any single territory, although Trinidad must certainly be credited with transforming the music into its present form.

Therefore, when we think about the music styles and languages of our region, we should resist the tendency to think of them purely in terms of nationalities. In a region as young as ours, if we continue to think about our culture in strict nationalist terms then we will proceed to obscure the fact that we all share common African, Asian and European heritages – which in many ways make our languages and cultures strikingly similar. Obviously, in most of our societies, the African aspects of our cultures are the most apparent and compelling, and so those of us who doubt that there exists this fundamental African link in all the cultures of our region, as seen in the music, should think again. I am, therefore, recommending that you listen carefully to the various music styles of our region and of Africa, some of which include calypso, *zouk*, *salsa*, *soukous*, *jùjú*, *merengue* and *compas*. Peace!

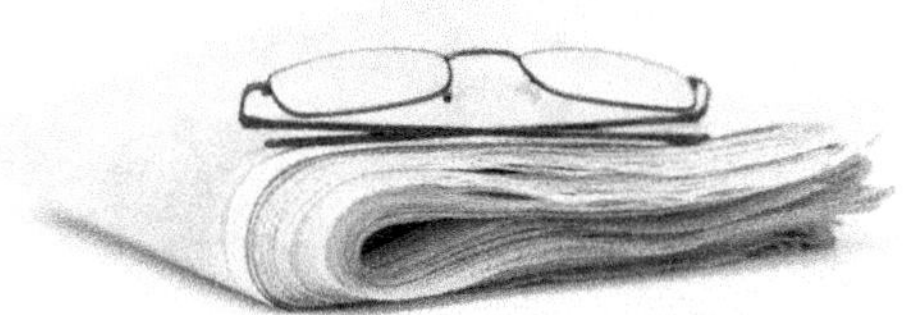

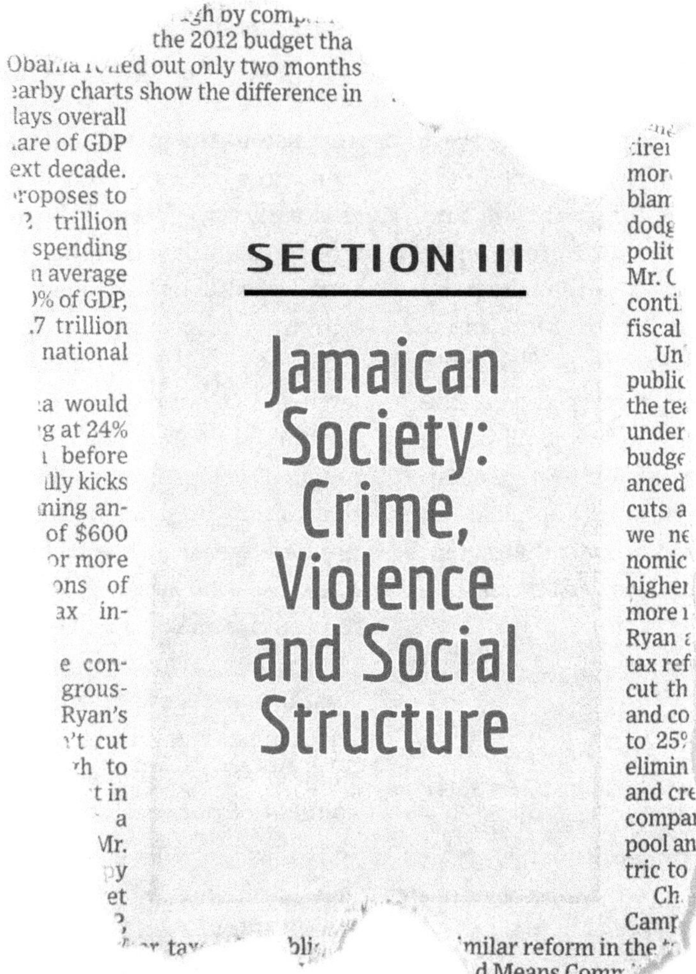

SECTION III

Jamaican Society: Crime, Violence and Social Structure

Introduction

Section III is the largest in the book and is divided into chapters which probe issues pertaining to crime and violence, education, sex and gender roles, and values and attitudes within the Jamaican society. Chapter 5 examines statistics relating to crime and violence, particularly homicide rates and other community related acts of violence. The chapter scrutinizes whether aspects of our popular culture, as well as elements of our political system, contribute to the spate of violence being experienced across the country.

In chapter 6, the articles explore how the issues of leadership, legitimacy and accountability are almost always used together when one explores matters relating to governance. This chapter looks at the ineffectiveness of public leaders – including the police – and the extent to which they are willing to accept responsibility for the outcome of their decisions and actions.

Chapter 7 discusses the system of formal education in Jamaica. It analyses the performance of Jamaican students in standardized examinations such as the Common Entrance and the Caribbean Secondary Education Certificate (CSEC) examinations. The author submits that factors such as the extent of teacher training, teacher/pupil ratios, declines in investment in school facilities, as well as the physical infrastructure, affect students' overall performance in exams. Chapter 8 looks at the extent to which attitudes to sex and gender have been changing in the Jamaican society. The ninth and final chapter in this section discusses "values and attitudes" in relation to the various changes in speech, dress, music, conduct and other norms – both private and public – that regulate a person's behaviour in Jamaican society today. Chapter 5 examines statistics relating to crime and violence, particularly homicide rates, and statistics for other community related acts of violence. The chapter scrutinizes whether aspects of our popular culture, as well as elements of our political system, contribute to the spate of violence being experienced across the country. In addition, the chapter zooms in on the extent to which other social and behavioural issues, such as parental neglect, low self-esteem, alienation, and poverty, have a positive or negative influence on criminal activities. [See also Section IV: Chapter 6: "Capital, labour and feudalism", Tuesday, November 16, 1993.] Collectively, the articles present the view that violence in Jamaica, unlike in the rest of the Caribbean, has become a "pathological" behaviour, and that this is due to the nature of the Jamaican society itself. Interesting comparisons and contrasts are made between poverty in Jamaica and Black poverty in the US (see "A conspiracy of poverty"), and approaches are proposed to resolve the underlying problem (see "Ending feudalism", "Inner city renewal" and "Taking control") and, also, to reform the police and criminal justice system (see "Reforming the police force", part 1, Tuesday, February 17, 1998, and part 2, Tuesday, March 03, 1998.

Chapter 5 Crime, Violence and Social Social Structure

- The price of progress
- The anatomy of violence
- When violence becomes pathological behaviour
- Out of many, many people
- Culture, the media and the people: Violent display
- Rhetoric and reality
- The Jamaican "caste" system
- A conspiracy of poverty
- Ending feudalism
- True democracy
- Free speech and freedom of the press
- Crime and science
- Inner city renewal
- Taking control / Education for the few
- Sports and progress
- Reforming the Police Force: Part 1
- Reforming the Police Force: Part 2

The price of progress

(WEDNESDAY, APRIL 07, 1993)

The spate of violence and voter intimidation that has come to characterize Jamaican elections (and society in general) is indicative of one thing: the country has a malformed civil society. By civil society I refer to those institutions within society which promote order, socialization and stability, and help to check the power of powerful groups. One reason why this situation persists is the fact that there is a large group of dispossessed people within the society who can be co-opted by the political system to form "states within the state".

Another reason is the presence of what analysts call garrison constituencies, which are in the de facto sense little states operating within the larger political system.

In this regard, garrison constituencies resemble fiefs which characterize some semi-feudal societies in Latin America, and also some which existed in nineteenth-century Europe. Within these societies, there is a landed class who ensures that the citizens conform to the demands of the landlords, through force and/or patronage. The unfortunate result is type jockey for land and power. Those who do not pay homage to the landlord are punished. In the Jamaican sense, the landlord would be the representative for the constituency who, through patronage, ensures the allegiance of the people. The people on the other hand, in order to make sure that this clientelistic relationship continues, "protect" their landlord [politician] by any means necessary. Of course, this situation only survives if you have a large enough concentration of poor and deprived people who have been forced to see no alternative to the current conundrum. In this regard, for the people in these areas, protecting their turf is very rational even if killing others is involved. Obviously, from a Machiavellian standpoint, this situation is also highly rational for those leaders who benefit from this status quo.

Liberation

How, then, does one rid the society of this type of backward political arrangement? Security arrangements and protests by citizens are important steps in the right direction. However, the more fundamental step must be the "liberation" of these sections of the society, psychologically and economically. Garrison constituencies have to give way to free open progressive residential areas in which people can work, and are not subjected to the barrage of propaganda from political parties. People must be educated and have access to jobs and housing. The role of the Urban Development Corporation should be expanded to replace the clientelistic relationship between the politician and the people. As long as people's livelihoods are tied up with the election of a politician, disaster will continue. The price of progress in this situation, then, must be massive investment and restructuring of the economic and social relations of these areas by the private sector and non-governmental organizations. The role of government should be as a facilitator of this process, through the provision of infrastructure, security and investment incentives; the strategy must be pursued on a bipartisan manner for the people to cooperate.

When this change occurs, civil society will come into being, and the "state" mentality of these constituencies will begin to disappear. Any policy which treats this matter with less than firmness and seriousness will not lead to constructive change and the development of a civil society in Jamaica. The government and the people of this country should begin the process now.

In the meantime, what of the short run? I believe that the country should look seriously at drawing on foreign observers from regional and international sources during the next general elections. There are many who will object to this position because of nationalist sentiments. However, we must be realistic; the Jamaican political system is too malformed to simply rely on the will of the political leadership for positive change. Many people in Jamaica do not realize that with the probable exception of Guyana (where, incidentally, violence has not reached the proportions that obtains in Jamaica) the type of violence and dislocation which takes place here during elections represent an anomaly within the English-speaking Caribbean. As long as the civil society remains underdeveloped within the country, corruption and chaos will continue to reign.

The anatomy of violence

(WEDNESDAY, MAY 05, 1993)

I was shocked as my eyes fell on the woman lying on the ground while her attacker, some alleged boyfriend (in what I gathered to be his characteristically cavalier manner), walked off in the company of a pack of cheering misguided boys. A few concerned citizens tended the battered girlfriend whose face was by now bathed in blood and dirt, while the hustle and the bustle of the midday downtown market continued as if nothing had happened. Some of the women took the man's side: "Is her fault; she deserve to dead." Others took the woman's: "If it was me, I would shoot him in his blood***** head". It stuck me then that the words spoken by these women appeared just as violent as the event my eyes just had the misfortune of witnessing.

I am sure that some of you will read these few lines and then shrug since you consider the woman to be lucky. Why? Because you can point to an even worse case of battery and thuggery. Something must be wrong.

It has now become a cliche to say it, but I will nonetheless: Jamaica is in many respects a violent society. Research by criminologist Dr Hyacinth Ellis shows that Jamaica leads the region in violent crimes. Within the past three decades, the rate of violent crimes in Jamaica has skyrocketed. In 1958, the rate of murder/manslaughter was 4 per 100,000; in 1968, it moved to 6 per 100,000; in 1978, it was 16 per 100,000; and in 1980, it was 43 per 100,000. The year 1980 was of course a special case, but what the heck, a murder is a murder, motive notwithstanding. Jamaica is now competing with places such as Washington D.C., dubbed the "murder capital" of the US. If the present trend continues, who knows? The Palestinians and Jews in the Gaza Strip may be in for some stiff competition. Something must be wrong.

Dramatic increase

It should be noted that the dramatic increase in violent crimes in this country came in the post-independence era. The data show that in the 1940s and 1950s, Jamaica was no different from the other Eastern Caribbean countries with respect to violent crimes. However, things changed dramatically during the 1960s and have gotten worse. By way of comparison, Dr Ellis puts the Jamaican situation more cogently: "while Barbados and Trinidad are likely to be concerned about relatively high and increasingly high levels of property crimes, Jamaica holds a reputation for dangerous crimes, compounded by frequent use of the guns since the mid-1960s". It should be noted that in 1980, guns were used in over 70 per cent of the homicide cases, while shooting with intent was recorded as 105 per 100,000 of the population. (By the way these statistics are based only on the reported official cases.) Something is wrong, somewhere.

All of this begs the million-dollar question: what is responsible for this high level of violent behaviour in the society? Let me say that this issue is very complex, and trying to find causes of any phenomenon, especially an elusive issue such as violence, can become a very haunting experience. My aim here is to add my voice to the current debate.

Many explanations have been advanced to account for the violence in society. These include, according to the late Carl Stone, increased urbanization; increased unemployment; an increasing inflow of guns from the USA; increased income inequality; and increased migration, which weakens the family bonds and family ties, disorganizes households and leaves a generation of youth without either adequate parenting or discipline. There can be no doubt that crime is a product of social, psychological and economic factors – all of which are exacerbated by the tenuous and volatile political climate which hovers over the country.

Qualitative element

But there is a qualitative element to violence in this society that I want to explore; an element of violence which almost seems to have a life of its own, and which at the very same time is a very passive sort of "violence". Take for example the way in which two friends meet each other on the streets. Forming what has now become the characteristic finger-shaped gun these two friends point and greet each other with: "Bow! Bow!" One friend (or foe) may occasionally blow off his imaginary nozzle and proudly replace this "gun" under his shirt. Take another example: a motorist stops in the middle of the road to exchange greetings with another motorist while the cars behind him explode in a chorus of honks, loud enough to make the walls of Babylon surrender. The driver glances back at his critics and in the most energetic gesticulation proceeds to tell them what they can do with their stares, snares and horns. The horns continue, and then the driver moves off, cursing his critics for making unreasonable demands on him. This type of behaviour is certainly not atypical of the society. Some may not consider it to be violence, but if one sees these within the context of human interaction, there appears to be a recurring pattern of passive violence in the society. Unfortunately, it is this behaviour which I think we take for granted and underestimate, since we see violence only in terms of the actual physical confrontation. The fact is that the everyday interaction of many Jamaicans is characterized by this passive violence.

Riding in a minibus during peak hours is such a dehumanizing experience that it becomes painful. The conditions under which many people make a living in this society bring them face to face with confrontation and aggression on a daily basis. People who have to deal with this situation every day eventually become hardened by it. How many Jamaicans feel shocked at the events on the 7 p.m. television news, which is often punctuated with episodes of murders around the country. What is the difference between the news and the obituaries?

Poverty

Let us be clear here, poverty by itself cannot explain the level and nature of violence in this society. There are many very poor Jamaicans who have never committed a violent act. In my view, the type of violence we see in this country is the result of factors which have created a kind of thinking that does not, in many instances, recognize violent acts. Violent behaviour, therefore, takes on a life of its own.

Part of the problem of violence in this society has to do with the fact that the country has a malformed civil society. Institutions of order and justice have authority but little legitimacy. Respect for the police comes from the fact that they have guns. Therefore, when civilians also have guns, they lose this respect and they begin to shoot back. The high degree of deference for people with status or titles in society should not be mistaken for the legitimacy of these titles. More than any English-speaking Caribbean country, we in Jamaica tend to distinguish ourselves by titles. Titles often bring with them authority and power. The high degree of deference many poor people have for individuals with titles comes, to a large degree, from the way in which they live in fear of authority. I am not necessarily referring to fear of physical harm, but also fear of losing a job or fear of not getting some of the goodies from some benevolent master (or mistress). (It is somewhat like the type of fear that drives people to go to church: the fear of perishing in Hell). However, whenever there is the possibility of overcoming this fear, people will challenge the authority.

It is therefore not surprising that garrison constituencies exist throughout the country. Garrison constituencies represent states within states. States within states will only emerge when people do not consider the "true" state to be legitimate, although it may be invested with authority. The sense of powerlessness is a dangerous precondition for violence. The increased prevalence of rape is one possible indicator of the level of powerlessness in the society. Rape is taken too lightly in this society. It is not seen for what it is: violence against women. It is one way in which threatened men seek to affirm who is in charge.

During the 1980s, the government freed up the economy and withdrew from civil society. As a result, people had to fend for themselves. This has produced a society in which individual "freedoms" have increased, but protection from the consequences of other people's freedoms has decreased. The state is actually withering away (with the taxation department intact, of course). In a society with a high degree of social and economic alienation, this is a recipe for chaos. The state must become more than just a tax collector; we need to develop a true civil society. Cool runnings.

When violence becomes pathological behaviour

(WEDNESDAY, MAY 25, 1993)

Ten-year-old David leaned nervously over the twisted gate that separated his home from the pothole- and weed-infested road. Gazing into the distance, he murmured, "I wonder what she will find to beat me for today. Every day, same thing, beat, beat, beat. Me can't please her." His trembling eyes caught a slim, weary figure coming in his direction, and he knew it was her. He rushed to the house and inspected the kitchen that he was ordered to clean up every day after school. David could find no fault with his work, for he had done his best; yet he knew that it was not good enough. He sat and waited expectantly. Soon, the verbal assault mixed with the peppered sting of slaps would be over with, and he could prepare to face another day of fire and brimstone.

This is not fiction. Unfortunately, this is the actual experience of a little boy who might eventually grow into a big man. This is the true story of the man you might sit next to in the office or on the bus. The man who might marry your daughter or your sister. The man who might father your grandchildren. The man you could very well meet one late afternoon in a deserted car park.

In many ways, this is the story of the life of too many of our children in this country. Of course, the story does not end there, for there is the mother's side. What the story does not include is her struggle to pay the utility bills and the rent, and to buy food, among others, on a mere 2,000 dollars per month salary. What the story does not convey is the abuse she has to put up with from her child's father in order to get money to support David.

Mental agony

The story also does not portray the agony she experiences at work due to poor working conditions, and victimization on public transportation. Actually, in her eyes she is not a bad parent, for she survives the best way she knows how. In many ways, she and her son are part of the most visible of the invisible in our society. She too can claim her holocaust.

Research indicates that there is a high level of child abuse in Jamaica. Last Sunday's *Gleaner* highlighted a story by Claire Clarke on the problem of increasing child abuse. Statistics indicate that violent crimes are on the increase. Based on Figure 1 below, we see that, save 1991, there has been a gradual increase in violent crimes between 1988 and 1992. Figure 2 shows that murder has consistently and rapidly increased between 1988 and 1992. What is alarming about violent crimes is the almost callous manner in which many of them are committed. It is as though human life has lost its value; similar to what has been occurring among the inner cities across the US, where violent crime is one of the leading causes of mortality among young Black males. This situation makes Jamaica very unique in the Caribbean. I believe that any attempt to characterize violence in Jamaica as simply an economic and political phenomenon is reductionist. This explanation ignores the interaction between the mind and the environment. Let us explore this issue.

One dimension of violence that many of my colleagues avoid dealing with (presumably for fear of offending others) is violence as a pathological behaviour.

Here I am not speaking of pathology from the strict medical or psychiatric sense. I use the concept of pathology here to refer to a process by which people come to view abnormal behaviour (both in terms of how it was viewed before, and how those on the outside view it) as being normal.

Normal behaviour

We live in a society in which violence has become part of everyday interaction. It is now normal to turn on the seven o'clock evening news and hear of people being murdered, or a body discovered in some gully or river. Insensitivity to violence and instruments of violence have already become the norm. Have you seen how police and soldiers handle guns when they are driving on the roads? Where else in the world, except for those areas in which there are civil wars, or actual police states, where police and soldiers drive around with rifles pointing out of the window of a Jeep. I have driven behind some of these Jeeps with the rifle barrels aimed directly in front of my car. Where else in the world do security forces travel with guns strapped around their waists or shoulders as though they were toys? But just to show how insensitive the society is to violence, not too long ago JBC Television showed a photograph of a policeman who was killed in the line of duty during the elections. The photograph reminded me of the gangsters in the famous bloody movie, The Untouchables. Here we have a television station beaming to children across the nation a picture of a man holding onto a rifle as though he was some type of don. The worrying part was not the showing but the nonchalance with which such a photograph was regarded. Could JBC not find a more appropriate photograph?

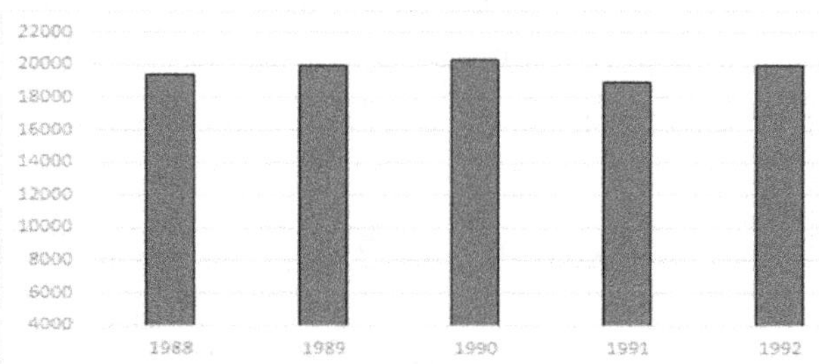

Figure 1: Total major crimes of violence (reported)

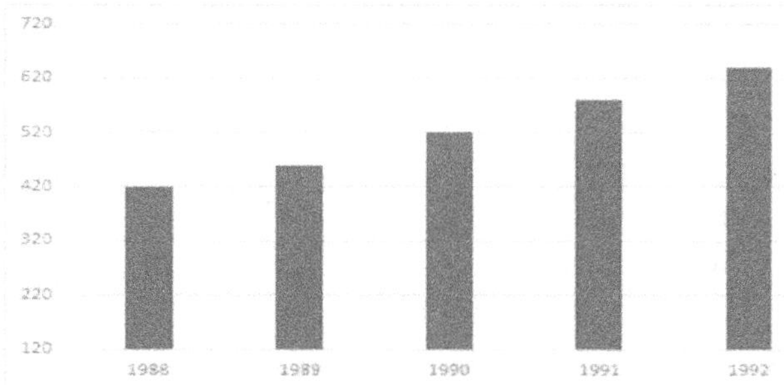

Figure 2: Murders (reported)

Acceptance

What this photograph did was reinforce the view of police work as basically having to do with confrontation rather than protection and resolution. In most other societies, JBC would have been flooded with calls and forced to act more responsibly. When events like this take place with little or no public outcry, it means that we have begun to accept such behaviour as normal. To the extent that this "normal" behaviour contributes to our own demise, when in the eyes of the world it is not normal, then we are dealing in pathologies.

The events that create violent behaviours are extremely complex and sometimes mind-boggling. These events associated with this new political era [emerges] has increased the level of alienation in society. Furthermore, according to the late Carl Stone, the return of overseas dons has made the crime situation more severe.

What we now need to realize is that violence has taken on a dynamism of its own. It is unreasonable to expect people to live in an environment of hostility and not have it affect them psychologically. Reductionist economic and political explanations cannot account for the high frequency of acid throwing, or robbers cutting you in the face after they have taken what they want. We are now dealing with cases where many people in our society have devalued human life and get some sense of relief from inflicting pain on others.

Survival

Indeed, political violence can also be pathological. Garrison constituencies are by definition alienated and ostracized from the rest of society. When survival in these areas becomes tied up with violence, pathologies are produced.

Let me be clear; I am not saying that all violence in Jamaica is pathological. However, I contend that much of it is, and is the result of a society which, by its structure, breeds violence. It means therefore that violence is not simply a police problem; it is not simply a government problem. It is the nation's problem. We need more than just the Private Sector Organisation of Jamaica (PSOJ) to speak to the government on electoral reforms (The Breakfast Club seems to equate private citizens with the PSOJ and the churches).

Out of many, many people

(WEDNESDAY, AUGUST 04, 1993

There can be no doubt that there are fewer and less severe social conflicts among the peoples of the Caribbean than in many other parts of the world. The Caribbean represents an interesting amalgam of different peoples and cultures. And while many people still cling to the view of M.G Smith in his 1965 publication, *The Plural Society in the British West Indies*, that what we have in many of our countries is a plural society, there is much evidence to support the existence of a more "creolized" type of social organization. We live in a region in which the cultures from Africa, Asia and Europe have combined to create something that is different from what one finds in other parts of the world. This we cannot deny.

But there is another dimension to our region – one wrought by its very evolution and fashioned by perpetual conflict and the jockeying for power. It is the social cleavages in our societies which have resulted in intense pain for large sections of our populations. These cleavages are a function of socioeconomic differences and colour. And, just in case you may be wondering why I continue to touch on these issues in my columns, just take a look around the world at the many ethnic conflicts, from Africa to Europe. We only fool ourselves if we continue to believe that we are free from such conflicts. Right now, in Guyana, and in Trinidad and Tobago, there have been increasing tensions between ethnic groups of Indian and African origin as the economic situation worsens in these countries.

Social divisions

There are four important social divisions in Jamaican society based on colour, religion, income and political ideology. A survey conducted by students in one of my classes at The UWI among people of lower St Andrew indicates that many Jamaicans are very discriminating in dealing with people. The sample included both lower- and middle-class respondents. The survey attempted to measure the degree of "social" distance between different social groups. That is, using a scale, respondents were asked a number of questions which would determine the extent to which they might exclude certain people from their neighbourhood, groups or families. The respondents were asked to rate a number of things about people with regard to income, religion, residential area and occupation. The higher the rating given, the less was the desire to increase contact with the person.

With respect to religion, it was found that respondents tended to give highest levels of social distance scores to people who practised "African-based" religions. That is, they felt greater prejudice against people who practised revivalist religions or Rastafari. Professional and skilled people were preferred over unskilled people for social interaction, and people from the ghettos were seen as least desirable for increasing social interaction. Interestingly, people of "mixed race" gave lower social distance scores to people of European descent than did "Black" people. That is to say, so-called "Brown" people felt closer to White people than "Black" people did. Another interesting feature of the findings is that women tended to be more discriminating than men.

While the findings from this survey cannot be generalized for Jamaica, it raises some interesting things about the nature of the society. It is a fact that we live in a society in which colour, education and income are important measures of social differentiation. It is a society in which people value what you look like and who you are more than what you are. Many of my friends relate stories about how they enter a business place to purchase an item only to be ignored for someone who looks "more important" (often meaning that the person has a much lighter complexion). This propensity to ignore people on the basis of how they look comes from business people who are either light-skinned or dark-skinned. This complexion thing has been haunting Black people ever since slavery.

Demonization

The demonization of Blackness represents the worst effects of colonialism. From Cuba to Brazil, the region has developed what I call a "Mulatto" mentality, so much so that in Chile, the attempt to eliminate the African presence resulted in mass miscegenation and the consequent elimination of people of African descent. In many of these societies (and also here in Jamaica), many light-skinned people who marry dark-skinned people feel that they are doing these dark-skinned people a favour. Of course, this feeling is encouraged by the society. Cubans, Black and White, were taught that the culture of their society is European, although anyone but an idiot who visits Cuba quickly realizes that this is nonsense. Fidel Castro recanted after he got involved in the African liberation struggles, and proclaimed Cuba to be Afro-Hispanic. But even today, this denial of the fundamental African aesthetic continues. An examination of the demographic information indicates that about twelve per cent of the population is Black. What a joke! A very conservative estimate of the Black Cuban population must be around twenty-five per cent, and this excludes the Mulatto population.

Even the problems in Haiti are connected to colour and race. Before "Papa Doc" Duvalier, Haiti was ruled by a Mulatto elite which discriminated against Black Haitians. Part of Papa Doc's support came from the Black elite who were opposed to the Mulatto dominance.

American scholar Chancellor Williams who specialized in African history once said that part of the explanation for the fall of Egypt from the hands of Black Africans had to do with "mulattoization" (see C. Williams, *The Destruction of Black Civilisation*, published in 1971). I find this thesis hard to accept in its totality. However, a reading of history tells me that there is some value in examining the role that this change in racial composition might have played in the process.

Let me make it clear that I am not arguing against miscegenation. My own view of human civilization would be inconsistent with such a position. My aim here has been to raise some issues which continue to afflict our society – issues which some people prefer to sweep under the carpet, and which continue to challenge the motto "Out of many, one people". Peace!

Culture, the media and the people: Violent display

(TUESDAY, AUGUST 17, 1993)

Like many other people, I got the opportunity to attend Reggae Sunsplash this year. For the most part, I found the event very enjoyable and was pleased with the easygoing atmosphere at JamWorld. However, I would be remiss if I did not address the issue of violence and coarseness which greeted the crowd on

Dancehall Night. While many of the artistes on that night performed well, it was also a night to sing about killing gays and informers and "dissing" the police. When artistes ran out of steam, they almost always reverted to the drivel of killing gays and informers.

This huge crowd was comprised of both so-called "uptown" and "downtown" people. Both had the same reaction to the music. Hence, we should not get trapped into believing that this is simply a low-class thing. There seems to be a subculture in Jamaican society which romanticizes violence. For many men, the symbolic display of violence, such as singing about shooting an informer, appears to be one of the purest forms of asserting masculinity and control. Among the women, this display appears to be associated with independence, and even sexiness. What next?

Subcultures of violence are often intolerant and ensure conformity through force or open humiliation. I can distinctly remember a point during the show when an artiste on stage threatened that anyone who did not hold a lighted object in the air would be considered gay. Well, next to me stood a young man who was intent on proving to the entire 60,000 people present that he was not gay. He huffed and puffed as he searched in vain to find something that he could burn. After his frantic search, he decided to confront his friend who had a lighter. Convinced that everyone was observing him, he ran towards a friend and yanked his lighter away. Now his friend, caught with his pants down, proceeded to grab another lighter from his female companion who was standing next to him. I have never seen two more relieved young men in all my life. It was as though their death sentences were just commuted.

Violent display

Now, I find the behaviour of the two youngsters very understandable, given the people's propensity to engage in violent display in this society. This sort of violent display represents a retreat from reason. Sadly, there exists in the society a situation in which violence becomes the first and sometimes the only way of resolving conflicts. As a result, possibilities for achieving common ground are stymied. It is not surprising therefore that there exists a civil society which remains relatively undeveloped. The high numbers of police shootings, gang murders, political wars and household conflicts are manifestations of a social structure which has yet to work our ways of resolving conflicts without resorting to violence as a first choice. It is for that reason that I believe that dealing with violent crime in this country will be difficult. Changes to the police force and political system will go a long way in dealing with the problem but will prove to be woefully inadequate. As much as the politicians and police influence society they also reflect it. Thus, to simply dismiss the police force or the political system as aberrations of the larger society is to misunderstand the dynamics of social relations. The world view which many Jamaicans share has in it a place for violence, which is different from that of Trinidad, Guyana or the USA. It is this world view which denounces, but at the same time romanticizes violence in music, art and folklore that we need to understand. I hope to address this issue at a later date.

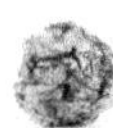

Rhetoric and reality

(TUESDAY, AUGUST 31, 1993)

Two weeks ago, I took a relative, who was returning to the US, to the Norman Manley International Airport. As she reached the check-in counter, I realized that there was no way I would be able to contact her again from behind the harsh dark glass which separated those inside who were travelling from their loved ones outside who were waiting amid pandemonium. To make matters worse, at the entrance of the check-in counter stood a number of soldiers whose job it was to keep away the large crowd of well-wishers, standing in the scorching sun, who were trying to say goodbye to their family members or friends.

Peering through the glass were many fathers, mothers, sisters, brothers, wives and husbands eagerly waiting to say their goodbyes. Standing in a depressing tiny space provided for "their kind", I watched these people touch their loved ones through the prison-style glass and embrace them mentally before seeing them disappear into another mass of confusion that awaited them at the immigration section.

It was then that it struck me – the Norman Manley International Airport was a fairly good metaphor for capturing the organization of the larger society. For the airport is neither built nor organized with people in mind; it is simply a structure to meet the minimum requirements of getting people in and out of the country. In this regard, it is no different from the transportation system, which operates merely to move people from one place to another at any cost. It is similar to the many edifices around Kingston whose architecture belie the fact that they were built principally to serve customers. It is similar to the police force, which apparently is there not to prevent crime but simply to catch criminals. It is like the various so-called "people parks" in Half Way Tree and downtown Kingston, empty of imagination, and perhaps influenced by the extreme pragmatism which led to the erection of high walls and concrete floors reminiscent of abattoirs. It is no different from the telephone company's decision to suddenly stop collect calls with little regard for public sentiment.

Mass politics

An examination of academic texts and writings in various media would give one the impression that, of the English-speaking Caribbean territories, Jamaica has the most distinguished history of mass politics. From the struggles of Nanny and the Maroons to Paul Bogle and the Morant Bay Rebellion, from Marcus Garvey to Michael Manley, the writers show that the interests of the people were advanced with revolutionary fervour like nowhere else in the English-speaking Caribbean. But is this claim more rhetoric than reality? On the face of the evidence, I have to come down on the side of rhetoric.

I will perhaps incur the wrath of many of my colleagues and readers for arguing that Jamaica has one of the least developed political mass movements in the region and a civil society which is perhaps more backward than those of most other Caribbean territories. It is these two factors which seemed to have encouraged empty people-centred political rhetoric and kindled spontaneous outbursts of community rebellions, too often confused as progressive mass action. Fuelling this situation is a massive gulf between the haves and the have-nots which, because of a lack of opportunities for upward mobility, creates the conditions for patronage and clientelistic politics. It is difficult to form truly national bodies, such as consumer leagues, in this country because of a value system which judges you on whether you consume at Peppers or at a bar in downtown Kingston. The end result of this type of social organization is the continued presence of political and economic elites, who are virtually untouchable by the law and who do just enough to keep the masses of poor people "quiet". Political and economic patronage perpetuates paternalism at all levels of the society. What therefore exists is not a progressive working class but divided tribes, many of whom see their existence as being tied up with the interests of a political party, when in reality what is needed is that they support radical transformation of the structure of power relations in society. Rebellious acts, such as drive-by shootings, are never aimed at the system of politics and economics which remain oppressive to many, but against one's neighbour or friend. It is this naked aggression among the people themselves, born of an exploitative system, which is mistaken for standing up for one's rights. The fact is that legitimate ways of confronting the powerful in society hardly work for the disenfranchised. And we wonder why there is so much crime.

Public pressure

One indicator of our undeveloped civil society is the lack of public pressure on government to deal with white-collar crime, which Colonel MacMillan continues to speak about. Yet another example is the lack of organized public outcry against the sudden implementation of taxes by the government during the recent budget presentation – a policy indicating that the government acts in an almost unbridled fashion. The other point, of course, is that the formal instruments of public opinion are in the hands of the powerful. Most importantly, however, is that there is no widespread consciousness among the masses of people that they can demand that the government fully and completely investigate white-collar crime, or should be sensitive to the needs of the public in constructing a budget.

From the sixties to the eighties, this country has heard the rhetoric of putting people first from all political parties. Yet the reality does not square with such rhetoric. In the 1970s, the heyday of "people" politics, research shows that there was redistribution of income in favour of the wealthy. This trend continued right through the 1980s up to the present. Dr Dillon Alleyne's study of the burden of taxation shows that sections of the middle class and the poor continue to pay a disproportionate share of taxes (see D. Alleyene, *Taxation and Equity in Jamaica, 1985-1992: Who bears the Burden?* published in 1999).

As capital exerts more influence on government policy, it would be wise for all to pay greater attention to the plight of the growing mass of marginalized citizens. For a time could well come when these citizens might no longer pay deference to the elites. It is then that rhetoric may be translated into reality. Peace!

The Jamaican "caste" system

(TUESDAY, JANUARY 11, 1994)

Recently, I was engaged in a discussion with a group of young people from different parts of Kingston about conditions in their neighbourhoods. They painted vivid scenes about conditions in their communities, and it was surprising how often lower-class and middle-class members of the group used the terms "uptown" and "downtown" in referring to relations between people. In their minds, uptown and downtown were as distant as earth was from Pluto.

Unfortunate division

The constant reference by "these people" to refer to someone from uptown or downtown highlighted part of the unfortunate division which currently haunts the society. It is a division which is so visible that one can almost tell which of the "towns" people are from by looking at their skin colour, texture, dress and mannerisms. It is a division so severe that I often get the feeling that we have replaced the British colonizers with our own local people. Indeed, the deference expected of "downtowners" by the "uptowners" is almost similar to that which the colonizers expected of their ignorant subjects. Correspondingly, the feeling among "downtowners" that "uptowners" owe them something is similar to the slave-and-master relationship of the pre-emancipation era.

For all of these reasons, to talk of a Jamaican class system may in some cases amount to a euphemism. To all intents and purposes, social intercourse within our society may more accurately be described as caste relations rather than class relations.

Now, I know that many people will raise eyebrows at this characterization of society, because a caste system is a system of social stratification based on ascription, while the class system is supposed to be a system based on individual achievement. Furthermore, over the years, many so-called downtown people have been able to move into the middle class either by the accumulation of personal wealth or by education.

But I want you to follow my reasoning here: I use the term "caste system" as a metaphor to represent a class system which is so harsh and so visible that people are constantly reminded where they fall on the totem pole. This is not to say that such reminders are conscious acts by individuals on all occasions. What is being argued is that intense class socialization is evident in virtually every sphere of everyday life.

Not trivial

Note that this issue of caste is not a trivial one if one wants to understand our society. Jamaica is, arguably, the most class-conscious of all Caribbean countries. Yet, the country has remained amazingly stable over the years. This, notwithstanding the many antisystem movements which the society has thrown up since slavery. In fact, I would argue that it is precisely due to the intense social divisions in the society that we have the growth of antisystem movements which gave birth to Garveyism, Rastafari, reggae, and dancehall music. All these movements are responses to oppressive social and economic conditions. But they also represent a critique of the snobbery and contempt with which the middle and upper classes have historically treated those whom they consider to be less civilized than they are. In this way, Jamaica is very similar to the USA, where urban African-Americans have developed a way of life which in many ways conflicts with "mainstream middle America". The problems faced by inner cities in Jamaica are amazingly similar to those of the inner cities of the USA. What is perhaps different between the two societies is the role played by race, which further complicates the American situation. In the USA, the lifestyle and world view of inner-city African Americans are so different from those of "middle America" that the term "caste" rather than "class" may more appropriately describe the social relations between the two groups in society.

Sharp differences

Interestingly, the sharp differences between social groups in our society have not yet translated into large-scale revolts or upheavals similar to those which have occurred in other developing countries – some faced with less intense cleavages. Why? The answer to this question is multifaceted, and available space does not allow for an exploration of the full range of issues. However, I will briefly mention two important reasons.

First, there is political tribalism, which has ensured the persistence of a divided lower class. This division has negated the growth of class consciousness and prevented the possibility of a class-based rebellion. Second, more than any other country of the region, there is a national (Jamaican) identity which is evidenced through music, religion (viz., Rastafari) and a philosophy of resistance (from the Maroons to Merlene Ottey). Now this is a minor point. What is very interesting is that the forms of resistance which have given birth to art, music and philosophy have been frequently embraced by the political and economic elites for commercial, political or psychological reasons. Invariably, this acceptance occurs only after what is created gains external recognition. It is for this reason that the initial negative reaction to dancehall music by the elite is slowly giving way to national acceptance as more local artistes gain international recognition.

When symbols of resistance – such as reggae and Rastafari – become part of the national ethos, they lose their initial significance and become part of everyday life. This conflict and eventual accommodation reduce the possibility of class-based social rebellion, even in a society with a caste-like system of stratification. Peace!

A conspiracy of poverty

(TUESDAY, AUGUST 30, 1994)

There is much which makes the USA different from Jamaica, but there are many things which make these two countries so alike. One of the similarities is the level of poverty, which is often compounded by the difficult social lives of many of the inhabitants of the so-called inner cities. In both countries, the inner cities are virtual states within states, and usually the rate of violent crime is higher than in the larger population. To be sure, there is nothing inherently peculiar about residents of these inner cities. And, if we were to borrow a metaphor from Rex Nettleford, most of us "came from the cane-piece on our way to the great house". What really makes us different as a people are the different circumstances under which we gained our experiences. It is these circumstances which often help to determine our life chances. But why is it that the circumstances of the inner cities often lead its inhabitants to have very different life chances from others in the larger society?

Investment

Even the most casual observer of American and Jamaican life will be struck by the huge gulf in education, housing, employment and environmental conditions which exist between the inner cities and the rest of their countries – the remote rural areas being the exception. Also, government policies concerning inner-city areas is similar in both countries. That is, both governments often talk about what is to be done, but do nothing until election time comes around. During the last presidential election in the US, Bill Clinton met with the National Urban League and a host of other organizations which represent inner-city interests, and he made an amazing number of proposals which would help to rehabilitate the major US cities. The inner cities continue to deteriorate under Clinton's presidency.

But our government's record is not more flattering. With all the talk about investment and jobs for inner cities during the last election, the present government, like previous ones, has yet to deliver on these promises. Despite a plethora of so-called poverty alleviation programmes, our inner cities continue to deteriorate.

Now, there is an underlying set of factors at work, in both countries, which accounts for the perpetual decay of the inner cities. In the US, it is racism; in Jamaica, it is a combination of politics and classism.

A recent article published in the highly respected American Sociological Review argues that in the US, it is the discrimination in housing, education, and business which is the main factor affecting predominantly black residential areas. The current debates surrounding the O. J. Simpson case in the US media, and the recent case in New York in which a Black police officer was shot – while on duty – by a White police officer because he was mistaken for a criminal, are indictments on American race relations. The debates surrounding the recent crime bill which was passed in the US Congress indicate clearly that most White and Black Americans live in two completely different worlds. In the view of most White lawmakers, more jails should be built to put away criminals – a disproportionate number of whom come from inner cities and happen to be black. Very few of these lawmakers care to see the link between crime and circumstance. I am not convinced that American policymakers are genuinely concerned with improving the standards of living in inner cities. Further, the policies of several states with regard to taxation, policing, housing, education, banking, investment and transportation support my conclusion.

Consumerism

By the same token, I am not sure policymakers in our country are seriously interested in rebuilding our inner cities. This comes against the background that we live in a society increasingly trapped by the consumerism culture of a place like Miami, but which has the levels of poverty and productivity comparable to some sections of Haiti.

At the same time, the presence of large groups of poor people has provided the fuel for the political parties. Coupled with this, we seem to have in this region a penchant for Messiahs, and consequently all the Caribbean countries have had their share of messianic politicians, to varying degrees and with varying results. But in order for these Messiahs to continue in their roles they must have constituencies – preferably of poor people, huddled together with little hope of changing their circumstances by themselves.

This is not to say that these Messiahs, generally, do not have a genuine interest in changing the conditions of the people. The reality is that if there is no one to deliver, then there can be no deliverer. The absence of people to deliver is antithetical to the very existence of our political parties. This perspective might be regarded by some as cynical, but I see no other explanation for the present state of the inner cities – given the rhetoric about what needs to be done in order to transform these communities.

Another debilitating factor is that we live in a society which is so class-conscious that many among us have accepted the inevitability of the inner cities. Just as there can be no justification for the state of inner cities in the US, there can be none for those in Jamaica. What is required in both situations is large-scale investment in the communities. There needs to be a national plan borrowing elements from the Kingston Restoration Project, but with a real bipartisan commitment to stamping out patronage politics. Only thus can such an investment bear fruit. As was demonstrated in many parts of Boston and Chicago over the past five years, community policing and serious investment in education can make a big difference in a short space of time.

A host of poverty alleviation programmes as advised by the IMF will never solve the type of social and economic problems emerging from having people live in spatial environments which geographers have shown threaten continued civilized human existence. Some will ask where the resources will come from; others will say the Americans can afford such resources, but we cannot. I say, we cannot afford not to find the money. Peace!

Ending feudalism

(TUESDAY, OCTOBER 04, 1994)

Ticky ticky tuck
everyting stuck
Dem a look little wuk
Wha yuh name?
Me no know
Whe yuh goin?
Nowhere
What yuh lookin?
Anyting
Ticky ticky tuck
everybody bruk
What a luck
No wuk

— MICHAEL SMITH, "TICKY TICKY TUCK"

Last week, the opposition leader, Mr Edward Seaga, gave a radio interview on the situation in West Kingston which I found truly amazing. One could have interpreted this interview in many ways, including that it was perhaps in some ways an admission of the complicity of some politicians in sheltering criminals in their constituencies. More noteworthy, though, was the fracas which later erupted between the commissioner of police and Mr Seaga, clearly reflecting a type of desperation in a society which has sat by and allowed the development of what are now termed garrison constituencies.

The conflict over whether or not Mr Seaga gave Colonel MacMillan a list or set of names is symbolic of a larger issue which has plagued our country for many years – who determines where this country should go and how? In other words, we are dealing fundamentally with the issue of power and control.

Now it seems to me that the Seaga-McMillan conflict has only served to bolster the internal contradictions of our feudalistic political system and quasi-rationally organized police bureaucracy. Part of the reason for the contradictions is that some politicians seem to be losing control over their constituencies – to other power brokers – and they are scared.

Environment

Then there are the police trying to become more professional and service-oriented in an environment where the distribution of state power thins as we approach certain areas historically under the control [literally] of a politician or village caretaker. Now, what last week's events are teaching us is that, while members of parliament (MPs) should represent the interests of the people in their constituencies, the relationship should not be one where the MPs become godfathers. For such a relationship is in many ways similar to the feudal systems of Japan before the Meiji Restoration, or the current clan system which operates in Somalia – both of which have often led to great conflicts, especially when the feudal lords could not provide for the serfs. This type of arrangement loop brings with it a dependency relationship, and is ripe for manipulation by dons of all types who can easily move in and fill the void left by an increasingly animated state and politician.

But there is a larger problem which the society, not simply the politicians, must address if our country is to be rescued from future violent upheavals. Simply arresting gang members will not solve the problem, for others will spring up to replace them as long as there is an opportunity. What we are dealing with is not personalities, but a system of social organization which encourages the creation and maturation of such gangs. What is required is that we address this problem with an economic and social development agenda which embraces the entire country, and not just isolated sections.

Why is it that we only see the type of violence witnessed last week in certain parts of the country – mainly the inner cities? Do the people who live in these areas have different goals and aspirations from the other people of this country? Of course not. What has happened is that over the years many of our popular politicians have carved out pieces of these communities to guarantee their power base. This is the essence of feudalism. Feudal societies cannot be effectively served by a single state. Feudal societies are inherently unequal and are prone to the type of civil disturbances which so often characterize inner city areas. Therefore, a pact among politicians to turn in gang members in their constituencies without serious change to the economic and political infrastructure will amount to little more than complicity to prolong this status quo. What is required is a fundamental restructuring of parliamentary representation along the national development policies, targeting areas most prone to high unemployment and crime.

"Welfare-ism"

Let me elaborate. The type of community welfare-ism where the government gives a certain number of jobs to JLP and PNP supporters is counterproductive. What this does is perpetuate the myth and feeling among people in those areas that the political system is the answer to their economic problems. Why does the government not award contracts to people in, say, Red Hills, Beverly Hills or Mona Heights along political lines? The reason is simple: the survival of these communities does not depend directly on the political system. Furthermore, people in these areas, like so many others across the country, do not have to approach politicians to secure employment. Consequently, block allegiances and clientelistic attachments are not developed. Voting is more on substance rather than for survival, and there is no power vacuum when the politician is unable to feed the masses. Why does the same not obtain for a number of inner-city areas?

There has been a conspiracy within the political system to maintain these so-called garrison constituencies, and with them the type of dependent underdevelopment which is evidenced by the crime and virtual segregation of these areas from the larger society. People who have to depend on others to feed them often find that they have to give up independent decision-making. Consequently, when I talk about investment in these communities it is not only in terms of development of public infrastructure but also the inflows of private capital in the form of business opportunities. Serious human development in the inner cities will only occur when citizens have economic independence, which is coupled with political reform which moves away from the feudal practices of the past and towards the rationalism of the present. Peace!

True democracy

(TUESDAY, MARCH 07, 1995)

> I swear to the Lord
> I still can't see
> Why Democracy means
> Everybody but me
>
> — LANGSTON HUGHES, "THE BLACK MAN SPEAKS"

Having read the interim report of the Electoral Advisory Committee (EAC), it seems to me that there is an uncanny similarity between the problems it addresses and the leadership squabble presently affecting the Jamaican Labour Party (JLP).

However, there are nine very serious problems of interest outlined in the report which are associated with voting on election day, seven of which relate directly to thuggery and violence – often against the independent minded people in garrison constituencies. In the same breath, one of the complaints which has sparked the present conflict in the JLP is the perception that, even though there may be an appearance of democratic mechanisms within the party, the practice of electing the top brass to leadership is essentially undemocratic. In other words, while the "law" says one thing, the practice is different. As such, this party, like our political system, operates more on tradition than on rationality and democracy. Consequently, to challenge these norms and conventions becomes risky business. It is for this reason that we must not reduce the debate to simply whether or not the so-called "Gang of Ten" used the correct procedure to address the question of leadership of the party. If we do this, then we will miss the issue at hand – violating the unwritten rules of party organization, rules which are based more on tradition than on democracy.

Contradictions

Now, as we in Jamaica and the Caribbean begin to confront our almost ageing political systems with reform, we cannot escape being caught within the apparent contradictions. What both the report of the EAC and the JLP conflicts indicate is that a political system which relies on patronage and violence for its existence will have to face itself one day. And when politicians no longer have the capacity to feed, and hence reproduce, such a system, that system will collapse. Furthermore, tradition is easier to challenge when there is a legal and institutional framework and a rhetorical discourse which contradicts this tradition. Therefore, I am arguing that as long as there is, within the party and society, a rhetorical discourse about democracy, and a legal and institutional framework, regardless of how embryonic, which seeks to advance democratic rights, then it will only be a matter of time before someone conflates the rhetoric and the legal and institutional framework in order to challenge what is in essence a contradictory tradition. You see, in the not-too-distant past, we saw an example in Barbados where tradition was overthrown by a vote of no confidence in Prime Minister Erskine Sandiford. Unseating Mr Sandiford would have been much more hazardous were there not a framework and a rhetoric of democracy within the political system. By now, it should be clear that much of our regional party tradition is (un)usually characterised by the party leader's ability to exert tremendous influence over his followers – often times, by any means necessary.

Might I add, the UK does not have a written constitution, yet the political parties are far more democratic than their Caribbean counterparts. Even as we speak, a number of political parties in the region have in their constitutions references to the democratic process, but they hardly exist in practice. Likewise, the right of the citizen to vote, and to engage in freedom of association is clearly outlined in the constitution, yet on election day there are many thousands who dare not try to exercise these guaranteed rights. Despite this, we continue to listen to politicians as they invoke the principle of democracy as the basis for their right to rule.

Folk heroes

If we remember that our political parties arose during a period when poor and mostly uneducated black people were fighting for their rights, and that trade unions were later started by political parties championing the rights of the masses, only then can we begin to understand the fulfilment which democracy facilitates. Regrettably, what was to emerge in our region were charismatic leaders who established traditions in these organizations in order to protect their survival. By extension, these politicians had the minds of a largely poor and uneducated population to mould; consequently, they were able to make themselves into little deities and folk heroes, thus palming themselves off as indispensable to many of our people who were traditionally on the margins of society.

Regionally, the transformation in the education system, the growth of a larger Black middle class, and the diminishing importance of the state has eroded the need for the mystique of the nice sounding rhetoric and good-looking politician. In Jamaica, the creation of garrisons and the explicit co-opting of poor inner-city areas by politicians represented their last-ditch efforts to ensure their political survival. The continued reduction of political spoils because of structural adjustment, and the change in the global ideological landscape have meant that, increasingly, party leaders can no longer justify maintaining their positions either by personal threats or by their guaranteed position in parliament – often guaranteed by their garrisons.

Now, if we continue to reduce unemployment, while providing more opportunities for education and personal growth for our people in the inner cities and in areas stricken by poverty, then we can be assured that we are moving closer to ridding our society of political violence, corruption and mismanagement. Surely, this should improve our chances of building an electoral system free of fraud and other malpractices.

This, therefore, is the larger context in which the EAC report must be placed. If not, many of its very useful proposals will never be achieved. And it is also in this context that we should read the current JLP crisis. I suspect that the PNP's own crisis is not too far away. Peace!

Free speech and freedom of the press

(TUESDAY MAY 30, 1995)

The debates about freedom of speech have been raging within literate societies for a long time. And, even as we speak, there is heated debate raging in the US about the right of so-called militias to publish and to articulate views which, from experience, can be detrimental to that society. In North Korea and China, this debate about the freedom of the press is smouldering. For, while it is true that today's oppressive state laws regarding speech are a function of communism, China and North Korea's histories will show that these countries have for centuries developed cultures which are founded on limited individual expression. Therefore, even to this day, a tacit consensus exists in these societies where the individual's liberty is secondary to the survival of the collective.

In fact, it was primarily after the period of enlightenment in the 17th century that attempts were made to get rid of censorship in the Western world. It is clear, therefore, that freedom of speech and of the press emerged over time and that they are ideals for which societies must struggle. Indeed, the relative openness of the Japanese press is because of their interaction with and the influence of Europeans and the North Americans.

In Britain and the US, the crusade against censorship took two forms: first, there was an attempt to prevent government from reviewing, before publication, any manuscript; second, there was an attempt to prevent government from penalising authors, after publication, for making what may be termed forbidden statements. Perhaps the most important way advocates could guarantee freedom of the press was to ensure that production of written material was privately controlled, and that the state had as little involvement in the dissemination of news as possible. Indeed, advocates of freedom of speech have been consistently critical of communist and fascist regimes. You see, under these systems, the state tends to monopolize the production and dissemination of news. So insidious is the perception of the state's role in preventing freedom of the press that even Confucius, who advocated caution as opposed to free speech, once said an "oppressive government is fiercer than a tiger".

In our society, one of the fruits of free enterprise has been the mushrooming of the media. Theoretically, there is the view that competition will allow for the opening of more media enterprises, thus guaranteeing wider dissemination and variety. This is precisely what is happening in Jamaica. Coupled with this is the declining significance of political patronage and the emerging of a civil society which has the capacity to critique governments' policies with comparatively little fear of reprisals.

Disbanding old style with this newly emerging civil society comes the disbanding of the old, style politics. So, where political parties once operated in an environment with one or two major newspapers and radio stations (one of which would likely have supported them), they must now operate in an arena with many newspapers and radio stations which may not have declared political allegiances. Perhaps if this were not the case, the JLP leadership crisis of a few months ago and the current PNP visa scandal would have been less visible to the public.

But there is another side to the freedom of speech and proliferation of the media. When a society guarantees free speech to the individual, there is always the possibility that abuses may result from such freedom. Thus, freedom to write and publish damaging things about a group in one's society can result in negative consequences for that group. If this group is at a comparatively disadvantaged position in the society, then the consequences of damaging speech may even be life-threatening. For instance, influential intellectuals who support theories of natural inferiority of a group may inflict harm on that group because members of the public may be tempted to believe those theories. Now, because of the inability of the disadvantaged group to respond effectively to these theories, they must then suffer unduly. In societies where there is a great deal of social inequality, freedom of speech tends to favour the rich and powerful, who invariably have a greater capacity to manipulate information. Therefore, we should always remember that truth is not always self-evident; it is not hidden somewhere waiting to be discovered. Instead, truth is constructed, and often times what is accepted as truth is based on what is most persuasive and most often repeated.

Consequently, an abundance of privately-run media houses does not mean that the public will actually hear "the truth" from the press. What it means is that we get the creation of many "truths" from those who are most influential and can manage to perpetuate these truths. Furthermore, those who own and control the media will protect their own personal interests by bringing pressure to bear on journalists when journalists investigate issues which affect them. This is true of the media everywhere. As such, private control of the media in no way guarantees that the truth will be told or that issues will be dealt with more objectively. What private ownership of the media allows for is multiple interpretations of issues and the reduction of state concealment of information.

It seems to me that when we talk about freedom of speech or freedom of the press, we have to recognize that this comes with responsibilities. Since there is no guarantee that such responsibility will be forthcoming, then the society has to put mechanisms in place to prevent abuses of free speech. Legal mechanisms are necessary to promote free speech, and also protect others from the harmful consequences of free speech. Ultimately, however, our most effective guarantee for such a process is social and economic development at all levels of our society. Peace!

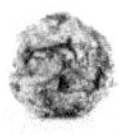

Crime and science

(TUESDAY, JUNE 13, 1995)

The growing incidence of violent crime in our society seems to have awakened a greater interest in crime-fighting methods. Consequently, the use of technological innovations and improved scientific techniques to assist in fighting this scourge is being contemplated. Against this background, Minister of National Security, K. D. Knight, announced that DNA testing might soon be introduced to assist with solving various crimes. In light of this – for the future – we in Jamaica could find ourselves looking for biological and medical explanations to violent crimes if we follow the lead of our American counterparts.

An article in the recent edition of the respected Scientific American journal entitled "Can science 'cure' crime?" looks at the link between biological factors and crime. One such reference to biological explanation is that a low resting heart rate bears some correlation to antisocial behaviour. A number of studies have, for example, found that problem children tend to have significantly lower pulse rates than their counterparts. Jerome Kagan, a Harvard psychologist, also advances the view that an inhibited "temperament" may explain why most children from high-risk homes grow up to become law-abiding citizens.

Study

Of note is that some years ago, a Californian businessman Everett L. Hodges spent more than one million dollars to support research which implicates manganese as a marker for violent crime. While research conducted by Louis Gottschalk, a psychiatrist, has found manganese to be 3.6 times higher in alleged felons. Critics have argued that the findings are inconclusive, and that they contradict many others which have found no such relationship.

Interestingly, experiments have been conducted in which prisoners were given various foods aimed at bringing about changes in their behaviour. One such study occurred in 1989 in which an experimental group was given vitamin and mineral supplements which were three times the recommended dosage. These supplements were aimed at reducing the prisoners' violent behaviour. In fact, the most cited study is one in which the link between violent behaviour and biological factors is said to have been traced to low levels of serotonin, a chemical which inhibits the secretion of stomach acid and promotes smooth muscle, and which also functions as a neurotransmitter in the brain. Nevertheless, none of these experiments has so far proven conclusive, and to date no one can say for sure how changes in diet or minerals affect violent behaviour.

Notwithstanding these difficulties, policymakers and researchers in the US and many industrialized countries still hold out hope that biologists and sociologists might one day develop a complicated model which can scientifically predict the most violent amongst us. In my opinion, this view seems a bit optimistic, given the fact that violent behaviour is a function of a myriad of factors. However, at present, the most persuasive explanations for the prevalence of violent behaviour are sociological. Psychological and biological evidence cannot yet satisfactorily explain the prevalence of violent crime among various social groups.

Furthermore, non-sociological explanations are

fraught with difficulty in cases where the social structure is oppressive as is the case with numerous societies. And if we take our own situation differences in life chances best explain why most of our society's violent crimes are committed by people from lower classes. We know from research that the more violent a person's life experiences are then the more likely it is that this individual will be tempted to use violence to resolve personal conflicts.

Inner-city renewal

(TUESDAY, OCTOBER 08, 1996)

Recently, interest in finding solutions to the increase in violent crimes in our society has led many people to seek developmental solutions for the inner cities – the areas most affected by such violent crimes. One such solution includes the provision of massive private sector investment through the setting up of businesses, along with the development of the physical and social infrastructure in the relevant areas. This idea is not novel and, for what it is worth, has been successfully implemented in a number of US inner cities.

While the US government has yet to seriously focus on transforming poverty-stricken inner cities into places where people can live and work with great dignity and less fear, these experimental programmes in economic empowerment have had a great deal of success. In cities such as Memphis, Harlem and Los Angeles, areas which have been designated empowerment zones, there has been a revival, because local and outside entrepreneurs are seizing the opportunity to invest in these communities. One incentive for entrepreneurs is the granting of tax breaks whenever they invest in these communities. In Memphis, the renowned Beale Street has been rejuvenated from a virtually dilapidated ghost town into a busy, active business and entertainment area.

Crime rates

These empowerment zones have also experienced reduced crime rates, and once more are attracting people from the suburbs. One of the amazing aspects of the American demographic scene is that some people are returning to the inner cities because there is a feeling that all is not lost there, and more so that life's "excitement" is not found in the suburbs. Interestingly, many of these inner-city areas much like those here in Jamaica, have given great works of art such as music and dance to the country and to the world. In other words, these areas have contributed in great measure to the wealth of the United States.

One of the largest income-earning industries is entertainment. The tens of millions of dollars earned yearly by record companies from the hardships of people from these areas (as reflected in the lyrics and melodies in rap and hip-hop music) is never shared with those who have created these art forms in the first place. Therefore, the effort at rebuilding inner cities in the US, though somewhat feeble, is well warranted, and the positive results are highly visible. US inner cities have given much more to the country than the country has given to them. A similar situation exists here in Jamaica.

Musical genius

You see, the contemporary musical genius of Jamaica comes from inner cities. All sectors of the society have benefited from reggae and ragga, whether we are talking about its incorporation into the tourism industry, or about the colourful hues which characterize textile and other forms of manufacturing. But those who benefit most from the entertainment industry in this country do not come from the inner cities, rather they are the uptown folk who control the night clubs, marketing and public relation firms, educational institutions, hotels, clothing and screen-printing enterprises, printing and publishing houses, restaurants and food retail outlets – to mention a few.

The selling of Jamaican goods overseas, and the country as a tourist product, is intimately tied up with a particular international image of our country which is due largely to the creative energies of the many dispossessed people from inner city areas. Thus, it seems to me that the rebuilding of inner-city areas should not be seen simply as a pragmatic response to rising crime and general social chaos, but also as a fair exchange, or compensation for the use of their people's intellectual property. Indeed, the individual artistes who have created the music, dance and social commentary for the benefit of the entire country, and by extension the world, owe their talent to the collective experiences of their peers and people in their communities, and as a result of this it is only fair that the compensation be community-focused. Against this background, the serious planning and careful public and private investment in the inner cities is warranted. These pivots for forward movement are long overdue. Peace!

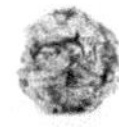

Taking control / Education for the few

(TUESDAY, OCTOBER 22, 1996)

For some time now, the problem of violence has been having disturbing socio-psychological effects on our society. Indeed, many of us know from personal experience that the level of violent crime in our society is far in excess of what is reported by official sources, since these statistics only reflect incidents which are recorded by the police. If this phenomenon is combined with continued economic instability, then you have the perfect recipe for an environment in which chaos and/or authoritarianism may eventually emerge – unless, of course, ordinary people intervene to deal with the crisis.

A content analysis of the print, radio and television news, along with other daily public opinion columns in national newspapers, reveals a disturbing pattern of a lack of control in people's lives. This discernible pattern is as a result of the feeling that the state is unable to maintain law and order, while promoting economic stability.

Even more disturbing is what seems to be a sense of pessimism among young people, especially those at tertiary institutions, about their future. You see, I have found that over the years an increasingly large number of university students are, upon graduation, less and less sure about their role in society. Also, there seems to be less tolerance for ideas about social responsibility and collective development.

Intolerance

Perhaps this intolerance for social responsibility and collective development has its basis in experience. The fact of the matter is that throughout the 1980s and 1990s, the formative years for these young people, they have been part of a developmental experience characterized by perpetual social and economic crisis. Whatever is the cause of this "new mood", it does not augur well for our society, for it is the youth who represent the future of any nation.

To be sure, this social and psychological malaise which currently afflicts our society cannot be cured given the current political arrangement, unless we sanction the emergence of a benevolent dictatorship. In my view, the future of our society is going to depend on the strength of civil society, which will have to stand up and take control.

Civil society refers to those institutions of people, ranging from the family to consumer organizations, in which individuals arrange themselves to force reforms in governance and help to decide what is to be done about issues ranging from transportation, public utilities, the electoral process through to the restoration of law and order, particularly in sections of the society which seem to be independent states.

No easy road

There is no easy road to such a process, but we are not without examples. The civil rights movement in the 1960s and the political and economic reform movements of Latin America during the 1980s were all born out of a desire by citizens to deal with crises in their societies. More recently, we saw the example of the Million Man March in the US, a symbolic gesture aimed at mobilizing black men to assume greater social responsibility for their lives and those of their communities. Although our concerns may be somewhat different, the individual responsibility is the same if we are to arrest a growing social crisis in our society. In the long run, the alternatives – authoritarian rule or total chaos – may be too costly.

Education for the few

It seems as though education in our society continues to be accessible to the few with money and influence. I understand that there are a number of young people who are finding it difficult to gain acceptance to certain schools to pursue A level studies. In almost every case, these young people who are turned away from schools are between the ages of 15 and 18 and have done well in the Caribbean Examination Council (CXC) exams. It would appear that the only factor which separates them from their peers who were successful in gaining acceptance to these schools is their "lower" social status, and the fact that they have no one to "put in a good word" for them. Here is part of the reason why there is a social crisis in our society. Peace!

Sports and progress

(TUESDAY, SEPTEMBER 30, 1997)

Historically, human beings have used sports to entertain, to interact socially, and to display physical skills and even religious prowess. The modern Olympics can be traced back to the ancient Greeks who invited participants from as far as Ethiopia to pit their strength against those of Greece and other nations. In

Egypt, sports were used by the Pharaohs to demonstrate their ability to rule and by extension their divinity. But in modern society, sports occupies an integral part of our existence, and thus a significant proportion of our time is spent either as participants or spectators of one type of sport or another. So important is sports to us that, primarily in the industrialized countries, competitive sport is a huge business run by large corporations. For all intents and purposes, organized sports have brought huge economic benefits to a number of industrialized nations; however, developing countries like Jamaica have little to show, economically, for the talent which they have released onto the world stage.

Perhaps the most debated side of sports is its political dimension. Nations across the world have used sports to draw attention to a cause, or to protest an issue. During the Cold War era, both the Soviet Union and the United States boycotted various international sporting competitions in order to score political points against each other. And both countries have used their sportsmen and sportswomen to highlight political concerns. In the Caribbean, C. L. R. James wrote about the role of cricket as a decolonizing force for the West Indies. Thus, despite others' attempts to decry the role of cricket as a social and political force within the region, and in some cases to try to substitute it with football as a future sport for our youth, it remains a potent force for the launching of our region onto the world stage. This, therefore, is the reason cricket remains, by far, the most successful sport ever played by the people of this region.

Camouflage

However, there is another dimension to sports, and it is that nations often use sports to camouflage serious problems and fissures within their societies. Countries which have had turbulent and divisive histories tend to rely on sports to whip up nationalist fervour and unity; thus, the US and the USSR have often relied on sports to project an image of national unity. Therefore, we can clearly understand why during the political and economic crisis of the 1980s, the USSR sent their athletes across the world to create an image of unity and strength. It must also be stated that communist countries invested heavily in sports, because success on the fields of sports was a victory against capitalism and represented good public relations at home. Indeed, it is regrettable that in both Australia and the USA, athletes are castigated by the ruling elites whenever they stand up for the rights of their oppressed ethnic groups.

Reliance

Unfortunately, I fear that we may be falling into the trap of believing that our success at sports can be easily transposed to other areas of national life. Too often, we rely on sports to solve the pressing social problems which our political system should be addressing. As such, we often spend an inordinate amount of time producing sportspersons, particularly in and from our inner cities, while failing to address the real problems faced by them in these very same communities. This is often done at the expense of developing the youths' intellectual capacities, and the end result is that you have very good athletes who do not have a future beyond the sports field. You see, the top sporting nations of this world do not need to produce the best athletes; they can simply buy them or give them visas. Their interest is in the economic control of sports, not simply the display of skills.

Now, while not overlooking the importance of sports to personal and national development, the idea that we can "play ourselves to stability, discipline and economic development" is utter nonsense. In light of this, it is fallacious to equate running a cricket, basketball or football team with running a country. Sri Lanka's cricketing successes belie the numerous political and economic difficulties which they are currently experiencing. Kenya's phenomenal success in middle- and long-distance running does not reflect that country's dismal political and economic performance. And Colombia's ability to produce, arguably, the world's most talented footballers year after year seems inversely related to the general quality of life of the majority of people in that country. That is to say, the more difficult the social and economic problems of that country, the more talented players they seem to produce.

There is no causal link between a country's ability to produce top athletes and its ability to properly manage its political and economic affairs. The fact is that a significant proportion of the world's top athletes have come from environments which are very depressed. Perhaps it is time that we get a sense of proportion and realize that success in any sport is not a sign of global greatness; rather, it is simply a sign of success in that sport. Furthermore, it is time that we become stakeholders in sports, and not mere participants. To do this, we need to encourage, develop and celebrate the cerebral process, and not just the physical or athletic prowess, of our athletes. Peace!

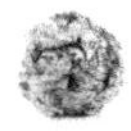

Reforming the police force: Part 1

(TUESDAY, FEBRUARY 17, 1998)

Recently, one of my colleagues at The University of the West Indies (UWI), Dr Anthony Harriott, presented an interesting paper on police reform in Jamaica at one of the many open seminars held on the Mona campus. In attendance were police officers, academics and others who have an interest in crime and justice.

The paper, which is based on research undertaken by Harriott, breaks new ground in terms of its depth and scope. The presentation looked at some of the reasons for the ineffectiveness of the police in reducing crime by focusing on some of the problems within the force itself. Also, the paper discusses the 1994 reform programme, based on the recommendations of the Wolfe and Hirst reports, while pointing to areas of success and failure, and also to policy options.

Political model

Harriott points out that, prior to the reforms of the 1990s, the police operated under a political model where control of the police force was achieved via networks of party-affiliated activists within the force. Hence, this approach to policing allows the political directorate to determine and influence detailed operational matters within the force.

Further, in a survey conducted by Harriott in 1991, officers reported widespread interference in the operations of the force, and according to Harriott, "some 67 per cent of those interviewed felt that the Minister of National Security routinely interfered with promotions...". Equally, some 20 per cent of those interviewed reported having had direct experiences of charges "brought against suspects dropped". Dr Harriott points out that the "political model", based on a highly centralized and rigid command, also fosters a police subculture "that celebrates and accords high status to those most adept at employing violence in the course of doing police work..."

It is against this background that we begin to understand why the reforms took place and why, as Harriott argues, the traditional "political model" of policing was in crisis and was unable to deal with the nature of criminal activities, which had changed radically. For instance, violent crime, as a proportion of total crime, moved from 10 per cent in 1974 to 41 per cent in 1984; so too had the murder rate moved from 18 per 100,000 in the late 1980s to 41 per 100,000 in 1997.

This pattern for violence in Jamaica parallels that of Latin American nations, while contrasting sharply with the rest of the Commonwealth Caribbean – the exception being The Bahamas.

Furthermore, the crisis in policing then and now is partly reflected in the inability of the police force to solve crime, in particular, violent crimes. For instance, Harriott points out that in the early 1980s, the "solution rates" for crimes against persons declined from 70 per cent to 60 per cent in the 1990s. During the same period, the "solution rates" for crime against property declined from 50 per cent to 30 per cent.

The statistics also reveal a more troubling feature, which is that the more serious the crime, the lower the conviction rate. He points out that in Western Kingston, which has the highest murder rate in the city of Kingston, the conviction rate was below 10 per cent up until 1995.

"New" criminals

Now, apart from the increases in crime, Harriott also zooms in on the new types of criminal organizations which have evolved in more recent times. These "business" units he posits are well organized, with large networks within which women and children have specialized roles and, by extension, are willing to protect the "business" and the "businessmen" – seemingly, at all costs. In the same breath, other manifestations of the crisis in policing, according to Harriott, include public resistance to law and the authority of the police; a general loss in confidence in the police and the entire criminal justice system; and an alarming increase in police vigilantism as a response to their inability to deal with the crime problem.

In my next article, I will look at some of these issues in more detail, as well as some of the reforms and options proposed by Harriott. Peace!

Reforming the police force: Part 2

(TUESDAY, MARCH 03, 1998)

The first part of this article about the exciting research being conducted by my colleague Dr Anthony Harriott pointed out some of the reasons why the police were ineffective in solving and controlling crime, and why the old model of policing, the "political model", was in crisis. Harriott, a criminologist at The UWI, points to a number of situations which indicate a crisis in policing, and which led to the reform measures instituted in 1994. But, before turning to these reforms, I would like to talk about a few of the manifestations of this crisis in policing.

According to Harriot, "vigilantism has become

progressively" institutionalized in the form of special squads. Now, for the period 1985 to 1994, police homicides averaged approximately 15 per cent to 20 per cent of all homicides in each of these years". He argues that while some of these are justified, this high rate of homicides is consistent with the pro-vigilante attitudes inside the force. As such, surveys conducted inside the force by Harriott in 1991 and 1994 indicate growing support for these pro-vigilante attitudes.

Another manifestation of the crisis in policing, according to Harriott, is the loss of the public's confidence in the force. He draws on the work of the late Carl Stone, where it was argued that "in 1991, 60 per cent of the population rated the overall performance of the force as poor. Another 48 per cent regarded the police as disrespectful of citizens' rights, 70 per cent regarded their behaviour as too violent, and 67 per cent as dishonest and corrupt". Indeed, it is interesting to note that these views occurred uniformly across the social classes.

Given these and other problems, reforms were introduced in 1994 which were based partly on the recommendations of the Hirst and Wolfe reports. These reforms included reducing the abuse of power and levels of corruption, depoliticizing the force, and improving the relationship between the police and the public. In other words, the new model of policing introduced was called the "professional model.

Improvement in discipline

In light of this, Hariott argues that one of the important achievements of the reforms was the dramatic improvement in the discipline of the force and the significant renewal of the officer corps, with 25 per cent being sent on retirement or on secondment or transferred from "sensitive positions". These officers were replaced with better trained and educated men and women "via the accelerated promotions programmes, university programmes and/or the force's performance criteria". Corruption in the force was reduced as new institutions in the force were created to investigate reports against the personnel in this organization. Equally, police vigilantism was actively discouraged through "a new internal code on the use of force, based on UN guidelines, which was adopted, and access to automatic weapons was restricted".

Depoliticization

Regarding depoliticization, Harriott claims that the changes which were made to the law have made it more difficult for the minister to interfere with the day-to-day operations of the force, hence the commissioner has more control over promotions and assignments. In the same breath, the organizational changes made in respect of the use of technology in the daily detection and resolution of crime have helped to improve the overall calibre of the police force. Likewise, the provision of a new fleet of vehicles has significantly improved the mobility of the force and their efforts at community policing, which by extension has improved the general quality of police work.

Despite the many changes and improvements introduced by the new model, Harriott argues that the professional model is limited and ultimately unsustainable. You see, the problem is that the "professional model", borrowed from industrialized countries, has not succeeded in controlling crime, because the resources required to keep this model going are substantial. Furthermore, according to Harriott, in the Jamaican situation "the ideology of professionalism limits the participation of citizens in crime control to being an extension, the 'eyes and ears' of the police... (and) weakens the crime control effort by excluding rather than harnessing the power of the people in crime control".

Harriott seems to advocate a "democratic service model" rather than the professional one. In this model, there is greater public involvement in the process of crime prevention, issues of accountability; redress in the form of compensation for wrongful treatment by the police; fairness and equal treatment of citizens; and openness, or access to information through the media and communities, are central.

Dr Harriott's research has added a new dimension to the discussions about crime and policing, and goes beyond narrow, partisan-inspired journalistic analyses to an objective look at the problems which afflict all modern societies. However, the challenge he faces when his research is completed will be to convince the policymakers to look at the big picture, rather than to pander to the concerns of private interests. Peace!

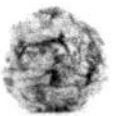

Chapter 6 Leadership, Legitimacy and Accountability

- The military option
- The power of the people
- Government and the people
- The buck stops there
- Leading and leadership
- Legitimacy and the police
- Hegemony and the state

Introduction

This chapter considers how persons in positions of authority relate to ordinary Jamaican citizens, when it comes to winning their confidence, maintaining law and order and soliciting their cooperation and involvement in matters which concern the community and the wider nation. (See, for example, "Hegemony and the state", Tuesday, May 20, 1997.) The chapter depicts the social order in Jamaica as "crumbling", "decrepit" and "decaying". (See, for example, "A crumbling social order" and "Legitimacy and the Police".) In general, these articles raise questions about the moral authority of Jamaican leaders, their "legitimacy", and also the extent of their accountability to the people.

Boxill theorizes that the institutions of political leadership and social control (such as the police force) were inherited, but not shaped by the struggles of ordinary Jamaicans. Ultimately, he believes that leaders lack legitimacy and authority in the eyes of many segments of the Jamaican society. This notion goes well beyond rival theories about what makes for popularity and unpopularity in leaders. (See "Leading and leadership".) Boxill concludes that the Jamaican society will continue to be on the periphery of world affairs as long as we have political and intellectual leadership which do not allow our citizens to release their creative potential.

The military option

(TUESDAY, JANUARY 18, 1994)

Is Jamaica in danger of moving to some form of military rule? Ridiculous as the question may appear, it is a legitimate one. Without diminishing the importance of the military's contribution to national development, I think that we should ask ourselves whether it is merely a coincidence that former or current military personnel are increasingly being asked to join the leadership of important parliamentary or civilian organizations in our society. Let me hasten to point out that I am in no way suggesting the existence of any form of conspiratorial action by any section of our society. I simply wish to discuss what appears to be an issue of concern to people with various interests in our society.

Military excursion

Indeed, the anglophone Caribbean has not been totally free of the military excursion into politics. In Grenada during the rule of the New Jewel Movement, the military played an important part in government. In Guyana, the Burnham regime used the military to maintain its virtual dictatorship. In Barbados, St Lucia and Dominica, the profile of the military in their societies increased in the face of perceived threats from external opposition forces. Here in Jamaica, the military has been involved primarily in military patrols and national emergencies.

Our army reputation rests on a perception that it is not tarnished by partisan politics, and that it strives to maintain a high level of discipline and professionalism – this in a country often characterized as suffering from rampant political partnership and indiscipline. However, there is a growing consensus among political scientists regarding the preconditions for the formation of military governments. Military regimes often come to power when military officers or governments believe that a crisis exists which cannot be solved by a civilian government – for example, when there is prolonged public disorder and hostility to government, or when there are threats to the survival of the military, or even in times of severe economic crisis and weak civilian leadership. Importantly, military rule may also develop gradually, when military concepts and strategies are adopted to deal with social problems.

The foundation

Now, if these political scientists are correct, then it stands to reason that we may be well on the way to laying the foundation for military rule in Jamaica. At present, there appears to be a growing perception, both of the economic crisis and of a weak political leadership. These, coupled with the disorder in aspects of civilian life and the high crime rate, are prompting people to find creative ways to survive or to beat the system. However, there is an important caveat to note here: as argued in a previous article, large-scale public protests have been stifled by the existence of a divisive two-party system; and also, this same system has effectively snuffed out the growth of class consciousness among the urban poor. Fundamentally, it is this situation and a nationalist ideology composed primarily of urban working-class symbolisms which have protected the society from social explosion. Here, I use "protected" advisedly, because the society has suffered enormously from tribal politics. These tribal conflicts have concealed a larger contradiction in our society. This contradiction is the serious disequilibrium between peoples' social and economic expectations and their achievements. Part of this expectation, particularly among the poorer sections of the society is fuelled by the fact that they see, daily, the ostentatious lifestyles of others, which conflicts sharply with their own squalor and sense of dispossession. It is unfortunate, therefore, that political tribalism has reduced the national debate on this major issue to ideological conflicts between JLP and PNP tribes.

Loss of legitimacy

As political apathy grows, and also as the political spoils become scarcer, the political system begins to lose its legitimacy, and the clientelist relationship upon which the politics of our society is built begins to degenerate. Therefore, political parties are finding it difficult to hold on to the type of partisan loyalties which existed in the past. This growing insignificance of the political system to people's everyday existence is a new social phenomenon.

An indicator of this delegitimization is the growth of, and boom in, the informal sector in Jamaica. I would also argue that the very presence and strength of this sector will play havoc with current government economic policy. Government policies are based at the moment on market mechanisms which have little relevance to the everyday lives of Jamaicans.

What options?

Now it seems to me that the government is realizing that the political system is losing its legitimacy. The question is, what are their options? To do nothing would leave the door open to the transferral of their fiefdoms to drug dons and other political movements. Unfortunately, there is not much that the JLP can do right now, since they suffer from the same limitations of vision as the PNP.

It seems to me that the government has tried to do two things to deal with a waning public confidence. First, it has re-examined the constitution and its provisions which speak to the political legitimacy question. Second, it has brought in the military personnel who possess the credibility in the eyes of the public to run institutions seen as politicized. Unfortunately, a few well meaning military people and a muted intellectual debate about the rights and future of our people cannot solve a looming national crisis, where people are trapped by archaic political processes and continued economic deprivation. It is highly likely, if consumer prices continue to increase rapidly and social cleavages continue to solidify, that an intensification in the current public disaffection and social chaos may lead to options which the society can well do without. To avert the risk of a military alternative, either by civilian consent or by force, there must be, at the very least, immediate political reform in which civil(ian) society plays a critical role to ensure accountability and performance, thus helping to drastically reduce the levels of poverty and social marginalization of the mass of the population. Peace!

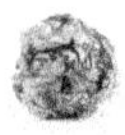

The power of the people

(WEDNESDAY, MAY 18, 1993)

Leahcim Semaj is right, the burden of change in the Jamaican society rests squarely in the hands of the people. This may seem at first to be a rather simple notion, but it is at the same time a powerful one. For it is powerful when it is taken seriously enough for people to act. This idea is not only powerful, but it is also frightening – frightening for those who hold power (political and economic) in society.

When ordinary people realize that they can, collectively, bring about change, they soon come to accept that they need not appeal to or beg those in authority for resources to survive. They soon realize their strength and begin to make demands for a better way of life. This is very subversive thinking. It is especially subversive and threatening in a society where the political system is based on clientelism and patronage. But it is worse yet when the people organize and collectively and seriously demand from those they have put in power amenities such as better roads, a bus system that works and protection form the excesses of others. Leaders shiver at the thought of people making demands in an organized manner. For organization not only signals seriousness but also longevity of organized action. Leaders hate movements of people which persist beyond the immediate spontaneous outburst of protest.

Ironically, although Jamaica was one of the few Caribbean countries which had a government during the 1970s that ostensibly championed the cause of the people, there is, perhaps more than any other country of the region, need for the people to have greater say in the running of their society. In other words, in this country, we have to go a long way to construct civil society.

Burning tyres

When people burn tyres and block streets to protest unfair police treatment or lack of attention by a government service, they do this because civil society is too undeveloped to meet their needs. They know that complaining peacefully will not yield them any serious response. When vagrants (the insane and otherwise) patrol the length and breadth of Kingston from sunup to sundown, this reflects the inability of civil society to meet the needs of the society. When people complain about the poor treatment meted out to them by the various public services, knowing fully well that they will be ignored, it says something very disconcerting about civil society. When you live in a society where there is little or no accountability then you can be sure that civil society is weak. If people are not made to account for their actions, then there is no incentive for them to act responsibly.

Now we see the importance of people power, because it is only when people demand accountability from their leaders, as they did in Brazil recently, that responsibility becomes the hallmark of governance. This country could do well with consumer organizations to check the excesses of the private sector. There is a need for a public utilities commission to deal with the carefree attitude of utility services cloaked in all of their monopolistic bliss. Such consumer movements should emerge from among the people and operate independently of political parties. When ordinary people begin to organize and force the powerful in society to listen and take action, accountability occurs, and civil society takes shape through legislation and norms. We would do well to remember that the civil rights movement in the US emerged from among the people and forced the government to change its laws and become more accountable to its most marginalized citizens. The surest way to improve the police, transportation, water services and education is for the people to organize community networks and challenge the orthodoxy of the day. So far, the media have been doing a fairly good job in articulating problems of crime, corruption, and many of the other concerns which plague society. However, we must move beyond this now. Communities need to organize themselves and, along with the help of experts in the various fields, offer solutions.

Organized pressure

The current attention being shown by the government to the transportation problem is the result of pressure from the media and the people. The people must now organize and demand better service, not only through protest but by providing alternatives drawing on their own experiences. If the majority of people who take the bus decided to stay at home to protest the poor bus service, someone – maybe someone important – will take note. If a well organized citizen's organization tackled the problem of health care by protesting the lack of drugs and proposing alternatives to what currently exists, someone important might listen and take note. If the people spoke out collectively, about crime and demanded immediate reforms to the police force, then both the opposition party, which has boycotted parliament, and the government will have to take note and act. The power of well organized collective action by the people should never be underestimated in society. Most of the freedoms which we admire the Americans for came through collective action of the people. In fact, political and economic systems never change on their own. From China to Russia to Haiti, people have come out in an organized fashion to demand better.

Let me reiterate that it is not enough to demand; we must also present solutions. As citizens, we already possess the expertise to make change, for we are the engineers, physicians, researchers, labourers, social workers, nurses, masons, clerks, carpenters, academics and taxi drivers. Imagine how much change can occur if the people pooled their expertise in a variety of fields to tackle the problem of health or education. The political system in the country cannot by itself create civil society, because by its very structure the political system negates such. Civilians, the people, the man or woman next to you on the bus, in the office, or on the road must create this. One love.

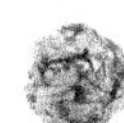

Government and the people

(TUESDAY, NOVEMBER 2, 1993)

For the past six months, I have been monitoring the price of an imported food item in the supermarkets. During this time, the cost of this item increased by almost 50 per cent. The astronomical rise in the price of the item led me to investigate the prices of some other food items; the revelation is that there are countless other items which have fallen victim to a spiralling inflation.

Part of the explanation given for the rise in the prices of these items is the fall in the value of the dollar. However, such price increases also seem connected to a trend in our society which dictates that consumer prices for almost any item – except postage stamps and bag juice – have a licence to run wild and unrestrained.

Some difficulty

Increasingly, the consumer is not only being battered by the high cost of living, but also by a barrage of taxes. The recent massive increases in property taxes is making it difficult for even the most patriotic citizen to rationalize these costs, let alone pay them. The sudden imposition of increases will probably ensure that some hardworking people who have property as security will be deprived of such assets because of their inability to raise relatively large sums of cash. The door is now open for speculators to move in and buy property at lower than market prices, because many people cannot afford to bear this tax cross. In the meantime, owning a house will continue to be a fantasy for most of our citizens.

There is something very unsettling about the ability of any government to, with a stroke of a pen, impose such conditions on its people. More intriguing is that there has not been any organized public outcry at the mass level, in the face of these oppressive economic conditions. Not long ago, riots erupted across Latin America when the governments of Venezuela and Brazil imposed stiff austerity measures on their people. In Jamaica, there is an endless verbal opposition – done individually – and with much apparent lassitude. The "organized" silence is almost as deafening as it is crippling.

Pushed out

What appears to be apathy is really a partial reflection of the vast number of citizens who have been pushed out of the formal economy as a result of structural adjustment policies which have lasted almost two decades. They have had to learn to survive in both the formal and informal economies, and it has not been easy. As people's life chances diminish in the formal sector, they gravitate towards the informal sector. The setting-up of shopping arcades and the imposition of the general consumption tax (GCT) were creative ways through which ostracized sections of the society were clubbed back into the formal system, invariably to raise the government's revenue.

Grown numb

We have been experiencing poor economic performance for so long that many have grown numb to any piece of bad news about our economy. Research shows that rebellions or revolutions are likely to occur among people whose standard of living has abruptly declined, not among those who have been experiencing a prolonged period of poverty. Abrupt declines in living standards are more often felt by the middle class. It is when the middle class finds a rapid decline in its standard of living that organized public opposition is likely to occur.

Interestingly, during the 1980s, as the size of the middle class increased, the gap between them and the poor widened. Therefore, we now have a social order in which a political elite presides over an ever-increasing socioeconomic gulf between the rich and poor. Furthermore, the presence of political tribes ensures that: (1) alliances are not created between the different social classes to challenge the political order in any serious way; and (2) the mass of marginalized citizens cannot organize nationally around common issues, such as better education or better health care, because they are too divided. Hence, there is a social order in which community organization becomes fractured, politicized, piecemeal, and disjointed. This produces patronage, and the privileged social groups remain isolated from the majority of the people, both in their lifestyles and in their thinking. By extension, the political system does not feel that it has to be accountable, because there is generally an absence of an organized public opposition; and where it does exist, it is not sustained.

Important watchdog

This is why the media, until serious changes are made in the system of government, have been and will continue to be the society most important watchdog. Newspapers and radio are perhaps the publics most consistent defendants. Daily talk shows provide avenues for public discourse on social and economic policy on the role of government. The absence of civil institutions, such as public utility boards and other mass consumer organizations, makes the role of the media even more critical in commenting on government policy.

However, Jamaica, like other parts of the world, is going through a period of change, and our people are questioning the ability of political systems to address their needs. The decline in the number of people who voted in the last general election is perhaps one indication of the frustration which we have with our polarized political system, and perhaps this is the beginning of its end.

We now need forward-thinking people who can transcend their privileges and class confines to work with the other social classes in the national interest. Governing is too important to be left to the government. Peace!

The buck stops there

(TUESDAY, DECEMBER 07, 1993)

As I watch the interactions between our people and follow the various scandals and controversies involving big businesses and the political elite, I get the impression that there is a growing tendency for individuals and organizations to shed their responsibilities. They do this by shifting the blame onto others, usually for actions which affect other people negatively.

Everyday behaviour

This tendency to blame someone or something else is characteristic of our everyday behaviour. I saw a motorist crash into the back of another person's car and try to defend his action by saying there was a shortage of road in the potholes (yes "road in potholes" is correct). Again, a cashier in a public-sector company tried to justify her cavalier attitude towards a long line of fuming customers by contending that she was hungry and, furthermore, her colleagues had decided to extend their lunch hour – as usual. Also, a businessman tried to rationalize an outrageous increase in the price of an item with the argument that the price of that item had failed to keep up with the rate of inflation. And a once-successful man explained his drunkenness by stating that his wife had turned him into an alcoholic. Then there are the politicians who blame the polls for their electoral defeat.

Perhaps the most distasteful attempts at passing the buck occur at the political level. During the recent ToJ debate, attempts by Breakfast Club members and other journalists to pin down those who were involved in activities which might be construed as being out of line with the public interest yielded responses which pointed in the other direction. Needless to say, those who were pointed to responded by pointing in other directions. Consequently, the issue has become muddled, and the public confused.

Notorious practice

One of the most notorious ways of passing on responsibilities is the appointment of commissions of enquiries. The Green Commission of Enquiry seems to support this position. The commission seemed to have blamed everyone and no one. But then, how many government-appointed commissions will be critical of those who gave them life?

What appears to be a fact of life in the societies of our region is that those who hold enormous political or economic power will always find someone to take the heat in times of difficulty. How many low-level civil servants have been burnt at the stake for the political ineptitude of our leaders?

Recently, our infatuation with statistics and figures has resulted in a differe type of blame. Technocrats and politicians are now blaming a sliding dollar for changes in monetary and fiscal policy. Some economists (and almost-economists) have now begun to reify the dollar; it is as if the dollar had a mind of its own. Thus, changes in prices and interest rates are explained in terms of relative changes in the exchange rate, and not in consumer behaviour or government policy.

Confusing rhetoric

Our bankers and technocrats continue to conduct many potentially simple discussions in such confusing rhetoric that even they are being mystified – along with their audience. Political, social and economic phenomena are not always easy to understand or explain; however, models and theories exist to help us make sense of the complexities. These models and theories are not meant to further confound us. If those of us who have formal training in the social sciences cannot communicate effectively with our people about issues which affect them daily, then I think that we have a serious problem. Consequently, we cannot be successful if the people we have to deal with, and for whom we are interpreting these complexities, cannot understand us. An idea expressed in simple terms is not necessarily a simple idea. If those in the private and public sectors continue to use language which allows them to escape responsibility for their actions, then there can be no accountability, and society will continue to be chaotic.

Be cautious

When people produce charts and figures to support an argument, we have to be careful. What does it mean for this society if there is a change in the inflation rate by two points? What really is the difference between 2-4 per cent and 42 per cent, particularly in an economy with a large informal sector, rapid fluctuations in prices, and grave disparities in income?

During the last presidential elections in the US, analysts, economists and political scientists were on the television analysing the impact of a one per cent and two per cent change in employment, inflation and other leading economic indicators deemed crucial for a Bush victory. These people whose job it was to study human society became trapped studying numbers, and they did not realize that a two per cent change in the index of leading economic indicators does not tell you anything about human needs or wants. The urge to hurl an index or some coarse statistical approximation at ordinary people, many of whom live outside of the very system from which these numbers are obtained, is the same as providing loopholes for escape during difficult times. One of my colleagues once said that physicians have to pay the price when they mess up; why is it that when those who run our economy make serious errors and create untold human suffering they are not made to answer to the people?

How are we to enter NAFTA (North American Free Trade Agreement) and do the serious things so cogently articulated by our educated talkers, when we have a society in which people at all levels have a penchant for passing the buck? How can we talk about fixing the problem when we do not even know who or what is responsible for the problem in the first place? Peace!

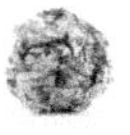

Leading and leadership

(TUESDAY, FEBRUARY 01, 1994)

In his column of January 28, 1994, Martin Henry states: "In politics perception is everything. In the polls, the most popular leaders are consistently the highest profiled, the most articulate and the most convincing, almost independent of quantifiable practical performance. And the most unpopular are the highest profiled, most articulate but least convincing."

I cannot accept the premise upon which Mr Henry bases his article. I disagree with his theory regarding what makes for popular and unpopular leadership, particularly since his theory contradicts the empirical evidence. Concomitantly, to argue that perception is everything in politics is not a discovery, since basically all human interaction is fundamentally a function of perception.

Mr Henry is setting up straw men when he links the lack of meaningful performance with popularity and fails to do the same with unpopularity. Indeed, the history of our region will show that the majority of the most popular leaders were also the same ones who were known for getting the job done. Errol Barrow, Eric Williams and T. A. Marryshow were not only extremely articulate and charismatic leaders, but they also made positive and concrete changes to the lives of the people. People were persuaded by the concrete achievements of these leaders, not simply by their rhetoric.

High-profile

Now, the fact that we have in our region a number of leaders who are not as articulate or charismatic as some of their predecessors is evidence enough to contradict the view that people are looking for extremely articulate and high-profile leaders. Erskine Sandiford of Barbados is neither a Tom Adams nor an Errol Barrow – in the profile or speaking department – but because of his exemplary record as a deputy prime minister and education minister, the electorate preferred him to Richie Haynes, a much more articulate and high-profile individual. The popularity of Prime Minster Patterson during the last election, as the Stone polls showed, was based partly on the public's perception of an experienced consensus-oriented statesman with the potential to move the country forward, without the need to resort to the type of suave rhetoric characteristic of postcolonial politics of the pre-1980s.

It is extremely simplistic to argue that the problem of unpopularity faced by the present government is the result of its inability to "sell" its many achievements to the public. To be sure, this government perhaps more than any other has made it a point to inform the public about its many accomplishments, as outlined in Mr Henry's article. Now, those of us who read the three major newspapers or watch the two television stations or listen to the numerous radio stations cannot miss the news items which deal with the work and achievements of the government. In fact, I would go as far as to say that the proliferation of media has provided more channels through which the government can "sell" its achievements and ideas – now more so than in the past. But the proliferation of media and the greater contact with the press also creates an antithesis – which is more rigorous public scrutiny and questioning of government policies. So, it is unfair for some commentators to argue that government should be complimented for fuller disclosures to the press as well as for greater freedom of expression, while at the same time ranting and raving about the criticisms which come with such a process.

Goodwill

I have no doubt that people are familiar with many of the changes and achievements made by the government. I also believe that the majority of the Jamaican people want the government to succeed – for there is much goodwill among the people for the government. However, you cannot blame people for not cheering when there is an enactment of an Act, or when a committee is set up by the government to look at and recommend treatment for some of the very important issues affecting our society. (To be sure, on the basis of their performance, some of these committees do not deserve to be cheered.) All of the technocratic advances made by the government have to be placed in context. For people will not develop a positive perception of the government simply because of the technocratic changes, especially when such changes do not make for tangible differences in their standard of living. When the mass of a population cannot afford a mortgage, or cannot get proper health care, or cannot afford proper education, or cannot sleep comfortably – unless they have their doors and windows tightly bolted and grilled – do you think that they really care about who is winning a war in the Gulf? The government and the opposition are both suffering from the "George Bush Syndrome". They are winning the wrong wars. Neither negative press nor unsophisticated public perception is the cause of government unpopularity. Popularity is a direct function of people's everyday life experiences. In the US, in spite of all of the negative press which Bill Clinton has received, he is still a very popular president. The reason is that he has a clear vision for his country and people, and they have started to see a difference in their standard of living.

I disagree with Mr Henry's view that Mr Seaga has seized the initiative in the areas he has identified. Furthermore, I believe that if an election was called today, the PNP would still win, but it would be a Pyrrhic victory. We are living in a society in transition, and our people are weary. They are weary from having to be constantly adjusting to the social and economic problems, to which the current political and economic systems seem to offer no solution. People do not expect their leaders to be superhumans. However, they expect their leaders to have a vision of the future and not piecemeal ideas which are blurted out as defence mechanisms. We expect our leaders to offer us hope, especially when the chips are down. But we also expect to see, especially in times of crises, positive, tangible and meaningful changes in our everyday lives. Peace!

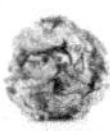

Legitimacy and the police

(TUESDAY, SEPTEMBER 20, 1994)

Recently, Colonel Trevor MacMillan gave a most interesting interview on television about his tenure as commissioner of police. The most intriguing thing about his interview was that Mr MacMillan did not see the problem of crime in Jamaica as a simple criminal justice problem, but rather as one peppered with a myriad of social, economic and political concerns. He also thinks that these problems, along with the pernicious problem of crime, require 'careful consideration before any far-reaching decisions can be taken. This is an enlightened approach informed by equally enlightened thinking.

However, one of the areas I believe the commissioner and the society must address, with a frontal assault, is the legitimacy of the police in the eyes of some sections of the public. Here I refer to legitimacy not in terms of the rule of law, but rather in terms of the responsibility which our people have placed on the police to maintain law and order. Any institution which has the authority of law to act but lacks the confidence of the people has a problem of moral legitimacy. Consequently, such institutions will have to resort to coercion in order to achieve their ends. South Africa before the end of apartheid, and Haiti under its military dictatorship are good examples of this posture. This is so because, in the eyes of the majority of people in these countries, the institutions lacked the moral authority to rule.

The problem of moral legitimacy faced by our police is especially acute among some of the poorer sections of our population. One telling sign of this is the frequency with which people in the inner cities mount protests about police brutality. Whether or not the charges of brutality are accurate, the fact that there is a perception that justice is not being administered is important and should be of concern. You see, for people to have confidence in any system, they must feel that they can trust the system to perform its role.

But the problem of police legitimacy among certain sections of the population is only one manifestation of the larger problem of legitimacy with regard to many of the institutions in our society. The perpetual reference to the crisis in values serves as commentary on the disequilibrium between what the official system says ought to be done in order for us to survive, and what our people feel they need to do in order to survive. Hence, it is senseless to tell bus commuters – who have to get to work at a particular time – to queue up when they know that they may get to work late if they have to wait because there are too few buses that run on an unstable schedule. Thus, you have a plausible explanation for the pushing which takes place when one tries to board a bus. Sadly, this has led to a situation where people have grown accustomed to forcing their way into the bus even when it is not necessary.

Not enough

Likewise, people may be unwilling to respond to an appeal to conserve electricity or water in an environment where they do not feel that by so doing it will lead to an improved service or an increased delivery of either service. Also, workers may not increase productivity unless there is an incentive. This incentive does not have to be monetary, since workers may be motivated if they see their company become more competitive. But why should you be interested in improving the competitive edge of the company to which you are employed if you cannot see the benefits for you, the individual? In other words, people will act in the interests of a group, organization or country if they see a convergence between their individual goals and those of the group, organization or country.

Now, if you perceive a conflict between the objectives of an agency and your own, then on the basis of experience it becomes more difficult to be persuaded that the agency is acting in your best interest. Therefore, it is not enough for the police to state that they are acting in the interest of any community – they must now demonstrate their concern in daily interaction with these communities. Those who argue that in order for the police to be effective, they must be as rough as the criminal have missed the point, since, if the police are to be distinguished from the criminal, they will have to rise above their present behaviour.

As I mentioned before, the problem faced by the police in keeping law and order is a societal one. The police operate in a society where the distribution of power is highly skewed in favour of those with economic and political capital. In an environment where there is a shrinking state, it seems that those who have little and those who are neglected by the state are being forced to find creative ways to survive. Thus, one can rationally account for the tendency in some communities to shelter people who, in their eyes, have helped members of the community financially or otherwise, but in the eyes of the state are criminals. In Colombia, where there are areas neglected by the state, drug cartels have provided schools, roads, electricity and jobs for their people. As a result, many people in these communities have developed stronger loyalties to the drug cartels than to the state. Therefore, an important part of the problem faced by the police in maintaining law and order is linked to the lack of legitimacy of the state in these communities. To talk about a single Jamaica is fine, if one does this through a comparison with other countries. However, the presence of communities which have all of the amenities and which support a lifestyle comparable to the norm in developed countries, when juxtaposed with living standards of other communities which are close by and, in some instances, even worse than what obtains in the slums of Haiti, represents a recipe for social chaos. It is this chaos which the police are being asked to transform into law and order. It is for this reason that the problem of law and order, in our society, cannot be treated as merely a criminal justice issue. Peace!

Hegemony and the state

(TUESDAY, MAY 20, 1997)

A well respected historian once said to me that one of the distinguishing features of Jamaica's history, when compared with the other Caribbean territories, is – perhaps with the exception of the 1970s – that the state has never really held hegemonic sway over the society. On the contrary, what existed, and continue to exist, in our society are competing and powerful hegemonies.

By hegemony, I refer here to leadership without the need for constant coercion. Indeed, both the colonial and postcolonial states have had to depend on cohesive measures to ensure that large sections of the dispossessed conformed to the dictates of the state. Unfortunately, for a large section of the population, the state has done little to represent their interests, and where through the subversion of the political competing states or garrisons have been created by the politician's "civil war" is likely to occur in defence of the preservation of these states.

The recent conflict in Tivoli Gardens is a reflection of the wider country, which depends on formal authority rather than legitimacy to govern – at least among some communities within the society.

Thus, given the reports about the police and army's misconduct in Tivoli, then it is likely that the state as a body, set up to govern those within, will have even less credibility in many parts of our society. You see, states cannot sustain their legitimate control over a society by simply depending on coercion. Thus, state legitimacy arises when people feel a sense of trust, feel that their rights will not be trampled upon, and ultimately feel that justice will be done.

Consequently, the situation in Zaire should be a clear lesson for us here in Jamaica. Notice that Mobutu Sese Seko was unable to hold onto power in the face of insurgency because he had lost all moral authority to govern. Mobutu, however, was kept in power by military forces although Zaireans had already lost faith in his ability to dispense justice.

And so, if justice is to be maintained, it therefore means that the security forces must always rise above the level of gunmen or criminals – even if this means that some of these gunmen or criminals will escape. There is no other way of assuring moral authority within the state, and without moral authority there can be no legitimacy. Therefore, citizens must hold the enforcers of our laws to a higher standard than we do the violators of our laws.

Most of us know that, fundamentally, the Tivoli incident is the result of the larger problems of the tribal organization of our politics, and the lack of economic opportunities for a vast section of our population. Few politicians would gainsay that these are but two of the most pressing problems facing our society. Yet, we continue to see few collective efforts to deal with these problems.

Given the traditionally adversarial approach to politics, which is primarily concerned with the scoring of political points, we are unlikely to see any changes to the political and economic management of our society. And so, it is business as usual for those touched or perceptibly untouched by the happenings in Tivoli.

Regrettably, under these circumstances, and in light of our present posture, the mistakes made in the community of Tivoli are bound to be repeated. Peace!

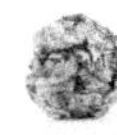

Chapter 7 Public Education, Social Class and Progress

- The (un)Common Entrance Exam
- Rights and privileges
- Development, education and the future
- Common Entrance (excerpt from "Caught in a bind")
- The education challenge
- The information revolution is here
- Education and the labour market

Introduction

This chapter places emphasis on access to education and in particular the importance of access to tertiary level education, especially since it serves to enhance productivity through the creation of an active supply of qualified workers in the labour market. The chapter also details that denial of access to tertiary level education does impact social inequality. The existence of gross stratification in the school system is also reviewed. The article continues by exploring the issue of stratification within the education system, noting that it is partly responsible for the grave inequalities in the society. This chapter is important, since it explores the fact that as a society we cannot separate formal education from the problems of crime, violence and productivity. (See the paragraph(s) sub-headed: Common Entrance in "Common Entrance (excerpt from 'Caught in a bind')".) Also covered are issues relating to credential bias, access to education beyond the primary level, as well as the role of ICT in the transformation of our education system.

The (un)Common Entrance Exam

WEDNESDAY, JUNE 23, 1993

As Mr Morris entered his home from his job as a gardener, he became deafened by the loud thud of his heartbeat. Today was D-day. Grabbing a copy of The *Daily Gleaner*, he searched frantically for his son's name. "Up and down, down and up, from side to side, diagonally, across, backwards", his tired eyes combed the pages in vain for Jack James David Morris. Falling to his knees in disappointment, Mr Morris looked up at his ceiling which had started to succumb to the recent onslaught of the heavy rains, then across the room where his eyes finally rested on the dejected face of his son who had been observing him for some time now. "I tried hard, Dad," said Jack. "I know," said Mr Morris. Rising to his, feet Mr Morris hugged his son majestically, and they both began to cry.

Mr Morris' tears were not so much for his son as they were for the many families like his – poor, semi-rural and proud – which would find it harder than everyone else to achieve social mobility, because society had created an educational system which was based more on class and status than on merit. Mr Morris knew that the reason why his son did not get into a high school was a function of their economic position and not his son's abilities. For Jack was a hard worker and clever, but occasionally he had to skip school and help his father work in order to earn an income to eat.

Fictitious

The characters in the foregoing are fictitious, but rest assured that the story is not! Last week, there were many Mr Morrises and Jack Morrises. These are the people whom the society, through an anachronistic Common Entrance exam, continues to alienate. The continued existence of gross stratification in the school system is partly responsible for the grave inequalities in the society. Conversely, the very stratification in the school system is a product of society. These structures, therefore, reinforce each other.

Let me state here a few reasons why I believe that the Common Entrance exam is partly responsible for inequality and marginalization of people. On May 5, 1993, *Gleaner* columnist Peter Espeut published an article titled "Education for the Few" in which he showed that fewer than half of those who were eligible to sit the exam in 1990 actually sat. In addition, of those who sit only 23 per cent get high school places. Factoring in those who go to private high schools, it is clear that fewer than 20 per cent of our eligible children get into high schools. What are we saying then – that the vast majority of children who did not pass the exam are not "bright" enough to handle a high school education? Certainly not. First of all, we know that the term "pass" is relative. Thus, the criteria for entering high school are fairly arbitrary and should not be linked in any serious way to merit. Secondly, the probability is that, proportionately, many more children of middle- and upper-class backgrounds will pass the exam than those from the lower class. We also know from research that what often passes as natural intelligence is really a function of socioeconomic status and the learning environment. For instance, many poor parents may not be able to send their children to school every day because of financial constraints. Many poor children do not live in environments which enhance curiosity and learning among children. Research conducted by sociology graduate students at The UWI has shown that performance in high schools in Jamaica is strongly related to geographical location and access to teaching materials, among other things. Consequently, the main reason why a large proportion of students from the lower class "fail" the Common Entrance exam has to do with their life chances. It should be noted that in the USA a disproportionate number of black and other "minority" students fail in school because of discrimination in its myriad forms. In Jamaica, the discrimination is not, fundamentally, ethnic in origin.

Educational system

But there is another sad dimension to the educational system. It is the labels that are attached to students who attend so-called new secondary schools. Not all new secondary schools or all-age schools produce poor students. In fact, some have produced some of

Jamaica's most successful people. The problem is that our status-conscious minds do not make the distinction between a child's ability and the school he or she attends. For many of us, what is true about the reputation of the school holds true for the child. This is known as the fallacy of division; our educational system has forced the entire society to commit this fallacy on a daily basis. As a result, many of our potentially outstanding children are lost in the system simply because we label them "bright or dull" on the basis of a school which they attend. Psychologically, labelling can be very devastating as it can negatively affect a child's self-esteem and, hence, performance. Research by social psychologists and sociologists has shown that defining people negatively will more often than not lead to negative behaviour.

Yet another dimension to the educational system is the fact that the society is credential-biased. In many instances, one needs a certificate to get a job or access to higher education. It therefore means that people who do not have the opportunity to obtain requisite credentials will be at a disadvantage in applying for certain occupations.

By the way, research in the USA has shown no serious link between certification and performance in many occupations; that is to say, it does not follow that obtaining the relevant certificate will result in better performance in many jobs. This is not to say that credentials do not serve a useful purpose; however, we must place them within context. Using credentials is one fairly effective way of allocating people to various jobs. However, in countries like Jamaica, it often results in increased inequality and alienation because so many, by virtue of their circumstances, rather than abilities, are denied access to such credentials.

Formal education

We cannot separate formal education from problems of crime, violence, and productivity in society. All of us have potential; however, the society makes it very difficult for many of us to realize this potential. Because the society is credential-based, the educational system plays a key role in alienating many of our productive citizens. People who cannot make it in the formal systems will be forced to find alternative ways, sometimes illegal ones. In many ways, therefore, the society has created an environment for criminal activity and demotivated workers.

Most poor people continue to use education as a source of upward social mobility. The recent budget is bound to make conditions worse for the people, especially the poor. What is even more disconcerting is that this country has one of the highest levels of social inequality in the anglophone Caribbean. The data shows that inequality in Jamaica worsened during the 1980s and 1990s. Increased inequality with the type of educational system that currently exists will further reinforce social divisions in society. The result can only mean more social dislocation, crime, and pain for the majority of the people in this country.

Many will ask what the solution is. What I know is that we can arrive at something which is better than what currently exists. There are much better models across the world to learn from. It is time for the country to restart the debate on this issue. Unfortunately, I am not optimistic, since many people who have passed through this system successfully – that is, the ones most capable of changing the system – are most likely to want to see it continue. Peace!

Rights and privileges

(TUESDAY, SEPTEMBER 07, 1993)

Last week, I listened to a guest on PSOJ Viewpoint expound the now trendy doctrine which says that tertiary education is a privilege, and not a right. He went on to argue that every citizen has a right to primary and secondary education, but not tertiary education. As I listened to the discussion, I was struck by the manner in which a small and influential (and often well-off) group of people in society have the ability to construct the social reality and sell it to the country as though such a reality were immutable. Let us do some deconstructing.

A right may be defined as a thing one is entitled to. A privilege, on the other hand, is a special right or an advantage. The right to education is an aspect of human rights agreed upon by various UN conventions. The idea of human rights, as expressed by the UN's Universal Declaration of Human Rights of 1948, and subsequent human rights conventions, has its origins in the philosophy of ancient Greece and Rome. The notion of human rights was closely tied up with Greek stoicism (a school of philosophy which held, among other things, that human beings should be judged according to the law of nature).

Natural law

It was, however, during -the 17th and 18th centuries that scholars developed more fully the concept of natural law. John Locke, a leading philosopher of this period, argued that certain rights were self-evident, since they existed in a state of nature before man entered civil society. Chief among these natural rights were life and liberty (freedom from oppression by the state). He also held that the social contract between citizens and the state empowered the state to enforce these natural rights, not to be invested itself with these rights. Furthermore, if the state did not enforce these rights, then there was justification for popular revolution. As time went on, the immutability of natural rights came under attack by conservatives and relativists. The relativism of Friedrich Karl von Savigny and Ludwig Wittgenstein brought into question the notion of the absolute truth of human nature. Conservatives such as David Hume and Edmund Burke believed that the notion of natural rights could lead to social upheaval. Following this attack, many theorists retreated from the idea of natural rights. The fundamental point made by this attack on the idea of natural rights was that the concept of rights was a moral one and not empirically verifiable.

In spite of the controversy regarding human rights, governments the world over have agreed through the UN that they should uphold various fundamental rights. For example, in 1977, Cyrus Vance, the then US Secretary of State, expressed his government's resolve to ensure various human rights, including the right to free speech, education and health care. What distinguishes human rights from other rights is the fact that they are "fundamental needs" as distinct from "mere wants". However, the question which this distinction begs is: when is something "fundamental" and when is it a "mere want"? Is there a bare minimum for something to be fundamental, and if so, what is it? On what basis does one decide that secondary education is a right and not a privilege, or tertiary education is a privilege and not a right? These are questions which cannot be resolved empirically. Interestingly, during the 1970s, it was accepted among Third World countries that tertiary education was a right, not a privilege. What accounts for the reversal of this situation in the 1990s? The answer is simple: as countries become more indebted there is less money for public expenditure. As part of their budgetary strategy, governments attempt to convince people that what they got in the past was a gift, and hence, the fact that they will not get it in the future is justified.

"New doctrine

Now the people have been fed with a number of fallacious arguments to support this "new doctrine" of educational rights. Here are two common ones. First, education can no longer be free, as it was in the past. What utter nonsense! Education was never free. Taxpayers put money in the government's coffers: the politicians and bureaucrats did not manufacture the money. It is one thing to say that the government did not collect enough for education; it is quite another to argue that education was free. But then, we have to ask: on what basis do we decide that the government did not collect enough taxes? Is it really a question of collection or allocation? Between the fiscal years 1989/90 and 1991/92, both capital and recurrent expenditure on Jamaican education fell, but this was not accompanied by a corresponding shortfall in taxes collected. Thus, it would appear that these ostensible financial shortages are more a problem of allocation than availability.

The second fallacy is that Jamaicans have been lucky in the past, because in the United States people pay for their education. What tragic reasoning! Why is it that we compare ourselves with the US only in such cases? One caller to the PSOJ programme argued that she pays to send her children overseas to study. My questions are: does she pay taxes in the US? Is she or the child a US citizen? Is her child entitled to all the other services provided by the US government, as a visitor to the country? If not, why single out education? Why point to America when we want to talk about asking people to pay, while ignoring the fact that there are countless ways in which university students can earn money to pay for their education, including very generous student loans? For those who simply cannot afford tuition costs, there is state assistance. We must stop comparing apples with goats.

Jamaicans now pay education tax, personal income tax and general consumption tax. Yet, they have to pay more from their pockets for services which they were taxed for. Furthermore, in many cases, the services for which people are taxed are not adequately provided. What moral justification is there for many citizens in Portland to pay taxes? In many parts of Portland, the alleged roads are better negotiated by horse than car, health care is appalling, transportation is abysmal and there is the virtual absence of employment opportunities. Tell these people who work and pay taxes that they get education for free.

To argue that economic problems will mean less expenditure allocated to education is very reasonable, though not necessarily acceptable. However, to justify change solely according to this "new doctrine" of rights is no more than ideological posturing. Peace!

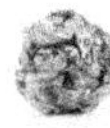

Development, education and the future

(TUESDAY, SEPTEMBER 14, 1993)

There are numerous theories as to why some countries develop economically, and others do not. They range from the classical theories of capital accumulation from Adam Smith and Marx, to the social-psychological approach of D. C. McClelland, and to the linear evolutionary perspective of W. W. Rostow's "stages of economic growth". In spite of their individual limitations, they all seem to have one thing in common: that is, the creation of surplus and its reinvestment.

The classical theorists have shown us that, in Britain, the mass of poorly paid wage earners originated partly as a result of the enclosure movement, which required the cheap labour that capitalists needed to earn a surplus, to reinvest and to produce more wealth. In many communist countries, this surplus was appropriated by the state and used inefficiently. In many capitalist countries, the surplus was ploughed back into the economy, which resulted in the creation of more jobs. Of course, much of Europe had begun their capital accumulation process through slavery and the colonization of lands in the so-called New World.

In many of the so-called newly industrialized countries (NICs) of the East, a mass of poorly paid workers exist in conditions no different from slavery. They provide the surplus that entrepreneurs need to reinvest in the country. In Mexico and Brazil, millions of people toil in the most inhuman conditions to provide profits for firms.

Surplus

Over the past three decades, in Barbados as in other Caribbean territories, the share of agriculture to GDP declined while that of manufacturing increased considerably. Much of this increase resulted from the establishment of electronic assembly and key punching firms from industrialized countries. One feature of these firms is that working conditions and wages are much worse than most other sectors of the economy. Indeed, it is not coincidental that the garment industry has been doing well in Jamaica, when other industries have remained stagnant or declined. Of course, the important factor here is what is done with the surplus.

So far, most countries in our region have failed on the reinvestment side. This is not unique to the Caribbean. In the US, under the Reagan Administration, it was thought that by not taxing capital gains, capitalists would have the means to reinvest in productive areas. The decline in the US economy throughout the 1980s was partly the result of capitalists, who instead of reinvesting, engaged in speculative activities, much like what is happening in Jamaica.

I guess that, if you look hard enough, there appears to be one theme running through this article. It is this: if economic development is to take place, there must be a mass of people who are willing to be paid low wages and who are willing to work in difficult conditions to create the surplus needed for reinvestment by the business class. This is the path that many in the East and the West have followed. Is this a realistic option for Jamaica?

Compared to most developing countries, wages in the Jamaican public and private sector are relatively high. When compared to many parts of East Asia and Latin America, industrial legislation is fairly advanced. Furthermore, Jamaica compares favourably with much of Latin America and East Asia, and even the industrialized countries, in regard to literacy and life expectancy rates. But Jamaica's close contact with North America has created consumption patterns and living expectations which are similar to those of this industrialized country. Likewise, our political system is based on universal adult suffrage, and civil society is at the stage where military intervention or political dictatorships are not the norm. To be sure, the presence of trade unions along with the consumption habits of the vast majority of the population would prevent the development of a large number of sweatshops found in (or associated with) Mexico, Brazil, South Korea and China. It seems unlikely that the option of mass labour exploitation, similar to what obtains in Thailand, Mexico or Brazil, is feasible. What is the alternative?

Robert Reich, US labour secretary, and author of The Work of Nations, argues that the global economy is weaving global webs in which skills and information are of critical importance. Already these webs have begun to take shape. They are dominated by people he calls symbolic analysts (people who solve, identify and broker problems by manipulating symbols). This group includes research scientists, civil engineers, investments bankers, management consultants, sound engineers, biotechnologists, organizational development specialists, architectural consultants and other professionals.

Economic development

The integration of global capital and the ability to move services across countries as a result of the communications revolution make the role of the symbolic analyst indispensable to economic development. Reich argues that well trained workers and modern infrastructure attract global webs of enterprise. Therefore, it is not accidental that Bill Clinton's campaign focused on education, health care and infrastructure. It is also not coincidental that he is in favour of NAFTA, even when a large number of liberal democrats are against it. Indeed, it is Reich's thesis of global integration that is the ideological guide for the Clinton economic policy. The Clinton administration is adamant that improved educational opportunities, improved health care, and an improved infrastructure are integral to America regaining her competitive edge.

In Daniel Bell's The Coming of Post-industrial Society, he proposes that theoretical knowledge will be the source of innovation and of policy formulation. This view is consistent with that of numerous futurists who argue that information will be the basis upon which societies will compete in the future. Competing in such an environment requires easy access to and an understanding of information technology. In such "information societies", education will serve to separate the haves from the have-nots. Societies in which education is not universally and evenly available will lag behind.

Jamaica is already part of the global web, through numerous transnational companies, such as International Business Machines Corporation (IBM) and Mitsubishi. It can take advantage of its geographical position and its literate workforce to compete in the manufacture and distribution of information technology. A number of Caribbean countries have attracted electronics companies and other similar service industries. Barbados' educated workforce has made it a good candidate for such investment. As the global web expands, capital will be attracted to the societies which offer the services of these symbolic analysts.

Researchers and engineers in East Asia and Europe are investing vast amounts of time and money in microelectronics and microbiotics, and are busy translating new insights into new services and products. Universities across East Asia and Latin America are bustling with activity as young people seek to enter the fields of computer engineering, marketing, management and social organization. In Argentina, Singapore and South Korea, more than one third of all nineteen-year-olds are pursuing a university degree.

Tertiary education

Unfortunately, Jamaican policymakers are not quite so convinced about the need for tertiary education to be readily available to all. Therefore, it is timely that I address two incorrect statements made by commentators about tertiary education in Jamaica. The first is that tertiary education is no longer important as a source of social mobility for Jamaicans. Nothing could be further from the truth. Research conducted by the late Derek Gordon, sociologist, and my own students at the UWI indicate a strong correlation between social class and education. All of the properly conducted research I have seen on this issue continues to indicate that, for poor people, education is an important facilitator for upward mobility.

Secondly, there seems to be a rather naive view that we should separate thinking from doing. However, this separation is merely clinical. Symbolic interactionists rightly contend that social action is itself a function of interaction, a process of interpreting and responding to the environment. It has also been suggested that the "doer" is of more value than the "thinker". This idea is sterile and reductionist. This is the wedge which creates the chasm between the university and the society at large. Indeed, if one looks at the data, one would find that the people who have been trained to "think", and continue to "think", are increasingly involved in highly paid and very profitable enterprises.

Selwyn Ryan and Lou Anne Barclay in Sharks and Sardines: Blacks in Business in Trinidad and Tobago found that some of the most successful black Trinidadians who were in business had the benefit of a university education. By extension, they have used their training as "thinkers" to start an array of companies; these include engineering, medical, management consultancy, scientific research and computer software businesses. In fact, the firms which employed 20 or more persons were invariable headed by people who had taken undergraduate, postgraduate degrees, or both. A clear example of the "thinker" doing things. In short, one does not exist without the other.

One of the arguments made against "free" tertiary education is that the society needs people to do manual labour, and other jobs which require little skill. The widespread availability of tertiary education would make this difficult. This is really not an argument but an ideological position which fundamentally denies people the opportunity to pursue their goals. In addition, the evidence does not indicate that countries which allow for free tertiary education have problems with occupational placement. I would ask those who still advance this argument to research the experience of Argentina, Venezuela, Barbados, Guyana, Antigua, Ghana and Costa Rica which all offer "free" tertiary education. As it stands, Jamaica is not providing enough skilled manpower to fill various important jobs.

This year, in a skills demand survey of 100 firms in the corporate area, conducted by students in one of my classes at the university, it was found that firms are suffering serious shortages of workers trained in accounting, management, marketing, engineering, and secretarial and clerical fields. In many instances, expatriates have had to be imported because trained people were not available locally.

The continued denial of adequate tertiary education to various sections of the population is bound to increase social inequality and deprive the society of necessary skills to compete in the global economy.

Many of the powerful people who today call for an end to free access to tertiary education themselves benefited from what they want to deny others. In a survey conducted by the late Derek Gordon and his assistant Jennifer Jones in 1992, it was found that a little over one fourth of university students come from the lower class. It was also found that those suffering economic difficulties were also from this social group. Further, their economic problems were often directly associated with their poor academic performance. So, as tertiary education becomes more expensive, it becomes less accessible to those who can least afford it – the lower class.

Resources

Jamaica has to find a way to create surplus and a way to reinvest it if we are to develop. The old ways of exploiting labour will not work for this society. We have to discover and properly use our resources. A resource is not self-evident; a resource is, in large part, an idea. The physical manifestation of the resource is only part of the resource itself. Oil was in the ground before people thought about how to exploit it. The way forward for Jamaica is to allow the creative energies of our people to flourish. Any industrial plan for our country must take into consideration the need for the entire population to have education beyond the primary level and free access at the tertiary level. This, along with incentives for reinvestment and the development of a crop of progressive professionals, can result in a bright future for our society in this age of global webs and symbolic analysts. Peace.

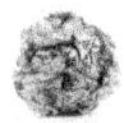

Common Entrance (excerpt from "Caught in a bind")

(TUESDAY, JULY 5, 1994)

At present, this country is experiencing one of the worst industrial climates in its recent history, and there is no indication that things will get any better in the near future. True, industrial disputes are not unique to Jamaica. However, during the spirit of privatization, the frequency, magnitude and the nature of these disputes are signs that something is desperately wrong with our economy. For if, in less than two weeks, we can have strikes by people who are in charge of some of the country's important services, such as petrol and electricity, then clearly something must be wrong.

The fact of the matter is that the government and the country are caught in a bind. The government has attempted to keep the rate of inflation down by adopting a high-interest-rate policy. However, there seems to be no complementary fiscal reforms aimed at keeping wages down – which is necessary for this policy to work. This is understandable, given that the skyrocketing rate of inflation has meant that the real spending power workers had has declined at an alarming rate. Therefore, it is unreasonable to blame the workers for demanding higher wages in this most trying situation.

Socioeconomic divisions

The fact is that if the government attempts to freeze our wages without reining in inflation, then one can expect a great social explosion reminiscent of the early

1980s or something similar to what happened in Venezuela during the nation's spirit of austerity in the 1980s.

In a number of countries in the region, such as Trinidad and Tobago, and Barbados, governments were able to reach agreements with the labour unions on how to contain wages for a period of time – a policy considered by all parties as being in the interest of the country. But given the gaping social and economic divisions and the politicization of everyday life, there seems to be little possibility of this type of social contract working in Jamaica. Further, because there is a perception that things will not improve, there is an absence of a collective national social responsibility. The prognosis, therefore, is that the chaos of everyday life is likely to continue.

Over the years, the basic problem which has faced the country is that while our consumption has increased, our output has either grown slowly or declined. This is a real conundrum. Increased industrial disputes will further reduce the meagre output, as workers lose important man hours to strikes and other forms of protests. We should note that to a large degree it is remittances from abroad (namely the US) that have been helping to prevent an even greater collapse of our economy.

Unrealistic

The efforts of the government to encourage more investment and output in the manufacturing sector should be complimented. However, the notion that the provision of rational incentives will lead to rational choices by manufacturers, and that others will suddenly switch to manufacturing, is nothing short of unrealistic. An incentive is as objective as it is subjective, and rationality is contingent upon one's experiences, commitment and perception of choices. These are the variables which guide the way human beings think. In light of this, we should ask ourselves why it is that the Asians or the Jews or some other ethnic groups in the Caribbean or the USA can seize business opportunities where others claim that no incentives exist? My argument, then, is that the problem of manufacturing and output is not simply one of providing incentives, but more importantly of providing the "appropriate" incentives. Appropriate incentives must be guided by an understanding of the motives of local entrepreneurs and a comprehension of the idiosyncrasies of local entrepreneurship. This begs the question: what are these appropriate incentives, and when do we know that we have finally found them? Answer: this is the part I am still trying to figure out.

Common Entrance

For yet another year, the Ministry of Education has placed the nation's children through the traumatic and iniquitous Common Entrance Examination (CEE). This exam is not only elitist, but it also reinforces the inequalities within our society. In the first instance, only a small number of eligible pupils took the exam in 1993. Of the 100,000 children eligible to sit the exam, only 48,144 were entered. Of that number only 10,900 or 23 per cent got high school places. You see, the Jamaican government only provides 10 per cent of the places for children of high school age. The other children must attend new secondary schools and all-age schools, or pay fees to attend independent high schools. Jamaica's CEE results do not compare favourably with those of other CARICOM countries. In both countries, there is talk about phasing the exam out. It should be noted that in Jamaica the number of pupils who pass the CEE is a function of the number of high school places available.

The society continues to play with a social time bomb when policymakers and the elite consciously perpetuate inequality through education. There is not one shred of evidence to substantiate the view that a child's potential can be known at age 11, following an abysmal primary school record. Were it not for other educational opportunities, the world might not have benefited from the immense talents of Albert Einstein. Our society is in part to be blamed for many of its education-related problems, having condemned the large majority of Jamaicans to an inferior and negatively labelled education. The Common Entrance exam should be abandoned for something more consistent with the objective of tapping the talents of the large number of cheated Jamaicans who are the backbone of the society. Peace!

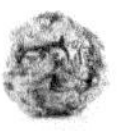

The education challenge

(TUESDAY, SEPTEMBER 13, 1994)

Unfortunately, the reports on the performance of Jamaican students in the CXC examination seemed to be a case of a country feeling the effects of past policies. And even though many positive developments have occurred in education – such as the higher literacy rates and the greater access of the population to formal education – it would appear that the structural adjustment policies and the management of the social sector by successive governments have had a negative effect on the quality of education provided to the population.

Compared to both industrialized and developing countries, Jamaica has a relatively high teacher-pupil ratio. This ratio is particularly alarming at the primary level. Errol Miller points out that up until the 1960s, the teacher-pupil ratio was roughly 1 to 56. However, during the 1970s, this was reduced considerably to 1 to 38. But, since the 1980s and up to 1987, the ratio has deteriorated to 1 to 43. Jamaica has the highest pupil-teacher ratio in the Caribbean, and one of the highest among developing countries.

In many ways, Jamaica compares favourably with many developing countries with respect to various aspects of the education system; but in others, it lags behind many countries, especially within CARICOM. The literacy rate in Jamaica is not too far below that of developed countries and the more developed countries (MDCs), excluding Guyana, of the CARICOM. But according to Errol Miller, in the late 1980s, we began to experience the decline in functional literacy.

One of the greatest problems facing the educational system in our country is the declining investment in schools' facilities, teachers and students. The government's expenditure on primary education has declined from what it was during the 1960s and 1970s. And while per capita costs increased after 1965, expenditure per student declined in real terms between 1980 and 1985 by 32 per cent. Between fiscal years 1989-90 and 1991-92, expenditure on primary education fell by 10.2 per cent. The evidence suggests that the shortfall in revenue is usually taken up by the parents of students and by private organizations. Jamaica does not compare favourably with many CARICOM countries in respect of its per student expenditure on primary education. Miller points out that Jamaica spends 60 per cent of what Belize spends, 45 per cent of what Saint Lucia spends, 41 per cent of what Dominica spends, 39 per cent of what St. Kitts spends, 17 per cent of what Trinidad and Tobago spends and 16 per cent of what Barbados spends.

This decline in the funding of schools has not only affected the physical upkeep of our schools, but it has also affected our students' performance. An analysis of the education component of the 1990 Survey of Living Conditions indicates that there is a strong relationship between students' academic performance and the school's physical facilities. That is to say, schools with better physical and teaching facilities are normally associated with better exam performance.

Part of the crisis facing the education system is a lack of adequately trained teachers. Poor working conditions and low salaries are in part to be blamed for the shortage of teachers. Jamaica has about 20,000 teachers from elementary to tertiary levels. The problem is, however, that many trained teachers do not remain in teaching because of poor working conditions.

University graduates as a percentage of teachers in high schools have fallen from about 50 per cent to 33 per cent, and in the new secondary schools there is a critical shortage of university-trained teachers. According to one analyst of the education system in the country, in none of the secondary schools do university graduates account for as much as 20 per cent of the teaching staff. The most serious shortage occurs in the areas of English, mathematics, the technical subjects, science and economics.

Since the 1970s, the performance of students in the O level and CXC exams has deteriorated considerably. With regards to the CXC exams, over the past five years our best results have been in Caribbean history. However, among the countries entering students for this subject, Jamaica ranks in the bottom three overall. The worst performance of Jamaican students is in the areas of mathematics and English, ranking only above Guyana. In 1993, Jamaican students were unsuccessful in 85 per cent of the 38 available CXC subjects, with only 40 per cent scoring a grade 1 or 2. Within CARICOM, only Guyana ranks below Jamaica in exam results.

Both the government and society face a serious challenge in regard to education. In spite of the efforts of the Ministry of Education to restructure this sector, much more needs to be done. The solution to the crisis in education is not easy, and therefore it will require the cooperation of all the interested groups in our society. That this should be done urgently cannot be overstated.

Manpower studies indicate that our country suffers from a shortage of trained personnel, especially in manufacturing, and in the service sector. And the research indicates that those countries in the region which have a strong educational system continue to experience higher standards of living than those which have comparatively weaker systems.

The recent appointment of a committee to review whether there is a need for an increase in electricity rates is a process which should be regularized for all public utilities. This process should take the form of a Public Utilities Commission where public hearings are conducted on request for increases in electricity and telephone rates. In a number of Caribbean countries, there are daily television broadcasts of hearings of their Public Utilities Commissions when increases are requested. The commissions are organized so that members of the public can object to rate increases by outlining their cases, even as utility companies make their stance for rate increases. Well run commissions are one of the few ways to protect consumer interests, especially in a monopolistic environment. Peace!

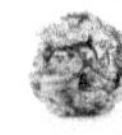

The information revolution is here

(TUESDAY, FEBRUARY 21, 1995)

Imagine if you could do one or all of the following: peruse the most recent romance or science fiction books by leading publishing houses in the USA; browse some of the world's most prestigious medical journals to learn about the treatments for a variety of ailments; read the latest news about the Middle East from the BBC or Voice of America or the New York Times; skim press releases from the US government before they are carried by the media; enquire about various vacancies and accompanying salaries in various companies in the US; or check the catalogues of overseas universities and colleges to find out about the courses being offered along with details about financial assistance and employment opportunities, and all this from the comfort of your chair at home or in your office. Well, you no longer need to use your imagination. For with a desktop or laptop computer, a modem, and a connection to the internet, your dreams can become a reality – right here, right now. These tools not only afford you the comfort of your favourite chair, but they also provide convenience, whilst the price in relation to the service is paltry.

This situation is made possible compliments of the heralded information superhighway of which we so often speak. It is a revolution which is slowly recreating the world, sculpting new dimensions within nations, and moulding a new ethos in the information-sharing arena. Those who see this technology as a new tool for the elite might be in for a rude awakening.

Legal concerns

Globally, legal concerns about copyright for published materials might be entering a new phase of confusion as more and more writers use the internet to transmit their ideas. That is, instead of relying simply on books, they put their information on the internet so that people with this service will be the first to get, and sometimes the only ones with, access to them. By doing this, it is difficult for a writer to claim copyright to the ideas as the protections which legal systems are expected to provide often trail technological advances.

The growing number of persons using the internet coupled with the growth and lure of electronic journals, books and clubs present the problem of ownership of ideas which will indeed become even more complex in the future. Furthermore, the internet is beginning to threaten the existence of publishing houses and the reliance on paper to transmit information – surely the environmentalists must be happy at the possible solution to pulp friction. Predictably, publishing companies are now investing in electronic publishing as a way of remaining competitive – in the future – since no one really knows where this new technology is taking us.

There is another dimension to this information revolution. It is fairly cheap and efficient for new converts to become a part of this new information process. The required tools are one's access to a computer that is connected to the internet, and an internet directory. Therefore, high schools with these amenities can search for books and magazines, without being concerned with the cost of and vagaries associated with airmail/snail mail.

Medical doctors, lawyers and business people can use the facility to get information on issues without travelling to overseas sources. Frequently, I find myself browsing the leading libraries in the US for information on events which cannot be obtained locally. Housewives or househusbands can use the internet to search for new and exciting recipes. What is good about the internet is that one can maintain communication with the world on a wide variety of issues at a minimal cost. You can follow what is happening on the world's leading stock markets or read news and sports in a variety of languages, almost at your leisure.

Local scientists

I believe that small, poor countries which have a fairly literate population, like Jamaica, can use this new information superhighway to its advantage. For instance, schools and other educational institutions can compensate for shortages of books and reading materials by using those assessable on the internet. The information on the internet can be used to create active data banks for the purpose of doing research, or to assist in assessing policy decisions. Investors interested in foreign investments can also use the internet to follow daily market trends and to determine investment prospects. Local scientists, engineers and medical personnel may be able to access information from training workshops as far away as Iceland geared at developing talents in a particular field.

This new information superhighway is also interactive; thus, the possibility exists for the arrangement of seminars, panel discussions, workshops, or it can simply provide fertile ground for the exchange of ideas and information.

However, one important caveat has to be made if we are to be optimistic about the possibilities associated with this information revolution. It is that our attitude towards education must become less elitist. We have to find ways to bring the majority of our population into this electronic age. Therefore, in our schools, computers and computer training should not be reserved for the so-called bright students. In short, we have to democratize the educational system. Neither should access to technology simply be reserved for the managerial staff in our companies.

If this information revolution, portrayed as some new electronic manifestation of genius on the rise, is marketed as a tool only for those on the cutting edge of technological developments, then we will run the risk of treating it as some new fetish of the elite. However, if we learn to see this new information revolution as another opportunity to expand our universe of knowledge, which will ultimately help us to improve ourselves, then and only then will we be able to exploit its advantages to the maximum. Peace!

Education and the labour market

(TUESDAY, MAY 2, 1995)

Last week, my colleague Morris Cargill pointed out in one of his columns that perhaps we might be producing too many graduates in the social sciences in this country. Whether or not he was serious, the statement led me to reflect on similar views which were expressed by politicians in different parts of the region some years ago. These views were expressed even though many of these same politicians were trained in the social sciences, and were paying foreign consultants, trained in the social sciences, large sums of money to help them run their countries.

Now, if Mr Cargill was suggesting that we need to train more people in engineering and other technical non-social science fields, then I have no quarrel with such an argument. However, the notion that we have too many people studying the social sciences is not consistent with either the demands of the labour market, or with current global trends in education. At any rate, compared to emerging economies in Latin America and Asia, the percentage of Jamaicans who receive tertiary education of any kind is very low.

Surveys

Manpower surveys which I have seen show that there is a serious demand for a wide range of social science skills, including organizational and administrative management; economic analysis; accounting; market research; and urban and rural planning, to name a few. Indeed, this need has been with us for many years, and as the structure of the labour market changes, the need for such skills will no doubt become greater. Already, there are predictions that within the Latin American and Caribbean regions, the swing in the global economy to automated forms of production, and the shift in manual labour to what is termed symbolic analytical services (e.g., management, industrial sociology and psychology, market research, advertising and public relations) will further increase the demand for training in the social sciences.

Experience

It should be noted that the experience of both industrialized countries and emerging industrialized countries is that as the economy expands, there are greater demands for people with training in the social sciences. In Japan, USA and Europe, the social sciences comprise the most popular field of study for those attending university. Latin American countries which have seen exponential growth in their financial markets now require graduates in a variety of financial and service-related fields – all sub-categories of the social sciences. The reality of business is that, as companies begin to grow, the management of people becomes central to maintaining organization competitiveness. It is for this reason that large corporations in the US and Asia invest large amounts of money in universities which have strong human-centred academic programmes.

There has also been a trend towards combining a social science education with an education in medicine, architecture or engineering. There is good reason for this. Many of the advances in health care are not due to new discoveries in medicine, but in developing ways of changing human behaviour that are consistent with supporting healthier lifestyles. One of the greatest misconceptions about public health development is that improved public health is a direct function of the number of physicians or hospitals in a country. Well, there can be no doubt that accessibility to qualified medical personnel is important for good health. However, the transformation which has been made in public health globally over the past 200 years has more to do with changes in human behaviour than with the availability of high-tech medical help. Current research on HIV/AIDS is being done within a multidisciplinary framework, where social scientists work along with medical researchers. Until there is a cure for AIDS, the changing of human behaviour will be the most important aspect of reducing the impact of the disease. It is for this reason that universities across the world, including The UWI, have drawn on the expertise of social scientists to deal with this disease.

Trend

Another trend in education, globally, has been the combining of a social science degree with training in engineering. Let me explain why this combination is not as strange as it may appear to be at first. During the 1950s and 1960s, the United Nations and international lending agencies embarked on massive engineering projects in a number of developing countries. The project teams were usually made of engineers, and a token social scientist – usually an economist. However, during the late 1960s and 1970s, most of these projects failed. From Egypt to Pakistan, these great technological edifices began to fall apart from lack of use and poor maintenance. What the planners failed to appreciate was that technological improvements will fail to have the desired impact, unless they can take cognizance of people's cultures and desires.

During the late 1970s and 1980s, social scientists were brought in to clean up the mess. It is now standard practice for development agencies to include social scientists in teams which participate in such development projects.

Our world is slowly moving back to an intellectual tradition in which disciplinary boundaries are falling apart. The integration of knowledge has reached such a stage that we can no longer seriously pigeonhole disciplines. As global changes continue to transform the old mode of work, we will need to train many more persons in the social sciences than we currently do. As for us in Jamaica and the region as a whole, we need to go a long way before the size of our tertiary-level educated work force is close to what obtains in a number of other industrializing countries in the developing world.

Wine and wind

To Mr R. Marshall Meghoo, while it is true that the type of dancing which I described in my column of April 20, 1995 is more logically associated with the word "wind" (that is, to go in a spiral or curved course), there is not yet a convention on the spelling of the word. Indeed, the most common and preferred spelling of the word throughout the Caribbean region is wine. This is one of the difficulties with words which have their roots in standard English, but really derive their meaning from our dialect or patois. Until someone puts together a dictionary of the West Indian languages, such words will always be open to different forms of spelling. Thanks, nevertheless, for your comment. Peace!

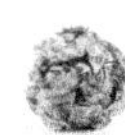

Chapter 8 Attitudes to Sex and Gender

Introduction

The articles in Chapter 8 cover the extent to which gender roles are shifting in the home and the workplace. They also examine the level of intolerance members of the society have towards homosexuals. On the one hand, the view exists that the behaviour of Jamaican men and women is changing as a result of their altered perception of their roles. On the other hand, the lack of sympathy and sensitivity towards homosexuality can be associated with fear and ignorance. Hence, the issue of sexual freedom is explored in the chapter. Within the context of relationships, the author ponders who is more likely to take on the role of aggressor. The chapter also highlights challenges women face in finding compatible mates, especially those who are in the professional ranks. The shift in focus away from relationships and into the world of technology is noted, especially in light of the fact that, while one group sees the computer as being a conquering device, the other sees it as having a utilitarian value.

Sexuality, sensitivity and sensibility

(TUESDAY, JUNE 08, 1993)

Last week, I had the good fortune of attending the gala performance of One of Our Sons Is Missing. It is an excellent play, one that I think all Jamaicans should see. The play dealt with two very complex and indeed sensitive issues, AIDS and homosexuality.

The thing I found most interesting about the play was the apparent schizophrenic response of the audience. I was often shocked by some of the responses of the older women in the audience to the fact that Miguel, the main character, had contracted AIDS. Instead of offering words of compassion, many of them used statements which would suggest that both Miguel (and his friend) deserved to have caught the virus as some sort of punishment.

I was surprised because, somehow, I thought that older women, particularly those with grown children, would be more compassionate. I did not have the same expectations about men, because our society socializes men to repress compassionate acts.

On the other hand, it was clear that the audience as a whole was moved emotionally by the story as they gave one of the most spontaneous rounds of applause to the play I have seen in a long time. The play struck a chord in the audience. Let us explore this apparent contradictory response.

During the course of last week, the talk shows were flooded with calls from people giving their opinions about homosexuality. Most of the callers were clearly opposed to such behaviour, fundamentally on moral grounds.

Most people used the Bible to justify their beliefs; in fact, one woman who said that she was a Christian argued that homosexuals should be eliminated. About a month ago, another woman, also claiming to be a staunch Christian, said the homosexuals should be shot; she then went on to use the Bible to justify her views.

There are two things which strike me about these responses. First, compared to other Caribbean societies, and in fact most societies I am familiar with, the position taken by Jamaican women towards homosexuality seems rather extreme. In most other societies, the tendency is for women to be more sympathetic to homosexuals.

Second, the level of violence expressed in the comments clearly exemplifies two problems in the society. The first is the inability of people to discuss controversial issues without resort to intimidation and violence. The second is outright fear of confronting the issue of sexuality. Thus, instead of discussing the issue in a rational way, there is the tendency to hide behind biblical quotations, even though these may be taken totally out of context.

I believe that we do not yet have a society in which people can honestly and openly tackle problems associated with sexuality. The machismo cult is so strong that men often feel the need to assert this manhood, even if violently so.

The construction of men and women as two separate genders is only a clinical distinction. In reality, there are emotions which men and women share in common. Some societies allow men and women to express those sides; others repress them.

Among the Navajo Indians in the US (a group in which there appears to be very little homosexual behaviour), hermaphrodites are seen as superior to both males and females because they embody the best of both sexes. In this society, the body and emotional strength of the female are respected much more that in Western societies.

The attempt to construct a masculine ideal which is based on an extreme clinical distinction has resulted in serious male-female problems, particularly in Western societies, like Jamaica, which exist on the economic periphery. In such societies, you have a large number of rape and abuse cases in the name of male dominance and control.

I believe that the violent reactions of some men to homosexuals is more out of fear than anything else, that is, fear of not knowing who they are (or not being able to identify them in their communities or in the wider society). Thus, in order to make it clear to others that you are a man, you take the most extreme position.

Research has found that a large number of men who become abusers of homosexuals were themselves tending towards such homosexual behaviour. To kill is a form of redemption and a reassurance of masculinity. This is purely sick behaviour.

I often ask the question: why is it that you have a society with the highest per capita number of churches anywhere, while at the same time one of the highest levels of violent crimes anywhere? More worrying is: why is it that someone who reads and preaches the ten commandments every day opts to kill a person because he is homosexual?

Let us admit it: there is something wrong with this type of behaviour. Something very wrong. Mind you, people have the right to disapprove of homosexuality. To be tolerant of other human beings does not mean that you approve of a particular type of behaviour. Many of us tolerate various religions, even though we disapprove of their tenets. But to want to kill in the name of this belief is sick.

Let me share a story with you. Some time ago, two young neo-Nazis attacked a man they believed to be homosexual. The man was brutally beaten and left crippled. It turned out that this was the same physician who, a few years before, had saved the life of one of the young men's parents and rescued the same young man from an acute disease only a year before. The physician had done nothing wrong to the two young men.

At every point in history, various societies have relegated people whom they viewed as being different to the position of non-humans and thus not fitting of humane treatment. How can we forget African slavery? In the 19th century, the status quo in many parts of the world supported Black slavery. In fact, scientists justified the exploitation of Africans by using biological and religious explanations.

How many people know that the Ku Klux Klan in the US places Blacks, Jews and gays in the same category. You see, as far as the Klan is concerned, all three of these groups are deviant minorities in the society. But it should be noted that there was a point in history in which some Europeans in the United States, who are now considered to be white, were once seen as deviant, sub-human groups by "other" European-Americans. As a result, they were treated badly, and many were killed.

Here is a quotation about how southern Europeans were viewed, taken from the book A Piece of the Pie by well-known American sociologist, Stanley Lieberson: "... the Mediterranean peoples are morally below the races of northern Europe is as certain as any social fact" (date, 25). The Northerners seem to surpass the southern Europeans in innate ethical endowment. A comparison of their behaviour in marine disasters shows that discipline, sense of duty, presence of mind, and consideration for the weak are much more characteristic of northern Europeans.

Medical doctors went as far as "proving" that the Caucasians from the South were inferior. What is the great irony here? Later in the twentieth century, European scholars reclaimed these people as bona fide Europeans, in order to establish that they were the creators of civilization. Be careful how you read history books!

I am saying all of this because human beings have a way of using religion or science to justify some ideological position. What we must realize is that truth is not necessarily absolute. Furthermore, there are some things which we do not fully understand, even though we may disapprove of them.

What we as humans in this society need is tolerance and compassion. There is too little of it around; people are too easily provoked into violence and extreme actions. The society needs to sit down and honestly discuss the issues of sexuality. We have in the country staggering cases of spouse abuse, child abuse and rape. These are all crimes of violence, most committed by men in a society which does not allow men to be more expressive.

The society has created a form of masculinity which seems to elevate aggression at all levels of the society. It has also created a society in which many women have come to accept this type of behaviour as maleness. As a result, many women view abuse as normal behaviour and socialize their male and female children within these dangerous categories.

But there is another dimension to this sexuality debate: the deafening silence of many people in society who can shed light on many an issue. It is unfortunate that we live in a society in which people cannot express a position without having labels attached to them.

Part of the problem with the society is that groups are so segregated that any time someone takes a position he or she is labelled as a supporter of that group. The other problem is that the society does not promote independent thoughts, even in the university. The late Professor Carl Stone was castigated by many a learned person for expressing views about politics which went counter to the norm, even when the norm was simply a figment of people's imaginations.

One of the reasons why there is so much intolerance has to do with the fact that people fear change, especially with regard to their value system. People feel threatened when you disagree with their construction of reality. Many avoid debate because their beliefs are sometimes the only thing they have to hang on to. But, more importantly, people are fearful when their ideals are threatened, especially by logical and rational discourse.

Western scholarship has given us a way of constructing reality in which we see things in categories; we can only deal with "yeses" and "nos", not "perhaps". We cannot deal with uncertainty. There must always be a right and a wrong, a good and a bad. Sometimes this search leads to extreme behaviour, like in the Jones Town tragedy, or the Waco event, or even the political and ideological conflicts of the 1970s.

Intolerance is the highest form of ignorance. The neo-Nazis, Ku Klux Klan and other extreme racist groups all have two things in common: fanatical attraction to ideologies in which there is one truth, and a view of the world in which ignorance is the rule.

Let us struggle against ignorance. Peace!

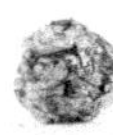

Male and female relationships

(TUESDAY, SEPTEMBER 28, 1993)

One of the most interesting things about behaviour is the relationship between males and females. In Jamaica, as in other parts of the world, this relationship has been the subject of much research by academics and commentators.

Academics in the Faculty of Social Sciences and the Women's Studies Programme at The UWI have, over the years, produced some excellent research in this area. This perennial topic, male-female relationships, was the subject of a recent survey by a group of undergraduate students at The UWI. The sample for the survey comprised 200 workers in the manufacturing and service sectors who had had tertiary education or post-secondary certification. Further, they were working professionals from the parishes of Kingston and Manchester, between the ages of 25 and 55, and they occupied either supervisory or managerial positions within their respective companies. Forty companies were randomly selected, and persons in these companies were interviewed on a number of topics related to male-female relationships. The sample consisted of 96 males and 104 females. Here are some of the findings.

Work-related issues

Both the males and the females agreed on a number of issues related to work. For instance, when asked whether both husband and wife should work in the same organization, 80 per cent said yes, while 20 per cent said no. There was no significant difference between the males and the females in their response to this question.

With respect to equal pay for work, 92 per cent of the respondents said that genders should be paid equally for the same type of work performed. Male and female responses were almost equal on this issue.

Authority

Regarding women in positions of authority, there seemed to be some disagreement between the males and the females, since 89 per cent of the females, compared with 51 per cent of the males, felt that women should be encouraged to hold executive positions in corporate organizations. These results indicate that, within the business sectors surveyed, some men still feel uncomfortable working with women in top management positions.

However, one should be cautious in drawing inferences, since the results also show that 63 per cent of the women and 64 per cent of the men preferred male bosses to female bosses. This is particularly surprising, given that the majority of the women interviewed wanted to see more women in executive positions. It should be noted, however, that both the males and the females (83 per cent) felt that more women should enter the more traditional "male" occupations.

The evidence suggests that some stereotypes regarding women at the workplace may be changing. The majority of the respondents rejected the idea that males make better managers than females (53 per cent disagreed, 33 per cent agreed, 14 gave no response). The females tended to disagree more with this premise than the males did.

It is the men, rather than the women, who still seem to see a conflict between the woman's involvement in the home and her involvement at the workplace. The majority of males (63 per cent) agreed with the view that, the more educated a woman became, the less involved she was in the home. On the other hand, 66 per cent of the women disagreed with this view. It would appear that the men felt that more education for women meant that they would take jobs which required them to spend more of their time at the workplace. It is not clear, from the survey, whether respondents saw this as something negative.

Personal relationships

The fact that women working outside of the household was having an impact on their relationships is beyond dispute. The majority (71 per cent) of both males and females felt that professional women preferred to delay marriage. Furthermore, the majority (89 per cent), equally distributed among the genders, felt that professional women tended to be more independent than non-professional women.

There still appear to be some traditional expectations of men and women entering relationships. For instance, the overwhelming majority of the respondents (85 per cent males, 95 per cent females) felt that males should initiate an intimate relationship. It is interesting to note that there also seems to be a serious problem of infidelity among men. The majority of both men (66 per cent) and women (76 per cent) said that men tended to engage in extramarital affairs more often than women.

Notions about earning power appear to be changing, since 65 per cent of the men and 55 per cent of the women said that it did not matter who in the relationship was earning a higher salary.

People seemed divided over the importance of social status in a relationship. From the sample, 50 per cent of an equal number of males and females did not feel that it was important whether both partners came from the same socioeconomic background for a relationship to work.

It would appear that ideas about household chores are also changing: 73 per cent of both males and females felt that household chores should be shared by both people.

It should be noted that these findings cannot be generalized for Jamaica as a whole, nor even the working population in Kingston or Manchester. The sample frame is restricted to particular types of people in two parishes drawn from the manufacturing and service sectors.

The value of the exercise is that the findings give some idea about how some men and women feel about a number of personal and job-related issues. It is clear that as more women move into the professional space and move up the professional ladder, society will have to adjust to this change. The men, in particular, will have to adjust to the changing texture of male-female relationships. What is encouraging about some aspects of this data is that some males have begun to accept that they have to do more in the home, and that females deserve to be paid not less but equally for the same work performed.

Some of the worrying aspects of the findings relate to the apparent male discomfort with women in executive positions, perceptions of male infidelity, and contradictory notions about women in positions of power. Perhaps these are issues which can be best deal with through more detailed research. Peace!

NOTE: The survey referred to in this column was conducted and analysed by the following people: C. Ezra Bogle, Juanita Reid, Leopold Morris, Jennifer Knight-Johnson, Mavis Blake Reid, Dorothy Griffiths, Hazel Hutchinson, Beverly Wedderburn, Lorraine Vernal and Violet East.

Devaluing male sexuality

(TUESDAY, MARCH 15, 1994)

The world is witnessing a phenomenal transformation in the nature of male-female relationships. Particularly in Europe and the US, the enforcement of laws governing sexual abuse and harassment continues to forge a new context for relationships between males and females. The basis for this change has to do with the well established view that men and women occupy different social and economic positions in society. On average, women earn less than men and are more likely to exist in poverty. Because men control the means of production, they have more to say than women in the construction of gender roles in our societies.

Issues

Perhaps one of the issues which are taken for granted in the current gender debates, especially in the Caribbean, is a view that sex is more important to men than to women. For men are seen as basically promiscuous and unfaithful, while women are seen as preferring romance to sex, and are deemed more faithful than their spouses.

The way in which society perceives males and females is linked to our construction of gender roles. There are many instances throughout history when women have been treated as chattels and as objects to be dominated and conquered. Perhaps the most celebrated aspect of this domination is sexual conquest. The baldest example of this domination and conquest is rape. Rape, in my mind, is not about sex, but about domination, conquest and violence.

But there is another side of this situation I believe lies at the heart of the battle of the sexes. When men place so much significance on conquering the female sexually, they are by extension devaluing their own sexuality. Females know this and often use sex to bargain in relationships. Thus, females in relationships with men may threaten to withhold sex as a means of bargaining. Men who fall prey to the process devalue their sexuality and themselves. Those who pay for sex value themselves even less.

Over the years, feminists and women's movements in the Western world have contributed to the process through which women have been able to improve their economic position in their respective societies. In the countries of the Organisation for Economic Co-operation and Development (OECD), most of the jobs in the service sector employ women.

Economic freedom

Likewise, in the USA and the countries of the Caribbean, most of the newly created jobs employ women. Even though these jobs pay the women less than they would pay their male counterparts, the ability to earn an income has led to a new economic freedom for women, which has resulted in fewer women depending on men for survival.

This economic independence has also meant more choices for women, especially with respect to their relationships. Women in Jamaica and across the world are shattering the stereotype of the passive female who waits for a male to make the first move. Many women enter relationships, but they have no desire to settle down. At the extreme, there are those women who can afford to pay men for sex. This change in gender roles is hauntingly depicted in the movie Boomerang in which Robin Givens becomes the aggressor and Eddie Murphy the object of her sexual desires.

Yet, with all of these changes the stereotypes persist – the promiscuous and dominant male versus the docile and morally upright female. Many feminists will willingly acknowledge the presence of the aggressive female in the workplace and on the sports field. However, they always retreat to the moral high ground when it comes to the sexual behaviour of the female.

Sexual freedom

Female sexual freedom is always seen as dysfunctional, and is thus rationalized as being a function of difficult economic times or the consequences of sexual domination by men. What these advocates of women's equality do not realize is that stereotyping reinforces these ideologies, thus creating more gender conflict.

This often happens because these traditional ideas do not reflect the new developments in gender roles. Males who are accustomed to being the aggressors find it difficult to deal with an aggressive and confident woman who does not need to exchange sex for the security of being supported by a man. Alas, these men have two problems. One, they are unknowingly devaluing their sexuality or their sexual desirability to women whenever they resort to cheap favours and trickery. Two, they are unable to deal with women cast in the roles of aggressors and who openly state their sexual desires.

Let us not forget that, in recent times, some men have begun to feel emasculated because they no longer dominate economically, in which case the women can now determine the basis for sexual intimacy. This often results in tension and conflict. Consequently, many women prefer to live alone rather than become embroiled in situations with which they are unwilling to contend. Those men who move with the times have revised their roles and use their sexuality as a basis for exchange and negotiation in relationships with their women.

Reality

A discussion about male-female relationships has to reflect the reality of everyday life. The change in the economic viability of our women's increased presence in professional contexts and the change in sexual behaviour and attitudes compel this reflection. For increasingly large numbers of women, like men, have made conscious decisions to engage in relationships which are based primarily on sexual satisfaction. If our society continues to socialize our young people into believing that the men, not the women, are always the ones to "get lucky", the men's sexuality will continue to be devalued and gender conflict will intensify. Peace!

Is there a man shortage?

(TUESDAY, MARCH 22, 1994)

Because of the overwhelming response from my readers, I have decided that this week's column should be a follow-up to last week's. In addition to this, some of my readers have asked me to address the issue of there being a shortage of men in our island. This article is therefore intended to satisfy both situations. For, indeed, this topic has been the source of inspiration for many singers who constantly lament the lack of eligible men for women. The topic has also attracted debate from among some of our prominent thinkers.

In his column of March 9, 1987, Carl Stone disagreed with Errol Miller who argued that educated women will find it increasingly difficult when looking for eligible husbands if the sex imbalance in our schools continues. Is it really the case that there is a man shortage in Jamaica?

Not uncommon

One of the arguments used to support the idea of a shortage of men in our society is that there are far more women in the population than there are men. In fact, it is not uncommon to hear men arguing that there are two women for every man in Jamaica – the rationalization for having multiple sexual liaisons. Likewise, some women have also used this argument to rationalize their relationships with married men. Indeed, it is correct to say that women outnumber men, but it is also true to point out that the difference is very small – no more than two per cent. In most Western societies, it is normal to have a slightly larger female population. This disparity is more evident in the elderly population of our society. The main reason for this situation is females tend to live longer than men.

Another argument used to support the male shortage thesis is that an increasingly large number of educated and professional women are having a difficult time finding compatible mates. Indeed, many point to the fact that more girls than boys get into high schools, and that the same obtains for tertiary institutions. The University of the West Indies speaks eloquently of the sex imbalance. However, another reality regarding this issue does not seem to support the original thesis. In both the public and private sectors, men continue to hold the top positions, while our women tend to dominate the areas of teaching (kindergarten, primary and secondary), health (mainly nursing) and clerical occupations. In his 1987 study of social mobility in Jamaica, Derek Gordon found that women by virtue of their occupations tended to be more concentrated in the lower middle class. He estimated that while less than 12 per cent of the male labour force was in the lower middle stratum, it was a whopping 27 per cent for the females in the same group. Likewise, among the lower class, men tended to be employed in the more rewarding and prestigious occupations, specifically, those which require skills.

More likely

Now these data are very interesting, for they indicate that if there is a problem with women finding compatible mates it would be primarily among those in the lower middle class. I say this for two reasons. First, women are more likely than men to marry someone above their social class. Because of this, upwardly mobile men have more opportunities to find mates than upwardly mobile females. The former is not as restricted by the same social norms as the latter, who usually marry within or down the socioeconomic ladder. In view of the comparatively faster mobility of women into the middle class, it seems to me that the women's choice of men is restricted purely by social norms rather than by a shortage of men. In other words, what is often called a man shortage is nothing more than problems related to the traditional attitudes and ideologies of gender roles, which have lagged behind the changes in the socioeconomic conditions of women.

Critical dimension

Now the norm of women marrying up and men down is a critical dimension in this issue of male-female relationships. This pattern in relationships is based upon an ideology of patriarchy in which the man is supposed to be earning more than the woman, so as to afford him a higher social status than his wife or girlfriend.

This is the difficulty many upwardly mobile women face, if they marry down socially. At this point, they must confront males who may not be comfortable with their spouses or girlfriends earning more or having comparatively higher status jobs than they do. There is an abundance of research to show that the source of much of the tension in many a relationship lies in the fact that the woman earns more, or that she has a higher status job than her mate; you see, gender roles still dictate that the man be the main income earner.

Therefore, in summary, I would say that statistically there is no man shortage in Jamaica. However, from a sociological standpoint, it is the women in the lower middle class who perhaps now face limited choices in finding eligible mates, because the social norms discourage them from getting involved with men from the lower socioeconomic groups. Thus, the notion of "a man shortage" is but a function of the gender roles in our society – a society in which ideologies of power and the use of this power still favour men. It is the fear among men about who should be in charge and the uncertainty among men regarding their own selves which best account for what ostensibly is a man shortage. Peace!

Men, women and computers

(TUESDAY, JUNE 28, 1994)

"Men typically imagine devices that could help them conquer the universe. Men think of machines as extensions of their physical power."

"Women want machines that meet people's needs, the perfect mother. And one who can be turned on and off at the flick of a switch."

"Men want to force computers to submit. Women just want computers to work."

(Quoted from Time magazine, May 16, 1994)

The new technological and information era is creating yet another area of controversy – the apparent conflicting approaches of men and women to the use of computer technology. Researchers across the United States, Japan and Europe are discovering that it is not as easy to attract women to the fledgling areas of computer programming and computer use, in general, as it is to attract men. Further, when women are involved, their socialization by the larger society impacts on how they approach the use of computers when compared to men. In the US, as in the Caribbean, computer programming is a predominantly male occupation; notwithstanding the fact that the first computer programmer was a female named Ada Lovelace. While women have made much headway in a number of the "hard" sciences, like chemistry and biology, they continue to remain on the periphery of physics and the other areas closely allied to computer-oriented professions. A survey which I conducted in 1992 showed that in Jamaica, there is a growing computer software industry, but there are very few females involved in the design of the software. Clearly, part of the reason for this lack of female involvement in computer-centred occupations has to do with the socialization of our females, beginning at the primary school and continuing through to university. Sociologist Ronald Anderson points out that in the United

States, boys and girls are equally interested in computers until about the fifth grade. After the fifth grade, the different appreciation posture for computers between girls and boys begins to develop.

Conquer

The most intriguing thing about computer use by males and females has to do with the notion that men with computers seek to conquer, while women are more interested in getting the job done. Put another way, men tend to be seduced by the technology, whereas women tend to be more interested in the utility of that technology. Researchers also argue that this difference is manifested in internet communication. For example, female electronic mail (email) messages are said to be more cooperative in spirit. On the other hand, male emails tend to be more aggressive and aimed at competition. In sum, these male-female differences indicate that while men communicate with their computers, women tend to communicate through their computers. Now, given the advent of virtual reality and what the researchers say – if it is correct – what are the implications of this phenomenon on the male-female communication process?

Virtual reality allows the user to "leave" the outside world and enter into another one created by the computer. And with the help of a piece of equipment called an EyePhone the user is able to feel as though he or she is surrounded by the image with which he or she is interacting. If the user moves his or her head, the image moves as in real life – look left and it shifts right, and so on. The glove, also a part of the new interactive process, "empowers" the user to alter objects in the computer-generated scenery. The potential uses of virtual reality seem only to be limited by the imagination. At present, the technology is used primarily in interactive video games which are concerned with event simulation. Also, attempts have been made to apply it to urban planning and design and automobile manufacturing. Now, it is not at all inconceivable for virtual reality technology to allow men to escape their surroundings more often or allow them to attempt to manipulate their environment even more. This may happen, especially, in the wider society where some feel threatened by the reduction of "male power". This could spell even more problems for male-female relationships in the future. However, the important point to be made is that male-female relationships are not static; they are always changing.

Utilitarian value

Perhaps we run the risk of exaggerating the differences between men and women if we ignore the changing socioeconomic positions of each gender, especially in Caribbean countries. It is quite plausible that as time goes on more women might come to see the computer as a conquering device, while more men may begin to see it in terms of its utilitarian value – thus closing this gender gap.

I am sure our society will see it necessary to debate these issues as the new information catches up with us. Some of us in Jamaica, and in particular at The UWI, are already part of the new information superhighway. Here, we sometimes communicate through cyberspace. Soon, communication by the telephone and through the postal service will become a thing of the past as these technological changes continue to envelope the rest of society; the issue of gender orientation will be more vigorously debated. The reality is that technological revolutions change relationships between people.

Postscript: Recently, the, Japanese prime minister resigned after he was threatened with a vote of no confidence. I wondered how many of the region's politicians, especially those leaders preparing to meet at the CARICOM Summit in Barbados next month, gave any thought to the event, particularly in light of the historic no confidence vote against Sandi. Peace!

The gender gap

(TUESDAY, MARCH 21, 1995)

Last week, while travelling along one of the corporate area's main highways, I observed two men harassing a schoolgirl. Both men reached out from the back of a motor vehicle and grabbed at the arms and buttocks of the girl. Obviously shaken by the experience, the girl screamed a number of expletives at the men and then lamented the stupidity and irresponsibility of men. Now, this is not the first time that I have witnessed such an incident on our roads; however, this incident remained with me because of the visible disgust that this girl felt towards the men. The incident also reminded me of another one: last year I asked a group of female students at The UWI why their male peers were not performing academically as well as they were. A number of them replied that the men were more interested in having fun than in using their time productively. They also admitted that while the women also had their fun, they were more interested in progress.

Yet, in spite of these incidents which speak to a perceived growing irresponsibility and mediocrity of men in our society, I have been observing the hard work and discipline of a number of male students at The UWI, and an increasing number of fathers proudly taking children to health clinics, shopping malls, schools and day care centres. Are we witnessing some change in the conditions of women and men? And are perceptions of gender roles changing in our society?

Well, on one hand, we might argue that little has changed for women if we look at their earning power in the workplace. Women continue to earn less than men even when they are more qualified. The situation is especially acute in the private sector where, according to a 1993 study by UWI economist Dillon Alleyne, on average the hourly wage of women is only about 67.3 per cent of what men earn.

But there are many cases where women are faring somewhat better. Our workforce is one in which women are slightly more educated than men. In addition, the late sociologist Derek Gordon in a study some years ago found that men were more likely to experience downward social mobility than women. In other words, women were more likely to remain in the middle class when they arrived than were men. We should note, though, that this situation has more to do with the definitions of middle and lower class rather than with the earning power of the job. For, while males usually gravitate towards manual jobs, the women are often encouraged to take up clerical, nursing or teaching occupations. Manual occupations are usually categorized as working-class occupations, while clerical and other service-oriented occupations are seen as middle-class.

We should note, however, that over the years many women have been able to break into traditional male occupations such as law, medicine, business and engineering. With the exception of engineering and perhaps business, by the year 2000, these professions could very well have more females than males working in them. However, we should caution that in these professions there is a high level of occupational sex segregation. For example, in medicine, one might find that women are well represented as paediatricians, but not as heart surgeons. As in business, the predominantly male positions tend to attract higher salaries and more prestige.

Given all that we have said so far, how does society perceive the roles of men and women? Unfortunately, there are very few studies which have looked at this issue. Nevertheless, the results of the study which I did about two years ago indicated that, overall, many working-class and lower middle-class young people are fairly liberal about male-female roles. Many young people in the society feel that it is the duty of both the man and the woman to do a variety of household chores. However, it should be stated that chores such as preparing the meals and shopping were still perceived by many as being the responsibility of the woman, while paying the bills that of the man. What we have here is a somewhat complex picture in which gender roles seem to be somewhat flexible, while on the other hand in many areas they remain very traditional.

It seems to me that the actual roles and perception of these gender roles in our society are constantly changing. Technological developments will certainly heighten these changes. As these changes occur, we need to address their ramifications. A study by UWI economist Ashu Handa shows that, in Jamaica, the absence of a potential female decision-maker in the household affects the welfare of the child. We also know that families in which the child is cared for by both mother and father stand a better chance of succeeding in society.

There are many men who feel that they are being pushed to the margins, because women "are taking over". This position is based more on insecurity than on facts. The reality is that women are aggressively moving into many areas of life once regarded as the purview of men. However, this situation is not the cause of many of the problems in education and loss of status that many of our young men are experiencing. That being said, though, we should not sweep the issue under the carpet. There is clearly a tension about gender roles in our society, and it seems to be affecting men more than women. We need to probe the issues more. Peace!

Women, men and moral authority

(TUESDAY, JUNE 6, 1995)

The reports of corruption among public officials in our society have led many commentators to postulate that this is as a result of our failed or failing political and economic systems, which are responsible for maintaining our social and ethical fabric. Incidentally, these systems are male-dominated. The implication of this situation for our society is that men have less moral authority for leadership than women. The view that women generally tend to be less confrontational and less ego-driven than men has fuelled the argument that if there were more women in politics, there might be fewer wars and fewer cases of poverty and social dislocation.

Perhaps the most commonly highlighted area of difference between men and women has been linked to the differences in the language each uses to express sexuality. So, it has been argued that females tend to use less assertive and less aggressive language than men when they recount, speak about, or identify with acts of sexuality. Likewise, females tend to use fewer expletives than men.

However, given the rapid social changes in our society, we have to be careful of not overstating the case. Indeed, research is beginning to show that roles and behaviour which were once associated with females may no longer be so gender-specific. Perhaps we are fast approaching the time when many of the views we hold about the specificity of male and female practices will have to be revised. Therefore, let me share this piece of information with you. Earlier this year, three students (Richard Leslie, Deborah Duperly-Pinks and Camilta Robert-Henry) in one of my classes at The UWI conducted a study on graffiti in school toilets and public conveniences in Kingston. One reason for this study had to do with the growing prevalence of graffiti in the country. Now some of you may ask, what does graffiti in toilets have to do with our discussion about gender and moral authority? Well, the prevalence of graffiti in public places is a fairly good indication of the type of society in which we live. Across the world, the greatest concentration of graffiti is normally associated with poor and depressed areas, and invariably the writings deal with issues which are of interest to the young people in these communities. What is written on walls often reflect people's thoughts and is a journal of their daily experiences.

In this study, the students randomly selected nine public conveniences, two high schools and two tertiary institutions. The writings on these walls included references to sexual, religious, political and violent issues. What we discovered in a content analysis of these references is quite interesting. We encountered a staggering 750 incidents of graffiti in the thirteen restrooms. In general, there seemed to be more graffiti in female than in male restrooms. In most cases, the writings sought to convey sexual and romantic notions. Interestingly, in the public toilets and those found in high schools, there was more graffiti by females, than males, relating to sexual issues and that is contrary to the popular wisdom; females were just as or more sexually explicit in their writings and illustrations than males. The writings of the females exhibited a greater willingness to conquer than males. The males tended to focus more on political issues than did the females – such as which party or politician they preferred.

Instructive

Now these findings are very instructive to anyone looking at the changing landscape of attitudes and values in our society. For while this research does not permit us to make any definitive statements about values among male and female populations, it nonetheless points to interesting areas for further exploration. For instance, in what other areas of social life do women reflect the same apparent aggressiveness as they do in matters relating to sexuality, and why?

To be sure, it would appear that the nature of gender relations among the youth and in the society in general have changed considerably over the years. In many cases, this has been a good thing. Women must have equal access to all forms of authority and to the opinion influencing and formation processes. However, it cannot be a foregone conclusion that their presence in the corridors of power will automatically usher in a new moral, social and political order for which our society yearns. Peace!

The trouble with men

(TUESDAY, DECEMBER 3, 1996)

In September of this year, *The Economist* carried a lead story entitled "The trouble with men", quite an unusual lead story for a publication with a name like *The Economist*. But, despite its title, one of the attractions of the article was the prominence it gave to the seemingly imminent demise of male social and economic dominance in the Western world. Indeed, for quite some time now, different groups of people ranging from anthropologists to novelists have been making observations about the gender transformations across the world.

Here in Jamaica, persons such as Errol Miller, Alston Barrington "Barry" Chevannes and Janet Brown, to name a few, have been studying this phenomenon of gender changes for a number of years. And, if you are an employer or you work in the area of education, you cannot help but notice the significant gender changes that are occurring in the labour market or in the classrooms.

Important issue

While we should be careful not to get melodramatic about the issue, it is equally important for us not to underestimate its impact on society. You see, the change in the relative status of men is a compelling topic for people from all walks of life. Some weeks ago, I had a discussion with an elderly lady from an inner-city community who told me, point blank, that she now prefers girls to boys. Even though girls can also be bad, she said, they will always be more responsible than boys -- that is, girls will bring in an income and they also do housework.

Interestingly, about a month ago, two of my colleagues at The UWI, Mark Figueroa and Ashu Handa, did a presentation on the effects of male socialization on the performance of males in schools, which stirred a great deal of discussion. Likewise, Rex Nettleford has written a most provocative piece on the Caribbean Black male for a recent edition of Essence magazine. Both bodies of information will, I am sure, provide food for thought. But back to the Economist article. This article raised some very interesting issues. One of them was that the trend observed here in Jamaica and throughout the region is also a feature of Western society. Everywhere across Europe and North America, females are outperforming males, particularly in school and university. Furthermore, while the labour market has been increasingly friendly to women, more men are falling outside of it. But hold on, you might say, men still earn more than women. True; however, women are catching up very fast.

Socioeconomic status

Now, the situation which I have just described occurs to varying degrees according to one's socioeconomic status. In other words, middle- and upper-class men continue to find good jobs and earn higher incomes, while lower-class, less educated men are the ones who are fast losing jobs and whose incomes are diminishing. Part of the reason for this is linked to the changing structure of the global economy which is relying more on brain and less on brawn.

You see, most of the new jobs being created globally are in the service sector and in areas traditionally dominated by women; for example, computer and data processing, child care, business services and health services. Yet, despite the warning signs and as women continue to break into male occupations, men continue to resist entering "female" occupations. Part of the reason has to do with the fact that so-called female occupations tend to be low-paying; but, that is half of the story. Society's machismo culture has also contributed to men not entering these occupations. How many mothers or fathers would permit their sons to take up nursing as a profession? Consequently, women are educating themselves so that they can occupy the higher-level jobs. Further, those women who are unable to pursue higher education, unlike most men, are much more willing to accept low paying jobs.

Economic forecast

One point which cannot be overemphasised is the rapid rate at which the world is moving towards more knowledge-based industries which require education, increasingly at the tertiary level. So as our young men continue to drop out of school at an alarming rate and as they seem to show less interest in higher education, so too must our society recognize that as a cause for concern. All of the economic forecasts for the global economy, which I have seen, for the early part of the next century show that an education will make the difference between those who get good jobs and those who do not. Also, now that women are equipping themselves with an education, more now than ever before, it will mean that they will be better placed than men to fit into the labour market of the future.

In a sense, and quite unfortunately, the chickens are coming home to roost: the very machismo image that men have constructed to maintain dominance over women in the world is creating its own contradiction, and by extension the male's demise.

The failing of our males is first a failing of our society. But it is also a failing of the way in which men have been traditionally, and even to this day continue to be, socialized – by our men and our women.

If we want to pull our boys from the brink, we should rid ourselves of the bankrupt notion that we should "tie the heifer and loose the bull". Peace!

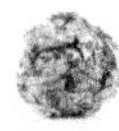

Chapter 9 Values and Attitudes

- Whose crisis of values?
- Arrogance, ignorance and dogmatism
- There must be a better way
- Ethics in business
- The death of idealism
- Who pays the taxes?

Introduction

The ninth and final chapter in this section discusses "values and attitudes" in relation to the various changes in speech, dress, music, conduct and other norms. Many social commentators are of the view that there is a crisis of values affecting the society in general, and our young people in particular. This crisis is attributed to a decline in religious or moral values and a rise in individualism. Like the other commentators, the author admits that behavioural norms are changing rapidly in the Jamaica we know today; and that the society is right to be concerned about such changes. (See, for example, "The death of idealism".) However, he notes that what is being observed is a challenge (by the underclass) to the legitimacy of the leadership of the ruling class, and to traditional Christian values, which the ruling class is attempting to inculcate in the society ("Whose crisis of values?"). The author suggests that there is no empirical evidence (in spite of the challenge) supporting the position that there has, in fact, been a radical change over the years from traditional (or established) values among Jamaican young people or in the underclass ("Arrogance, ignorance and dogmatism"; see also "There must be a better way").

Also included in this chapter is an article entitled "Ethics in business", and another, "Who pays the taxes" (originally published on Tuesday, March 10, 1998), which provide research data about the extent of tax avoidance and tax evasion – particularly among large and medium-sized business corporations in Jamaica – and raise the question of how fairly the burden of taxation is distributed among those persons who live and work in Jamaica.

Whose crisis of values?

(TUESDAY, FEBRUARY 08, 1994)

To my knowledge, there has never been a period in human history when people did not lament the decline of the values in their society. I can vividly recall this scratching comments of my parents, teachers and members of the church, and others, on the decadence of the adolescent – this, as they compared their times with the times of my youth. In taking the moral high ground, they would often and fondly reminisce about the purity of their childhood, ostensibly, a period when there was great harmony and respect for each other.

Interestingly, I now find myself engaging in the same type of nostalgic wanderings when I observe the behaviour of today's adolescents. However, if we reflect, we will realize that there is no period in human history which has been spared the debate about the decline in societal values. To be sure, Hinduism, Buddhism, Judaism, Christianity, Islam, Rastafari, socialism, communism, Reaganism, Thatcherism and Clintonism were all responses to what was perceived as the moral decay in particular societies.

Now I am not suggesting that we should not be concerned about the changing attitudes and behaviour in our society. For if our society is to function with any degree of stability, there must be some fundamental values which are shared by all. We should also note that consensus over values is arrived at through a normative process, hence all value systems are open to challenge.

Religious values

What I find particularly disturbing about the current debate on values is a plethora of reductionist and sterile arguments regarding the decline of religious values or the growing threat of individualism to society. Many religious zealots hold the view that there is a crisis of values, and that this is a direct result of people abandoning Christian principles. As far as they are concerned, you cannot have morality unless you have religion (read: Christianity). This is indeed foolishness! For, while there can be no doubt that religious ideas do influence our behaviour, we must be equally aware of the impact the socioeconomic environment also has on our behaviour. Remember, people had values before they had Christianity. Secondly, Christianity is a creation of the human mind. So-called Christian values are the product of people's experiences. Thirdly, Christians, like other groups of human beings, have historically been responsible for some of the worst human tragedies known to man, African and Indian slavery being the most recent. Research by social scientists shows that Western societies which professed to be more religious also have much higher crime rates, greater inequality, poverty, and a higher divorce rate. Further, though not conclusive, the evidence suggests that countries tend to become more religious as social and economic problems worsen.

The other factor blamed for the so-called crisis in values is the growth in individualism. There is no doubt that people have become more individualistic over the years, but it is a response to people's concrete situations. To make matters worse, we are being told that we should depend less on the state and more on our initiative. All this is happening as IMF- and World Bank-inspired policies lead us towards the construction of an economic philosophy which says that the people must orient their lives more towards the market and less towards the state and society. However, common sense and experience tells us that the more stratified the society, the more imperfect the market. Now, if the government does not protect the welfare of its citizens, and if the market cannot fulfil their demands, then we are going to have chaos. Yet our religious and business leaders lament the "me-first" mentality of our people. It seems as though we want to have our cake and eat it.

Popular culture

Very often, discussions about values are traced to expressions in the popular culture. Many commentators attack dancehall music and the so-called vulgar fashions for the lowering of the moral standards. They talk about sexual overtones in popular local dances, although they "wine down" (out of rhythm) during carnival. They scold the young for being promiscuous, but are enthralled by popular US television talk show *Real Personal*, which makes committed heterosexual relationships between two persons seem boring and passé.

Ironically, it is a generation of the 1960s (the decadent era of sexual liberation and rebellion) who now condemn popular expression in music, dress, dance, speech and sexuality. Let us not forget that the 1950s gave birth to rock 'n' roll, an art form that was condemned as being demonic and symbolic of the second coming of Christ. Many of the people who celebrate reggae music as Jamaica's gift to the world would not, in the past, be caught dead singing the rebellious songs of Big Youth and Burning Spear. Many who now splash red, gold and green colours over store windows or clothing or any other item which we now manufacture were sympathetic to the authorities who often prosecuted the Rastafarians during the 1960s.

There can be no doubt that our society is in a state of transition. The social and economic relationships between males and females are changing. Admittedly, the prolonged and intense social and economic hardships have forced people to use some rather unorthodox ways to deal with their problems. The challenge to norms of dress, speech and personal intercourse by the less privileged sections of our population is in a sense an assertion of their own legitimacy in a society undergoing these changes. If there is a crisis of values, it is more among the elite of our society – the people who often articulate what are acceptable values. The elite is faced with the problem of perpetuating the virtues of so-called traditional values in an environment which is hostile to the existence of such values. Peace!

Arrogance, ignorance and dogmatism

(TUESDAY, MARCH 01, 1994)

In his overly ambitious article titled "PM's campaign for value", published February 13, Sunday Herald columnist Ian Boyne engages in what has now become a hallmark of mediocre discourse in our society – personal attacks and insinuations against commentators. I am intrigued by the passion with which Mr Boyne approaches the topic of values. Indeed, it may well be such zeal that accounts for Mr Boyne's seemingly narcissistic feeling that he is in a position to determine the competence of academics at The UWI.

However, Mr Boyne's imputation that my motive for writing the column on February 8 was to discredit the prime minister's conference on values and attitudes is harder to fathom and excuse, since there is absolutely no legitimacy to such a view. From what is discernible from his rather meandering sermon, Mr Boyne makes a feeble attempt to defend the view that individualism and the decay in traditional values have resulted in a social crisis, and that those who have attempted to change our values (to what I am not sure) are doing the right thing.

The notion that the Jamaican value system is now characterized by rampant individualism is an unsubstantiated view on the part of those who make the observation. While it may be true that people have become more individualistic over the years, as in all societies where there is a growing urban population, this individualism is no greater than in most other societies. This individualism is certainly not very different from what obtains in Trinidad or perhaps in Barbados. Even if this individualism were greater, one cannot logically conclude that it is bad for the society.

Indeed, the view that there has been a radical change over the years from so-called traditional values is not supported by empirical research. We need to make a distinction between values and behaviours. Values are central beliefs of a culture that provide a standard by which norms can be judged. While values influence behaviours, human behaviour is also determined by a complex set of factors. Therefore, we cannot determine whether or not people's values have changed by simply making inferences from their behaviour. Studies conducted on various aspects of Jamaican attitudes and values show that the majority of Jamaicans still aspire to traditional middle-class lifestyles. For example, in a recent study which I conducted for the United Nations Population Fund, on sexual attitudes and family life in lower middle- and working-class areas in Kingston, it was found that virtually all the young people in the study preferred to have a nuclear family with two children, disapproved of male and female promiscuity, and believed that men and women should share household responsibilities, among others. The findings do not indicate any large-scale shift in family values, except that women want to assume greater control over family life. Furthermore, statistics show that the divorce rate is declining among younger couples while on the increase among the older ones.

Hard work

Carl Stone's work attitude survey, along with others conducted by my students at The UWI, indicate that most Jamaican workers continue to believe in hard work as a key to success. Furthermore, analysis of education data by some of my colleagues continue to show that the majority of Jamaicans believe that education is critical for the development of society. Increased student enrolment in university and other territory institutions over the years, and the proliferation of private educational institutions do not support the view that people are abandoning education as a means to success.

I agree that we should address the crudity and callousness which have come to characterize social intercourse among some Jamaicans. But we must be careful not to commit the economical fallacy. What may be true about part of the society is not necessarily true about the whole of it. Furthermore, if we want to explain phenomena such as an increase in violent crime, or poor behaviour on buses, we should eschew simplistic and reductionist explanations such as those adopted by Mr Boyne.

Violent Crime

In his recent book, The Jamaican Crime Scene: A Perspective, criminologist Bernard Headley points to the fact that explanations for the persistence of violent crime include sociocultural, economic and political factors. There is no evidence to support the view that the majority of Jamaicans value or support the use of violence against each other any more now than 15 years ago.

Any discussions about the state of social intercourse in our society has to be grounded in people's everyday life experiences as much as in an examination of values and attitudes. We live in a society which has been structurally adjusting for almost two decades. Poverty has increased, inflation is rampant, and the quality of social services has declined. People have to pay more for education, suffer inhuman public transportation, and contend with the health system which is woefully inadequate. This is a society in which unemployment is highest among the 14 to 24 age group, and the gap between the haves and have-nots continues to widen. This is a society in which the burden of taxation falls on those least able to afford it – those who have little hope of owning a home. But this is the same society in which poor people (particularly women) have been able to create opportunities in the informal sector because of little hope for employment in the formal sector; where parents are finding the most creative ways of educating their children; while large numbers of young people are sacrificing meals in order to pay for tertiary education; in which people get to work on time and immaculately dressed even though they have to endure the indignities of public transportation. This is the same society in which people patiently wait every five years to vote for a government.

It is commendable that Mr Boyne has taken a keen interest in public affairs. However, I do not think that his penchant for dogmatic points of view, emotional colourations or fallacious reasoning will get us very far. If we want to change values for the better, let us begin with ourselves. Peace!

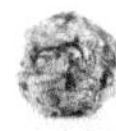

There must be a better way

(TUESDAY, OCTOBER 11, 1994)

"Who is a patriot? Here, he is a person who loves his country. He is not a person who says he loves his country. He is not even a person who shouts or swears or recites or sings about his love of his country... A true patriot will always demand the highest standard of his country and accept nothing but the best from his people. He will be outspoken in condemnation of their shortcomings, without giving away to superiority, despair or cynicism..." (From Things Fall Apart by Chinua Achebe, published in 1958)

No. 1

A car and an extremely large truck – obviously built for the superhighways of North America – are travelling in the same direction on the narrow roadway. But the driver of the truck, in his haste, attempts to overtake the car in front of him. Unfortunately, he collides with the side of the car, and continues his threatening journey along the chaotic highway. The driver of the car pursues the truck and catches it after a tiring chase. In the exchange of unpleasantries which follows, the truck driver denies knowledge of the accident even when confronted with indisputable evidence of the collision. What is to happen next will most definitely escalate the problem.

No. 2

A car breaks down almost at the centre of a four-way intersection. The driver and his two passengers get out and proceed to repair the car, completely oblivious of the lines of traffic trapped behind, in front and to the sides of the car. Motorists, however, instead of insisting that the driver move the broken-down vehicle to the side of the road, meander acrobatically to get past the car, or perhaps past each other – it is hard to tell from the confusion. Within an hour, there are two accidents in the area of the intersection, and a long line of fuming motorists are sentenced to wait in the bizarre heat of the morning sun.

No. 3

A man collapses in an area where there is a large number of construction workers. He lies on the ground groaning from what appears to be most excruciating pain. Two young men look at the man on the ground and joke with each other that the man perhaps fell because of lack of food. They continued to chip away at the concrete blocks, quite content to ignore the man who is now bleeding profusely from the left arm.

No. 4

At a function which has attracted a large middle-class audience, the Governor-General walks in. A third of the audience stands on his arrival. The remainder remains seated, either unsure about what to do on such an occasion or engaged in seemingly intense chit-chat.

No. 5

A woman visits a government agency to purchase an item. She is told by the clerk in the office that the item has been sold out for over a month. With a quizzical look on her face the woman reluctantly retreats from the office, convinced that she had seen another person leaving the same office with the item a few minutes before her. As the woman is about to leave the premises of the agency, the clerk in the office signals for her to stop. The clerk approaches her and then suggests ways in which he could help her to get the item she requested earlier, for a price, of course.

Now after reflecting on these five actual events, I thought to myself, how can we be asking of the children what we as adults do not practise? For values and attitudes are not only formed by philosophy and religion; they are formed fundamentally from experience. Therefore, children will not become disciplined and patriotic by just being preached to about these ideals. As I sat and continued to contemplate the situation, the words of Chinua Achebe rang aloud in my mind: "civilization does not fall down from the sky; it has always been the result of people's toil and sweat, the fruit of their long search for order and justice under brave and enlightened leaders" (*Things Fall Apart* by Chinua Achebe). Peace!

Ethics in business

(TUESDAY, OCTOBER 18, 1994)

Recently, I participated in a seminar on business ethics in which the participants tried to grapple with some of the issues associated with ethical business practices.

After the seminar, I reflected on some of the comments of the participants – all of whom work in major private-sector companies. And it occurred to me that some business people do commit acts considered to be unethical in the normal course of their daily business activity. Indeed, those of us who have had some experience in business know how easy it is to give into the temptation to engage in some form of unethical behaviour. Herein lies the unfortunate irony; many of these business people are often quick to chastise the government and politicians for corruption.

Unethical practices

About eight years ago, my brother and I owned a retail food outlet which I managed for about a year. During a very lean business period, I was tempted to (and did on one occasion) dilute the fruit juice with water in order to make them "stretch", although I knew that by doing this, I would be compromising the standards which we had professed. Fortunately, I gave up running the business because I needed more time to concentrate on my studies. I say fortunately, because I was tempted to adopt even more unethical practices which would have improved our profit margin – while reducing the quality of our products.

About two years ago, while conducting a study for CARICOM on cross-border investment in the region, I had a discussion with a Trinidadian businessman who told me that one of the reasons why Black Trinidadian business persons are not as successful as business people of other ethnic groups is because they are too honest. He told me that business is not about honesty and integrity; it is about making profits without getting into trouble with the law. Interestingly, I have heard this view echoed in Guyana and Barbados.

There seems to be a school of thought which says that, to make it big in business, one has to engage in unethical behaviour at some point. Regrettably, the little empirical evidence which exists indicates that many people feel that business persons behave in very unethical ways. Michael Williams, a lecturer in management at The UWI, writing in the most recent edition of the Caribbean Labour Journal, states that, in a survey of local business organizations, the majority of the respondents perceived Jamaican businessmen as being unethical. Although Mr Williams' survey was just an exploratory study and therefore cannot be generalized to the entire country, there is good reason why such a perception would be widespread. Consider the following quotation which is taken from an article written by Trevor Munroe, and which appeared in a 1992 edition of the Caribbean Labour Journal.

Figures provided by the Revenue Board in January of this year (1992) and relating to the period April to December 1991 suggest a startling problem of dishonesty ... the data indicate that the average self-employed person (including the doctor, lawyer, architect, insurance agent and own account business person) report earnings of less than \$19,700 a year, about \$379 a week. The data suggest that the salaried worker and employee received, on average, higher earnings (\$23,197.00 per annum compared to \$19,700; or \$446 compared to \$379 per week) than the self-employed. Even more startling is the fact that the same data suggest that the average taxpaying company declared an income of just over $82,000 per year.

Work ethics

Clearly, many business persons are not truthfully reporting information for tax purposes. Thus, a commonly held view of the unethical Jamaican businessman or businesswoman is not totally without foundation. Many business persons feel that we live in an environment which is not conducive to ethical business practices. They argue that it is because of serious bureaucratic obstacles and poor public sector work ethics that they are being forced to occasionally act unethically in order to succeed. Furthermore, rampant unethical behaviour is as a result of the lawlessness and disorder in the society. Unfortunately, in our society, this kind of behaviour is esteemed, rewarded and, by extension, allowed to flourish. But even in cases where such behaviour is punished, it is a proverbial slap on the wrist. And so, the unethical business habits persist.

In the US, during the mid 1980s, a *Wall Street Journal* survey reported that four out of ten executives said that they were asked to behave unethically while on the job. A study of Fortune 500 companies in that country also showed that the overwhelming majority of executives admitted to having engaged in unethical behaviour to get ahead professionally.

Also, studies indicate that there are four main factors which influence ethical behaviours of people who work in or own organizations: first, the organization's policy on ethics; second, the general ethical standards of one's profession; third, one's peers in the organization; fourth, and most importantly, one's superiors.

I am by no means suggesting that business persons are more unethical than anyone else in our society. However, what I would like to point out is that very often our business leaders stand up to criticize political leaders, drug dons and those convicted of criminal acts; but they do this without realizing that they too may be a part of the problem. Peace!

The death of idealism

(TUESDAY, JANUARY 14, 1997)

Ian Boyne's article "Decadent Dancehall Mirror's Society", which was published by this newspaper on Sunday, January 5, highlights an important social and development problem faced by our society today – the disappearing set of core values which hold society together. Now, I am an avid fan of dancehall music, but I must admit that in recent times I have found some of the music rather troubling. Not so long ago, I took a visitor to a popular "uptown" nightspot to "get a taste of the culture", only to be confronted with a group of performers whose music advocated misogyny and violence. To my surprise, the women in particular at the nightclub could not get enough of the crudest performers.

In relating this and other experiences to a number of persons associated with the entertainment industry, I found that they expressed similar concerns to mine. Like me, none of them made their views public. Perhaps it was out of fear of being labelled "anti-people" or snobbish, or prudish and "not with the times".

Hence, as Boyne correctly observes, part of the dilemma faced by our society, like so many others in many parts of the world, is the seeming lack of what I call "a moral centre". This of course begs the question: why do we in Jamaica find ourselves in such a predicament? I will venture a few ideas.

One of the features of the so-called urban "Black culture" (Western or pop culture) of the Western diasporic Africans is the tendency for commentators to take almost diametrically opposing positions regarding its acceptability. One group of people tend to dismiss dancehall, hip-hop and rap as faddish and decadent, while others embrace these music styles as true expressions of the human soul. The two groups are essentially involved in an ideological battle. On the other hand, those who embrace these genres but abhor their occasional dangerous messages fail to speak up because of fear of being seen in a similar light to those who hold the music in contempt. Consequently, the failure to critically and constructively examine our own cultural utterances leads us to justify almost any form of expression as being "part of the culture", as though this automatically makes such expressions useful.

Two more reasons

But there are two more compelling reasons for the seeming lack of a moral centre to which I refer. The first one has to do with the fact that political and economic elites in the society have even less moral authority now than in the past. Hence, those who make the laws and policies lack the legitimacy to lead, or to be taken seriously by the masses of the people. Arguably, the most respected group of people in our society is the Rastafarians.

Part of the reason for this lack of regard for the elite by the masses of the people, especially the so-called rebels of the inner cities, is the shocking level of inequality and political apartheid that exists in the society. Indeed, there can be no moral justification for the current social conditions which exist in places such as Rema and Arnett Gardens, to name a few. The society as a whole, but particularly those who have the capacity to bring about change and some semblance of normal existence in these occasional "Gaza strips", have much to answer for. How do we expect to have a moral centre when we live in a society which accepts the existence of communities which are treated and, in some way, resemble the Bantustans in South Africa which we decried?

The second compelling reason for the lack of a moral centre is related to the fact that we seem to have surrendered our souls to a crude form of "free-market" economics. If the 1970s was known as the period of idealism and socialist experimentation, the 1980s and 1990s may be termed a period of extreme pragmatism and right-wing dogmatism. Many of our "thinkers" and policymakers have surrendered their minds to the ideas of a few philosophers who tell us that, to achieve economic development, liberalization must be accelerated at the expense of social progress. The notion of a fully deregulated economy is premised upon the idea that there is clear predictability to human behaviour: implement a few measures and people will behave in the prescribed manner. I wonder, do these defenders of this crude economism know something about human behaviour that behavioural scientists, whose job it is to study human behaviour, do not?

Now, while it is true that poverty has always been with us, we now have a set of economic theories which rationalizes its existence. Nowhere in the world is there a society which has eradicated poverty without serious state intervention. Where serious poverty persists in the rich countries, it is due to the conscious lack of attention paid to the affected areas by the state. Inner cities in Britain and the US come to mind.

But ideological deregulation is more than an economic concept; it is a philosophy which has permeated all sections of the society, reducing almost every aspect of our lives to an absurd economism. Hence, our discussions about education, transportation, health, food and art are ultimately reduced to economic questions.

Ironically, given this ideological venom, not only has our economic performance not gotten much better over the decades, but the quality of human life has also not improved appreciably for most people in the society. Now, how can there be a moral centre when virtually every human concern becomes an economic one? When everything and everyone has a price!

Unfortunately, I am not sure when we might be able to recapture this moral centre, or who will lead this process. To be sure, most policymakers will not act unless people force them to do so. Perhaps the safest bet is for each of us to begin working on ourselves. If our existence is based upon simple economic pragmatism, then we might continue to hobble on from day to day. There can be no vision where there is no idealism. Peace!

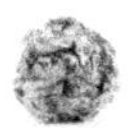

Who pays the taxes?

(TUESDAY, MARCH 10, 1998)

Some weeks ago, the president of the Jamaica Chamber of Commerce (JCC) was reported as saying that more ways should be found to collect taxes from micro-enterprises – such as snow cone vendors – across the country. At the same time, the chairman of SuperClubs is also reported to have said that no new taxes should be raised until the existing taxes were collected. While the government, for its part, has introduced a new tax compliance bill which will give new powers of search and confiscation to tax officials.

Now, all this talk of taxes has led me to ask the following question: why is there such a great interest in taxes, suddenly? Who really bears the burden of taxation in our society? For the answer to these questions, I sought out my colleague Dillon Alleyne, a lecturer in public finance in the Department of Economics at The UWI. You see, Dr Alleyne has spent a decade studying our tax system and he has even written a book on the subject. The book, which provides great insight into the nature of the Jamaican taxation process, should be available to the public later this year through its publishers Canoe Press, University of the West Indies, and the Consortium Graduate School of the Social Sciences, UWI.

According to Alleyne, the great interest in taxes at this time seems to be linked to our growing internal debt; the unanticipated budgetary outlays through FINSAC to aid our shaky financial sector; and the need for additional revenues to meet social needs in a period of stagnation. Given the foregoing situation, there seems to be some concern among members of the private sector that tax rates may have to be increased to meet our various national demands, hence the suggestion that the tax net be widened to capture the micro-enterprises.

Misplaced

However, according to Alleyne, the JCC president's focus on the small vendors is misplaced for a number of reasons. Dillon Alleyne points out that, a long time ago, the political economist Adam Smith said that it was pointless to pursue revenue if the costs were greater than the returns. Thus, to Alleyne's mind the effort to collect taxes from micro-enterprises will be too costly and therefore counterproductive. The second reason why the focus on the micro-enterprise is misplaced, according to Alleyne, is that the main sources of government revenue leakage are in the large- and medium-sized enterprises, where the government's audit procedure is weak and sporadic and, in some cases, non-existent. He goes on to point out that, in fact, in many of these incorporated enterprises, there is a high level of non-compliance through evasion (not paying taxes at all) or through avoidance (using existing legislation to limit tax payments). In the same breath, certain sectors such as the hotel industry and certain financial enterprises, like insurance companies, under the current legislation, are able to significantly minimize their tax payments. Evidently, the practice of avoidance and evasion are made easy because of the structure and design of the income tax machinery.

Most of the estimates of the tax burden for the corporate sector reflect a substantial divergence between the statutory rate (the rates companies are legally obligated to pay) and the effective rate (the rates some of these companies actually pay). But as Alleyne says, in discussing corporate taxes, most commentators tend to talk about the statutory rate rather than the effective rate, the latter being the more meaningful under the circumstances.

By way of example, Alleyne continues to argue that rough estimates of potential revenue to total revenue collected in 1991-92 indicate that for individual taxes, the self-employed contributed as little as 15 per cent of potential revenue, and only 27 per cent of those registered filed returns. In the case of the GCT, which represents a fairly successful collection effort, the filing rate was 76 per cent in 1992. The rate of filing in relation to company taxes was only 20 per cent. Now, the total taxes collected versus the potential (what should have been collected), was a mere 26 per cent. This massive underpayment of taxes by the corporate sector has resulted in a situation where the bulk of the taxes come from consumers, many of whom are already on the PAYE (Pay As You Earn) tax roll, which constitutes the significant portion of income taxes.

Supportive

In light of the foregoing, attempts at ensuring greater statutory compliance should be continued and, in this regard, Alleyne is supportive of the present tax administrative programme which is aimed at ensuring greater tax compliance. This programme should lead to more efficient collection of taxes and the "widening" of the net to include those corporate entities which should be paying taxes. However, Alleyne also thinks that tax rates should be reduced for those who are already paying taxes, like the PAYE payers. Equally, he feels that a system should be introduced to reward those who pay promptly, and punish those who are tardy or refuse to pay.

The emphasis on compliance should be continued at the sectoral level, rather than spreading our meagre resources across the tax units simultaneously. This should ultimately lead to more efficient collection of taxes, which by extension should result in a reduction in taxes all around. Our statutory corporate and income taxes are high, according to Alleyne, especially when compared with some Latin American and Caribbean countries.

I have a strong feeling that even if compliance is significantly increased, given the difficulties in our financial sector, tax relief as advocated by Alleyne would be a long way off. Nonetheless, let us hope that the policymakers are listening, as there is much food for thought. Peace!

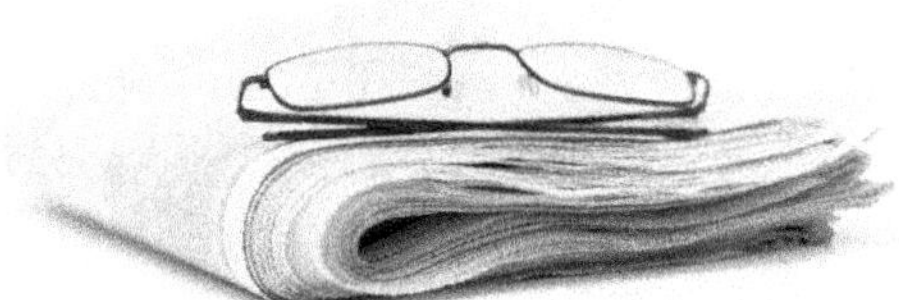

SECTION IV

Economic Development in Jamaica and the Caribbean

Introduction

One of the major issues raised in Section III is that of the slow rate of growth of the Jamaican economy and the related question of what the government and private sector must do to increase worker productivity. This section spans three subsections and covers a number of areas relating to development within the Caribbean region. The section looks at one of the basic pillars of development, that of enhancing productivity. The matter of the factors of productivity is explored, as well as its overall impact on the growth and development of the Jamaican economy.

Also explored is the role of the international lending agencies in the growth and development of the developing south. In fact, the section explores theories of development as outlined by international financial institutions, as well as how they influence the respective debt burdens among countries of the developing south. What is concerning is whether the official position and policies of the IMF and the World Bank (that the state should stay out of the market and allow pure market forces to dictate the process of production, distribution and consumption) are appropriate or even relevant. There are some schools of thought that suggest that countries of the developing south are expected to adopt the more formalized models developed by the more developed north to turn around the economic and social spaces within which they exist. Matters relating to the sustainability of the tourism sector are also explored. In this section, the author explores the impact of structural adjustment policies on the sector, as well as on the environment. The question of whether the tourism sector is the answer to the question of growth and development of Caribbean societies is also explored.

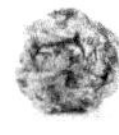

SUBSECTION A

Economic Development in Jamaica

Introduction

In subsection A, Boxill argues that both the now discredited socialist policies of the past and the free-market policies once pressed upon Third World countries by the World Bank and IMF were both extreme positions. Secondly, he also contends that "the state sector" – a term with a broader meaning than the term "government" – must play an integral and proactive role in social and economic development. And, thirdly, he stresses that the government "must define its role and that of the other sectors of society to ensure collective responsibility and consistent action" (see "The role of the state" p. 153, this volume). Our problem in Jamaica and the Caribbean, he suggests, "is not technical, it is philosophical. We need a vision" (see "Ideology and development" p. 156, this volume). In addition, the author posits that the shift in government policy away from an emphasis on the public good towards an emphasis on the good of the individual (a shift done "partly out of necessity and partly because of a change in global ideology consistent with the market model" which assumes that society is "an aggregation of individuals) has negatively impacted the Jamaican society.

Chapter 10 On Productivity

➢ Compete with whom?
➢ Work ethics and development
➢ The illiteracy problem

Introduction

The chapter explores the extent to which factors such as regional and international competition, local competition as well as competition in the private and public sectors affect productivity. It also considers the impact work ethics and illiteracy have on productivity. (See "The illiteracy problem", published Tuesday, September 23, 1997.) On a more specific note, Boxill suggests that an examination of the factors affecting productivity cannot be had without the scrutinization of other areas of the productivity equation. These factors include "the long and dehumanizing experience of catching a bus, or the pain the worker suffers in seeing a physician to attend to her son, or the woes a family experiences in obtaining a reasonably priced house to rent" ("Compete with whom?"). Ultimately, Boxill's goal is to turn the discussion away from productivity as something which is solely tied to performing a technical task in a nine-to-five job, and towards the softer everyday activities of human behaviour influenced by their experiences and world view. (See "Compete with whom?" and "Work ethics and development".)

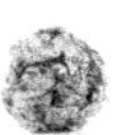

Compete with whom?

(WEDNESDAY, MAY 12, 1993)

The words have now become deafening: "We have to be more productive to compete in the global economy." Just turn on the radio or the television, open the newspapers or just listen to the latest expert in economics (suddenly almost everyone in the society has turned expert economist), or tune in to some talk show, and you will be told that we are not competitive in business (what a discovery) and why we need to be more competitive. Many will even tell you what to do to make the country more competitive in NAFTA, LAFTA, CAFTA and who knows which other -TA. Gimme a break.

Some (like the executive director of the PSOJ) tell us that we do not have the right policies in place to encourage businesses to be more productive (yeah, right). Others lament the lack of creative entrepreneurs, and still others blame an ineffective and myopic political system. (Listened to The Breakfast Club lately?) Some academics (bless their hearts) will tell you that we need more trained managers, and better infrastructure, and appropriate technology and relevant skills, and markets, and a proper mix of fiscal and monetary policies, of course. The business sector will complain about the lack of affordable credit, high taxation, high wages and the proverbial lethargic government bureaucracy. (Not surprised, are you?) And you actually wonder why the country is so confused.

Okay, granted, there is some truth to all of the above reasons given for why this society is not as productive as it could be. The more important question, though, is what are the most important factors that we should isolate and deal with, in order to improve productivity? Let me share with you some ideas I have on the matter. I want to turn the discussion away from productivity as something which is tied to performing at technical task in a nine-to-five job and see productivity simply as behaviour.

Astronomical bill

Only last week I got a bill from the National Water Commission (NWC) which showed that I owed some astronomical sum for the consumption of water. I almost fainted at the sight of the bill, but reason told me that if I showed the bill to the commission, they would immediately concur with my view that it was an error. I was wrong, to make a long story short (and believe me, the story is extremely long and ridiculous). The people at the commission eventually agreed with me, but not before disconnecting my water for two days and passing the matter from person to person, demonstrating a level of incompetence that almost made me collapse in shock. It would appear that the different sections of that organization operate independently, creating sheer agony for the consumer. The situation is tantamount to the head not knowing what the hand does, and the stomach not being coordinated with the bottom. And we want to compete with the world?

But the encounter brought up more than the problem of incompetence. There is also the problem of service (or the lack thereof). For instance, there were no apologies for, nor the faintest recognition of, what they had done. I am not trying to single out the Water Commission; all of us know that this behaviour is characteristic of the public sector. In fact, it can get worse. There seems to be a policy among public servants never to look at customers while they speak with them, or never to say "thank you", "excuse me" or "please". The treatment of customers in the public service is so horrible that one wonders how people continue to maintain their calm in the ever-present long, meandering and pointless lines which seemed to be a hallmark of every public sector organization. It would appear that, if there is not a long confusing line of bewildered people, then the agency is not doing its job.

The fact that there is corruption in the public sector is not surprising. Sure, part of the problem is linked to poor remuneration and working conditions, but the other aspect is that the formal channels are so poorly organized that it is more rational for people to go through the informal ones. Just go to any public sector agency and try to get information. If you have the courage to go in, you might encounter an information section. Four out of five times the information desk will be unable to tell you anything besides very routine common-sense things. Worse yet, if Mr X is not at work, then "yuh salt", for Mr X alone has all of the information about everyone in the line. If Mr X dies today, it will be sheer chaos in the place. We have too many organizations pretending to be organized. No wonder people prefer to go through informal channels, even illegal ones, to get things done. I believe that if we can cut 25 per cent of the inefficiency in the public sector, we can pay off 25 per cent of the national debt.

Clearly there is a problem with skills and work ethic in the public sector. Many of our workers do not recognize that they are providing a service for human beings. Many are unable to, because of a lack of skills. Even worse, many do not see a link between what they do and the development of their organization and country. Of course, one of the reasons why the public service remains inefficient is because there are some people in the society, some important people and some not so important, who get things done without standing in lines or confronting the woman behind the counter. These people seem to like the idea that they do not have to suffer the humiliation like the rest of us plebs. So, who are we competing with?

Sometimes worse

Now, I do not want to give the impression that things are much better in the private sector. Private sector organizations treat customers with the same amount of disdain, and sometimes worse. Furthermore, the private sector has the additional problem of employing a large number of people who are ill-equipped to perform their jobs. The result is oftentimes poor or mediocre workmanship or service. Pray, tell me who can we compete with?

As if things were not serious enough, we have a situation where the infrastructure in the society is decaying. Roads cannot accommodate the traffic, and bus transportation is dehumanizing, as the state continues to abandon the people in the name of an ill-defined free market economy. We are creating a monster – a society with a high degree of social alienation. For some people, work is not a means to contribute to society, but a way to get back at the system. When the insurance teller or clerk snaps at the customer who wants to query a financial matter, this may very well be a form of rebellion against a system which pretends to serve people, but does little for the very teller who works in it. Powerless people have a way of using whatever little authority they have to attain some worth. The intoxication with guns by many people in our society is the worst manifestation of powerlessness and alienation. The sad thing about this type of behaviour is that, increasingly, we are beginning to view disrespectful behaviour as the norm. What are we competing with?

It should now be clear that when I speak of increasing productivity I am speaking, fundamentally, about the potentials of labour power (until robots take over). Too many of our pseudo analysts see productivity simply from the management side. They overlook on the productivity equation the long and dehumanizing experience of catching a bus, or the pain the worker suffers in seeing the physician to attend to her son, or the woes a family experiences in obtaining a reasonably priced house to rent or buy. I know of a case where a teacher was forced to leave her workplace and her residence because of the fear of criminals. When civil society is unable to protect its citizens, why should they be concerned with production? How does increased productivity, or getting into NAFTA, or competing in a new global economy impress a worker when he cannot link these great ideas with an improvement in his or her daily existence? When the firm's profit increases, does the worker also get an increase? When the worker gets an increase, can she spend it without being robbed of the items she buys by someone who will never be caught by the police? Or can she put these few dollars away in a bank for a rainy day without the fear of devaluation? Who is the worker really competing with, the outside world or her daily existence? When we talk about increasing productivity, we are talking fundamentally about changing worker attitude and behaviour. For a group, or a firm, or a nation to perform at its best, the people must feel that they have common interest. They must feel that they have a stake in whatever they are doing. They must feel respected. Human beings are driven by more than economic incentives; they are also driven by emotions. Just examine your own feelings after you have read this article. Peace!

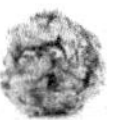

Work ethics and development

(TUESDAY, JULY 19, 1994)

On a recent trip to Saint Thomas in the US Virgin Islands, I was confronted with questions about what conditions explain the differences in work ethic and the levels of economic development among nations. My experiences in the Virgin Islands seem to reinforce some ideas I have had about these issues. I will use this opportunity to share some of them with you.

St Thomas is about 32 square miles, with a population of just about 50,000 people. The US Virgin Islands are territories of the US and as such are subject to the laws and bureaucratic control of the US federal government. Now, one of the most interesting things about the island of St Thomas is the nature of its infrastructure, which to all intents and purposes is very metropolitan. For although there are no skyscrapers or superhighways, the basic outline of the road system reflects a metropolitan influence. Likewise, virtually all the major stores found in St Thomas can be found on the mainland. These are a few of the things which set the island apart from many others in the Caribbean. By mainland standards, it is not well off, but, interestingly, St Thomas is not a part of the "Third World". For if one takes in per capita income, its level of consumerism, its standard of health and its physical infrastructure into consideration, then one cannot consider St Thomas a Third World island. At any rate, if it were to be considered Third World, it would have to be at the upper end of the scale. Notwithstanding this high economic ranking, there is a remarkable similarity between the work habits of those born on the island and those of their Caribbean counterparts in the other territories. What is even more interesting is that in many ways these habits contrast with the habits of those persons who originally came from the mainland to work on the island. So, on the face of it, Virgin Islanders from the US mainland seem, in general, to be more businesslike and efficient, as opposed to the "natives". Of course, there are exceptions. However, I found "native" Virgin Islanders to be much more laid-back, easygoing and less efficient than the mainlanders.

Apparent difference

In a society which is much more disciplined than Jamaica, there were numerous instances in which the work attitudes paralleled many of those found in the Jamaican public and private sectors. Therefore, the obvious question is: what is it that explains the apparent difference between the mainlander's work ethic and that of the "native" islander? Surely, in the case of the Virgin Islands, it cannot be explained simply in terms of salaries, since workers are fairly well paid and the labour laws in these islands make it harder for workers to lose their jobs than on the mainland.

I believe the difference has to do, in large part, with people's world view. That is, their values, norms and folkways have helped them to grasp their reality – all societies have their unique ways of interpreting their reality. But those countries which are deeply entrenched in the global capitalist economy and whose people out of necessity or conviction compete each day in it, seem to have much more in common than those countries whose economies are not as entrenched or whose people do not feel this entrenchment.

You see, for countries to compete successfully within the competitive world economy, high levels of efficiency are required, since productivity is the key to success. But production and distribution are only one side of the equation; consumption represents the other side. Now, in order to deal with consumption, companies have developed very sophisticated ways of meeting and creating consumer needs. Consequently, efficiency becomes much more than how fast one produces an item on the assembly line; in fact, with time, it becomes a part of one's psyche – one's life. Therefore, capitalist development is not only about capital; it is also about ideas and attitudes – that is, how people think about something before or while they are in the process of performing the task. If longevity is the objective, competitive industrial capitalism requires a set of norms and values which can reproduce and support a system in which efficiency and order are the norm and not the exception.

Daily experience

Whether this efficiency is achieved through competition as in the West, or through collaboration as in the East, for efficiency to be achieved, it has to be part of people's daily existence. As such, the technologies developed to ensure increased efficiency and better service are merely extensions of people's ideas of themselves and their societies. In the developing countries, we often adopt some of these technologies, but we are unable to effectively use them because we are not part of the ethos which gave these creations life in the first place. In short, the meaning attached to work for the mainlander in St Thomas may not be the same as the "native" Virgin Islander's ideas about work. This is because the world view which each brings to a task comes from a different set of experiences and therefore foments different notions about what is important to and for existence.

Thumbs up to JBC for their coverage of the World Cup! The idea of a football bar was sensible, and made it easy to watch the matches. It was also good that they included females in their commentary team. On the other hand, CVM's studio setting was too tacky and unnatural, particularly last Sunday when the commentators appeared in tuxedos. Give me a break, CVM!

Thumbs up to CVM for the recent series entitled Royal Palm Estate. Although there were problems with the programme – for instance, the acting was very uneven – I found myself riveted to the television set on Sundays. Both the script and the technical aspects of the series were fairly good. This programme is indicative of what is possible in our region. Although no polls were taken, from listening to people I got the impression that CVM received high ratings for this show. I eagerly await the next series. Peace!

The illiteracy problem

(TUESDAY, SEPTEMBER 23, 1997)

Despite the much vaunted success of the recent attempts made by the Ministry of Education to expand educational opportunities, illiteracy remains one of the most serious problems which we face in this country. The 1994 National Literacy Survey, coordinated by sociologist Dr Louis Sterling, showed that only 57 per cent of the population is functionally literate, 18 per cent can be considered literate, 3 per cent has basic literacy skills, and 21 per cent can be classified as absolutely illiterate.

The report defines functional literacy as "the ability of a person to engage in all those activities in which literacy is required for effective functioning in his/her community and also for enabling him/her to continue to use reading, writing and calculation for his/her own and the community's development". A person classified as literate has "the ability to read and write a short, simple statement, with understanding, on his or her everyday life". Basic literacy refers to having nominal literacy skills, below the literate level. The report also found that a significantly larger number of women were literate than men, and illiteracy among the rural population was around 30 per cent. What is even more shocking is the fact that about six per cent of those who attended (though not necessarily completed) the most prestigious high schools in the country were judged to be absolutely illiterate.

Indeed, these figures do not compare favourably with our CARICOM neighbours who, with the exception of Haiti, all have illiteracy rates well under 10 per cent of the population.

Compromise

One of the problems with such high rates of illiteracy is that productivity levels and quality of work are seriously compromised since workers find it difficult to follow written instructions required for problem solving. In a world where technology is so integral to everyday life, being able to read and write has become central to survival. Mundane things, such as connecting a VCR to a television or replacing an old car part, require an understanding of the English language, since we often need to follow instruction manuals. Our country is plagued with mechanics who are unable to read or write, and who have to rely either on intuition or experience, or both, to repair vehicles. We are often forced to employ masons and carpenters who are unable to follow architectural designs; and frequently, we are transported by bus and taxi drivers who cannot read road signs. Is it any wonder why there are so many road accidents, or why constructing a building is often a traumatic experience?

Although controversial, education research has shown that there is a relationship between literacy and the ability to think logically. Generally, less literate groups are said to have greater problems with logical thinking. Therefore, these groups exhibit more aggressive or violent behaviour, especially in urban settings. Social science research also shows that societies with better living standards and higher productivity levels tend to have higher literacy levels – except in cases where unfree or exploited labour is used. One caveat: researchers are not here claiming that illiteracy is a cause, but rather they argue that there is a significant and interesting correlation between literacy and a society's productivity and standard of living.

Unfortunately, my daily experience tells me that the problem of illiteracy is much worse than what the statistics show, and there is little indication that this problem will improve in the immediate future. If we are serious about development, then we ought not to make the education of our people a partisan matter. Before we can do anything about the problem, policymakers first have to acknowledge that a significant level of illiteracy exists throughout the society, and that it is a critical problem which requires urgent attention. Peace!

Chapter 11 IMF and World Bank Policies

- The role of the state
- Ideology and development
- The past, present and future
- A budget without vision
- Morality, vision and progress
- The budget and cricket
- Public and private interests
- That World Bank report

This chapter explores the impact that policies of the World Bank and IMF have on the growth and development of Third World developing states. The chapter zeros in on a much debated issue among some of the poorer regions of the world (specifically, Jamaica, the Caribbean and Latin America): the issue of debt and the social, economic and political effects repayment has on respective countries. What is concerning is whether the official position and policies of the IMF and the World Bank (that the state should stay out of the market and allow pure market forces to dictate the process of production, distribution and consumption) are in fact sound. The chapter explores the extent to which the policies of these international lending agencies can stand up to scrutiny.

The role of the state

(TUESDAY, JUNE 29, 1993)

A number of readers have requested that I write a column on the role of the state in development. One reader in particular said he felt as though the state had abandoned the people, especially in light of the recent budget. From travelling around the country and speaking to people, I get the feeling that many citizens have actually lost confidence in the ability of the government to pull the nation out of its present economic conundrum. This does not have to be so, if we recognize that the state sector has an important role to play in the development of the nation.

Just as there were those who once believed that the state should be in control of the commanding heights of the economy in the society, there are also those ideologues who argue that the state should stay out of the market and let pure market forces dictate the process of production, distribution and consumption. Both positions are extremes with serious limitations, although increasingly the latter has come to dominate development thinking throughout the world. The attempt to emasculate the state to the extent that it has become withered and feverish cannot be in the best interest of the country. Also, to reduce the role of the government to that of a tax collector is the last thing that any developing country needs.

Before I continue, I would like to make the distinction between the government and the state. The state here refers to a set of institutions comprising the legislature, executive, central and local administration, judiciary, police and armed forces. The government is therefore only one component of the state.

Since the 1980s, particularly after the collapse of communism, many analysts and politicians the world over retreated from the view that the state should be the main player in economic development. Spencerian notions of "the fittest survives" and Adam Smith's theoretical construct of the "invisible hand" immediately took on renewed meaning as countries moved to "free up" their economies. The Marxists, socialists and social democrats beat a hasty retreat as they saw the Soviet Union crumble and capitalism triumph across East Asia.

Free market

Critics of Marxism suddenly gathered more energy and many Marxists converted to "free-marketism" overnight, many shouting down the state as a piranha. The IMF and World Bank consultants quickly became demigods. Such was the situation that if anyone uttered the word "state", it resulted in swift condemnation for being out of touch with the present reality. As Thomas Kuhn would argue, a new paradigm came into being. In effect, a new way of explaining and dealing with reality took over.

However, the question now posed by this new paradigm is: who will do the work that the state once performed? Two answers have emerged. First, turn over business to the private sector and, second, discontinue the social programmes previously carried out by the state. That change includes reducing the state from the role of providing social goods, such as education and health, and letting the market forces dictate what to do in this area. The problem: after almost ten years of pursuing some of these policies many developing countries are now asking where they went wrong.

Policies

They wonder for two reasons. First, economic conditions in developing countries have become even more oppressive, with little hope of getting better; and, second, they look around the world and realize that no industrialized country has been pursuing the same policies that they (the developing countries) were advised to pursue by the experts in the industrialized world. In fact, so serious has been the situation in developing countries, following structural adjustment policies, that the IMF has now acknowledged that the state should play a role in the provision of basic public services if a country is to progress.

If my knowledge of history serves me correctly, all the great ancient civilizations had one thing in common – strong proactive states. From the Indus valley of India, to the Ming Dynasty of China, to the Phoenicians of the Middle East, to the Mayans of South America, to the East African empire of Meroë to the great land of Timbuktu in West Africa, and the fabled Great Zimbabwe of southern Africa, there was no mistake about the role of the state in the progress of these great nations. From the American Revolution, to the Haitian Revolution, to the liberation of Latin America, there was no mistake about the centrality of a proactive state to political development. From the great transformation in England which ushered in the Industrial Revolution, right across France and Germany and stretching east to Japan, there was no mistake about the role of the state to social and economic development. The writings of Barrington Moore Jr., historian and social scientist, on the development of democracy and economic development, point to the centrality of a proactive state in these processes. Indeed, one cannot mention the so-called Japanese miracle unless one pays attention to the conscious act of the Meiji government, which was restored in 1868 following the fall of the Tokugawa Shogunate. The Meiji government engaged in a process of Western industrialism, facilitated both by the setting up of Western-style universities in Japan, alongside universal and compulsory education, and by a set of government policies which enforced discipline and consensus and encouraged productivity. By 1894, approximately 60 per cent of all eligible Japanese children were attending school. By the turn of the century, all of them were. So much for the miracle!

Recently, the father of the so-called Korean miracle (notice how the word "miracle" has come to mean anything we are still grappling with, and which others have ostensibly succeeded at understanding) came to Jamaica to share his views on economic development. Dr Park's presentation suggested two things to me: first, that government must take a proactive stance with respect to productivity and economic development; and, second, that the "Lewis model" of industrialization worked for some people. Dr Park was adamant that in Korea as in many East Asian countries, the state played a key role in both encouraging and regulating private-sector growth. Unlike in Jamaica and some other developing countries, those governments ensured that the state was linked to the development process instead of playing a spectator role.

The election of Bill Clinton in the USA shows that even in America, often seen as the quintessential free-market economy, Americans understand that the state must be at the centre of the development process. A cursory look at the Clinton-Gore manifesto shows that they sought to address virtually every aspect of American life. Americans believe in the market but they, like any sensible group of people, recognize that it is suicidal to ignore its limitations.

To suggest that there are limits to the market does not imply that one has to embrace any form of totalitarianism as an alternative. Experience has taught us that this would be a regressive step. However, what is an inescapable fact of life is that if there were no state, there would be more chaos than that which currently exists. What this suggests is that there should be mechanisms in place to ensure that any nation as a whole is not left to the whims and fancies of the powerful few or many. The more fundamental point, however, is that there is no way a nation can progress unless the state plays an integral role in the process. One cannot expect the private sector to provide infrastructure, such as education or health, for these are all public goods. It is not enough for a government to collect taxes and resolve disputes. It is not enough for the government to divest public services and then referee disputes between workers and managers. The government must define its role and the role of other sectors in the society to ensure collective responsibility and consistent action. At present, no one in this country seems sure where the government stands with respect to a development agenda. Hence, it is not clear where the other arms of the state fit into the development puzzle. From time to time, we hear the government saying that they will leave "it" to the private sector, while the private sector says that it needs more space to manoeuvre. I suspect part of the reason why many governments play it shy is that they have no clear vision for the future. Unlike the fairly optimistic period of the 1960s and 1970s, people are no longer clear about where the society should go. As a consequence, there is a tendency to fiddle around and fill up potholes rather than design new road systems, to speak metaphorically.

The word "govern" comes from the Greek verb kubernan which means "to steer". A government is fundamentally concerned with guiding a nation. This is a job not for a referee, but for a captain. When people elect leaders, they do so with the expectation that these leaders have a vision for the future. As the saying goes, where there is no vision, the people perish. Peace!

Ideology and development

(TUESDAY, JULY 6, 1993)

At various times in human history, societies have been faced with crises, some seemingly so unsolvable that cynicism and hopelessness have begun to reign. There have also been periods when solutions seem to be in abundance, when almost every developmental problem faced by people has a solution.

I want to suggest that in the post-World War II era, solutions to problems faced by developing countries were in abundance. From India to Ghana, the solution to economic "backwardness" was decolonization. But even in industrialized countries, there was also some optimism; in Europe, it was widely held by intellectuals and policymakers that one way to prevent national conflict and promote economic development was to form regional blocs. In one sense, this signalled, in theory, the end of narrow nationalism. Among the Soviet camp, the Council for Mutual Economic Assistance (COMECON) was formed in 1949; for those in the Western camp, there was the formation of the European Economic Community (EEC) in 1957.

For developing countries, there were, broadly speaking, two basic development options – capitalism or socialism/communism. (Those who wanted the best of both worlds opted for the hybrid of democratic socialism). These two basic options were pursued with vigour from blueprints, which were supplied to developing countries by either the USA or the USSR. Many developing countries opted for socialist regimes.

There was something very attractive about Marxist socialism. For one, it offered a way of conceptualizing reality; hence, diagnosing the problem was very easy. Furthermore, it supplied the answers to very complex problems – solutions which were attractive since they guaranteed "milk and honey" in the future. In many ways, Marxism appealed to the more idealistic among us. It appealed to many who wanted to see better come to our people; it appealed to our humanity.

For many leaders and intellectuals in developing countries, the strength of the Marxist analysis lay in its ability to make sense of their own reality. Oppressed by colonial powers and powerful elites for centuries, it made sense to conceptualize the basis of many of our national problems as being a function of the existence of social classes, or external imperialist domination, or both. We in the developing world were beginning to put our experiences in some clear ideological framework which could be easily articulated to the masses.

New order

But there was more. Across the world, there were examples of this thinking in practice. Cuba had started a new order and seemed to be doing well, and Julius Nyerere in Tanzania embarked on an optimistic path of African socialism. In many ways, socialism and its variants offered hope and optimism. More importantly, poor struggling nations just out of the clutches of the mother country were beginning to redefine their reality and begin a new day.

But there was a downside: in many ways Marxism-became tantamount to a religious dogma. Its strength was its very weakness; that is, it offered a solution to everything. Furthermore, many Marxist ideas were elitist and often brought out the most authoritarian tendencies among human beings. Another problem was that socialist thought, while recognizing the importance of production, instead emphasized distribution and consumption. In many ways, Marxist ideas were their own worst enemy.

Competing with Marxism and its variants, ranging from democratic socialism to African socialism, was capitalism. Advocates like Milton Friedman held the view that the free market was the only way in which economics could develop and maintain democracy. "Free to choose" was the basic idea governing this development option. Condemning socialism as totalitarian and counterproductive, the USA offered up itself as an alternative model of development. Unfortunately, many of those who became takers seemed to be either despots or sheer murderers. These were the Duvaliers and Mobutus, among others. Not that these people pursued free market policies – in most cases they did not. What the capitalist world was interested in was alliances to stamp out the encroachment of communism.

There is an important convergence between communism/socialism and capitalism. Both of them represent ways of thinking about the real world. Both offer solutions to problems. Both are ideologies. Ideology for many people is a "dirty" word, but in fact we cannot function seriously without ideologies. I mean, by ideology, a set of loosely or tightly held beliefs, attitudes and opinions. In this sense, a religion is an ideology. Pan-Africanism and regionalism are also ideologies. Ideologies not only help us to make sense of our reality, but they offer solutions to problems we encounter.

Since the fall of the Soviet bloc, Marxist ideology (as well as the many variants) has provoked serious criticism. Free-market capitalism has become the one viable way of structuring our world. But free-market capitalism has yet to deliver on its promises to a number of poor countries, particularly those undergoing structural adjustment like Jamaica.

You see, there is a certain tragedy with the way in which we have adopted free-market capitalism in our region. It is almost by default; there seemed to be no alternative. In many ways therefore, especially for our policymakers in Jamaica and across the region, "free-marketism" is not intuitive. The ideological conviction is not there; hence, apart from debt obligations, there is little consistency or clarity of thought and policy with respect to development along free-market lines. The fall of socialist ideas has led to a serious vacuum among many of our thinkers and policymakers. Obviously, those who seem to have less of a problem are those who have for a long time believed in the assumptions of the free market.

The fact that socialism has fallen into disrepute and free-market capitalism has not yet delivered is partly why piecemeal, uncoordinated policies are the order of the day. Human beings are in many ways creatures of ideologies. We need a way to make sense of our reality, so that we can offer up solution to our problems. The absence of such ideology at this point has left many of our intellectuals unsure about the legitimacy of many of our ideas, and plunged our policymakers into a conundrum.

No longer, for example, do we say with conviction that the cause of crime is inequality. In spite of the plethora of hurry-come-up "expert economists", none of us can speak with much certainty about the mighty dollar. People talk about productivity daily, but do not know how to deal with it. I submit that we have crossed the Rubicon in terms of developmental thought. Just look at the number of consultants we have in this country. They come from every continent, consulting on every matter, from the vaguely important to the trivial.

Groping in the dark

Some of these consultants are paraded on KLAS' The Breadfast Club, and are questioned as though they hold the solution to our problems. We are fast becoming like Tanzania, where UN consultants run the country, but yet the people are getting poorer. We have consultants who get rich from studying the poor. What an abomination! Suddenly, we seek a technical solution to problems of philosophy. Such occurrences are signs of a country groping in the dark.

I submit that part of the problem we face in this country, and indeed the region, stems from the fact that we have discarded many of our former assumptions about the "human spirit" and have not replaced them with anything viable. Hence, we are unsure why parts of our society have become "killing fields"; we are unsure why people do not work harder; and we are confounded by the gyrations of the "boom-boom-byes".

Our problem is not technical; it is philosophical. We need a vision. If there is to be a vision, there has to be an ideology upon which we can draw to make sense of our reality and offer solutions. Unfortunately, this vision is not only absent among our political leadership, but also among those who provide the theoretical basis for policy – our intelligentsia. How else would one explain the absence of a Department of Philosophy at The UWI? Peace!

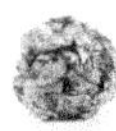

The past, present and future

(TUESDAY, NOVEMBER 9, 1993)

A recently concluded series of radio programmes centred on how Blacks were perceived by whites in ancient and modern times. The subject is not simply one of academic worth, but also one which has far-reaching implications for how people construct their lives in the present. The discussion indicated that "truth" is not a totally objective phenomenon, but is fundamentally a function of how people construct their reality. Furthermore, it was suggested that those who made this truth are often those who have the power to do so. In the case of Africa, European colonialism and the lack of a literate tradition in many

African societies allowed for the creation of stories which were far from the truth. Of course, much of the nonsense about simple-minded Africans running around in loincloths with spears persists even to today in cartoon series, such as Phantom, and in at least one children's television commercial. Such predatory programmes poison the minds of our young ones.

It is now time

I think that the time has come for us to stop looking at how people have viewed us. It is now time for us to start paying attention to how we view ourselves and others. By focusing on how Europeans saw Africans or other peoples, we run the risk of establishing the views of Europeans as the basis upon which we develop "truths" about others. However, by looking at both sides, we not only balance the picture, but we can also start to move away from the image of Black people as victims. This victim perspective is very negative and does not lead people to take greater responsibility for their action. The victim image is part of the ideological and philosophical crisis which now shrouds scholarship and politics among Blacks in America and among Blacks in the diaspora.

Of equal interest is the matter of relationships between Africa and non-European countries. Indeed, the much talked about South-South relations are nothing new. History will show that countries which are now called developing or underdeveloped were engaged in important economic relations in the past. From East Africa to China, and from Mali to Saudi Arabia, important trading routes were well established prior to the coming of the Europeans to Africa. Guyanese-born anthropologist Ivan Van Sertima and the distinguished British Africanist Basil Davidson have made references to the fact that there were even trading links between the Native Americans and Africans long before the voyage of the Niña, the Pinta and the Santa Maria.

Relevant

This information regarding the trading links between different parts of the world is relevant to the manner in which we construct our models of development and by extension how we define ourselves. Without this information, many of our theoreticians who ultimately influence our policymakers and commentators (whether they believe in the free market or a state-led economy) make assumptions about what was, and what is possible, from a position of misinformation or ignorance. For instance, the debate about the success of the "Asian Tigers" is always premised on the belief that the "correct" models for industrial progress are those of Europe and its protégé, Japan. Our problem is that we tend to confuse the process of industrial development with the country or the region in which it occurs; therefore, many people do not realize that it is possible for the process of industrial development to take place under different circumstances in other societies. By not making the distinction between the country and the process, we run the risk of seeing the consensus model of East Asia as an aberration from the European norm.

Differences overcome

Some time ago, US and European academics and policymakers criticized South-South cooperation because of perceived historical differences and the southern countries' low levels of economic progress. The truth of the matter is that many of these differences had been overcome and many of the current ones are superficial. Furthermore, because poor countries have been conditioned to see economic progress in terms of categories constructed by Western Europe, they tend to lose their creativity and vitality in the pursuit of economic cooperation.

The burgeoning trade between countries of the South should not now be seen as an aberration, nor

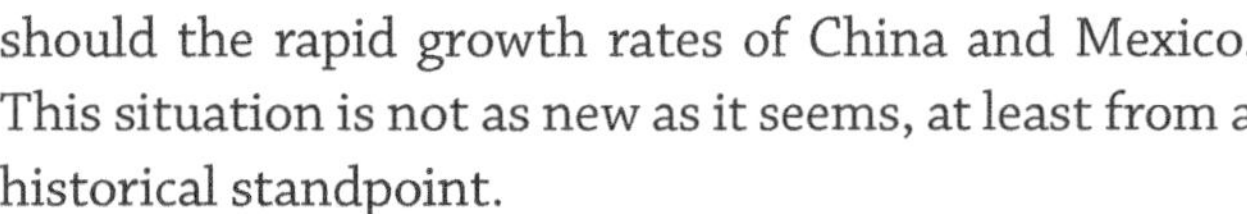

should the rapid growth rates of China and Mexico. This situation is not as new as it seems, at least from a historical standpoint.

I find the discussions about the various economic miracles a bit disturbing. Even more disturbing is the attempt to transpose models of development from one country to another. I know of no model of economic development drawn from the experiences of another country which has been successfully applied to other countries, as is. The reason is that economic development is about more than economics; it is about social, political and cultural syntheses, and many more issues which cannot be comfortably accommodated in economic theory. All the modes of economic development arise out of hindsight. No wonder development economics fell on hard times!

None convincing

Unlike some of our policymakers, I am not convinced by the notion of laws of economics, as obtains in physics. Not that I believe that such laws are not possible to arrive at; it is just that, at present, there is none that I find convincing. And if there is anything approaching such laws, there are too many assumptions for them to be truly practical in real life. If I am correct, then we need to take a hard look at our local structural adjustments programme, as well as the rhetoric spouted by our leading policymakers about economic development. In short, economic development, like any definition of ourselves, has to be a hybrid and not a mere transplant. Peace!

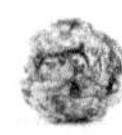

A budget without vision

(TUESDAY, MAY 3, 1994)

To make a poor country richer is not easy.... It doesn't take much to start an ambitious program of development projects on a foundation of foreign loans and hope. Until the day of reckoning, the process may even be exhilarating.... Those whose only goal is a balanced budget also take an easy path. Their task is to balance interests in society so that nothing much happens.

— NAOMI CAIDEN & AARON WILDAVSKY (1990)

Last week, the new Minister of Finance Dr Omar Davies delivered an interesting budget speech. It was charged with a great deal of enthusiasm, confidence and passion – a rarity in Gordon House these days. And, thus, it was within this framework that Dr Davies attempted to persuade the nation that his presentation was aimed at promoting growth with equity. Now, there were some who expected the government to launch its usual tax crusade under the guise of a budget, but they were able to heave a sigh of relief after the minister's presentation. Consequently, and with few exceptions, the commentators concluded, it was a good budget.

Expected

But what they really meant was that it was a good budget, given what they had expected. In my view, this budget manifested a slight shift away from the sterile and oppressive budget of last year. Nonetheless, the presentation was aimed more at placating and appropriating, rather than at seriously stimulating growth while producing equity.

There were high praises for the following proposals:

the concessions to operators of small businesses and to low-income earners; the increase in the sum paid to pensioners; the increase in the minimum wage; and the government's intention to improve the tax system in order to net more revenue.

Yet, despite these apparent advances, the budget was really the government's attempt to rescue its plummeting popularity from an increasingly dissatisfied society. And in attempting to accomplish this objective, the government avoided its usual harsh methods of exacting tribute from its workers. This time, they cleverly shifted money from one group to another.

The increases in pensions and wages were made at the expense of PAYE workers who still have to purchase gasoline, which now attracts a new tax. Furthermore, the small concessions which were made to low-income earners, pensioners and small business operators were responses to the pressure placed on the government by various interest groups, including the media. These increases and concessions were long overdue, given the current level of inflation in the country and the need to stimulate investment. Also, we await the concrete improvements in the tax system, given the high levels of inefficiency in the public sector. Now, the government did not increase the GCT because of the massive inflows into the government treasury in previous years; plus, an increase could well have prompted a tax revolt.

Assumptions

One of the heroic assumptions being made about the present budget is that there will be little change in the value of the dollar during the new financial year. But unless something dramatic happens in the manufacturing and agriculture sectors, there is very little chance that the dollar will retain its current value.

However, my most serious concerns with this budget are that it does not provide us with a vision of where Dr Davies expects the country to go, nor does it articulate a clear philosophy which will guide the country's development. It seems to me that an attempt was being made to have the numbers add up – after 50 per cent of our money was set aside for debt repayment. In the same breath, the issues of transportation, roads, education, health or crime were not addressed, even though they certainly relate to growth and equity. How then can we seriously say the budget is geared towards growth with equity?

It is nothing short of a joke to reduce equity to merely moving tax thresholds – which by the way are still way below our inflation rate. You see, the problem with equity in this country has more to do with the creation and maintenance of wealth rather than with redistribution.

Morality, vision and progress

(TUESDAY, NOVEMBER 1, 1994)

A few months ago, I had the unfortunate experience of taking a few friends to the St Ann Parish Hospital for emergency medical attention. Although I was concerned about the lack of medical personnel and the corresponding lack of attention for my friends, I could not help noticing that we were in an environment where suffering was the norm.

On the hospital premises were a set of dilapidated buildings and a number of men and women who were patiently waiting for medical attention. One could see the agony on their faces as they waited to see the one doctor who was on duty. Incidentally, I was told that the other doctor who was on duty was on a break, probably trying to recuperate from overwork.

Outside, on the veranda of one of the seemingly abandoned buildings sat an elderly man. As he rocked back and forth in an old chair he murmured, "Things can't go on like this." He repeated these words about five times and then he gave a somewhat puzzling grin – as if he was laughing at his tolerance and that of those around him who were waiting to see the physician.

Trance

Drawn by this man who now appeared to be in a trance, I went over and spoke with him. I sat on a step next to him and tried to strike up a conversation. I learned that he was 72 years old and had journeyed six miles in order to take a relative to see the doctor. He had been there at the hospital since 5 p.m. – it was then close to midnight. This old man was not really in a talking mood, but nonetheless I coaxed him on. I discovered that he was a labourer who had spent nearly his entire life helping to feed our country. Yet he had little to show for his sweat and hard work. He talked about the difficulty of making ends meet and the virtual impossibility of people like him owning a decent home.

Moved

Interestingly, at no point in our conversation did he blame anyone for his problems. He seemed more concerned about where he had gone wrong. He felt that if a man worked hard all of his life and contributed to his society – so that other people could benefit – he should not have to suffer in his old age. I was moved by the testimony of this old man. Moved, because when I looked at the faces of those waiting to see the doctor, I could see them asking the very same question.

I remember this occurrence well, because two days later I heard a discussion on the radio about the state of the economy. I was struck by the speaker who said that the market forces would soon work things out in the housing market. I thought to myself: if there are persons in the top 20 per cent of income earners who find it difficult to own a house, how then is it possible for this old man to own one? I began to wonder, who are the people purchasing the houses in this country? How can the social fabric of our society not tear apart when people who have worked so hard all their lives cannot afford to buy a house? How can this fabric not tear apart when real estate is basically another way of redistributing income from the have-nots to the haves?

One colleague of mine has dismissed this type of reasoning as a misunderstanding of the market and said that we should not make economic decisions based on what we believe ought to be. My own view is that we are in danger of making the market into a fetish. We will continue to fool ourselves if we believe that the reason why the country is facing its current economic crisis is that market forces are not working properly. The notion that we will, somehow, solve our present social and economic malaise by simply depending on the objectivity of economic forces is to my mind extremely facile, if not dangerous. Economic theory cannot be used to justify the crazy housing situation facing our society.

Economist Samuel Weston argues that "[I]t is not so easy to argue past the point that giving policy advice almost inevitably means asserting one's own values" (Weston, 1998, p. 40). This is because economic and other social scientific theories merely provide developmental options – policymakers choose which ones they wish to pursue. The decision to choose a path of development is basically an investment in someone's vision of what ought to be. Therefore, policymaking is more about what ought to be than what is. Determining what ought to be is a moral issue. To quote Weston again: "... an economist who would tell us, explicitly or implicitly, what is ethically desirable for society may have no more formal preparation for that role than the guy who pontificates at the corner saloon".

Priority

There are many negative and positive effects of a country subsidising agriculture, yet some governments do it and others do not. Despite harsh economic circumstances, countries such as Cuba and Barbados have resisted moving away from free universal education. In the United States, the government continues to pump money into space research, even though many critics claim that the money could be better spent. In all of these cases, policy decisions were based on what policymakers felt ought to be given priority.

Not too long ago, before the emergence of Japan as an industrial power, Western scholars felt that their way was the only way to achieve industrial development. For me, the lesson about industrialization in East Asia is fundamentally about making choices based on some idea about what the future should be. Japan began its industrial revolution by following Western technology and industry; but the government also saw fit to institutionalize universal education – something which the Western nations did not pursue, despite their more advanced industrial development at the time. In other words, while the Japanese did not ignore certain objective realities of industrial development, they made choices which were based on a vision which they had of the future. Put another way, they were guided by a particular type of moral conviction which has in turn guided their progress.

What is the point of all that I have just said, and more so its relevance to the old man I encountered at the hospital? It seems to me that part of our problem is the lack of moral conviction about what ought to be, especially in the minds of many of our experts and policymakers. The disappointments of the 1970s seem to have turned us into people who no longer care about what is right and wrong, or what is desirable and what is not. We have educated ourselves in enough jargon to justify the abominable housing conditions in our country and the swelling ranks of homeless children and beggars in our streets. Too many of us have surrendered our intuition and common sense to very inhumane and frighteningly pragmatic notions of development. People have suddenly become dispensable in the name of achieving macroeconomic stability, and in fulfilling the other fetishes we have created. Yet we continue to wonder why the social fabric is tearing.

Economic and political analyses will help to provide options for us, but in the final analysis, we have to make our own choices. Very often, experts or policymakers speak without being convincing. This is partly because they have not convinced themselves, nor have they developed any serious moral commitment to their particular positions. In an environment where there is moral bankruptcy, there can be no clear vision of the future. Consequently, policymaking will remain piecemeal and chaotic, and people will be easily swayed by nice-sounding arguments, no matter how dangerous.

When most of us think of great leaders, we think of those who have been able to inspire their people into helping to transform their societies. We think of people who had clear thoughts about what ought to be. We think of people whose lives revolved around a set of morals which were the bases for determining a vision for the future. What we need is consensus about where we believe our nation should be heading. And not just in economic terms, but more importantly as part of a larger human family, as people with desires which transcend the immediate material achievements. For what then is the value of discussing what is, if we do not know how to use it to inform and work for what ought to be? Peace!

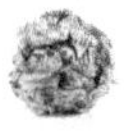

The budget and cricket

(TUESDAY, MAY 9, 1995)

While the West Indies cricket team was about to receive a crushing defeat at the hands of the Australians, Prime Minister P. J. Patterson was making his budget presentation to the nation. Arguably, it was one of his finest presentations and Mr Patterson jokingly appealed to the elements on the West Indies' behalf, but fate was unresponsive and nature unmoved, and thus the better team won the match. The lesson from the Australians to us as West Indians was that success demands hard work, dedication, discipline and, above all, a vision.

While there were elements of all of those factors in Mr Patterson's budget, not unlike West Indies cricket, the government's policies seem to lack a clear vision.

Budget

For the record, I thought that there was much to be pleased about in the budget presentations of both Mr Patterson and Minister Davies; and from all indications, it seems as if Dr Davies has turned out to be a great asset to the government. I am also encouraged by the acknowledgement – belated though it is – by the prime minister of the centrality of efficient government to the development process. And, hence, the recent budget signalled the intention of the government to move away from the naive notion that if they free up everything then Jamaica will grow. Specifically, I am encouraged by the recognition that there is a need to improve infrastructure, particularly roads. However, I am still a bit hesitant on the question of incentives for the private sector, since I have always been perplexed by the mindset of some of our traditional private sector professionals.

Despite the foregoing, I am not sure that there was a cohesive policy framework within which the presentation was made.

To me, it is foolhardy to have a programme of repairing roads in the Corporate Area unless it is part of an urban development plan. Concomitantly, an urban development plan without a transportation plan is bound to lead to disaster. As such, it continues to amaze me that the government continues to treat transportation as another problem to be solved rather than as an essential conduit in its industrial development process. After all, an intense cerebral exercise is not necessary to recognize that it is virtually impossible to have an efficient and effective public transportation service that is entirely privately operated. This is more so in a country which has high population densities in its urban areas and where the majority of workers – often from these areas – earn relatively low wages. The experiences of every industrialized country and of most of the newly industrialized countries show that governments are intimately involved in the provision of public transportation. These governments rightly acknowledge the relationship between transportation and production. Consequently, there is no reason why commuters should be made to suffer the indignities of our public transportation because it is easier and trendy for the government to pass the matter on to a private sector company whose primary interest is to turn a profit, rather than provide a good service.

It is also with a sense of unease that I noticed that Mr Patterson's references to human resource development and tourism were not clearly woven into the fabric of general national development. Instead, we got a piecemeal presentation of a collection of important policy issues. The government should have linked the issue of transportation with tourism and human resource development in a more direct and definitive way. Are these issues as disparate as they appear? Does it make sense to simply widen a congested road, when this could lead to even more chaos in an area where in two years there will be a major shopping centre? Would it not be better to (re)construct better and new highways over a ten-year period in anticipation of the projected growth in population and industry? Should we not be more than concerned with long-term infrastructural development, rather than the "pitchy patchy" projects which are aimed at filling gaps rather than expanding opportunities?

It seems to me that it is precisely in the area of long-term planning that we seem to fall down most, and this is true for our politics and our cricket. In the case of the latter, a number of people in the region have been calling for a more structured approach to its administration. This would involve the development of the game and players before, during and after they represent our region. As such, many writers across the region have argued, quiet convincingly, that our success in cricket is due primarily to our talent, skill and enthusiasm for the game.

Undoubtedly, the People's National Party has within its ranks many talented, skilful and enthusiastic politicians. As with the politicians, many of our cricketing administrators seem to have a strange aversion to long-term planning and to the viewing of things in their totality. I fear that Mr Patterson's outstanding budget presentation could well fall victim to such an unenlightened posture. Peace!

Public and private interests

(TUESDAY, NOVEMBER 5, 1996)

It appears that the confusion in our society, as we continue to struggle with the notion of what must be done in the public's interest and what must be done in the private individuals' interests, will be with us for a very long time.

As part of the developmental strategy in the 1970s, there appeared to be the tendency for the government and sections of the intelligentsia to emphasize public concerns over those of the individual.

There were good reasons for this: since Jamaica, like most of the postcolonial states in the developing world, had to find ways to improve the lot of the mass of expectant and dispossessed people. Second, socialist ideas which gained currency during this period emphasized public interest over individual ones. As such, Jamaica's experience with socialism during the 1970s was certainly not unique; almost all postcolonial states, from Asia to Latin America, adopted some version of socialism to deal with the present problems of underdevelopment.

Thus, the argument that socialism is responsible for the current economic difficulties faced by our society is not only facile, but also of very little analytical use. One would indeed have to account for why other societies like India and Indonesia have done considerably better, economically, than Jamaica, even though they adopted many aspects of the socialist model of development, which in many cases were not dissimilar to those chosen by Jamaica. But I digress.

Individual needs

During the 1980s, we witnessed a shift away from an emphasis on the public good to the good of the individual. This was done partly out of necessity, and partly because of a shifting global ideology consistent with the market model, which puts forward the idea that society is an aggregation of individuals. This philosophy assumes that to satisfy the needs of the community in, say, housing and education, we simply have to address individual needs. Here is where I part company with this type of economic reasoning. The fact of the matter is that government policy cannot be premised simply on individual preferences. You see, public policy should respect and accommodate individuals, but cannot and must not be dictated solely by them. Thus, government policy has to be premised on some notion of the public interest, which may or may not be reconciled with those of each individual.

Illegal fires

Now, it seems to me that it is precisely this inability to distinguish between private and public interests that is at the heart of much of the chaos which we see around us daily. This wanton disregard for public concerns by individuals is demonstrated by the numerous illegal fires started by decent middle-class people as they try to get rid of their garbage, even though garbage disposal services are available. The fact that these fires affect the neighbours next door is of little consequence to those who wish to burn their rubbish in their yards in order to clean their premises. Interestingly, far too often those who are affected by the billowing clouds of smoke refuse to take action against the perpetrators of this grossly unhealthy practices, because they themselves do not have a sense of public rights. More alarming is the fact that many people have begun to accept this type of individual indiscretion as normal, especially since they too will soon have their opportunity, at a later date, to exercise their own inconsiderate will of "smoking out" other people.

Take another example: this is an example of the bus owners who decorate their buses with pictures, paintings and slogans which are not only offensive to many adult commuters, but are also inconsistent with the values which many parents, teachers, commentators and policymakers try to teach our children on a daily basis. One gets the impression that bus owners, like so many in the private sector, are unable to recognize that they provide a public good and thus should be sensitive to public tastes. But there is also the other side to this picture, which is that commuters are so thankful to get a ride on the bus that they are willing to put up with these "minor" offences. And, so, the crisis in public transportation has now led to a situation in which both bus owners and members of the public have begun to accept this inappropriate bus graffiti and the emotional assault as normal.

More to the point is the collusion of some commuters with bus and taxi drivers in their reckless driving on the roads. Many commuters see no problem with bus and taxi drivers "bad driving" other motorists, since this allows them, the commuters, to reach their destination on time. They would put it this way: "It does not matter what happens to other motorists; as long as I reach my destination on time, more power to the driver."

Another example of this confusion between public and private interests is reflected in the outrageous exchange rates charged to tourists and local customers by business people in tourism areas such as Ocho Rios and Montego Bay. In some shops in Ocho Rios, tourists are charged the equivalent of J$40 to one US dollar when they wish to buy items in Jamaican dollars.

Of course, when these tourists discover the level of theft which takes place in these businesses, they paint the business sector in the country as being corrupt and chaotic. Indeed, those business people who charge outrageous prices simply see their actions as a clever way to make money. For, as far as they are concerned, who cares if the ignorant tourists spend their money elsewhere – that is, if he even returns to this country – and who cares about the idea of a business person who has a responsibility to the larger public.

Implicit in all that I have said so far is that many of the problems which we see in our society today cannot be blamed on any single group of people, even though some people certainly share greater responsibility than others. If the politicians have been able to divide and rule, it is perhaps because, in the minds of many of us, the notion of community is expendable. In other words, we have not taken steps to make our leaders accountable to the public at large, because the concept of community is not important to us, particularly to the elite. Consequently, it is not the politicians who will change this society, but organized people, civil society, the community.

Privatization bug

To be sure, the current social crisis is exacerbated by the fact that we have unleashed a privatization bug in an environment where the sense of community or public interest has been eroded. Thus, how do we seek greater accountability for the community when the very notion of community itself has been subverted by emphasis on private interests. Increased private interests can only be a good thing if steps are taken to protect the public from the excesses of those very private interests.

What we have in Jamaica over the last decade and a half is a growth in private interests and a decline in the importance of community and public interest. It is the fallout from this process which in my view partially accounts for the chaos around us. Therefore, what we need is a rebirth of community, of collective conscience, of civil society that cuts across class and colour. If you think carefully, it really does take a village to raise a child. Peace!

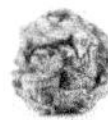

That World Bank report

(TUESDAY, JULY 29, 1997)

State spending now constitutes almost half of total income in the established industrial countries, and around a quarter in developing countries.

— *WORLD DEVELOPMENT REPORT* (1997: 2)

I must admit that I have become sceptical about reports written by international agencies which claim to speak about world development. Therefore, my views regarding the recently published World Development Report are no exception. You see, not so long ago, the World Bank, IMF and other leading institutions began raging about sustainable development; this after they had colluded with governments and business people across the world to wreck the ecological structure of the earth. But having finally recognized, after countless years of lobbying by environmentalists, non-governmental organizations and ordinary citizens, that unbridled economic planning was not the end all to modern civilization, and that it was not truly sustainable, they have reluctantly accepted the proposition that something must be done about this untenable situation.

Omniscient ones

After groups of consultants and academics were commissioned by some UN agencies and other bodies to conduct a series of studies on the impact of economic reforms on the environment, many of the World Bank's omniscient officials are now going around to developing countries telling the people and non-governmental organizations how the "new" development model should be implemented. Interestingly, in recent times, they have switched their attention to the issue of governance and the role of the state in development. Presumably, in a few years, the omniscient ones will be again telling us what we have known for years, and indeed should have been doing all along.

But, back to that very momentous report. I am less struck by a seeming change in the bank's disposition towards the role of the state, than I am by the lack of clarity which it evidences. Also, I sometimes get the impression that here is an attempt to salvage a development philosophy which contributed to the crude economism of the 1980s which had decimated societies across the world.

The report states that "an effective state is vital for the provision of goods and services... Without it, sustainable development, both economic and social, is impossible. Many said much the same thing fifty years ago, but then they tended to mean that development had to be state-provided. The message of experience since then is rather different: that the state is rather central to economic and social development, not as a direct provider of growth but as partner, catalyst, and facilitator" (*World Development Report,* 1997, 1).

I am not sure what is meant here by the use of the terms "catalyst", "facilitator", and "partner". These terms appear to conceal more than they reveal. For instance, is a state which "owns" a subsidized transportation system or housing scheme a provider or facilitator? And, if this state is being defined as a provider, how can it be defined as being ineffective, if it provides good service to the populace?

Equally, the report admits that "[w]hat makes for an effective state differs enormously across countries at different stages of [each country's] development." Even with their admission of the existence of enormous differences, the report flatly rejects the state as provider. Presumably, at no stage can a state be effective if it acts as a provider of growth. What then of the Chinese state and the older states in many parts of Asia? Are we therefore saying that the state is inherently incapable of providing development?

I raise these questions not because I hold a brief for state-led development, but rather because, given our experience in this region, it is imperative that civil society be more actively involved in the development process. You see, I am concerned with these questions because as citizens, especially in developing countries, we continue to allow institutions like the World Bank to dictate our development discourse far too much.

Unfortunately, oftentimes, policy documents of lending agencies are authored by young upwardly mobile men who have spent the better part of their lives in the artificial environment of an Ivy League university. Their research, therefore, ignores the essential contact with real people. Consequently, as we look back at research done on this issue of the state, one would find countless reports written by academics from our region and other developing nations which raise the very same issues as does this bank's report. But legitimacy of our ideas comes only after they have been published in some international document.

In fact, I can personally testify to observing confrontations with officials from the World Bank, other lending institutions, local academics and policymakers on the role of the state during the mid-1980s. I have participated in several international meetings where representatives from developing nations were ignored or mocked because questions were raised about the dogmatic manner in which issues relating to the role of the state and poverty were dealt with. At some of these meetings, talking about the vulnerable and about social capital (a crude term used by economists to integrate aspects of human society in economic models) was considered to be part of a socialist agenda not suitable for the so-called cutting-edge discussions on development.

If we look at this debate about the state from a historical standpoint, we will see that all of the countries which have achieved high levels of economic development have done so under a strong state. The minimalist state advocated by the IMF during the '70s and '80s took hold only in rhetoric in industrialized countries. Even after the Thatcher and Reagan (so-called) revolutions, the states in both the UK and the USA played a far more important (some say intrusive) role in those societies than in most of the developing nations which were significant participants in the structural adjustment programmes. This may come as a surprise to many, but if one looks beyond the rhetoric of socialism in the 1970s to the actual policies, one will find that the development process in, say, Barbados was, and continues to be, more state-directed than in Jamaica.

The World Development Report does not represent a fundamental shift in the thinking of the World Bank, but it represents a belated attempt to deal with the very difficult and complex aspect of development. For this, the bank is to be credited; but then they have a responsibility to help repair the global social decay that they have helped to engineer. Peace!

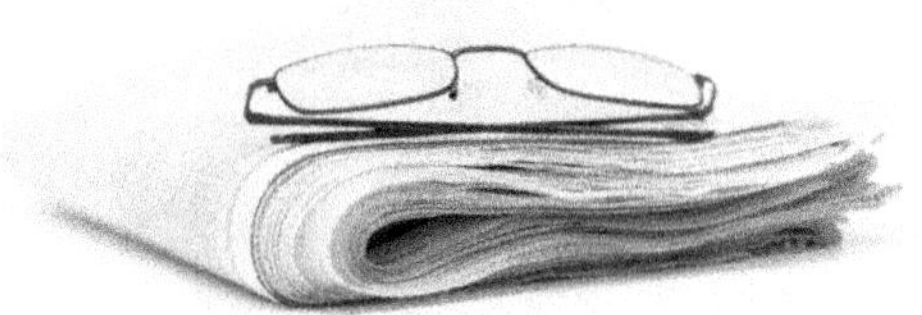

SUBSECTION B

Economic Development in Jamaica and the Caribbean

Introduction

As a follow-up to the previous section, this section explores the models of development outlined by development agencies as well as countries of the developed north. In addition, the articles in this section examine trade and economic relations between countries of the South. Also explored are factors which contribute to growth and development among countries of the developing South. Emphasis is placed on the history of South-South trade and economic relations in an attempt to provide readers with a new perspective on the economies of India and China and on their rapid growth rates, and also on the burgeoning trade between many countries of the South. The author notes that development within and among countries of the developing South will be dependent on the extent to which these countries embrace existing technological advances, in a sustainable way.

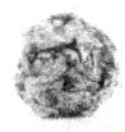

Chapter 12 Development Models

- ➢ Theories and reality
- ➢ The muddle of models
- ➢ The question of development
- ➢ A new development model
- ➢ Opportunism and the Asian saga

Introduction

Articles in this chapter warn against any wholesale attempt to "transpose" models of development – regardless of their origin – from one country to another. This chapter adopts the view that "economic development" has to be a hybrid and not a mere "transplant" as it is "about more than economics; it is about social, political and cultural syntheses, and many more issues which cannot be comfortably accommodated in economic [or social] theory" ("The past, present and future", p. 158, this volume). "The muddle of models", "The question of development", "Theories and reality" and "Opportunism and the Asian saga" (pp. 173-181, this chapter), are all variations on this theme. Sections of this chapter encourage countries of the developing South, in particular, to preserve their natural environment ("A new development model", p. 177, this chapter) in their pursuit of economic development. They are encouraged to adopt sustainable development practices.

Theories and reality

(TUESDAY, DECEMBER 21, 1993)

I swear, the next time I hear a discussion on the economy by technocrats and policymakers, I shall either vomit or have a massive seizure. These highly prescriptive discussions have now become a bit too predictable: reduce liquidity, bring down inflation, and exports will increase, and so on and so forth. Why is there this compulsion to tinker with these most nebulous things in an economy where one does not know how much money enters and how much leaves? Why is it that technocrats and policymakers continue to focus simply on stabilizing something called a dollar in order to bring about economic development?

I ask humbly (well, almost) what is a dollar? What the heck does it represent? If the value of the dollar is linked to our capacity to export and earn foreign exchange, what is the use of continually tinkering with the interest rates, liquidity, and all of the other things which now serve to obscure rather than to elucidate the situation? Let me suggest a part of the reason, for what it is worth: policymakers and technocrats have made abstractions into reality and turned paradigms into truth. They are victims of "formal scholarship".

Recently, I had the rare opportunity of listening to a lecture delivered by one of the world's leading development economists, Gerald Meier. Professor Meier, clearly an extremely able man, and one sympathetic to the plight of the suffering South, gave an interesting talk on development in the South and the problems which the discipline of development economics now confronts. Now, I thought this was an incredibly creative way of saying: "Well, we 'tried a thing' in the past, but we now realize that we need to know more about our people if we are going to 'try another thing', since we can help only when we know enough about what makes them tick."

Economic transformation

To say it is this policy or that policy which should be adopted to bring about economic transformation is not good enough. This is saying to me that there are limits to the rationality of the economic theory which we hear spouted by the plethora of MBAs on the talk shows. It also says that the attempt to extrapolate from the experiences of others to our own context must be done with the utmost caution. There are no immutable laws of economics that I know of, and for that reason, when we think of policy prescriptions, we must be sensitive to our situation, and with this knowledge we can then go on to "try a thing" from there. What is our situation?

At a seminar some time ago, a former central bank governor of Barbados said that he paid close attention to what people were saying on the streets rather than relying on official statistics to make policy. Some people sniggered. I think he was making sense. In a small country, one can afford to do this, and more often than not this approach may be more rewarding than relying on a set of impotent numbers. Barbados does not have much of an informal sector like Jamaica. In Jamaica, virtually everyone is in both the informal and formal sectors. Large department stores buy from informal commercial importers, and some workers engage in pilferage. There is no section of the society which does not occasionally pilfer something from someone.

Agricultural products

When I was young, my family had a small business. My mother retailed goods, while my father produced a wide variety of agricultural products commercially. What was interesting was that my father had more discretion in determining prices and profit margins than my mother, for her prices were not only determined by demand, but by the production function of companies which produced the items. Thus, the more efficient and creative my father was in producing, the more profitable the business – as long as there was a market. Furthermore, by producing, he was adding not only to the wealth of the household, but also to the wealth of the nation. The most my mother could have done to compete with my father – which she did not, bless her heart! – was to sell fewer goods for the same money or engage in propaganda (commonly called advertising).

Now, we have in Jamaica and much of the Caribbean an extremely large and powerful section of the economy tied up with my mother's side of the business (reselling foreign goods) – except that the players are less scrupulous than my mother, for she was one of the few Christians who took their Christianity seriously. These less than scrupulous people shuffle their money in and out of the country, and they are shrewd at it. Except for the fact that some earn interest through speculation and give loans for investment – I might add at some of the most usurious interest rates – all that is really happening is the passing of money from one set of people to another. No new wealth is being created, not one iota. I remember earlier this year hearing the stock market gurus arguing that the market reflected what is happening in firms: well, should we not now be seeing the large-scale closure of firms island-wide? Why is this not the case?

I do not wish to cast moral stones at those who seek to make a quick buck, nor at those who wish to milk their fellow man dry. After all, swindling each other is what capitalism is about: better yet if you enjoy it. Even the beggars are becoming crafty at making up stories to swindle a few more pieces of the paper we call dollars. The fact is that business people will put their money where the grass is greenest, especially in the short run. Thus, unless there is a radical policy shift away from the mundane talk of dollar stabilization and tight liquidity to the introduction of incentives for greater productivity in the economy, nothing will save us. For we will continue to face the outrageous cost of food, the massively overvalued real estate, the outlandish mortgages and ridiculous interest rates. Let us begin to listen! Peace!

The muddle of models

(TUESDAY, APRIL 19, 1994)

For some time now, many of our policymakers, commentators and academics have been discussing models of development which seem to lead us to very few convincing policy options with which we can effectively work. There have been mass media discussions about the South Korean model, the Costa Rican model, the Mexican model, the Chinese model, and why they succeeded. To be honest, the only model which seems to make sense to me is the Pulse model.

The debate about models of development begs the following questions: first, if there is something so universal about these models, why is it that we find it so difficult to adopt them? Second, if there is something so universal about these models, why is it that there are so many? Or is it that whenever a country or a region becomes economically successful, a new model is created? Note, all of these models are hindsight constructs. Twenty years from now, we may be talking about a Jamaican model or a Nigerian model or an Ethiopian model. By having a plethora of models, are we not implicitly accepting that much of what is termed economic behaviour is "culturally" relative, and hence particular and peculiar?

We have heard the argument that the problem is not the absence of common characteristics among these models, nor is it that there are no common features which we can draw upon and use in our reality, but that the political system prevents the implementation – which is pointless in the development debate. How then does one end up in this bind? You see, to abstract the political and cultural practices from the "laws of economic development" is to promulgate the view that economic behaviour can be separated from political and cultural behaviour. But when is an act purely economic, political or cultural? In my view, there can be no incontestable, empirical answer to this question.

Therefore, the problem – if you agree with my line of reasoning – is that these well touted models do not adequately reflect an understanding of human behaviour, and hence the claim of universalism becomes groundless. You see, most of our models which seek to predict behaviour of any sort are limited by what we understand, or do not understand, about human behaviour in the first place.

An example

Let me give you an example. Before the last US presidential election, I watched the economic and political analysts on television and was intrigued as they spoke about the state of the US economy. But what I found most intriguing was how these analysts used their models and a set of coefficients to determine whether or not the economy was growing, and to what extent such growth would lead to a Republican victory. In fact, one analyst constructed a model which he used to predict the reelection of George Bush. He was so convinced about his numbers that he appeared on television to defend his model. I do not think the public takes him seriously anymore. In my view, what appeared to be the problem with these analyses of the economy and electoral behaviour was that an analysis of behaviour was not well articulated nor indeed understood.

This particular analyst – through his analysis – dealt with the deficit and inflation in the most abstract terms, in much the same way that we speak about the dollar in our country. The analyst was captivated by the two per cent growth rates, although people were losing their jobs and there was a feeling that George Bush had no clear vision for the country. I do not think commentators in this part of the world will make such a mistake, given that we are not in a position to abstract ourselves from the everyday reality. Let me make it clear: I am not suggesting that we all become relativists, for this will not get us anywhere.

Modest claims

However, we are forced to be modest in our claims of universalism with respect to economic behaviour, given our experience so far. Staying the course as per our present experiences in Jamaica may make sense in Germany or England or even St Kitts, but the peculiarities of the Jamaican scenario makes it questionable.

Unfortunately, too many of our theories of economic progress start with assumptions which we do not critically examine. And, therefore, we have policymakers operating within an alien historical framework which they do not question. If our models are based on the historical experiences of others, what kind of successes can we expect? Much of what is often termed scientific truth is a function of political agendas, which can only be understood within the context of history. We only have to think about some of the debates on genetics and medicine which have been influenced more by social circumstances than by scientific rigour.

If we have been passed down theories which derive truths from other people's experiences – experiences which often impinge upon our own – are we not inhibiting ourselves when we use these theories? Let me make it clear again that I am not denying the fact that all societies share certain things in common, or that we should learn from other people's experiences. The more important issue is determining points of divergence – a very difficult task.

In the 1960s when development economics was popular, we in the so-called Third World internalized a number of theories which had little to do with our experience. To a large degree, modernization theory has its roots in the racist philosophy of colonialism.

Notion of progress

For you see, thinkers such as Marx and Weber thought very little of the development experiences of non-White peoples. Their notions of progress led to linear and narrow views of development which resulted in a number of present-day experiments which have subsequently destroyed the economies of many developing countries.

Thus, when we have a South Korea or Hong Kong which achieves economic growth, we treat them as anomalies, instead of legitimate processes which have in them the normal characteristic, as did the British Industrial Revolution or the period of American industrialism.

There is a lot that Jamaica shares in common with the world, but there is much that is unique about this country. The sooner we understand this, the less inclined we will be to fish around for somebody else's model of development when the solution requires a comprehension of ourselves. Peace!

The question of development

(TUESDAY, JUNE 7, 1994)

Last week, I listened to Wilmot Perkins on his call-in radio programme as he discussed the issue of development and its relationship to the urban-rural ratio. In sum, he argued that the societies which have developed significantly have the majority of their population concentrated in the cities, while a smaller group remained in the rural areas and focused on agriculture. This is partially because the mechanization of agriculture had released the majority of the population to become wage labourers in the cities. The cities were where the industries were present. Implicit in Mr Perkins' comments was the suggestion that such was the direction Jamaica should follow – if it is to develop.

The observation made by Mr Perkins, though important, is not new. Historians and political economists, including Karl Marx and Max Weber, have often pointed to the British Industrial Revolution as an example of this urban bias in terms of population distribution. W. Arthur Lewis won the Nobel Memorial Prize in Economic Sciences for putting forward a model of development which suggested that industries should be developed to absorb the large labour force in the region which could not find optimum employment in the agricultural sector. In general, this view continues to be the orthodoxy for social science theories on development the world over.

With that being said, let me issue an important caveat. While the evidence largely supports the view that developed countries have larger populations in the cities, we must see this phenomenon as a consequence of the development process and not as the cause. And even with this caveat, we have to be very careful, since there are numerous exceptions to this pattern.

Portugal, which has six times the per capita income of Jamaica, has 30 per cent of its population concentrated in cities, and has a significant proportion of its population in the rural or semi-rural areas. Note, also, that the distribution of the rural and urban populations differs significantly among the world's fastest growing economies in East Asia. For instance, the urban/suburban populations of these economies are as follows: Taiwan 71 per cent, Singapore 100 per cent, Thailand 18 per cent, Hong Kong 93 per cent,

Malaysia 35 per cent, Indonesia 26 per cent and China 41 per cent. And among the Organisation for Economic Co-operation and Development (OECD) countries, there are important differences in the size of the urban/suburban population: for example, Italy has 72 per cent, the USA 73 per cent, Switzerland 60 per cent, an urban-rural ratio of almost 50%, which makes its population distribution closer to that of the developed countries than to the developing countries. By contrast, Haiti, the poorest country in the Western Hemisphere, has a similar urban-rural ratio to Indonesia, while poverty-stricken Nicaragua has an urban-rural ratio not very different from that of Switzerland.

Now, the relative contribution of agriculture and industry to the Gross National Product (GNP) varies both among the Newly Industrialized Countries (NICs) and the already industrialized countries. As this table shows, Jamaica is no different from these countries in terms of the sectors and their contribution to the GNP.

Country	% GNP Agriculture	% GNP Industry	% GNP Service
Mexico	9	39	5
Indonesia	26	31	4
Singapore	1	35	6
Thailand	17	31	5
Trinidad	3	42	5
Taiwan	6	52	4
Japan	3	44	5
Jamaica	6	54	4
USA	2	30	6

These figures show that the basic structure of the Jamaican economy, in terms of the contribution of the different sectors to the GNP, is not significantly different from the developed or the leading developing economies in the world.

Developmental conundrum

It seems to me, therefore, that the question about the direction in which our country should move rests with our level of productivity and the extent to which value is added to a commodity for sale, and should not rest with the relative distribution of populations in our urban and rural areas. You see, Jamaica's rural population is not very large, even by a developed country's standard, and if we encourage large city populations in this society without providing adequate infrastructure and jobs, then we will be heading for a developmental conundrum – Nigeria and Brazil are clear examples. While the mechanization of agriculture in most cases increases productivity, it does not always address effectively the issue of development; and at any rate, large scale mechanization is not the only way to proceed in the short run.

The Chinese, under the reformed leadership of Deng Xiaoping, managed to increase national output manifold by returning farms to families and by making modest improvements to their agricultural technology. Large scale production and mechanization was not adopted as was the case in England and the United States. Research throughout the Caribbean region has shown that the small-scale producers have had a much higher level of productivity in certain crops than the large-scale producers. I agree that mechanization of agriculture is important, and in most cases necessary, but this is dependent on the type of crop, the terrain of the geographic area and the working patterns of the population.

The problem of development in Jamaica is not only linked to an unclear development agenda and poor infrastructure, but also to the plethora of businesses engaged in paper transactions rather than adding value through the production of commodities for local consumption and export. In addition, with few exceptions, the productivity levels in both the public and private sectors are low. I agree with the view that much of the debate regarding the development of the country is always too locked in with balance of payment, devaluation and other mundane matters. The policymakers need to seriously consider the long-term macro-picture. Peace!

A new development model

(TUESDAY, FEBRUARY 28, 1995)

The public outcry about the planned shipment of plutonium via the Caribbean to Japan is most interesting. I am almost sure that 15 years ago a similar such shipment would have taken place without notice. Furthermore, instead of embracing members of Greenpeace, an organization whose main concern is the preservation of the natural environment, many, especially politicians and policymakers, would want to dismiss them as more lunatics. Despite the seeming intransigence of France, Britain and Japan in regard to the shipment of plutonium, countries which make up the OECD have been challenging the developing countries to take a more holistic view of mankind and the environment, much more than the industrialized countries have done in the past. Furthermore, many industrialized countries seem to be in the Vanguard of the struggle to have what is known as sustainable development.

The interest in sustainable development by developed countries and by powerful environmental movements will most likely affect the nature of the North-South relationship in the future. There seems to be the desire by the North to impose various environmental standards on the South as requirements for a continued trading relationship. The recognition by people in both the industrialized and the non-industrialized countries that continued pollution and destruction of the natural environment will lead to greater natural and economic disaster has led to the feeling that a real development cannot occur unless the environment is protected, and that this must happen while not deterring economic growth. This desired situation can only happen if we factor issues of environmental renewal into our new development models.

This new thinking

This new thinking has strong implications for countries of the South. And some have even argued that this new situation has given the South greater bargaining power in global trade and politics. On the other hand, some believe that this situation will only limit the options for growth and economic development available to the South. Regardless of the position one takes, it is clear that the developing countries have to be more prudent in the ways in which they approach the exploitation of nature in the name of progress. Traditional development models have invariably led to mass destruction of forests and to air pollution and soil degradation.

The path to economic success once pursued by industrialized nations is now under attack by the very same industrialized nations. In a matter of years, the structure of the General Agreement on Tariffs and Trade (GATT) and the policies of the multilateral lending agencies, such as the World Bank and IMF, will be influenced by environmental concerns. The groundwork is now being laid. Perhaps new lending conditionalities are in the making by these agencies.

What does this mean for poor countries? It means that they will have to construct a new theory of development. It means balancing environmental concerns with economic development. It means a comprehensive revision of our old models of growth. You see, we should no longer simply propose manufacturing or tourism as an engine of growth without looking at the environmental implications of such a proposal.

In short, we must be able to embrace a production process which uses energy-efficient technology, thus polluting less and resulting in the minimum of soil destruction.

To argue, as Arthur Lewis did in the 1950s, that agriculture has to be commercialized and export zones created – without a clear idea of the environmental ramifications of such policies – has become unattractive and inelegant as a development strategy.

Soon, we will have to discard certain types of mineral exploitation if we are to resolve what is to happen to the environment in the long run. This is not to say that pollution will cease. But what will happen is that countries will have to become more judicious in mining their resources.

It is almost certain that developing countries will face the greatest difficulty in dealing with this new status quo. Some analysts argue that these countries will benefit from this situation, since sustainable development will result in the safeguarding of the natural resources we will need in the long run. But what will happen in the short run? What will poor countries like India and Kenya do with rapidly growing cities and slow economic growth? Third World countries have some of the largest cities in the world, and the lowest per capita income as well. Therefore, to what extent can poor countries save their forests, for instance, when they can obtain revenue from the sale of lumber? How can they avoid growing in lucrative and yet destructive cash crops, when economic pressures are unbearable? Industrialized countries seem to be ignoring these issues as they discuss issues of sustainable development. This they do as if one can separate these issues from issues of trade, the debt crisis, and other global politics.

There are those who feel that the more things change, the more they remain the same. For instance, the decision by OECD member states to ship plutonium across the world, in spite of the opposition from those likely to be affected if something goes wrong, is not unexpected and is yet another case of "Do as I say and not as I do". They also contend that the industrialized countries have depleted their forests and polluted their atmosphere in the name of progress. Yet developing countries cannot and must not pursue a similar path to development – because of the notion of our common density as creatures of this world. Meanwhile, they continue to remain impoverished.

If the rhetoric of sustainable development is to work, the survival of the whole world must be linked to the survival of individual countries, and in particular poor countries. In short, a greater concern for the welfare of the South by the North must be the signature for the new status quo. Peace!

Opportunism and the Asian saga

(TUESDAY, JANUARY 13, 1998)

BEFORE:

"What is happening in Asia is by far the most important development in the world today. Nothing comes close... The modernization of Asia will forever reshape the world as we move toward the next millennium."

— JOHN NAISBITT IN HIS MUCH CELEBRATED BOOK, *MEGATRENDS ASIA* (1995)

"Malaysia has proved that privatisation works."

— HARVARD ECONOMIST, JEFFREY SACHS, QUOTED IN NAISBITT (1995)

"Tales of success of Asia's 'Four Tigers' are legendary. The world watched in awe as Hong Kong, Singapore, South Korea, and Taiwan leapfrogged over the industrial stage and pushed full force into the information age."

— JOHN NAISBITT, *MEGATRENDS ASIA* (1995)

"Indonesia, the framework for growth has been established by a determinedly orthodox group of economists who have concentrated macroeconomic stability and opposed subsidies."

— *THE ECONOMIST* (JUNE 24, 1995)

"All around the world, economic prospects seem glum at best – except in East Asia, Hong Kong, Singapore, Taiwan and South Korea, the so-called Little Dragons that first began coming of economic age in the 1970s, have been joined by a new generation of legendary fire-breathing beasts – Thailand, Malaysia and Indonesia. The Super Seven, once known as minor-league producers of junk jewellery and throwaway toys, are leading the world in economic growth."

— *TIME* (SEPTEMBER 14, 1992)

"It is precisely this kind of can-do attitude that is giving the Seven the most rapid spurt of economic development in history. There will be bumps along the way, but continued economic progress is inevitable – and will be increasingly enjoyable."

— *TIME* (SEPTEMBER 14, 1992)

NOW:

"After years of extraordinary growth, East Asia's emerging economies are showing signs of fatigue. Are they exhausted? Or just resting before springing forward again?"

- *THE ECONOMIST* (MARCH 4, 1997)

"Asia's economic rise came to an end. Malaysia's prime minister, Mahathir Mohamad, introduced tough reforms while blaming foreigners for the crisis, which began with Thailand and set off currency devaluations and stock market crashes throughout East Asia. Kim Dae Jung, South Korea's president-elect, said that he was shocked that what had been the world's 11th largest economy was close to bankruptcy."

— *THE ECONOMIST* (JANUARY 3, 1998)

"If Asia's governments fail to cure their sick banks, their economies' crisis – and its implications for the rest of the world – could grow much worse."

— *THE ECONOMIST* (NOVEMBER 15, 1997)

"Bailing out East Asia's banks, it must be made clear, will be neither easy nor cheap. Robert Zielinski of Jardine Fleming, an investment bank, estimates that the non-performing loans of South-East Asian banks alone will peak at $73 billion".

— *THE ECONOMIST* (NOVEMBER 15, 1997)

"In one important respect, however, Asia's illness is harder to treat than Latin America's was. Latin America had a robust United States to act both as purchaser and benefactor – buying the region's exports once its currencies had depreciated, and speeding financial assistance by direct and indirect means. This is the role that Japan might have played in South-East Asia. But it cannot. Far from being the answer, Japan is part of the region's current problems".

— *ECONOMIST* (NOVEMBER 15, 1997)

Contrary to what some writers in the media are now opportunistically arguing, very few people, including internally renowned economists, predicted the current economic crisis in Asia. If there were many who saw the crisis coming, they certainly did not convince investors from around the world who for years have seen Asia as a safe place in which to invest their money. Nor was this negative prognosis reflected in the changing US policies which now see Asia as the number one part of the world to court. (Incidentally, I recall that in the late 1980s and throughout the early 1990s, Guyanese economist, and former deputy director of the Consortium Graduate School of Social Sciences, C.Y. Thomas, was repeatedly criticized by neoliberal thinkers and others for arguing that East Asian economies could not sustain their development path, that a crisis was inevitable.)

Beyond the political overtures made to Asia by western investors – from Europe to Australia – there are volumes of articles and books by financial analysts and social scientists from around the world on the reasons for the unprecedented success of the Asians. Such explanations range from motions of superior intellect and unique culture to unorthodox or orthodox (depending on what one chooses to focus on) approaches to capitalism. I have in my files numerous articles and speeches made by foreign and local economists and quasi-economists (and I can also recall the numerous programmes on morning talk radio) which point to the virtues of East Asian capitalism, with more than a hint that we in the Caribbean should follow the example of these countries in order to develop.

Indeed, it is no secret that respected economists, including Jeffrey Sachs, felt that the East Asians were on the right path to economic development. In his lecture at The UWI in February last year, Sachs pointed to the East Asian economic strategy as the way forward. Here was a region with high rates of economic growth as a result of the openness of their economies.

Crisis

There was no hint that a crisis or even difficulties were looming. Far from it, as he used East Asia as an example of what was possible for "closed" backward economies in this part of the world, only if they opened up.

Perhaps, more than any other, the debate over the nature of the "Asian Miracle" exposes much of the opportunism, intellectual dishonesty and weaknesses of social scientific thought. In the halcyon days of the East Asian miracle, neoliberal social scientists would point to the speedy deregulation and privatization as indicators that the East Asian model was in line with orthodox Western economic thought. (Incidentally, since the crisis began, many now amazingly argue that these economies were not deregulated enough.) On the other hand, those who opposed neoliberal ideas pointed to the high levels of government involvement in these economies as an indication that the market needs to be tamed for economic development to proceed. Here I am reminded of a popular saying by one of my professors while I was a student in the US: "A way of seeing is also a way of not seeing."

Confusion

There is a great deal of confusion and disagreement over the causes of the crisis and the solutions to it. There also seems to be as many explanations as there are analysts. Without a doubt, there will be the tendency for some to return to the attractive simplistic explanations, such as, the Asians were not practicing "true" capitalism, whatever that may be.

But the more serious analysts will study the situation carefully before there is a rush to invoke religious-like slogans from a black box of answers. At the moment, there is heated exchange among the affected Asian governments, academics, and IMF officials over the probable effects of IMF policies on some of these countries. What is clear, however, is that given the centrality of that region to the global economy, Western policymakers may be forced to bail out these economies. If this happens, yet another miracle may be in the making. Peace!

Chapter 13 Globalization and Economic Development in the Caribbean

- Capital, labour and feudalism
- Caught in a bind
- Capital, competition and the Caribbean

Introduction

This chapter acknowledges the growing interdependence of the world and what it means for the development of critical sectors within the Caribbean region. The author notes the extent to which tourism is shaping the pace at which globalization occurs. The chapter goes on to examine whether the type and quality of infrastructure utilized within the tourism sector can challenge the sustainability of both the environment and the tourism product. The chapter discusses how the clearing of farms and forested lands, wastewater disposal practices, as well as how the removal of coral reefs in areas surrounding major ports of entries affect the natural environment. The author concludes the chapter by noting the need for Caribbean countries, particularly Jamaica, to implement fundamental changes to enhance the sustainability of the tourism sector. These changes involve tapping into the unique cultures of the region, and engaging in sustainable environmental practices whilst increasing the community's involvement in the process.

Capital, labour and feudalism

(TUESDAY, NOVEMBER 16, 1993)

Fundamentally, economic development has to do with the relationship between capital and labour. If there is one thing which all the discussions on the Asian and Latin American models of economic development have taught us, it is that all the countries which have made important economic strides over the years have succeeded because they were able to make the relationship between capital and labour work in the national interest. This begs the question: why is it that in Jamaica we have not succeeded in making this relationship work in the national interest? Follow me closely!

Jamaica resembles a society in transition from feudalism to capitalism; modern feudalism, that is, not the type found in Latin America or pre-industrial Europe. By feudalism I am talking about a situation in which large segments of our society are "governed" by political elites (as distinct from the government) and/or neighbourhood "dons". This situation has meant that to a large extent the relationship between constituents (serfs) and political elites (landlords) is a reciprocal one. Therefore, the politicians provide the spoils, and the constituents provide the votes. Note, this type of relationship occurs primarily with the very poor sectors of society. Note, however, that not every part of the sector subscribes to such a relationship. Importantly though, the sectors who subscribe are large enough to influence electoral outcomes.

Defence at all costs

Now if electoral outcomes depend more on this feudal relationship, where politicians ensure allegiance through the provision of spoils, then their political tenure has less to do with their ability to function or to obtain national consensus and accountability, and more to do with their ability to maintain this allegiance from their constituencies. If the survival of people who reside in these highly politicized areas depends on their landlord winning a seat, it is highly "rational" for them to defend their fiefdom at all costs from "external" threats. In this type of political arrangement, both the landlord and the serf win. The question is: at whose expense?

Now, if we have a political system in which the winner of an election "takes it all", where is the incentive for both major political parties, who prey on the marginalized in these urban and rural areas, to abandon this feudal relationship or eradicate poverty? If there is a political system in which the elected representative does not have to answer to the entire nation in order to maintain power, where is the incentive for accountability? Ask yourself, why is it that there has been so little protest over the zinc affair? Is it not in part because we live in a society so partisan and so divided that any form of action which may be to the detriment of one fiefdom may be to the benefit of another, even though collectively we may all suffer in the long run? Therefore, it will always be easier for elected representatives to raise revenue through taxes, than it would be for them to develop policies which would increase productivity. All this is simply because our elected representatives are not answerable or accountable outside of their fiefdoms.

Alienation

The presence of fiefdoms and the deep gulf between the haves and have-nots continue to alienate labour and capital while we try to pursue a nebulous development agenda. But if we can get a national consensus from labour and capital about the direction of our country, then this development agenda will cease to be nebulous and fictional.

There are only two ways to get labour and capital to work together – by coercion or by volunteering. Realistically, the latter is the only real option we have. But how do we achieve this accommodation when the vertical and horizontal cleavages in society hinder any notion of national good? Further, even if this ethos existed, we would still have to deal with the fact that the macroeconomic framework and the attitudes of our traditional business elite are somewhat incompatible with conditions of sustained industrial development.

Poverty

In sum, our country is faced with two very serious problems which retard development and economic progress. First there is poverty, which has created a reservoir of disaffected people who can be easily co-opted in the name of survival by people who find pleasure in being treated as demigods. The extreme wealth gap and the subsequent marginalization have created different class "cultures" which may be incompatible. Contrast the lifestyles of the "aristocracy" of the hills and the "commoners" of the urban slums and you will see what I mean.

The second problem is the spectre of the multiparty (in reality two-party) Westminster system which is based on the notion of "the winner takes it all". This has failed to make our political leaders accountable to the public and dedicated to promoting national interests. I therefore ask: if the political leadership is not accountable to the people, how will it be possible for us to arrive at and enforce any agreement on the policies which can create a climate for cooperation between capital and labour in the national interest? Peace!

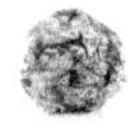

Caught in a bind

(TUESDAY, JULY 5, 1994)

At present, this country is experiencing one of the worst industrial climates in its recent history, and there is no indication that things will get any better in the near future. True, industrial disputes are not unique to Jamaica. However, during this period of privatization, the frequency, magnitude and the nature of these disputes are signs that something is desperately wrong with our economy. For if in less than two weeks we can have strikes by people who are in charge of some of the country's important services, such as petrol and electricity, then clearly something must be wrong.

The fact of the matter is that the government or country is caught in a bind. The government has attempted to keep the rate of inflation down by adopting a high-interest-rate policy. However, there seems to be no complementary fiscal reforms aimed at keeping wages down – which is necessary for this policy to work. This is understandable, given that the skyrocketing rate of inflation has meant that the real spending power of workers has declined at an alarming rate. Therefore, it is unreasonable to blame the workers for demanding high wages in this most trying situation.

Socioeconomic divisions

The fact is that if the government attempts to freeze our wages without reining in inflation, then one can expect a great social explosion reminiscent of the early 1980s or something similar to what happened in Venezuela during the nation's period of austerity in the 1980s.

In a number of countries in the region, such as Trinidad and Tobago, and Barbados, governments were able to reach agreements with the labour unions on how to contain wages for a period of time – a policy considered by all parties as being in the interest of the country. But given the gaping social and economic divisions and politicization of everyday life, there seems to be little possibility of this type of social contract working in Jamaica. Further, because there is a perception that things will not improve, there is an absence of a collective or national social responsibility. The prognosis, therefore, is that the chaos of everyday life is likely to continue.

Over the years, the basic problem which has faced this country is that while our consumption has increased, our outputs have either grown slowly or declined. This is a real conundrum. Increased industrial disputes will further reduce the meagre outputs, as workers lose important man hours to strikes and other forms of protests. We should note that to a large degree it is remittances from abroad (namely the US) that have been helping to prevent an even greater collapse of our economy.

Unrealistic

The efforts of the government to encourage more investment and output in the manufacturing sector should be complemented. However, the notion that the provision of rational incentives will lead to rational choices by manufacturers, and that others will suddenly switch to manufacturing, is nothing short of unrealistic. An incentive is as objective as it is subjective, and rationality is contingent upon one's experiences, commitment and perceptions of choices. These are the variables which guide the way human beings think. In light of this, we should ask ourselves why it is that the Asians or the Jews or some other ethnic groups in the Caribbean or the USA can seize business opportunities where others claim that no incentives exist? My argument, then, is that the problem of manufacturing and output is not simply one of providing incentives, but more importantly of providing the "appropriate" incentives. Appropriate incentives must be guided by an understanding of the motives of local entrepreneurs and a comprehension of the idiosyncrasies of local entrepreneurship. This begs the question: what are these appropriate incentives, and when do we know that we have finally found them? Answer: this is the part I am still trying to figure out.

Common Entrance

For yet another year the Ministry of Education has put the nation's children through the traumatic and iniquitous Common Entrance Examination (CEE). This exam is not only elitist, but it reinforces inequalities within our society. In the first instance, only a small number of eligible pupils took the exam in 1993. Of the 100,000 children eligible to sit the exam only 48,144 entered. Of that number, only 10,900 or 23 per cent got high school places, I see; the Jamaican government only provides 10 per cent of the places for children of high school age. The other children must attend new secondary schools and all-age schools, and pay fees to attend independent high schools. Jamaica's CEE results do not compare favourably with those of other CARICOM countries. For instance, in Trinidad and Tobago there was xx percent pass rate in CEE in 1993; likewise, in Barbados over 75 per cent of the candidates passed the CEE. In both countries, there is talk about phasing the exam out. It should be noted that in Jamaica the number of pupils who pass the CEE is a function of the number of high school places available.

The society continues to play with a social time bomb when policymakers and the elite consciously perpetuate inequality through education. There is not one shred of evidence to substantiate the view that a child's potential can be known at age 11 following an abysmal primary school record. Were it not for other educational opportunities, the world might not have benefited from the immense talents of Albert Einstein. Our society is in part to be blamed for many of its education-related problems, having condemned the large majority of Jamaicans to an inferior and negatively labelled education. The Common Entrance Examination should be abandoned for something more consistent with tapping the talents of the large number of cheated Jamaicans who are the backbone of the society. Peace!

Capital, competition and the Caribbean

(TUESDAY, JANUARY 17, 1995)

Those who believe that foreign investment is not coming into the region and transforming the economic landscape should take another look at the evidence. The recent decision by the government of the twin island Republic of Trinidad and Tobago, to sell 51 per cent of the shares of the British West Indian Airways (BWIA) to the Edward Acker group eloquently argues this point. Acker, an American entrepreneur, has reportedly acquired the single largest block of shares in this regional airline, much to the displeasure of a number of Caribbean businessmen. The parliamentary opposition in Trinidad is livid. They have accused the Patrick Manning administration of a lack of transparency and have vowed to fight him on this issue.

Those leading the accusations are concerned about what they termed the possible Americanization of the airline. They strongly believe that the regional character of the airline will be lost, and as a result, Caribbean destinations may not fall in line with the operational plans of the Acker group. They also argued that national and regional private interests were willing to surpass the Acker offer. So, for now, there is a great deal of disquiet over the future of the airline and, particularly, the future of the many jobs within the region which the restructuring of the airline is sure to affect. Nevertheless, the question being asked is, why did the government rush to sell the shares of BWIA to the Acker group, given the overtures of regional investors?

Meanwhile, Antigua's prime minister, Lester Bird, has accused Caribbean governments of abandoning the Leeward Islands Air Transport Services (LIAT). These comments were made after it was announced that the region will have a new airline, the non-Caribbean owned sunrise airline. Supporters of LIAT feel that the new airline could snuff out the old carrier in the long run. However, Mr Bird argues that LIAT has served the region well, especially since it has continued to serve uneconomic routes, all in the best interest of the region. In his views, LIAT has been and continues to be the conduit for regional integration. On this point Mr Bird and I agree. But one wonders if he is not also distracted by the jobs his country will lose if LIAT folds; after all, the airline is headquartered in Antigua.

Let us add another dimension to this regional investment picture. Private sector interest in St Lucia and Barbados are nervous about the decision by the large American chain store Kmart's intention to establish outlets in their countries. Already, plans are on the way to construct a large Kmart mall in Barbados. Interestingly, Barbados has more shopping malls per capita than perhaps any other English-speaking Caribbean country. Be that as it may, large retailers in both countries are of the view that they will not be able to compete with the low prices and variety offered by Kmart.

Some months ago, I got a call from a store owner in Saint Lucia seeking advice about what could be done to counter the plan by Kmart to establish a store there. My understanding is that after the Saint Lucian Chamber of Commerce held a number of meetings to discuss the issue, the Kmart operation will still go ahead. But here is an interesting twist to the retail outlet issue. Julie'N Supermarket, one of Barbados largest retail outlets, recently decided to sell its store in Saint Lucia, because of a spate of robberies against its business. Julie'N's presence in Saint Lucia has always been controversial since it offered, arguably, some of the most modern shopping facilities in the island, and its prices were extremely competitive. Consequently, sections of the local private sector have always expressed its unease with respect to Julie'N being in Saint Lucia. Some commentators have speculated that the targeting of Julie'N in Saint Lucia by robbers was not accidental.

Julie'N is now investing in a massive shopping mall in Barbados, reputed to be one of the most modern in the entire region. It is sure to compete with Kmart's outlet, which is also supposed to be very modern. The picture becomes clearer.

There are other events which could be highlighted, but let us stop here for a moment and ponder what is happening. Clearly, we are witnessing a movement of capital into some parts of the region. Interestingly, however, it is not moving into the area of manufacturing. We need to ask ourselves why is it that American firms are choosing to invest in air travel and retail outlets, rather than use the region as a source of primary extraction as it did in the past, or for cheap labour to manufacture products. I will not venture to answer this question just yet. But I would like to suggest that it has to do with the process of globalization and the desire to embrace the region – at least parts of it – as an extension of the American economic spare, primarily as consumers, not producers.

A more interesting angle from which to observe these developments can also be identified. It is this: while sections of the regional private sector are calling for free trade and divestment, they are unable and in some cases unwilling to compete with other regional or extra-regional companies when competition presents itself. And, in a bid to restore respectability to our finances, Caribbean governments are in the process of blindly divesting national assets with little regard to the consequences of their decisions. Mind you, I am not against divestment; what is in question here is the manner in which it occurs. Unfortunately, a complete misunderstanding of our history and of the current processes of global capitalism has led to a "school" of economics which encourages a ludicrously passive role on the part of the state in this development process.

This situation is not unknown to us in Jamaica, where our government has turned the entire ground transportation system over to the private sector when there is not one developed or newly developing country which has gone this route with success.

It is clear that with all the ranting and raving about NAFTA, and even with the formation of the Association of Caribbean States, we are still ill-prepared for the wind of change which these agreements will inevitably blow our way. Yes, our status in the world economy is changing – from producers of primary products to consumers and distributors of finished products. How is this for progress? Peace!

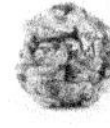

Chapter 14 The Tourist Sector

- The truth about tourism: Part 1
- The truth about tourism: Part 2
- Crime and tourism
- Crime and the crime rate

Introduction

The chapter seeks to examine the factors that affect the Jamaican tourist industry, especially since the sector is a major source of income, employment and wealth. Most of the articles within this chapter seek to determine whether there is any link between crime and tourism. The author submits that, before arriving at a conclusion on the link between tourism and crime, one should examine the extent to which publicity of events affect the perception of any possible correlation between crime and tourist arrivals.

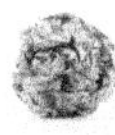

The truth about tourism: Part 1

(TUESDAY, JUNE 14, 1994)

It is not uncommon to hear commentators and public opinion makers arguing that the increase in crime is causing a decline in the visitor arrivals to our country. Popular talk show host Wilmot Perkins, for example, continues to argue that the level of violent crime in the country is seriously impacting on visitor arrivals.

There can be no doubt that a society which has a high level of crime runs the risk of crippling its tourism industry. However, such an argument does not automatically mean that crime in Jamaica has led to a decline in this industry. In fact, if tourist revenue and arrival statistics are anything to go by, then there appear to be little relationship between the level of crime and tourist arrivals in the country – so far.

The period which saw the most drastic increase in violent crimes in Jamaica since independence was between 1968 and 1980. During these years, the violent crime rate steadily increased, becoming almost five times what it was in 1968 by 1980. Between 1968 and 1979, total crimes per 100,000 increased by more than 40 per cent.

Nevertheless, during this same period, we saw a significant increase of more than 40 per cent in stopover arrivals. Between 1975 and 1977, there was a sharp decline in this number. Interestingly, during this period, while stopovers declined, cruise ship arrivals increased dramatically.

However, between 1975 and 1977, Jamaica lost

important revenue from the tourism sector since arrivals declined by almost 40 per cent. It should be noted, however, that this was the period in which the state of emergency was in force and American visitors were discouraged from visiting the island. Immediately after the lifting of the state of emergency in 1978, tourist arrivals increased by about 39 per cent. Interestingly, though the violent crime rate continued to climb during this period, reaching its peak in 1980, tourist arrivals also increased up until 1980 – the year of the general elections. It is not surprising that arrivals in both the stopover and cruise ship sectors recovered in 1981, immediately after the elections and has continued right up to 1994.

Crime rate

Even though the overall crime rate continues to be high, with no sign of decline in the major urban areas, the number of visitors to the island has continued to increase during the 1980s and into 1990s.

The most significant fall-off was witnessed in 1988 – the year of Hurricane Gilbert. The number of visitors to the island for 1993 was almost three times what it was in 1979. In 1993, there was a 3.4 per cent growth in visitor arrivals over 1992, due in no small measure to the recovery of the North American economy.

Contrary to the view that the tourism industry is in trouble, the year 1993 saw an increase of 7.7 per cent in stopover arrivals, resulting in a 10.7 per cent increase in gross visitor expenditure over 1992. Stopover visitors for the months of January and February, 1994, have been up when compared to the similar periods in 1992 and 1993.

In addition to this, the industry witnessed increased investment in the region of 500 additional hotel rooms. Between 1968 and 1993, there has been a dramatic expansion in employment in the accommodation sector and a steady increase in foreign exchange earnings. Employment in the accommodation sector has increased steadily in all of the major tourist areas, except Kingston.

There have been two areas of decline in visitor arrivals, and these are with armed forces and cruise ship passengers. This decline in the armed forces is not significant, since this group has traditionally accounted for a very small proportion of our tourist arrivals. The other area of decline has been in the cruise ship sector which, having increased steadily over the two decades since 1968, declined by 3.1 per cent in 1993.

Note, however, that this decline was not unique to Jamaica – eight other countries in the region also experienced a decline in their cruise ship arrivals. In 1993, with the exception of Puerto Rico and the Cayman Islands, Jamaica had the smallest decline in cruise ship arrivals.

If one looks at the overall performance of the tourism sector in Jamaica, it compares favourably with all other Caribbean territories which are seriously involved in tourism. In 1993, only the Bahamas received more tourists than Jamaica.

Based on the available data, it does not appear that Jamaica's high crime rate is causing a decline in the tourist industry – so far. The situation might have made the all-inclusive hotel more attractive to tourists, but it has not stopped them from coming.

This situation is not unusual; the state of Florida and the city of Washington, D.C., in the US continue to attract large numbers of visitors despite their highly publicized crime rates. The same is also true of the Dominican Republic – a country which has had to deal with an upsurge in criminal activity in recent years.

Three factors

So far, it would appear that three factors can explain the reductions in visitor arrivals to Jamaica over the past two decades. First, there are natural disasters, such as hurricanes, which disrupt the utilities and other normal services. Second, the downturn in the economies of the countries of the visitors would obviously make it more difficult for them to take vacations. Third, and perhaps most significantly, there is political conflict – the state of emergency between 1975 and 1977 and the 1980s election succinctly address this point.

Now, I do not deny that crime may have deterred some people from visiting the country, or that criminal activity aimed at tourists will not certainly make them less enthusiastic about coming to our shores. However, my main point is that the evidence so far does not support the view being put forward by public opinion-makers that crime is the cause of a decline in the tourism sector. Perhaps we might assess what effect crime is having on the non-all-inclusive hotels and services and even speculate about what could happen to the tourism sector were the crime rate much lower. Peace!

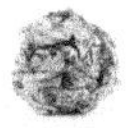

The truth about tourism: Part 2

(TUESDAY, JULY 26, 1994)

In his opinion commentary of July 8, 1994, Mr Geof Brown argued that my analysis of the relationship between crime and tourism was methodologically flawed and by extension incorrect. He then attempted to find support for his thesis: that crime is the single largest factor responsible for the decline in tourist arrivals since 1968 and on to the present. Let me reiterate, I stand by my article of June 14 and vehemently disagree with Mr Brown's criticisms of my methodology, as well as his thesis about crime and tourism. What is clear is that Mr Brown seems to have overestimated his own understanding of the methodology I used to arrive at these findings.

To be sure, his attempt to explain a causal relationship between crime and tourism is not methodologically sound and contradicts detailed statistical analysis of the data. Regrettably, this is not the appropriate forum for one to engage in a debate about methodology or the philosophy of science. Nevertheless, it is imperative that I point out that, while one of the conditions which researchers use to establish causation is correlation, correlation does not mean that there is always causation. In other words, the absence of correlation is a legitimate basis upon which to reject direct causation. However, the presence of correlation does not mean that there is a causal link between the variables under examination. To be sure, there are a number of other issues which we need to consider in determining causation – not least of which are alternative explanations to the observed correlation. From an empirical standpoint, there are a number of statistical tests that one would have to perform on the data to arrive at causal statements.

Position

I will now make my position clear on the tourism and crime issue. Based on an analysis of the data – an analysis which I am quite willing to share with Mr Brown and with tourism officials – there seems to be a weak direct relationship between relative changes in the crime rate and changes in tourist arrivals. That is to say, if we do a longitudinal analysis (1968-1993) of the relationship between the crime rate, aggregated or disaggregated for violent crime or crimes against property, and tourist arrivals, the relationship will be less than moderate – meaning it would be weak. Put another way, if we compare the rate of change in tourist arrivals with the rate of change in the crime rate, total or disaggregated, we do not see a consistent pattern of inverse variation between crime and tourism. While the violent crime rate shows the most consistent variation with cruise ship arrivals, the relationship is neither substantive, nor is it statistically significant.

Now, further detailed statistical analysis of the data from a causal perspective indicates that changes in the crime rate have over the years had very little impact on tourist arrivals. However, what is clear from the data is that the Canadian and UK markets account for a large degree of changes in rates of visitor arrivals. In fact, changes in Canadian arrivals account for about a 40 per cent variation in the stopover arrivals in the period herein under examination, while the UK arrivals account for about 9 per cent of the variation. Interestingly, it is mainly the changes in the Canadian and European markets which account for the relative declines in tourist arrivals so far this year. For instance, while stopover arrivals for the period January to June saw an overall increase of 15 per cent over the same period in 1992 and a 3.4 per cent increase over 1993 for the US, for Canada there was a 10.2 per cent decrease over 1992 and a 4.8 per cent decrease over 1993. Changes in crime rates do not account for these differences.

Comparisons

It has been argued that relative to other Caribbean countries, Jamaica's tourism is on the decline because of crime. One has to be wary of making such comparisons, since many of the industries in this region are not entirely comparable. Furthermore, for this year up to May, Barbados has been experiencing an increase in its crime rate, but it has also recorded larger increases in arrivals than Jamaica.

Another look at the data will indicate that the largest and most mature tourist markets in the region, which include Puerto Rico, the Bahamas and Jamaica, have been having the smallest relative increases in the stopovers this year. Likewise, a further look at the data will show that, even though declines were experienced in the months of April, May and June of this year, the pattern of tourist arrivals from a numerical standpoint is the same as the spring seasons of 1992 and 1993. Just a word of caution: comparing 1994 with other years can be problematic, because we are comparing essentially monthly data with annual data.

As I have argued before, I am not suggesting that crime does not have an impact on tourism. Clearly this would be absurd, especially in the Jamaican context. But the causal link between crime and tourism, though intellectually appealing, is theoretically and empirically complicated. My hypothesis is that where crime is seriously linked to tourism, it is not through increased crime per se, but through the publicity about particular crimes. This is a separate variable from the crime rate itself. In other words, it is perfectly possible that if the crime rate is on the decline and there is a murder of a high-profile tourist, negative publicity will affect people's perceptions of the country. Cancellations of bookings which some hotels will experience would not be due to an increase in the crime rate but rather to the publicity associated with the particular crime. While crime and the publicity about crime can be related, they are separate things which we need to disaggregate. An examination of the data shows numerous periods when there are sharp increases in the crime rate and large increases in tourist arrivals. Recently, a tourist official in the Virgin Islands pointed out to me that some years ago, adverse publicity about the murder of an important official on one of the islands resulted in the temporary decline in the industry. This is despite the island being considered one of the safest tourist destinations anywhere in the world. Therefore, what we are dealing with is perception feeding reality.

Limited data

Really, though, just how important is crime to the tourists who visit Jamaica in terms of preventing them from returning? The data on this issue are very limited; however, they give us some insight. A survey conducted by the Ministry of Tourism in 1992 shows that more people considered harassment, bad driving, poor road conditions and poor service as being more serious problems than crime. In fact, only two per cent of those surveyed considered crime to be a problem. But even if this figure were much larger, there is no sure way of knowing if this perception will lead to them not returning. These results are similar to those found in a recent survey regarding the perceptions of Jamaica by tourists. Of those who felt that they would not return, when asked what would prevent them from returning, the overwhelming majority identified harassment, poor facilities and personal financial problems. A number of them also mentioned the fact that they did not get what they saw advertised. Very few identified crime as a serious factor.

In Barbados, a number of surveys conducted on the tourist industry cited crime as a potential problem, but not one indicated evidence that an increase in crime was causing a decline in arrivals. In fact, well over 90 per cent of those surveyed consistently had a positive impression of the island. Additionally, an analysis of the crime rate and tourist arrivals for Barbados showed no causal relationship between the two.

Important sector

Tourism is a very important sector for Jamaica, and for this reason we need to understand what is happening to it. In the most recent edition of *Annals of Tourism Research*, one of the top scientific tourism-focused journals, there is a useful discussion about some of the problems one faces in trying to understand the tourism market. We need to engage our research in some of these issues.

Further, we need to be familiar with some of the techniques of analysis, such as life cycle analysis, which are widely used in developed countries to interpret data gleaned from the tourism market. Also, it is clear that the government's macroeconomic policy and the competition from places such as Cuba and Eastern Europe are inextricably bound up with the future of our tourism industry. One final point: the government is investing huge amounts of resources in the tourism-centred areas, when the reality is that crime is more of a problem outside these areas. Let me be clear: I want our visitors to be safe and free of crime and harassment; however, separation of the natives from the visitors can be deemed an overkill. Until we understand that we are dealing with a rapidly changing industry and a complex set of issues, I fear that the discussions about tourism will become as trivial and ideologically charged as the discussions about politics. Peace!

Crime and tourism

(SUNDAY, MARCH 5, 1995)

For some time now, tourism officials and media personnel in Jamaica have been arguing that the cause of the fall-off in tourist arrivals to Jamaica for the years 1994 to 1995 is due to the country's rising crime rates, in particular the violent crime (see, for example, Geof Brown, "Tourism: Not the Whole Truth, Dr Boxill," *Daily Gleaner*, July 8, 1994).

In an article published in the *Daily Gleaner* on June 14, 1994, I challenged this view and suggested that there is very little empirical basis for arriving at such a conclusion. In this paper, firstly, I present more empirical evidence to support the view that there is very little relationship between the crime rate and tourist arrivals in Jamaica. Second, I suggest the possible negative links between crime and tourism. Third, I outline what are some of the additional issues which should be tackled to make tourism more sustainable.

The main data used in this paper are crime rates and tourist arrivals, both computed from official sources, from the year 1969 to the year 1993. I have also decided to place more emphasis on violent crime rates than on total crime rates, since Jamaica's non-violent crime rates are not significantly different from those of the other English-speaking Caribbean countries.

Crime and tourism: A look at the data

A look at Figures 1 to 3 show that the pattern of tourist arrivals for both stopovers and cruises does not seriously vary with either the violent crime rate or the total crime rate. Indeed, if we compare the pattern of arrivals from the major destinations, the United States, Canada and the United Kingdom, with the pattern of the violent crime rate or the total crime rate, we observe that there are no clear patterns of inverse relationships to suggest that crime is impacting on arrivals negatively

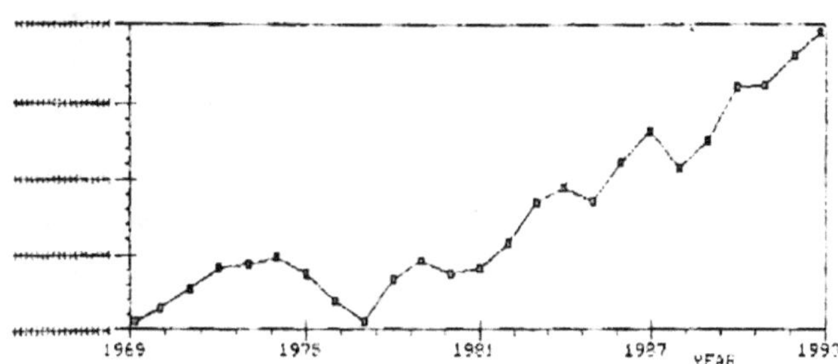

Figure 1

Figure 2

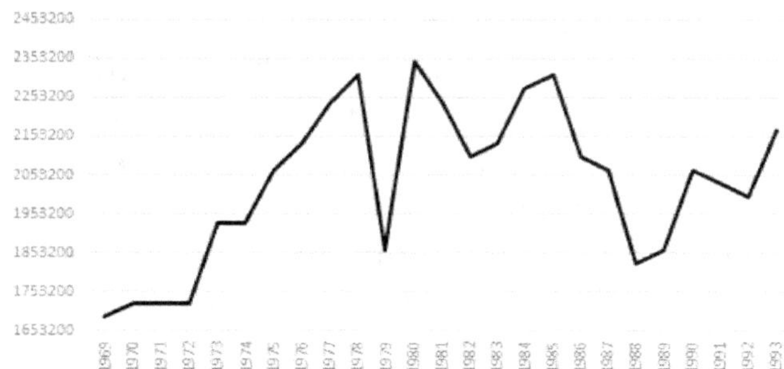

Figure 3

In order to arrive at a more sensitive measure of the correlation between the violent crime rate and stopovers, I computed the change in the violent crime rate and the change in stopovers for the years 1970 to 1992, and then examined the relationship. The relationship between the percentage change in the violent crime rates and the percentage change in stopovers comes out negative (r=-.11). However, the Pearson correlation coefficient is very small. This result implies that, while there is a relationship between the violent crime rates and stopovers, this relationship is extremely weak.

Figure 4: Percentage change in stopovers and violent crime rate (lagged for one year), 1970-1992.

To determine whether there is a causal link between crime and tourist arrivals, a simple linear regression was constructed. The model is as follows: Y=a+bX+c, where Y = percentage change in stopover visitors, and X = percentage change in violent crime rate. The r-squared for this model is .02, indicating that only about two per cent of the variation in the changes in stopovers is a direct consequence of the changes in the violent crime rate. Indeed, if we lag the impact of the crime rate on stopovers by half a year or one year the results will change little (r-squared = .03 for a lag of one year) (see Figure 4).

Implications of findings

Let me make it clear that I am not suggesting that crime does not impact on tourism. I am simply arguing that, on the basis of the longitudinal data, it is incorrect to contend that tourist arrivals seriously vary with increases in the crime rate.

Perhaps during the 1970s and particularly in 1980s, the high crime rates may have prevented many potential tourists from coming to Jamaica, but even this conclusion has to be contextualized. What tourists responded to during the 1970s was not adopting a political ideology deemed inimical to the preservation of human rights and the stability of the Caribbean region. Therefore, the state of emergency that lasted from 1975 to 1977 was more of a political factor than one relating to crime. The reason I say this is because, by 1978, after the state of emergency was lifted, tourist arrivals increased by over 40 per cent, even though both the total crime rate and the violent crime rate increased by over three per cent.

The notion that tourists are not coming to Jamaica simply because of crime is certainly not borne out in the exit surveys conducted by the Jamaica Tourist Board. In a 1992 survey conducted by the Board, only two per cent of those surveyed regarded crime as a major problem in coming to Jamaica. The largest numbers of responses were in relation to harassment and poor physical infrastructure as the most serious problems they see in Jamaica as a tourist destination. Indeed, a survey conducted by me in 1994 corroborates the Tourist Board's findings.

What, therefore, is the relationship between crime and tourism in Jamaica? My hypothesis is that where crime is seriously linked to tourist arrivals, it is not through increased crime per se, but through adverse publicity about various types of crime. In other words, it is quite plausible for a reduction in the crime rate to be accompanied by a decline in visitors' arrivals due to adverse publicity in the overseas press about a specific incident or incidents. To be sure, the years 1971 to 1974 saw an increase in the violent crime rates as well as an increase in stopover visitors. It should be noted, however, that sometimes, even in the face of adverse publicity about crime, some countries still have booming industries, since visitors weight safety considerations against their desire to visit the country.

Peru and Russia are examples of countries which have seen increases in violent crimes accompany increases in tourist arrivals. Indeed, in Jamaica between the years 1987 and 1993, increases in the violent and total crime rates were accompanied by increases in stopover arrivals.

It is, therefore, clear to me that we must exercise much more care in jumping to conclusions about the impact of crime on tourism in Jamaica. Certainly, the less crime we have, the better for the industry and the society as a whole.

However, we should spend more time examining other factors which might have a greater impact on tourist arrivals, such as marketing strategies, the life cycle of the industry, the competitiveness of the industry, and the social development of our country, to mention but a few.

Crime and the crime rate

(TUESDAY, SEPTEMBER 3, 1996)

Recent discussions about crime in our society have been very instructive. If we use the radio talk shows and news broadcasts as a barometer of the extent to which the authorities are likely to get a handle on the problem, it appears that things are not looking too good. It seems that the police and the relevant ministry are at a loss to find solutions to the problem. And while it is true that crime is a worldwide phenomenon, it is difficult to make meaningful comparisons with other countries, as some of our commentators and politicians want do in their analysis, simply by juxtaposing the particular crime rates. And this tendency is more pronounced whenever we experience a sudden escalation in barbarism.

The crime rate is a statistic which, by itself, reveals nothing substantial about the nature of the problem in the specific society. Crime rates are the results of the efficiency of any law enforcement system, cultural practices, levels of reporting, and the definitions of what is a crime. As such, it is quite possible for the rate of certain crimes to fall because of the reclassification of these crimes or, equally, because of low levels of reporting and recording.

In certain parts of Asia, for instance, relatively low official figures on rape exist. This is a direct consequence of cultures which discourage the reporting of such an act. In some developing countries, heavy workloads and abysmally poor working conditions have led law enforcement authorities to reclassify particular types of violent offences as less serious crimes. In other societies, these changes have been made to legislation which have the aforementioned effect, and are also aimed at reducing the prison population.

But a closer look at the nature of crime in any society

must consider how vulnerable to crime its citizens are, and also the effectiveness of its law enforcement teams in dealing with these crimes. Societies which have booming private security industries reflect a fairly high level of vulnerability – at least by those persons who are served by the security industry. When these private security personnel can be seen toting rifles, as is commonplace in our society, this is an indication of a relatively high level of vulnerability.

Societies in which law enforcement officers do not carry weapons during routine patrols are likely to have comparatively lower levels of vulnerability than those where revolvers and rifles, and perhaps tanks, are part of the normal policing exercise. The no-gun-carrying police phenomenon is true even for those societies which have comparatively high violent crime rates, since the people have confidence that the law enforcement officials can and will protect their interests without routinely resorting to deadly force. Additionally, high violent crime rates may be restricted to a particular section of the society where such areas are controlled by drug traffickers or gangs, and by extension have little effect on the larger society.

Against this background, if we were to use the violent crime rate by itself to locate where Jamaica falls on the global crime rate scene, then our terms of reference and process of analysis would have to be more astute than what presently obtains, failing which, our analysis would be highly problematic and our findings inaccurate.

Footnote: The recent concern expressed by Opposition Leader Edward Seaga about the seeming immanence of foreign domination of certain sections of the local economy is interesting. However, such comments seem somewhat inconsistent with the much-heralded market economy models touted by both the JLP and PNP, which eschew nationalist ideals and even limited regionalism (like CARICOM).

If, as has been argued by exponents of these models, there is a certain "natural" movement of capital within a global economy, which is characterized by a plethora of free trade rhetoric, why then should we worry about foreign investment? Seems as though we are going around in circles. Peace!

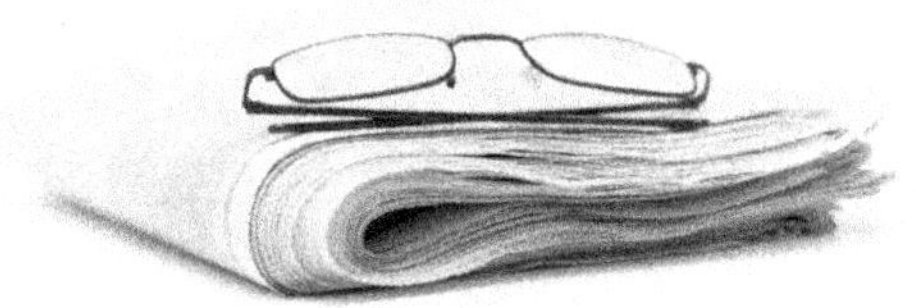

SUBSECTION C

International Development and Structural Adjustment

Chapter 15 Environmental Pollution, Poverty, Structural Adjustment and the Environment

- Killing us slowly
- Structural adjustment: Global lessons
- The community and tourism
- Jawaiian music and tourism

Introduction

This section has one chapter, Chapter 15, which looks at the extent to which the structural adjustment policies implemented in the 1980s impact the fiscal parameters within which countries of the Caribbean operate, and in particular Jamaica. Emphasis is placed on the extent to which countries within the region experienced a deceleration in economic growth and the measures implemented to deal with the resultant impact. In addition, the section gives careful consideration to the environmental impact of structural adjustment, and the extent to which an adoption of the structural adjustment policies is necessary for the development of countries of the developing South.

Killing us slowly

(TUESDAY, DECEMBER 14, 1993)

From just casual observation, it appears as if the number of people in Jamaica with lung and bronchial tract problems is increasing. On the basis of discussions I have had with medical and environmental researchers, there seems to be a strong case for linking increased health problems with the pollution in Jamaica.

In a paper titled the "State of the environment and health in Jamaica", Dr Homero Silva, sanitary engineer, states that the greatest concentration of air pollution is in the city of Kingston, and in other areas where there are companies inadvertently involved in either chemical or dust pollution. To make matters worse, emissions from factories and motor vehicles helped to contribute their fair share of pollution to the city – leaded gasolinc bcing a major source of atmospheric pollution.

Lead pollution

According to Dr Silva, since March 1990, the ECD (Environmental Control Division) monitored the area northwest of the city: findings indicated that lead concentrations in the air were two to seven times higher than the recommended limit. Although unleaded gasoline has been introduced, its use is still not as widespread as it should be. One only has to drive through Liguanea, Half Way Tree, or Parade to see the number of people trapped in carbon monoxide, often the result of traffic congestion.

This pollution wórsens in areas close to garbage dumps. Recently, the smoke from the Riverton City dump cloaked sections of the city, creating a nightmare for the citizens, forcefully reminding us of our scant regard for our environment. We are yet to realize that setting fire to such dumps is a sure way of destroying our health. Dr Silva in his report points out that "air sampling in the area of the dump found levels of particulate matter to be four to nine times above the recommended limit. In the Spanish Town area, residents complained about upper respiratory problems which seemed to be linked to the emission of sulphur dioxide from a chemical plant situated in that community.

Taken for granted

Now, it would appear that many people take for granted the costs associated with atmospheric pollution. Perhaps this is why people all over the country burn their garbage indiscriminately. Particularly in residential areas, people think very little of lighting a fire, which often creates a smoke nuisance to anyone who lives in the immediate vicinity, while at the same time polluting the environment.

What are the costs of this pollution? Gaseous and dust pollution often create serious medical problems. Inhalation of carbon monoxide, carbon dioxide, sulphur oxides and nitrous oxides causes direct physical damage to the tissues of the lungs and bronchial tract. In areas not properly ventilated, acid fumes often cause physical damage to the lungs and eyes. Carbon and lead from factories and motor vehicles, and dust and silicates from strip mining and quarrying can also affect the lungs. The intake of lead can result in brain damage, deformities and congenital birth defects.

The costs of air pollution to personal health are unquantifiable; likewise, also, are the financial costs to individuals and the state. Why should the nation want to incur such costs at a time when the health system is in virtual chaos?

What can we do? A large part of the problem associated with air pollution has to do with poor urban planning, increased vehicular traffic, ineffective emissions testing, the growth of pollution industries, and public ignorance.

Urban planning appears to be irrational and piecemeal. There seems to be little relationship between the growth of businesses, road networks and the transportation system. The Liguanea-Matilda's Corner intersection is a case in point. The powers that be seem unable to understand that one cannot allow the growth of businesses in an area without changes being done to the archaic and extremely irrational road systems. Ever wonder why everyone driving a vehicle is in a hurry, but always late for appointments?

Influx of cars

But the necessity to improve the country's infrastructure becomes even more apparent with the influx of cars into the country. The importation of these cars is directly linked to the dismal state of our public transportation system. However, unless something drastic is done to improve the physical infrastructure of our country, owning a vehicle could become a liability. In other words, soon, it might be easier to walk or ride to work than drive.

With the increase in the numbers of vehicles on the road, it is now essential that emissions testing be conducted more rigorously. Currently, there are some serious questions which need to be asked about these tests.

Little concern

Jamaica is not a country with a large concentration of polluting industries. The problem, however, is that these few industries are located in the most curious spots, and their locations indicate little concern for the well being of people, either by the government or by the private sector. Yet, there is talk of an industrial policy. Any industrial policy which is not linked to proper urban planning and serious monitoring of pollution sources will create nothing less than a death trap. The public must be made to know that many of their health problems have to do with the chaotic environment in which we live. This consciousness is dawning in areas such as Harbour View, which are most afflicted by air pollution.

The people must get involved. Experience both locally and internationally – particularly on environmental matters – has shown that, when public pressure is brought to bear on a government, only then will any action be taken in the interest of the nation, rather than in the interest of special groups. The alternative is for us to be killed slowly. Peace!

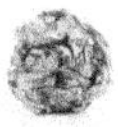

Structural adjustment: Global lessons

(TUESDAY, DECEMBER 20, 1994)

Some months ago, a World Bank official who visited Jamaica commented on the high level of poverty in our society. When he was told that the situation was in part the result of the conditions attached to the loans from lending agencies, such as the one he represented, he proceeded to defend the Bank's position by arguing that countries which negotiate loans from the World Bank are not forced to implement the policies which they eventually pursue. Since this event, however, we have been told that the IMF and the World Bank have broadened their narrow view of structural adjustment to include improvement in the social sector. This position could change again very soon.

Two weeks ago, Dr Dillon Alleyne and Professor Al Francis of the Department of Economics at The UWI and myself attended a conference in Brussels sponsored by the influential World Wildlife Fund. We were one of the many teams presenting seminal studies which looked at the impact of structural adjustment on the environment and on the living standards of countries implementing structural adjustment programmes.

Countries represented at the conference included Mali, Tanzania, Pakistan, Zambia, Cameroon, Vietnam, Venezuela, El Salvador and Jamaica – all of which have adopted a significant structural adjustment programme. Also present at the meeting were representatives from the World Bank, the European Commission, leading academics from British and American universities and members of powerful environmental and non-governmental organizations. The gathering sought to examine and interpret empirical evidence with respect to (a) if and how the policies associated with structural adjustment programmes affected the living standards and the ecological conditions of particular countries; and (b) how this phenomenon can be changed.

Evidence

The evidence showed, with few exceptions, that most of the countries which have implemented structural adjustments have had experiences not wholly unknown to Jamaica. Here are a few of these findings:

1. Deterioration in the social sector, especially education and health
2. Rapid urban growth leading to homelessness (the exception being Zambia)
3. A resurgence of repressed diseases because of the decline in public health and increased urbanization
4. Severe social inequality and an increase in violent crimes
5. Deterioration in the quality of underground water supplies
6. Contamination of surface water and rapid deforestation
7. Either stagnation of, or a retardation of, the export sector (this was not true for all countries)
8. Air pollution as a result of an unregulated industrial sector

Our study, like many others, made a link between structural adjustment policies and attendant deterioration in education and public health. One of the most compelling arguments against the manner in which structural adjustment policies are conceived and implemented is reflected in the data on the indirect impact of these programmes on the environment. Our studies reveal that Jamaica could be headed towards a serious underground water contamination problem if steps are not taken to regulate and address the matter of the construction of hotels and the treatment and disposal of sewage. Again, there are serious problems associated with the dust and chemical emission from bauxite sites, and with land degradation and water contamination from the production of coffee. The African, Asian and Latin American studies also linked deforestation to structural adjustment policies.

It is only a matter of time before questions relating to the environment are integrated into the policy framework of these lending agencies. Already, the evidence is mounting, and it is expected that within the next year or so the findings from these studies will be used as ammunition to fire the change of the narrow economistic approach of these lending institutions. At present, developing countries tend to experience the worst natural disasters and, unfortunately, we have the most to lose if we do not deal with our social and ecological problems; so, there are some who wonder whether environmental concerns will lead to new lending conditions by international funding agencies. Countries such as Mali, El Salvador, and Ethiopia are paying a high social and economic price for man-made ecological problems. At this moment, Zimbabwe is re-examining its policy on eco-tourism; they have found that quick expansion of this sector has led to a virtual decimation of the very animal population which supports this industry. In Jamaica, we have estimated that the potential economic and public health threat of the uncontrolled expansion in the tourism and coffee industries are enormous. Our study suggests ways of increasing coffee revenues without damaging cultivation practices. It also recommends that the resources of agencies like the Natural Resources Conservation Authority (NRCA) be increased so that it can do a better job of monitoring the local environmental situation across the country. However, we are aware that Jamaica will not solve many of its current ecological problems if the social and economic conditions remain oppressive. Peace!

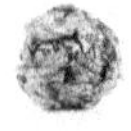

The community and tourism

(SUNDAY, MARCH 19, 1995)

Although Jamaica has witnessed a tremendous inflow of revenue from tourism, not enough of this revenue has been invested in the communities within the main tourist areas. This situation has basically created tourist enclaves, the sustainability of which is seriously in doubt. The conflict between the growth of the tourist industry and the local communities has resulted in a situation where hotels provide top quality accommodation for visitors, but just outside these accommodations some people live in abject poverty.

Many of those who live in poverty migrated to tourist areas because of perceived employment opportunities in the tourism sector. However, for many, this migration was not accompanied by the acquisition of appropriate housing and other human settlement facilities. The result has been the growth of squatter communities which have contributed to unsanitary conditions in many communities. Within these areas there are large numbers of unemployed and underemployed youth who seek to make a living either through the selling of services (ranging from the legitimate to the illegal, such as sex and drugs).

The scramble to make a living is so serious that visitors frequently complain of harassment from locals seeking to sell their wares. In a survey conducted by the Tourist Board in 1992, it was found that almost two out of every three tourists interviewed complained of being harassed by locals.

In addition, the majority of those surveyed identified harassment as the biggest problem they faced while staying in the country. Most of this harassment was in the form of people aggressively trying to sell their goods to visitors in order to secure an income.

Perhaps the most visible manifestation of

enclave-type tourism, and the consequent neglect of communities, is the sustained deterioration in the physical infrastructure of popular tourist towns such as Ocho Rios, Montego Bay and Port Antonio. Residents in Port Antonio consistently complain about poor roads and utilities in their communities.

Visitors to Jamaica often complain that one of the negative features of the tourism sector is the country's poor physical infrastructure. In July 1994, a group of travel agents visiting the country stated that the level of poverty which tourists see on their way from the airport to their hotels could have a damaging effect on the tourists' psyches, because it could create feelings of guilt, thus preventing them from returning to the country.

During the 1980s, our country witnessed a sustained growth in all-inclusive accommodations for tourists. This type of accommodation ensures that the tourist is provided with a variety of quality services without necessarily interacting with the community. A number of national and regional surveys have however found that shop and taxi owners complain that these types of accommodations deny them, and the community, of business.

There is also tension among residents in tourist areas regarding the use of beaches on which hotels are located. In many instances, hotels supply staff to maintain beaches and charge a fee for public use, presumably to defray the cost of maintaining the beaches. However, many residents feel that they are being denied access to the beaches by the hotels.

Tourism and the environment

Numerous environmental problems are associated with the expansion of tourism in Jamaica. Some of these problems have been documented in the United Nations Environment (UNEP) study entitled "Regional Overview of Environmental Problems and Priorities". According to the study, coral reefs are blasted to provide channels for the passage of small crafts into marinas and boating basins. Canals are also cut into residential subdivisions, and poorly designed marinas become septic sinks because of poor water circulation, often induced by shoaling which prevents tidal flush.

In addition, many hotels are without proper sewage treatment facilities. As a result, the raw sewage from the hotels is routinely dumped in ocean waters near to beaches used by tourists and locals for recreational purposes. In some cases, the waters become polluted with faecal coliform and other pathogenic bacteria.

A second problem identified by the study is the frequent use of beach and road vehicles by guests and locals – these vehicles destroy dunes and dune vegetation, thereby contributing to beach erosion. Finally, the study refers to the frequency of large recreational outings by tourists, often to offshore islands, and to caves; such expeditions disturb the wildlife and can destroy the fragile habitat of aquatic life. In general, the environmental problems associated with the growth of tourism in Jamaica include the destruction of reefs, water pollution, sand erosion, and poor sewage disposal. Clearly, there are serious questions about the sustainability of the Jamaican tourism sector unless major changes are made.

Solutions

It is clear that fundamental changes have to be made if tourism is to become sustainable in Jamaica. In 1986, stopover visitor expenditure in the island supported over 250,000 full-time jobs, and every 2.32 stopover visitors supported one job opportunity. However, as the evidence indicates, there is a question as to how long these benefits can continue, given the level of harassment, deteriorating infrastructure and environmental degradation.

To deal with the social problems, there is a clear

need for investors in the tourism industry, along with government, to invest in the provision of proper infrastructure (such as roads, utilities and public parks) in tourist areas. It is also in the interest of everyone for investors and the government to provide affordable housing for the ever-increasing populations in those areas.

To protect workers and organize the activities of the informal economy, while at the same time controlling harassment of tourists, there is need for effective regulation of the plethora of small vendors along tourist areas, perhaps through a licensing process. However, for this to work, vendors should be able to advertise their goods and services to tourists through or with the assistance of hotels and the Tourist Board. Anything less than this will not succeed, given the fiercely competitive environment where there are large numbers of vendors selling similar items, occasionally to the chagrin of the hotel owners and tourism officials.

Increasingly, newly established companies are required to conduct environmental impact assessments (EIAs) before they begin operation in Jamaica. Hotels in tourist areas are now required to do this.

Since the construction of hotels will have an impact on the environment and the people in it, it is important that the public also get more involved in the development of tourist areas. The establishment of hotels along coastal areas, especially in parishes such as Portland and Westmoreland, tends to affect people's livelihood through the reduction of fishing and other agricultural areas. Specifically, the discharge of effluent in the sea, and the blocking off of coastal areas once accessible to locals, for example, can lead to reduced employment opportunities for those in traditional occupations, such as fishing or farming.

Of course, the hotels also bring with them prospects of new jobs and ultimately a larger population in the area. But all of these changes produce potentially serious problems which should be addressed before the hotels begin to operate. There is a need for citizens to engage in debating the merits and demerits of different kinds of tourism in their areas, so that they can more readily cope with changes which will ultimately occur when hotels are opened. Such involvement can result in more preventative action by the citizens, and hence the long-term stability of the community. The alternative can be abrupt changes and alienation of citizens, thereby reducing the possibility for concerted community action when serious problems arise. Peace!

Jawaiian music and tourism

(TUESDAY, OCTOBER 14, 1997)

A few days ago, I received a package from a colleague who is a professor of ethnomusicology at a university in Hawaii. The package contained an audio tape and a video tape of what is popularly known in Hawaii as Jawaiian music. Jawaiian music, which is the contraction for Jamaican-Hawaiian, is reggae with a Hawaiian flavour. Now, most of the Jawaiian songs which I have heard are remakes of recent and old songs done by either local or British artistes. In most cases, the quality of the music and the interpretation of the original songs are good.

As in other parts of the world where reggae has been

indigenized, the more conservative "classical" reggae styles are preferred over the rapping-type dancehall music. Thus, the preference would include the music of Dennis Brown, Bob Marley, UB40, Steel Pulse, Jimmy Cliff and Luciano, to name a few. Despite the much-vaunted success of dancehall music producers internationally, this type of music, even more than rap, is still very much the music of the "outsider", the music of the very young and those on the margins of their society. Whenever and wherever dancehall music has succeeded internationally, it has had to be combined with a good singing style along with decipherable lyrics, or it has had to be fused with hip-hop or rock music to create a crossover sound.

I am not sure how popular Jawaiian music is in Hawaii, but there seems to be a significant audience among the youth there – as is the case in other Pacific countries. A clear indication that reggae music has "come of age" is that it is often combined with other forms of music from other parts of the world to produce something new, while at the same time reflecting the culture of those who have "appropriated" this art form. Hence, today we have the varieties of reggae which include, for example, ragga, ragga soca, reggae-calypso and Jawaiian reggae.

Tourism

These days, it is customary to speak about the benefits to be derived from ecotourism; however, like any other tourism product, the development of ecotourism must be accompanied by significant societal changes if it is to be successful. Countries with significant sustainable ecotourism industries have relatively low crime rates in the areas where the tourists visit, and fairly good infrastructure such as roads, water and transportation. Therefore, ecotourism will not take off if tourists are not made to feel secure; and as well if the infrastructure and transportation outlay are so bad that visitors are forced to give up their independence and conform to inflexible time schedules.

New Zealand, which has one of the best eco/community tourism industries which I know of, has gone as far as to provide parks and lookouts throughout the country where tourists and locals can enjoy the vistas for miles around from an uninterrupted vantage point. Equally, the New Zealand government encourages its citizens to get involved in the industry by providing bed-and-breakfast accommodation for tourists.

According to some tourism analysts, in the future, the most effective and sustainable type of tourism, internationally and here in Jamaica, will be more small-scale, cultural and environmentally oriented. This does not mean that the large-scale, "sea-sand-sun", all-inclusive model is dead, nor is it dying; rather the large-scale, all-inclusive model will continue to command a sizeable section of the market for the foreseeable future. However, unless this type of tourism is closely monitored, it can result in devastating consequences for the environment through pollution and the destruction of the underground and coastal waters and coral reefs. I have seen data which indicate that, if we are not careful, we can create an environmental catastrophe with respect to coastal pollution from these large hotels and the surrounding communities, the latter of which often falls outside of the formal economy. Likewise, in the long run, this type of large-scale tourism does not bring as much benefit to the community as does small-scale, community-oriented tourism.

However, the one basic fact which we need to face is that no tourism model will be sustainable in an environment of economic uncertainty, high crime, poor infrastructure, and a deficient transportation system. Indeed, it is mind-boggling that the government has not yet made the connection between the availability of a proper transportation system and an increase in efficiency and productivity. With this in mind, sustainable tourism planning cannot be done in a vacuum; rather, it must be linked with the other positive developments taking place in the society. Peace!

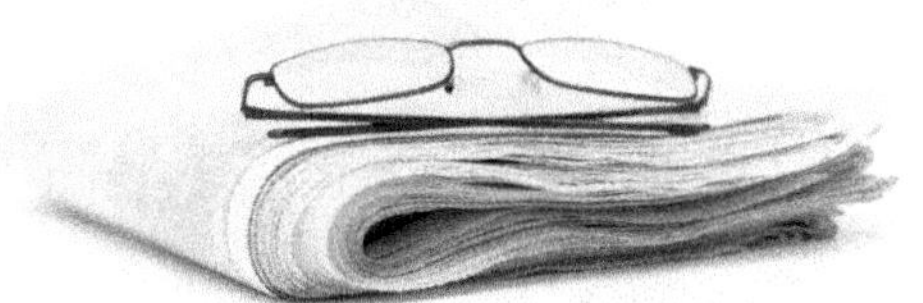

SECTION V

Jamaica and Caribbean Regional Integration

Introduction

Regional integration occurs when two or more countries cooperate on issues relating to trade, policy decisions, and economic growth and development with a view to build greater resilience and scale whilst enhancing bargaining power. This section covers content relating to Caribbean regional integration. The first chapter in this section, Chapter 15, titled "Jamaica, CARICOM and the Media", examines in detail the extent to which citizens across the region have bought into the idea of regional integration. The author reviews the impact of regional integration and the possible benefits that could accrue were CARICOM to be expanded to include non-English-speaking countries of the Caribbean. Issues relating to trade polarization in favour of the Most Developed Countries (MDC) of the English-speaking Caribbean are also explored. Recognizing that the media remains a force to be reckoned with, the author explores the level of apathy sustained by the Caribbean media in their deliberations on the matter of regional integration. Finally, the section concludes by revisiting the benefits of having regional integration within the context of the new development taking place within the region.

Chapter 16 Jamaica, CARICOM and the Media

- Culture, the media and the people/Informative
- Why regional integration makes sense: Part 1
- Why regional integration makes sense: Part 2
- West Indian political union in '97?
- More on political union
- Commentators and the public
- Talk shows and air travel
- Caribbean integration and Jamaica's future

Introduction

The chapter analyses in great detail the importance of balancing and supporting information presented in the media with factual and expert knowledge from both local and regional personnel, whilst providing a forum for the wider citizenry to express themselves. In addition, a call is made for commentators in the region to place greater emphasis on regional policies and institutions, especially since they are known to play a very critical role in promoting greater access to information within the public sector. Finally, the benefits of having cooperative management of air travel, as well as the possibility of a Caribbean regional political union, are fleshed out.

Jamaica and CARICOM

(TUESDAY, JULY 13, 1993)

Last week, the 14th CARICOM Conference of Heads of Government took place in the Bahamas. The meeting dealt with a number of issues, among them closer unity between Barbados, Trinidad and Tobago, and Guyana, and the establishment of an Assembly of Caribbean Community Parliamentarians.

A few of the local talk show hosts and social commentators seem petrified at the thought of a politically integrated region, including Jamaica. In fact, one talk show host went as far as to suggest that the establishment of the Assembly appeared to be a way to enter into a political union through the back door. Now, while I agree that the relatively poor performance of CARICOM in implementing a number of policies justifies some degree of scepticism, I also think that CARICOM should not be judged by the experience of Jamaica. For instance, some people have argued that the establishment of a Caribbean Court of Appeal should not be pursued because of the questionable state of the judiciary in this country. While I share their concerns, I think it is fallacious to argue that, on that basis, the countries of the region should not proceed with examining the possibility of setting up such a court. It is not true to state that what obtains in the Jamaican judiciary also obtains in the rest of the region. Of course, this also holds for other aspects of society.

Trade links

Historically, countries of the Eastern and Southern Caribbean have had links through trade and the movement of people. If one examines the family background of many Barbadians, Trinidadians, St Lucians, Grenadians, and Guyanese, one will notice a network of lineages that exemplify the historical interaction of these peoples. In addition, there has always been trade between these countries among hucksters (whom Jamaicans call higglers). Thus, there is a historical bond between the people which makes the issue of integration more than academic.

I think that it is unfortunate that many Jamaicans who influence public opinion in the media do not see the country's interests tied up with those of the rest of the region. The notion that Jamaica should cast its net up north instead of east and south appears to be rather short-sighted. If one examines the record of the regional integration movement, one will find that the countries which have benefited most from trade are the so-called More Developed Countries (MDCs) – Jamaica, Trinidad and Tobago, Guyana and Barbados. In fact, the nature of trade right up to the 1980s indicates a case of trade polarization in favour of the MDCs. If one looks at the prospects for cross-border investment and the size of the Jamaican economy, its comparatively more developed capital market could result in important advantages for the country in a region which is more closely integrated. At present, Jamaica, and Trinidad and Tobago are the greatest beneficiaries of cross-border investment in the region – closer integration of both trade and policy-making would perhaps benefit Jamaica more than the rest of CARICOM. The attempt to widen CARICOM to include larger markets such as Cuba, the Dominican Republic and Haiti presents a number of even more important opportunities. The recently signed CARICOM-Venezuela agreement, if taken advantage of by regional manufacturers, could result in import monetary rewards, especially for a country like Jamaica which has one of the largest manufacturing sectors in CARICOM.

Benefits

It is not impossible for Jamaica to look up north while at the same time looking to the rest of the Caribbean. In reality, all Caribbean countries look north. The question we have to ask ourselves in this country is: what is the best way to look north? The weight of the evidence shows that Jamaica has more to benefit from doing so together with an integrated region.

While I remain sceptical about the Patrick Manning proposal for a union between Guyana, Trinidad and Tobago, and Barbados, there is indeed some credit to such a proposal. The experience of the OECS has shown us that countries which have pooled their resources and have a well regulated monetary system, which is not subjected to the whims of an individual nation state, are the ones most likely to do better economically. The Eastern Caribbean Central Bank is perhaps the most efficiently run central bank in the region. The so-called MDCs, particularly Jamaica, could learn from them.

Investment

There is no reason why CARICOM governments have to invest vast sums in embassies and high commissions all over the world. The negotiation of the CARICOM-Venezuelan agreement is an excellent example of what could be achieved through regional cooperation.

I think that the time has come when Jamaican policymakers must decide where they stand with respect to closer ties with the countries of the region. To suggest that regional leaders are trying to bring political integration through the back door is indeed very misleading; it is a propaganda which the Jamaican public can do without. It is also misleading to suggest that Jamaica would not benefit much more from a closer relationship with CARICOM. Starting with Bustamante, Jamaican politicians and some social commentators have continued to treat regional integration negatively, even though the record does not justify such treatment. Jamaica has benefited immensely from functional cooperation (namely, in the areas of health and education) and trade, and has been able to use CARICOM as a platform for its foreign policy. On its own, the Jamaican economy has performed the worst in the region for the past two and a half decades. While there are many problems associated with CARICOM, the reality is that Jamaica has more to gain (perhaps more than any other country) than lose from greater integration, even political integration, with the rest of the region. Peace!

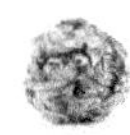

Culture, the media and the people/Informative

(TUESDAY, AUGUST 17, 1993)

Like many other people, I spend a fair amount of time listening to the radio. One show which I find very useful is The Breakfast Club on KLAS. Its international segment is especially informative. However, the programme is fast becoming a little elite club of business persons and commentators who exchange the same old ideas on a daily basis. There also seems to be some compulsion to have politicians on the programme to speak on almost everything in the society. I am not sure that their participation enhances the discussions. Very often, participants on the show are party to a process called groupthink, a situation whereby everyone agrees on basically everything. The show's hosts and participants spend most of the time discussing the economy in the most mundane fashion. Many of the analyses appear to lack any empirical basis and amount to little more than speculation. Seldom does one hear a serious intellectual element to these discussions of the economy, except of course from some American professor who has spent some time in his little office with a little computer analysing faulty statistical data.

I often wonder why the Club never includes in its programme a discussion of regional issues, using regional experts. Yes, there is the occasional link with Trinidad and Tobago, but there are many other countries in the region which deal with issues which affect the welfare of Jamaicans. Why is there this resistance to discussing regional issues in Jamaica? Why is there an unwillingness to tap the large pool of competent experts who live in the other territories? And, yes, there are regional economists who work at The UWI in Trinidad and Barbados who can actually engage in serious discussions on a variety of issues.

Too often, well intentioned groups engage in discussions without doing their research. Sometimes they manage to reinvent the wheel and waste the public's time. A typical example is the New Beginning Movement's seminar on a currency board system for Jamaica. It would appear that these "New Beginners" know nothing of the work that has been done on this issue many years ago by a number of leading regional economists. Why did they not involve people from the Eastern Caribbean Central Bank who have had the most recent experience with this matter? Are Jamaicans not interested in learning from their neighbours? Perhaps we live in a society so insecure that even our so-called leaders have little confidence in themselves. How sad. Peace!

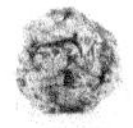

Why regional integration makes sense: Part 1

(TUESDAY, MAY 16, 1995)

At the 25th Annual Meeting of the Caribbean Development Bank, Prime Minister P. J. Patterson urged the Caribbean Community to move towards a single regional market. This is not a new pronouncement. The idea of a single common market economy was agreed upon by the Heads of Government prior to 1992, and reiterated in the report of the West Indian Commission. So, with the constant talk of NAFTA and of an industrial policy, Mr Patterson's statement could not have come at a more opportune time. Unfortunately, over the years, much of the talk about economic integration – not to mention political integration – has been met by a great deal of cynicism, particularly by journalists and some members of the educated elite.

Admittedly, there is some basis for such feelings, especially in light of the failed West Indies Federation, and the many inadequacies which exist today with the operation of the CARICOM Secretariat. Despite these shortcomings, it is important that we make a clear distinction between performance and worth. To say that there are problems within CARICOM does not mean that the movement is worthless. Furthermore, one can develop very persuasive arguments supporting or refuting further economic integration within the region – it depends on one's vision. As such, the question of whether there should be further regional integration should not be based simply on the examination of "hard data" alone. This is because the interpretation of this data is in part a function of one's experience and more importantly one's vision.

Benefit

Those who argue against greater integration within CARICOM often make the claim that small poor countries cannot benefit from integrating their economies. Indeed, this argument is severely flawed, more so, in light of the experiences of other developing countries around the world and particularly in our region where the closely integrated economies of the Organisation of Eastern Caribbean States (OECS) have outperformed the larger and less integrated ones. To be sure, integration within CARICOM does not preclude closer ties with those up North, or in Europe.

Furthermore, experience has taught us that collective negotiation with respect to trade and economic agreements, such as the Lomé Convention, are more beneficial than bilateral negotiations. Experience has also shown that countries which have strong ties to a collective of nations are better able to influence decisions in the international arena than when they venture out alone. As such, we should bear in mind that the force of the collective has more impact when opposing powerful nations such as the USA or Japan.

Now with the talk about joining NAFTA gaining momentum, I cannot see how either Jamaica or Trinidad will gain entry on their own, given the difficulty encountered by the larger and more developed Latin American countries. Indeed, analysts who understand the NAFTA process recommend that entry to NAFTA for CARICOM countries be negotiated collectively.

The other argument often used against closer regional integration is that CARICOM has offered very little tangible benefits to the ordinary man. Nothing is further from the truth. CARICOM has had tremendous successes in the areas of education, health, agriculture, and science and technology; these being but a few of the fruits of this functional cooperation through integration. Institutions within CARICOM which are progeny of our pooled resources include the Caribbean Examinations Council, the Caribbean Broadcasting Union, the Caribbean Meteorological Organization, and the University of the West Indies. In addition to these achievements, the 1970s saw Jamaica, Barbados, and Trinidad and Tobago being the greatest beneficiaries of intra-regional trade.

Incidentally, there are many within CARICOM who support the movement towards a single market and economy without the participation of Jamaica. They cite Jamaica's experience in the Federation as the basis for such a posture. Therefore, it is important that we put Jamaica's retreat from the Federation in proper perspective. My research shows that the decision to form a Federation lacked the strong ideological currency necessary for political and economic longevity. The Federation was doomed before it started.

Others in the Eastern Caribbean also refer to Jamaica's dubious record in the regional movement, particularly, under successive JLP administrations. There can be no doubt that Jamaica under JLP governments has adopted policies which could be construed as being hostile to regional integration. However, this perception should be counterbalanced by the fact that the movement has benefited from the sterling contributions of both Michael Manley and P. J. Patterson.

Consequently, it does not make much sense for CARICOM to proceed with a single market without Jamaica's participation, if only for the need for greater diversity in production and the population market size. Such a market, when established, should also be accompanied by the free movement of labour and the abolition of the ridiculous travel documents required for entry into a CARICOM country. It is indeed shameful that it is easier for an American visitor to enter and work in CARICOM countries than it is for CARICOM citizens.

There is much that our politicians, policymakers and our economists (particularly those trained in America) can learn from West Indian cricket. The success of West Indies cricket has as much to do with the efficient use of talent as with a common sense of identity and purpose. The Germans, Japanese, and Americans are well aware of the link between economic pragmatism and nationhood. Perpetual economic pragmatism without a commitment to some "larger" ideal will get us nowhere. Peace!

Why regional integration makes sense: Part 2

(TUESDAY, MAY 23, 1995)

The reason why much of the discussion on regional integration has tended to be negative is that too often discussions have focused on the role of the politicians, rather than on the efficacy of various policies and institutions within the regional movement. Therefore, I want to focus on two issues which seem to have fallen victim to such reasoning. They are a monetary union and a Caribbean court of appeal.

Monetary union

Discussions about a monetary union are nothing new to our region. The period following decolonization saw the formation of a plethora of central banks across the region. Interestingly, those countries which opted to continue with some form of monetary union have consistently maintained greater macroeconomic stability than those which created their own central banks.

The creation of central banks in Trinidad and Tobago, Barbados, Guyana and Jamaica was seen as an opportunity to afford individual governments greater control over their economy. This desire for autonomy was most evident during the period of the 1970s when Guyana and Jamaica embarked on non-capitalist paths of development. Unfortunately, the governments of these countries invariably used their central banks to further their political ends. However, the so-called Less Developed Countries (LDCs) or members of the Organisation of Eastern Caribbean States retained membership in the Eastern Caribbean Central Bank (ECCB) – formerly the Eastern Caribbean Currency Authority.

This prevented individual governments from arbitrarily printing money or engaging in other activities detrimental to macroeconomic stability. This success has strengthened the argument in favour of monetary integration across the region. At a meeting of the central bank governors of CARICOM in June 1992, it was suggested that CARICOM should adopt a two-tiered approach to monetary integration. According to a report issued by the meeting "Category A would include those countries able to maintain 3 months' import cover in foreign exchange reserves for at least 12 months, and a stable exchange rate for 36 months, with a sustainable debt ratio, not exceeding 15 per cent".

Category B countries

The report further recommends that "Category B countries would be expected to subscribe to the disciplines of the stages approach which involves a series of well defined stages and a pre-determined timetable, the co-ordination of monetary policies, agreement on fiscal limits and the maintenance of exchange rate parities within bands which would be progressively tightened". In sum, what the report is acknowledging is that some countries are better prepared for monetary integration than others. Jamaica and Guyana are considered to be least prepared for entry into such a union because of their highly unstable macroeconomic situation. It should be noted that achieving monetary integration within CARICOM, no matter how desirable, will not be easy.

To be sure, monetary integration will not be popular among politicians who believe that political power should be acquired by any means necessary. Furthermore, monetary union is bound to drive fear into those nationalists who believe that such forms of cooperation will seriously diminish their country's autonomy. Finally, monetary union brings with it many costs. Two of them include high transitional costs, and restrictions on government fiscal programmes. Nevertheless, if a monetary union is approached creatively and cautiously, the benefits should be greater than the costs.

The idea of a Caribbean court of appeal has had much wider acceptance within the region than that of a monetary union, especially in the Eastern Caribbean. However, the idea has also been seriously criticized by commentators and intellectuals across the region. Although much of the debate has become rather muddled, it is still possible to distil two important areas of opposition.

First, it has been argued that a Caribbean court of appeal is likely to be subject to political manipulation by regional governments. Second, it has been suggested that our philosophy of justice in the region is not developed enough to ensure that people brought before the court will be treated fairly. Despite their importance, these arguments cannot be proved or disproved unless a court comes into existence and cases are brought before it. Furthermore, experience has shown that, as institutions become more regional and less under the control of individual governments, it is more difficult for them to be manipulated by politicians. The Eastern Caribbean Central Bank is a case in point. At any rate, the success of a Caribbean court of appeal will rest not simply on the decisions of politicians, but on the strength of civil society.

Admittedly, civil society is not uniform across the region. Civil society is fairly strong in places like Trinidad and Tobago, and Barbados. Here in Jamaica, while it is emerging, serious social inequalities continue to fetter its growth. Consequently, we should guard against committing the individualistic fallacy by arguing that what is true about a particular country is also true of all other countries in the region. For instance, what may be true about the criminal justice system in Jamaica may not necessarily be the case for St Lucia or Grenada. It is therefore regrettable that much of the discussion about a regional court of appeal has been based more on what obtains in Jamaica rather than in the region as a whole. At a more intuitive level, I find it difficult to digest the argument that we – some six million people, who by world standards enjoy a fairly high degree of individual and political freedom, and whose history of slavery and indentureship has allowed us to give to the world some of the greatest philosophers of freedom and democracy – are unable to sustain a credible court of appeal. Some of the world's leading scholars in jurisprudence come from this region; we have no shortage of intellectual talent in this area. Furthermore, there is also no reason why a Caribbean court of appeal could not call on the services of other jurists from other countries to strengthen the court's integrity and independence.

Perhaps it might be useful to remind readers that the Caribbean Examinations Council did not come into existence without opposition. During the 1970s, there were many who thought that regional educational standards would fall if the region offered its own exams. I recall the many predictions of gloom and doom that were made by eminent scholars and popular commentators when it was suggested that we in this region were quite capable of testing our own educational skills and intelligence.

It seems to me that there are valid reasons to be concerned about a Caribbean court of appeal, especially in light of the uneven record of our criminal justice system. Let me make it clear that I support the idea of a regional court of appeal only in a context where governments and the people are prepared to attend to deficiencies in the administration of justice in all the territories. But we should also acknowledge that the strength of the Privy Council in the UK is based on its experience over its many years of existence.

The Privy Council is not a sacred entity; like all human endeavours, it has its limitations. The same is true of central banks. We in this region will never know what we are capable of achieving if we are afraid to act in our own best interests. Peace!

West Indian political union in '97?

(TUESDAY, DECEMBER 31, 1996)

Recently, I have noticed an increased interest in and coverage of regional issues in the local press. Part of the reason for this situation seems to be related to a concern with the effects of global economic changes on countries in the region. Also, out of sheer economic pragmatism, many business people and some politicians are interested in maintaining links with other countries in the Eastern Caribbean because of the "banana issue". Banana is an important export for Jamaica and many other Caribbean countries, and losing preferential access to European markets could prove costly for all those who earn income from this export. Interest in the rest of the region has also resulted from local concerns with the effects of drug smuggling throughout the region, and the controversial Shiprider Agreement.

However, to his credit, Prime Minister P. J. Patterson has placed Jamaica back at the centre of regional development. The one area in which Mr Patterson has been remarkably successful is that of foreign policy, particularly within CARICOM. Both he and Mr Owen Arthur of Barbados have become the de facto leaders of the regional integration movement, taking over from Trinidad and Tobago, and Guyana. Both leaders have sparked renewed interest in CARICOM and integration across the region. With Suriname joining the fold, and others knocking at the door, there are those who argue that now is the time to deepen the movement towards greater economic and, eventually, political integration. I believe that, sooner or later, we in the region will be forced to put the issue of political integration back on the table for serious examination. The sooner we do it the better for us.

It is not my intention to make a case for political integration of the region in this article. I hope to do this in future articles. However, for those who may be sceptical about the idea, I suggest that they peruse the many reports, academic studies, books, speeches and literary works which has dealt with the issue over the past fifty years. To begin with, I would recommend a report written in 1972 by the late W. Arthur Lewis, entitled "Towards an Eastern Caribbean Federation". Arthur Lewis, the region's most respected economist who was saddened by the break-up of the West Indies Federation in 1962 never gave up on the idea of a political union of the West Indies. Throughout his illustrious career, he authored many works which sought to explain why political unification of the region was better than the flag independence which our little fiefdoms now struggle with.

William Demas, the respected Trinidadian economist and regionalist, also set out the case of political unification, beginning with the OECS countries, in a book entitled *Seize the Time: Towards OECS Political Union* in 1987. There are also publications by the late Eric Williams proposing a political union of the West Indies, excluding Jamaica, written during the 1960s. Presumably, Williams' decision to exclude Jamaica was related to Alexander Bustamante's role in the break-up of the West Indies Federation. A later article by Williams in 1973 included Jamaica in a proposed new federation. Recently, there has been talk among regional technocrats and politicians about the viability of a political union of Guyana, Barbados, and Trinidad and Tobago.

Scare tactics

It should be noted that both Lewis and Demas were fighting against a tide of politicians (there were a few exceptions) who duped people into believing that each of their little nations was better off than other countries in the region. Some politicians also used scare tactics to reduce popular support for political integration by suggesting that closer integration would lead to massive migration of people from other territories into their countries. We have now reached the stage where our petty insularities have led us to make some remarkable claims of uniqueness. For instance, almost every Caribbean country makes the claim that sorrel, the popular beverage drunk during the Christmas season, is unique to their "culture". Intellectuals who are supposed to know better often make too much of the seeming uniqueness of their country's dialect, dance and music.

I suppose that, as postcolonial people living in small vulnerable nation-states, we needed to construct our separate identities for self-esteem purposes. Unfortunately, many politicians, keenly aware of this need, have exploited it by helping to construct mythical histories of uniqueness. And so, all of the countries in our region constantly refer to the uniqueness of their struggle against slavery, their labour movement, their dances, and sometimes even their cricketers. If you are someone who is familiar with the countries in the region, these claims of distinctiveness seem rather exaggerated.

There is now an emerging leadership in the region which is in a unique position to change these silly insularities for the benefit of the people. I find it astonishing that citizens of this region accept that an American citizen can enter almost any Caribbean country with a driver's licence, while a CARICOM citizen has to use a passport. This is discrimination which works in favour of the politicians, not the people. Politicians are aware that if Barbadians, Trinidadians or Antiguans feel that Guyanese or St Lucians will take away their jobs, then the possibility of devolving national power to a larger supranational authority is less likely to receive support from the people.

I hope that some of us in the region will take the lead and move the integration process to a higher stage in the coming year. It is likely that if this were to happen other countries would eventually fall in line, as per the history of CARIFTA and CARICOM. Happy New Year!

More on political union

(TUESDAY, JANUARY 07, 1997)

This week, I continue my discussion of political integration by looking at the ideas of one of the region's foremost thinkers on this topic: the Honourable William Demas. In many ways, Demas is ahead of his time in his thinking about political union in the West Indies. Almost a decade ago, when he was in the forefront of the attempt to form a union of countries which make up the Organisation of Eastern Caribbean States (OECS), I recall that I was very sceptical about the idea. At a panel discussion organized by Professor Norman Girvan at the Consortium Graduate School of Social Sciences at which K. Dwight Venner – then Financial Secretary of St Lucia and now Governor of the Eastern Caribbean Central Bank – spoke in support of the idea, there was much criticism of the proposal. When asked to respond to Venner's proposal at the time, I argued that such a union would have contributed little to the development of that region. In addition, I also felt that a political union of that sub-region would not have worked, because based on polls that I had conducted in two OECS countries around that time there seemed to be little support among the people for the idea.

On reflection, I think that both Demas and Venner were correct in their assessment about the benefits and need for a political union of the OECS. Just an aside: in recent years, I have tended to explain away my initial opposition to the idea of political union of the OECS by pointing out that, at the time, I was an overly exuberant graduate student.

As time progressed, opposition mounted against the idea for political union of the OECS and regional governments did little to advance the process, even though their rhetoric told a different story. It seems to me that OECS governments at the time were not themselves interested in the formation of a political union, since this would have whittled away their power.

Benefits

Nonetheless, as I examine the case for political union of the OECS and the wider Caribbean more closely, I am more convinced of its benefits. In his book *Seize the Time: Towards OECS Political Union*, Demas examines the many arguments for and against political union of the OECS. He identifies possible benefits from having larger populations, bigger market economies, more access to capital, greater access to scientific and technological research and a larger pool of skilled labour. He also discusses the prospects for saving money from having fewer embassies and external representatives. Interestingly, one of the problems with CARICOM trade is that movement of capital and labour are heavily regulated because individual nation-states are concerned with protecting local industry and political power. In some instances, it is easier for CARICOM firms to invest outside of the region than within the region. According to Demas, political integration would make it much easier for CARICOM firms to invest and thrive within the region.

Politics and economy

But political union, according to Demas, can be justified on grounds other than economics. For instance, he argues that political union could contribute to greater respect for human rights in the region, because of the checks and balances that would have to be put in place with a federal structure of government. Indeed,

Demas and the late W. Arthur Lewis are thinking along similar lines. Here, Lewis had, since the 1950s, justified the formation of a federation on the grounds that it would likely guarantee human rights for the people of the region more so than if each state became independent. As it stands, there is no reason to doubt such a view.

There are, indeed, numerous other justifications for political union, some of which I hope to touch on in future columns. Those who believe that the idea of political union is an imposition on the society would do well to note Demas' observation that it is idealistic to expect that "by some spontaneous process the people would rise one day and demand political union" in either the OECS or CARICOM. Realistically, political union is an issue which those leaders among us with vision and courage will have to implement; after all, the people of this region did not rise one day and demand independence from British colonialism, nor did they rise one day and end the Federation! Peace!

Commentators and the public

(TUESDAY, JANUARY 06, 1998)

Two weeks ago, a friend of mine said to me that he hoped that during the new year, newspaper commentators and the radio talk show hosts would offer more in terms of solutions to our country's problems and less in terms of biased views. He also lamented the inordinate amount of influence these media personalities appear to have on public opinion. According to him, it is one thing to talk, it is quite another thing to run a country.

Well, I guess my friend is correct, to some extent. Talking about how to run a company and actually running that company are very different experiences, as many book-trained management consultants often learn when they have to run the company. Likewise, radio talk show hosts, commentators and academics who bemoan the performance of policymakers often have a rude awakening when they themselves become policymakers. Respected academic, Leslie Manigat of Haiti, one of Duvalier's fiercest critics, learned that removing Duvalier was one thing, but having to run the country afterwards was quite another. Manigat was ousted from power shortly after becoming president following the fall of Duvalier.

Another example of this occurred in New Zealand a few years ago, when their most popular talk-back radio host (as they are also called), decided to trade in the radio studio for a career in politics. However, she soon discovered that life was not as she had often described it while on the outside. When questioned by the media and people about actions that she had taken, which she herself had vehemently criticized while on radio, she confessed that things were not as simple as she had made them out to be while behind the microphone.

However, I do not know that my friend or anyone has anything to worry about regarding the influence which newspaper commentators or radio call-in show hosts have. To be sure, newspaper commentators in our society do not have much influence because we are still very much an oral culture; not many people read. We must also recognize that although many more people listen to the radio call-in shows, they seem quite capable of distinguishing between reasonable arguments and those which are based on prejudice and animosity.

The "fear" of the so-called power of radio talk shows is not unique to Jamaica. Just recently, I came across an article on the internet which was critical of a talk-back radio programme in Australia. As with all popular talk radio hosts, this one had a very clear, predictable and controversial perspective on his country's development. Permit me to quote the article by Steve Mickler at length: "Like many talkback presenters, Sattler routinely disguises the amount of control he has over almost every aspect of the programme. Particular points of view come to dominate the discussion of topics on The Sattler File as a result of the format of talkback radio itself, and the possibilities this creates for Sattler and his ilk to confuse editorial comment with more objective information. Readers of newspapers are attuned to the fact that the editorial column is not meant to be a neutral presentation of ideas. It is understood that editorials contain the views and opinions of the newspaper. Similarly, regular columnists are identified quite clearly as writers of opinion; some have the author's photograph or caricature alongside and even a disclaimer of responsibility by the newspaper printed underneath.

Enormous power

Straight news reports, on the other hand, while they may or may not have a 'by-line' to credit the reporter, are expected to be impartial and balanced presentations of the relevant facts pertaining to a particular story. In principle, they are not supposed to reflect the views, values and opinions of the reporter or the paper. But talk-back radio enables presenters more easily to conflate or confuse opinion with fact if they so wish. They have enormous power to establish the terms under which the topic (which they have chosen from among many) can be discussed at the beginning of the programme or segment. By framing issues in a certain way, credibility can be lent to some views, but not others" (*Talkback Radio, Antielitism and Moral Decline: A Fatal Paradox* published in 1995).

Now, while Mr Mickler may well be correct in his critique of talk-back radio, I really see nothing much to worry about in a democratic society where people are supposed to be able to think for themselves. Studies of talk shows in which the audience participates indicate that the most popular programmes are not necessarily those which are the most truthful, balanced, educational or constructive. Most listeners know this. Few listeners expect impartial comments from their favourite host on social and political issues. Listeners tune in to the talk shows for a variety of reasons – in particular, for entertainment, usually characterized by the clashes and confrontations between the host and callers. Many of the talk show hosts derive their popularity from being humorous and very opinionated. As one critic of Oliver Stone's new movie Talk Radio, which is based somewhat on the life and death of popular Denver talk radio host Alan Berg, argues, the show demonstrates that people are more likely to listen to hosts that they do not always agree with.

What some of the research indicates is that the most popular call-in talk shows in many countries tend to be those that are critical of their governments, take on influential interest groups like large corporations, and challenge the dominant political and cultural ideologies of the day. They also offer no solutions to the problems which they raise, and they routinely claim to be championing the cause of "those without a voice" and the national interest. One of the unstated objectives of many of these shows is to achieve high ratings in order to bring in more advertising dollars. What better way to achieve this than by being controversial?

Inappropriate

Howard Stern achieved meteoric rise in popularity across the US by mocking the establishment and articulating views which the society often considered to be racist, sexist and crude. Stern realised that the more he offended "the establishment", the more popular he became. Part of his popularity is the entertainment value he offers his listeners, both those he offends and those who adore him. Stern publicly expresses views which are considered inappropriate, or in bad taste. However, these views are shared by many Americans.

Rush Limbaugh, America's leading talk-back radio host, as well as Bill Clinton and the Democrats' fiercest critic, achieved his highest radio ratings in approximately the same period during which Clinton also received his highest ratings. Clinton went on to win the presidency on two consecutive occasions when his critics were also very popular. Evidently, there seems to be no positive correlation or causal link between the popularity of a particular radio or television call-in programme and the popularity of a government, or certain social and cultural ideas. Contrary to popular belief, radio talk show hosts are not as influential as is often claimed.

In my view, commentators and radio talk show hosts of all types have a duty to be responsible. However, they are not obligated to be impartial or to provide solutions to problems they raise, unless these are their stated objectives. I am sure that the public is quite capable of understanding the difference between just talking about something and actually doing it. To my friend and others, I say: let the talk commentators and talk shows be. Peace!

Talk shows and air travel

(TUESDAY, FEBRUARY 02, 1998)

A few weeks ago, I wrote an article on talk shows, which resulted in a fair amount of feedback from some readers of this column. While some agreed with the view that radio talk-shows (that is, talk-back radio shows) are primarily about entertainment, others, however, pointed to the fact that although they often listen for the entertainment value, these shows can be informative. I quite agree. Now, to make sure that readers do not get the wrong impression about how I feel about talk shows, here are a couple of good things about this interactive genre.

The talk show may help to advance the democratic process by providing a forum for people to express ideas about a wide array of issues. Although callers to any one talk show do not necessarily represent national sentiments on particular issues, they reflect the concerns of sections of the society. Especially in cases where these views are marginal, talk shows provide an important avenue for expression. Many of us mistakenly believe that the only views that count are those of the majority, as are reflected in public opinion polls. This sort of thinking can be dangerous, as majority views can be just as tyrannical as minority ones. Equally, majority views can result in a great deal of harm to minorities. Take, for example, a majority decision to make (Christian) prayer compulsory for school children. Such a decision not only discriminates against people of other religions, but, if rigidly enforced, could conceivably lead to a great deal of psychological harm for those pupils who are not Christians.

Another important role of the talk show is that it provides a forum for making public officials accountable. If we consider that public servants have a duty to respond to the concerns of citizens, then when these officials respond to the questions and criticisms of members of the public and investigative journalists, one is given a chance to better understand the issue at hand or the proposed policy or path to be undertaken. In many industrialized countries, government officials routinely appear on talk shows to answer the concerns of the public and the media. When and where such practices become institutionalized, they help to increase public awareness of many issues, and by extension advances the cause of accountability.

There can be no doubt that the various radio talk shows in our society have had a positive impact, in so far as forcing public officials to be more open about a number of public policy issues. Therefore, given the limited avenues through which citizens can have a say in the running of the country, talk shows provide a forum for a significant section of the population to ask questions, discuss their concerns and, perhaps in the future, contribute to the formation of policy. To the extent that hosts are responsible for facilitating these concerns, then this augurs well for the development of our society.

Air travel woes

Once again, CARICOM is caught up in an air travel crisis and questions are being raised about the wisdom of a few Caribbean countries subsidizing American Airlines instead of cooperating with regional carriers. The air travel issue in the region has been studied by consultants or discussed at "high level" meetings for many years, resulting in numerous recommendations from experts in relation to the benefits of cooperative management of air travel. The first of these studies was done by Steve DeCastro in 1967, in which he recommended the setting up of regional air travel arrangements, to save on unnecessary duplication of air travel facilities and airlines. However, during the era of decolonization, every one of our specks in this region wanted to have its own airline with planes adorned with the national flag. Yet not one CARICOM nation has been able to run an efficient or profitable airline.

Many global factors have conspired to make the running of an airline business rather difficult in this region. These difficulties have not been helped by decisions based more on "crony economics" and partisan politics rather than on sound business sense. Sadly, and with this in mind, almost every time there is a glimmer of hope that we in this region will learn from our past, something happens and our governments return to making short-term fire-fighting policies with questionable long-term benefits to individual territories. Let us hope that this is not one of those times. Peace!

Caribbean integration and Jamaica's future

(SUNDAY, MARCH 08, 1998)

Something is sweeping across the Eastern Caribbean region at a pace so rapid that the politicians there are beginning to wake up to it. It is a process characterized by the formation of entertainers from the different islands into groups bound for the markets in the metropole where the diaspora resides.

Groups like Burning Flames of Antigua, Krosfyah of Barbados, and Xtatic of Trinidad and Tobago all combined to perform before a common audience of marooned Caribbean people in the cities of North America and Europe. This is a process characterized by the movement of peoples in search of work, wealth, family roots, family trees and the discovery of self.

This is also a process in which investors led by the Trinidadians are purchasing properties and shares, from Antigua to Georgetown. These investors sense that they might be catalysts for a process that has been with us since the 16th century. The process is the closer integration of the Caribbean region, a process not directed by politicians, but which they are now trying to join.

The small island nations – or more accurately, according to the historians, the island communities of Caribbean people scattered across the region into our artificial nation states – seem to be coming to terms with their place in this modern world.

There was a time when I felt that it would not happen; I would look at the trade statistics, read the sterile works of academics and listen to the self-serving reports of journalists, and then ponder why we in this region have been so shortsighted as to eschew closer cooperation. But such a way of looking at the complexity of life can be myopic, if not dangerous.

For in trying to understand the Caribbean by simply focusing on a few empirical facts, as reflected in, say, the trade figures or the Caribbean Community (CARICOM) decision-making mechanism, I ignored my own lived experience, that of others, this phenomenal work of our artists, and the lessons of history.

Union

Therefore, this is not an analysis based fully on the hard "data" as social scientists know it. Rather, it draws on my lived experience from being part of the Caribbean family, and being in tune with Eastern Caribbean life in particular, which has led me to conclude that in the not-too-distant future the Eastern Caribbean region will form a political and economic union. Their example will be the catalyst for greater regional cooperation and integration from North to South.

Why

To understand what is happening across the Eastern Caribbean, one has to look at the history of the English-speaking Caribbean and, in particular, the Eastern and Southern Caribbean.

The (English-speaking) Caribbean is a region which, historically, was treated as a single administrative and political space by the British. Before the emergence of the decolonization era, the Eastern Caribbean region witnessed movements of people and resources relatively freely from territory to territory. Come the 1960s, fragmented pseudo-nationalist movements began to emerge and flag independence from Britain was achieved.

What emerged in the Caribbean were movements for psychological emancipation and economic progress rather than, strictly speaking, movements for national independence. These anti-colonial movements were aimed at overcoming economic and racial oppression. These were movements geared towards achieving "recognition", as Frantz Fanon would say.

In other words, these were not really nationalist movements in the political sense. This is why the Federation was the obvious means to an end. The fact is that the Caribbean had always been run as a collective entity. The Federation may have failed at the political level, but intellectually, at least in the Eastern Caribbean, the rationale for its existence was and remains quite sound.

But even with the end of the Federation and with the ushering in of flag independence, Caribbean people from the different countries still interacted to a large extent. Migration statistics indicate significant migration flows between the Eastern and Southern Caribbean.

However, flag independence now means that Caribbean people have to get passports to see their cousins in another country, whom they used to visit by simply taking a boat from Saint Lucia to Saint Vincent without the need for immigration documents. Also, Saint Lucian traders now require documents to travel to Barbados to sell their bananas, instead of sailing their boats to the Bridgetown Wharf as they used to do not so long ago. In other words, flag independence has reduced the historical connection between different countries by trying to create nationalism which belies the historical experiences of the people.

Changing times

But times are changing very fast. The Organisation of Eastern Caribbean States (OECS) has recognized that a collective approach to development is a sensible route to follow. History is on their side and so is common sense. The OECS will have to deal with the banana problem soon, and it makes no sense for them to approach this issue on an individual basis. Furthermore, their positive experience with the Eastern Caribbean Central Bank should be a lesson for those who wish to reduce the ability of politicians to manipulate the economy.

Recently, the Barbados government indicated its desire to join the OECS. Many Barbadians and OECS members welcomed the news. Both OECS and Barbados stand to benefit from greater cooperation. Barbados is at the crossroads of the Caribbean. It houses most of the regional and international organizations in the Caribbean and is really the hub of Caribbean travel. Its infrastructure and business facilities make it the ideal place for a magnet point within the region.

Even future travel between Africa and the Caribbean is likely to have Barbados at the centre. Barbados publishes most of the regional newspapers. There are no fewer than five nationally distributed papers in Barbados, three of which are regional in orientation; one – The Broad Street Journal – is dedicated exclusively to regional business. Barbados is 35 minutes from Trinidad and 45 minutes from Antigua by air. Realistically, there can be no talk of wider regional integration unless Barbados is involved.

The current Prime Minister, Owen Arthur, a man who was educated at the Mona campus of The UWI, and who worked in Jamaica during the 1970s, has realized this and has sought to capitalize on the strategic location of Barbados. Mr Arthur has already said that he intends to make Barbados the leading services centre in the region. So far, he seems to be succeeding. Peace!!

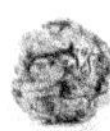

Chapter 17 CARICOM Policies

- The Cuban crisis and response
- The power of the Chinese
- Haiti, Cuba and the USA
- The importance of vision
- Rights and justice in Surinam

Broadly speaking, a policy can be described as a set of guidelines which outline courses of actions to be taken in response to a wide range of political, social and economic issues. Given that CARICOM is the single most important body responsible for promoting economic integration and cooperation within the region, it has a number of polices and guidelines that govern how it responds to specific situations, such as those concerning trade, foreign policy, and migration, among other policies.

This chapter addresses the increased visibility of China in the region, as well as the importance of taking a regional position on critical foreign policies, especially in light of the increased vulnerability of the region to internal and external forces. The chapter also considers the importance of having a unified plan on how to address the issue of rapid globalization, supported by long term plans geared towards negotiating bilateral and multilateral agreements, for example, the Shiprider Agreement. A quick glance is also taken at how countries in the region relate with each other. More specifically, the chapter looks at the extent to which Caribbean countries are eager to expand linkages with the neighbouring Cuba, as well as their willingness to lend their voices when confronted with matters that affect sister nations, for example the treatment of the Maroons and other indigenous peoples in Suriname.

The Cuban crisis and response

(TUESDAY, JULY 20, 1993)

As I descended the steps of the small shivering aircraft, I looked expectantly at the Cuban landscape. This was my fourth visit to Cuba, and the first since the end of the Cold War. But Cuba is no longer what it was during the early 1980s when I first visited. The world in which it now finds itself has changed. Abandoned by a splintered and ideologically transformed Soviet Union, and isolated by the United States of America, the Cuban government and society are now confronted by the reality of trading in a harsh capitalist world economy in which the accumulation of hard currencies – that is, the currencies of the industrialized countries – determines a country's buying power. In the era before the Cold War, Cuba conducted an important barter trade with the Eastern Bloc countries. This has all but disappeared.

Like other developing countries, Cuba is confronting an intense social and economic crisis. For the first time since the revolution, the country is faced with double-digit unemployment. It has seen a fall in its gross national product over the past five years, and the Castro administration has been forced to rationalize social services. The fuel shortage has led to a transportation crisis. The small number of motor vehicles on the roads is a vivid indication of how serious the crisis is. Ten years ago, it was not unusual to see near bumper-to-bumper traffic moving along the wide streets next to the Malecón. Today, one can virtually count, with ease, the number of cars which pass on these same streets. Of course, many of these vehicles which now travel this route are taxis which transport the growing number of tourists who now come to the country.

The Cuban government is actively promoting tourism since it represents an important source of foreign exchange. However, concentration on this sector has led to the development of a dual labour market in which those who work in the tourism sector tend to earn higher wages than those in the other sectors. As a result, many well educated Cubans take up very low-skilled jobs in the tourism sector.

Tourism

For instance, I was told of a case in which an engineer took a job as a porter, because of the potential to earn more money. Another problem associated with the growth of this sector and the decline in the country's economy has been the growth of prostitution. Although not high by Third World standards, it is growing.

The Cuban economic crisis has led to another phenomenon – the growth of a fairly large informal sector. This sector is an important supplier of many items which cannot be obtained on the official market. Many of the players in this sector are people who travel overseas (especially to Miami to visit their families) and return with goods. A conservative estimate of the monetary size of the Cuban informal sector puts it at about US$40 million.

However, what is interesting about the Cuban society is its response to the economic crisis. One is struck by the resilience and adaptability of the Cuban people. Although a difficult choice, many Cubans have turned to bicycles as an alternative form of transportation. Also, the type of hostility which has come to characterize social relations in many developing countries, such as Jamaica, is not present in Cuba. Although crime has increased on a per capita basis, it is nowhere near what obtains in Jamaica, Trinidad and Tobago or Barbados. Undoubtedly, people are disconnected, but the Cuban government has made sure that important services such as health and education are provided for all. Furthermore, the state has made sure that people do not starve. Hence, you hardly find beggars or vagrants in the streets. All in all, there is a certain dignity with which the Cuban people have responded to the crisis.

Welfare

I have always believed that there is much more to the Cuban experiment than Americans would have us believe. No matter what one says about the option which they choose, it is clear that the people are put first. Even in its most difficult times, the welfare of the people is still a central concern of the government.

How many of us can say the same about our own governments in the region? It would appear that it is this contract between the state and the people which has allowed Castro to maintain both authority and legitimacy. How many of our leaders in the region can honestly claim both legitimacy and authority? In this sense, I disagree with those critics who argue that Fidel Castro will fall due to some uprising of the people. I have no doubt that the Cuban people, as they debate their fate in this new world, will arrive at a suitable option for themselves, and will not be forced into some ideological quick fix by external "money suckers" or local ideologues who care not for the grave social and economic inequalities which continue to torment our societies, but only for the acquisition of the latest gadget from the metropole.

As we in the region debate regional integration, let us not forget Cuba. It is unfortunate that we in this part of the world have accepted, instead of finding out for ourselves, the propaganda of the American media about Cuba. The Caribbean Broadcasting Union has made inroads into reporting about Cuba. This is to be commended. Let us take advantage of the changes in Cuba as the Europeans and other Latin Americans are doing. There is much to be gained from trade and tourism, not to mention cooperation in health and agriculture. At the last Heads of Government meeting, CARICOM leaders acknowledged the importance of closer links to our brothers and sisters in Cuba for economic reasons. Unfortunately, this apparent thirst for a Cuban relationship seemed to have been spurred by talk of the Americans' interest in a soon-to-come post-Castro Cuba. Let us not allow other people to dictate our destiny. Let us seize the time and take advantage Cuba's geographical and cultural links to the region. Peace!

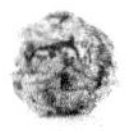

The power of the Chinese

(TUESDAY, MAY 31, 1994)

In a matter of days, the president of the United States, Bill Clinton, will have to make a decision about renewing China's Most-Favoured-Nation (MFN) trading status. Despite his rhetoric about human rights abuses and China's sharp rebuff of such rhetoric, it is highly unlikely that he will refuse the world's fastest growing superpower the MFN status for another year. It appears that the US, like its counterparts in Europe, has come to accept that China is quickly filling the gap left by the former USSR in superpower politics. China's record speaks for itself. While the world economy has been witnessing sluggish economic growth during the past couple of years, the Chinese economy has been growing at an amazing rate. In 1992, China's growth rate was propelled by a 20 per cent increase in industrial production. In the last quarter of 1993, the state-owned sector grew by 14 per cent. Furthermore, during the first quarter of this year, industrial output of joint ventures and private businesses was growing at an annual rate of 80 per cent. China will very soon become the world's second biggest economy after the United States.

American policymakers are well aware of the economic opportunities in China. Only last year, a number of top executives from the US secured joint venture arrangements with the Chinese which included: the manufacture of fibre optic cable, the production of personal computers, and the establishment of a new Hepatitis B vaccine factory. US exports to, and investment in, China are surging annually. In 1993, the US exported US$9 billion and invested US$5 billion in China. The Clinton administration can ill afford to lose such deals, as it could lead to the loss of tens of thousands of jobs in America.

But China is more than an emerging economic powerhouse; it also has a strong military and great technological capability. The Chinese have a satellite in space, are major arms manufacturers, and possess the world's largest army. In 1993, China spent US$7.4 million on defence. What is perhaps more intriguing about the Chinese situation is that unlike other communist nations it has successfully overcome civil unrest, maintained its rhetoric of communism, and implemented market reforms with a degree of success that is the envy of IMF and World Bank officials. What is it that accounts for China's iconoclastic success?

Sinologists

First, sinologists point to the fact that China is fairly ethnically homogeneous – about 94 per cent of the population are Han Chinese, with only 6 per cent making up over 50 different ethnic groups. It is believed that this homogeneity has prevented the type of ethnic conflict seen in Europe following the fall of communism.

Second, it has been argued that, unlike other communist countries, China implemented important social and economic reforms which prevented the type of economic collapse which occurred in the former USSR, Poland and Yugoslavia. The leader of this process was former premier Deng Xiaoping, who dismantled the inefficient system of communes and turned farms over to families. The result was a 44 per cent increase in output over eight years. He also implemented a number of market reforms which saw the development of joint ventures between the state and private capital outside of China.

Notwithstanding these reforms, the Chinese government has refused to implement a policy of "glasnosts" and "demokratizatsiya" along the lines of the USSR. Yet, except for the Tiananmen Square uprising of 1989, there have been few signs of large-scale social unrest in China. In my view, this situation is best explained by the culture and history of China. China has been a well unified country for thousands of years.

Ideology

Confucianism (and later modified versions of Taoism) lead the ideological basis for people to obey authority and pay particular attention to family and community. Perhaps it could be said that the totalitarian philosophy of communism was more relevant with regard to China's authoritarian and rigid social structure than it was in Eastern Europe.

It should also be noted that the approximately 50 million overseas Chinese who reside in virtually every part of the globe are the most important investors in China. Most of the overseas Chinese live in Taiwan and Hong Kong, which together with China account for a whopping five per cent of world trade. Sinologists are unlikely to be surprised by China's emerging superpower status. After all, we are talking about a country which has a long and extremely distinguished history. The Chinese, for instance, roamed the seas and reached the coast of East Africa long before the Europeans.

Chinese Columbus

Zheng He, the "Chinese Columbus", arrived on the East African coast around the early part of the 15th century. While Columbus set sail with three ships, Zheng He commanded 62 galleons, more than 100 auxiliary vessels and tens of thousands of men. Trade between Africa and China took place long before the Portuguese sought to plunder the East African coast.

For over a decade now, China has been increasing its visibility in the Caribbean. In Barbados, for example, Chinese technical assistance has been present in the areas of agriculture and large-scale construction. Given the increase in visibility of the Chinese in the global economy and in the region, it is perhaps time for a CARICOM policy on China based on serious ongoing research and collective self-interest. We need nothing less if we are to adequately deal with the experience and talent of a reborn China. Peace!

Haiti, Cuba and the USA

(TUESDAY, SEPTEMBER 6, 1994)

Last week in a radio interview, foreign ministers of Jamaica, and Trinidad and Tobago attempted to explain with very little success why they supported an invasion of Haiti.

It is unfortunate that our regional politicians have no clue about what to do about Haiti, except to follow Uncle Sam's orders. The problem which they face is justifying an American invasion of Haiti while not supporting one against Cuba. This contradiction will become even more apparent as anti-Castro Cuban-Americans, along with conservative republicans and salivating business people in the US, pressure the Clinton administration to get rid of Fidel Castro.

Let me make it clear that I do not believe in the notion of non-intervention. The presence of thousands of refugees clamouring to enter the US makes this idea unrealistic. In addition, US taxpayers still have to foot the bill when refugees come to their shores.

Furthermore, I do not support those who are against the invasion of Haiti simply on the basis of maintaining absolute consistency in international law.

Consistency should not be maintained for its own sake. However, as much as I want to see the present regime in Haiti go and Aristide returned to power, I find it difficult to support an American-led invasion of the country, not only because of US involvement in the country, but because of the implications of such an invasion for other countries, specifically Cuba.

Interestingly, there are those in US policy-making circles who are pointing to similarities between the Cuban and Haitian cases. Furthermore, the recent change in refugee policy towards Cuba, bringing it closer in line with that of Haiti, is causing commentators and interest groups in the US to point to similarities in the situations of both countries. Similarities in problems could well lead to similarities in solutions.

To be sure, the situations in Cuba and Haiti are not the same. True, both countries are without democratic regimes; however, until recently, Cuba's powerful state had over the years provided the majority of Cuban people with a standard of living far superior to that of most developing countries. Despite what we wish to say about the Castro regime, it had until the collapse of the Eastern Bloc provided proper health care, education and employment for its people. It is therefore disingenuous for people to claim that the Cuban government is solely to be blamed for the current economic crisis faced by that country.

The fact is that no Caribbean or Latin American country could seriously survive a US embargo without significant support from a powerful trading partner. If there were a US blockade of Japan today, that economy would go into a deep recession in a few months. The reality is that US leverage in the global economy is still enormous, and countries which are closer geographically to the US are even more at its mercy. But even without a blockade, and with net population movements to the US, the Jamaican economy is not that much better than Cuba's. Something is definitely wrong when the US can trade with China and Vietnam, and repeatedly negotiate with Haitian dictators, while refusing to talk to Cuba, except with respect to the refugee crisis which they encouraged.

Unlike the Cuban regime, the Haitian governments have not had a history of looking after their people. In addition, historically, Haiti has had a fragile state with its rulers leading a precarious existence. For instance, nine of Haiti's presidents were presidents for life, one committed suicide, one was executed, two were assassinated, and 22 were overthrown.

Haiti also has a complicated colour and class problem which can be traced back to the independence struggles in the late 18th century. This Black-Mulatto conflict was a contributing factor to the rise of Papa Doc's regime, and it also haunted Aristide's government.

As with pre-Mandela South Africa and the Philippines under Marcos, US policy towards Haiti was based on its security interests and not on those of the people. The US supported Papa Doc in return for military bases or guided missile stations in Haiti. During Haiti's first democratic election, the US supported Marc Bazin, a conservative economist who had the support of Haiti's elite.

It is therefore not surprising that after Aristide's victory, certain elements in the US policy-making circles started rumours to the effect that Aristide was insane. A serious investigation of these allegations, originally circulated by the Central Intelligence Agency and anti-Aristide republicans such as Jesse Helms, found that they were concocted. Aristide's militant nationalist stance during the election campaign seems to have offended the US conservatives.

In a recent interview on television, opposition leader Edward Seaga indicated his lack of support for the return of Aristide to office, referring to him as a madman. Aristide was given a mandate by 68 per cent of the Haitian people to govern their country. It seems to me that the Haitian people are the ones to determine whether or not Aristide should return to power. All indications are that the Haitian people want their president back in office.

On the other hand, those who clamour for an invasion of Haiti might find themselves persuaded to support an invasion of Cuba. It would appear that the US really has no interest in invading Haiti, for Cuba is a place where their interests lie. We could be setting up for the Cuban scenario by invading Haiti.

What the Cuban and Haitian crises dramatize most vividly is the extreme vulnerability of the region, internally and externally, and that the new world order is really nothing new. Above all, however, what is clear from the events is the emergence of a new pragmatism among our politicians, a pragmatism which has its roots in a lack of vision and a syndrome of dependence on the North. Peace!

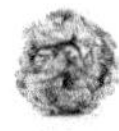

The importance of vision

(TUESDAY, DECEMBER 10, 1996)

Last week, two events occurred which led me to conclude that part of the problem of development which we face in the Caribbean is the sense of who we are in the world and where we are going as a people. The first event had to do with the announcement by Barbados' prime minister, Owen Arthur, that he will not sign the Shiprider Agreement – an agreement that, in effect, would have given the US authority to police the country. Mr Arthur was adamant that while his country is in favour of fighting the illegal drug trade, the methodology should be negotiated and not simply be a unilateral proclamation by Uncle Sam, and rightly so. For, while sovereignty is not an absolute, it does not mean that we in this region should simply surrender control over our lives to any superpower.

However, there is little that the people of this region can be proud of, given the way in which regional governments have approached this matter. You see, the history has shown that CARICOM has always avoided taking a regional position on critical foreign policy and security issues, and yet one of the objectives of the Treaty of Chaguaramas, which brought CARICOM into existence, was the need to have a coordinated and collaborative approach to foreign policy. Unfortunately, our regional political leaders seem to have a penchant for the short-sighted policy of negotiating bilateral agreements, which invariably work against them in the long run.

In this regard, both Patterson and Arthur should be lauded for their call for a regional position on the illegal drugs issue, since the illegal drug trade has significant implications for the development of our countries individually and collectively. To be sure, given the close proximity of each territory to the US and to each other, and the high degree of travel within the region, all the territories are likely to be affected in one way or the other, and as well by each other's activities.

Thus, it is high time for CARICOM to move beyond the rhetoric of regionalism and come up with a regional position on its role in the so-called fight against illegal drugs in this part of the hemisphere. And whether or not we agree with them, the Americans already know what their role is and how they would like this region to fit into their grand design. Regrettably, CARICOM countries collectively or individually do not seem to have as clearly defined a position or perspective as does the United States.

This brings me to the second happening: the Lester Thurow Lecture, which was delivered at the Pegasus Hotel last week. Although there were a few points which I would take issue with, what impressed me about him was his ability to combine abstract academic ideas with experience and common sense. He is certainly not a slave to theories or intellectual fads. Many of Thurow's ideas seemed to be informed by practical experience and a willingness to understanding people as human beings, and not simply as producers and consumers of goods and services.

An important point made by Professor Thurow was that Caribbean countries have to develop some sort of plan, or vision, if you will, as to how they will participate in the rapidly changing global economy. Thurow, an internationally renowned economist who was invited to Jamaica by the Mona Institute of Business, UWI, pointed to the fact that development is not haphazard, but rather a planned affair. He also stated that while Jamaica and the Caribbean can learn from the so-called Asian Tigers, we cannot replicate their development strategy.

Thurow made a number of important observations about the future of the global economy, one of which was the need for small states in the region to find what "worked" for them instead of trying to copy experiences which are culturally inappropriate. When asked about the role of ideology in the development process, he pointed to the fact that it was indeed important. After all, an ideology is a kind of anchor point from which one can articulate a vision.

To be sure, some of Professor Thurow's observations about the global economy are common knowledge, and many of the ideas he advocates for with regard to the region are not new. Some of our economists like George Beckford, Lloyd Best and C. Y. Thomas have been saying many of these things for quite some time. However, as a colleague of mine observed, it may in fact be a good thing to hear these ideas from an overseas academic, since our policymakers and elite groups seem to have higher regard for ideas which come from people in the metropole.

Against this background, we in this region have to stop being survivors who passively sit by and wait for events to unfold. Try as one may, there is no escaping this issue of vision. Peace!

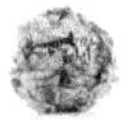

Rights and justice in Surinam

(TUESDAY, FEBRUARY 18, 1997)

Suriname is a sister CARICOM country in the Southern Caribbean which has been engaged in a perpetual battle between the indigenous and Maroon peoples and the state over the rights of these peoples in their country. Yet very little is heard about this very tense situation – perhaps because the main source of news in this region is the American media, which has little interest in such events, unless of course refugees begin to crawl across their borders. But according to a report from Forest Peoples Programme, an organization based in Britain, in November 1996, the indigenous people and the Maroons held their second Gran Krutu (great gathering), the purpose of which was to strengthen their relationship and to express their opposition to the sale of their ancestral lands to multinational mining and logging companies. So, despite what the Harvard religious economists tell us, not everyone wants to sell their souls to live like the people in Singapore or Taiwan.

Suriname, unlike most countries in this hemisphere, does not recognize that indigenous or Maroon people have any special rights to land or are to be given special considerations under the law. This is amazing, since most Surinamese are of African and Indian descent – groups that have fought for their own rights under the colonial law. Consequently, tribal and non-tribal Surinamese people have much in common.

The tribal peoples in Suriname suffer from the same threats of development that other indigenous people throughout the world are called upon to endure. These are: economic marginalization, high infant mortality rates, cultural destruction, high crime rates and the low overall survival rates. Already, the Surinamese government has granted concessions to mining and logging companies, which in effect allow these multinationals to encroach on peoples' lands. As such, logging companies including Berjaya Berhad, Suri-Atlantic and MUSA of Indonesia are said to have been awarded contracts for millions of dollars for logging. Might I add that, although the contracts have been suspended, many fear that it will not be too long before logging begins. After all, it is merely a suspension, not a cessation order. You see, Indonesian logging companies like those throughout East Asia are hungry for wood, and equally their exploits are well known in countries such as West Papua, where the indigenous people have been murdered or turned into modern day slaves in order to satisfy these companies' appetite for wood. This mass exploitation of the general citizenry has helped to fuel the booming Indonesian economy. Sadly, however, there are some Harvard economists who might applaud Indonesia's advances as a way for societies to develop and grow.

Lifestyles

Regrettably, the lifestyles of the tribal people are viewed through Eurocentric eyes; thus, there is a tendency to undervalue these peoples' worth in society and consequently to see them as obstacles to the "good society" that many of us so crave. Now, due to the seeming incompetence of the Surinamese government in monitoring the activities of the logging companies, many observers are becoming increasingly concerned about the rights of the tribal peoples.

To be sure, there are good reasons to fear the many multilaterals which have descended on the rainforest and on the other tribal lands in South America, for their initial impact on the quality of life of these tribal peoples and the environment has been devastating. One example is the Canadian gold mining company, Golden Star, which is said to be wreaking havoc on the environment and on the indigenous peoples throughout the region. Alas, you might remember Golden Star as the company which was involved in the OMAI mine disaster in Guyana, where some 4,000,000 cubic litres of cyanide-laced effluent was released into the Essequibo River. Equally, the Forest Peoples Programme states that Golden Star security personnel have been implicated in the threatening and harassing of committee members in Maroon communities, and villagers have also been denied access to agricultural plots and hunting grounds by the companies' security.

No one is disputing the need for Suriname to utilize its natural resources for the greater good of their society. Indeed, no one is disputing the involvement of multilateral corporations in such a process. However, what is in question here is the manner in which it is done. Therefore, as a sister CARICOM nation, we have an obligation to raise questions about the treatment of the Maroons and other indigenous people in Suriname, in the same way we have done in relation to Haiti. Regrettably, in an environment where sermons of total exploitation are being preached by people who have lived sheltered fairy-tale lives in expensive grey suits (those Harvard economists), such pleas might be seen as no more than a moral crusade. Fortunately, most of us know better, for we are a people who know what it is to struggle for justice and human rights; we can always rise above the Harvard sermon. Peace!

Chapter 18 The Caribbean Single Market and Economy (CSME)

- ➢ Repositioning CARICOM
- ➢ Fate of the single market
- ➢ Revisiting CARICOM
- ➢ Whither the single market?

Introduction

The CARICOM Single Market and Economy is an arrangement among CARICOM member states which creates an economic space through which skills and labour, goods, services, capital and technology can move freely across participating states. Though the idea of regional integration seems practical because of the proposed benefit of deepening the integration thrust, the chapter details mixed views. The chapter demonstrates that, on the one hand, there are those who welcome the CSME and identify models of economic development within the region that can be adopted by other member countries, while on the other, there is a great deal of hesitancy into making the CSME a reality. The chapter explores the impact the following factors have on integration of CARICOM member states:

- Lack of clear direction and policies
- Unfair competition
- Lack of conversation about the benefits and disbenefits of CARICOM
- Failure to identify areas of functional cooperation
- Impact of extra-regional trade

Finally, the chapter concludes by revisiting the benefits of having regional integration within the context of the new development taking place within the region.

Repositioning CARICOM

(TUESDAY, JULY 09, 1996)

The decision by members at the recent CARICOM Conference of Heads of Government (HOGC) to delay the implementation of the CARICOM Single Market and Economy should not come as a surprise to those following the process over the years. While a few member states have taken small steps to make the single market a reality, most continue to conduct business as usual. Countries like St Kitts, St Lucia and Guyana have invested a great deal of time sorting out internal political strife. All of the territories save, perhaps, Trinidad and Tobago are desperately trying to survive the vicissitudes of a dramatically transforming global economy. Additionally, the continued focus on internal political survival, at a time when CARICOM countries need to seriously re-orient their economies either away from the (or towards a more sophisticated) banana-sugar-paper and sea-sand-sun tourism development strategy, has resulted in the non-implementation of decisions made at the previous HOGCs. Of perhaps greater importance is the fact that not many of the leaders within the region are sure about the status of CARICOM, especially in the light of the existence of NAFTA, the Association of Caribbean States (ACS) and the newly formed World Trade Organization (WTO).

Interestingly, the initial hype made about NAFTA is slowly giving way to disinterest and perhaps even cynicism in some political quarters. The CARICOM countries which initially appeared most likely to join the free trade group – Jamaica, and Trinidad and Tobago – find themselves ranked below Barbados (in terms of level of attractiveness for entry), which has a comparatively smaller export sector. Furthermore, the windfall benefits anticipated from NAFTA by the poorer Latin American nations have so far gone primarily to the US corporations

In this rather confusing environment, I get the impression that many of the technocrats within CARICOM are not particularly clear about the future direction of the regional body. Such is not an environment terribly conducive to the implementation of single market policies within CARICOM

To achieve a single market and economy, the issue of harmonization of monetary policy will also have to be addressed. The widely varying views with respect to monetary and fiscal approaches to development across the region make it difficult for member states to agree on monetary policy. While policymakers in Guyana and Jamaica seem convinced about the virtues of having a weak currency, those in Barbados, the OECS states and, to a lesser extent, Trinidad and Tobago do not at all find devaluation attractive. And for good reason. There is not one shred of evidence to indicate that continuous devaluation has brought serious long-term benefits to either the Jamaican or Guyanese economy.

There seems to be a great proclivity among the many "experts" in the media here in Jamaica to preach about the virtues of keeping down labour costs and ensuring that the exchange rate is competitive, whatever that means. Yet they also want increased productivity from workers. Well, the Trinidad and Tobago economy is perhaps the most competitive in the region, even though labour costs there are much higher and their dollar is much stronger than ours.

It is not coincidental that there is a trade dispute between the Trinidadians and the rest of the region. Trinidad has the most robust export sector in the region. Part of the reason for its success has to do with a powerful indigenous entrepreneurial class in the country and a long-term approach to industrial development.

However, it is also true that, whatever their failings, previous governments there have expanded physical infrastructure and education, stabilized the food import bill, and provided numerous incentives for the development of a variety of industries which produce goods and services. Relatedly, a much smaller inner-city underclass does not provide the incentive for the type of feudal political structure which continues to stunt our growth here in Jamaica.

Having worked with CARICOM on a few aspects of the single market and economy process, I strongly believe that it is the right step for the region. However,

I also feel that much of what is occurring globally in terms of economic opportunities, especially in the computer and related services, is passing us by.

Here in Jamaica, our debates after two decades of structural adjustment continue to revolve around technical issues of money supply and exchange rate. A small section of the intelligentsia has captured the debate and reduced larger matters of progress to technical economic issues.

Let me make it clear that since no one has a monopoly on knowledge, this group has a right to articulate its views. To be sure, technical issues are also important and deserve to be discussed. What I fear, however, is the tone of the debate; it seems to me that much of what is discussed often does not reflect most people's everyday experiences or an intuitive understanding of what they see around them. In light of the recent HOGC, I now have some reservations about the effectiveness of the single market and economy, not because it cannot work, but due to the seeming conservatism among our political elites and economic analysts in the region who have failed to look beyond the USA and the banana-sugar-paper and sea-and-sand development model. Perhaps Trinidad and Tobago, the emerging economic powerhouse in the region, may be able to offer much needed guidance. Peace!

Fate of the single market

(TUESDAY, APRIL 29, 1997)

Much unlike like the John Major and Tony Blair debate over Britain's role in the new European Union, there is little discussion among CARICOM people or their governments about the proposed single CARICOM market and economy. Yet if this new plan is to be successfully implemented, it will mean that regional governments will have to make a number of important changes in the ways in which they relate to other CARICOM countries, and also change their posture about this proposed CARICOM Single Market and Economy (CSME).

The history of the CSME dates back to 1959, when the Heads of Government took the decision to create a single regional market and economy. Further progress was made on the matter at subsequent meetings, and in 1996, there was a special consultation on the CSME, presided over by Prime Minister Owen Arthur of Barbados. Therefore, in essence, the CSME seeks to ensure that firms across the region – from Belize in the west to Suriname in the southeast – would be able to compete with each other without the obstacle of national protections through tariffs or subsidies. Other areas of integration would include the integration of regional capital markets, namely those in Jamaica, Trinidad and Tobago and Barbados; the creation of a single regional currency; the free movement of capital and labour; and the harmonization of legislations which would give life to many of these objectives.

Indeed, there have been many technical studies on a wide range of issues in relation to the CSME. Some of these point to the fact that there will be no windfall economic gains to be achieved from the CSME, as most of the CARICOM countries' trade will continue to be extra-regional. However, were the governments to take the promises made at Heads of Government meetings seriously, and by extension work towards fulfilling them, then there is some evidence which suggests that much would have been gained in the areas of education, human resource development, regional travel and investment.

So far, a number of countries have adopted a few measures which could move the single market towards reality. For instance, eight member states have accepted forms of identification other than passports; however, Antigua and Barbuda, Barbados, St Vincent and the Grenadines, Suriname, and Trinidad and Tobago have not. Furthermore, all member countries, except Trinidad and Tobago, use common lines for citizens, residents and CARICOM nationals at their airports. Additionally, most governments have already devised legislation to allow UWI graduates to work in their countries without the need for a work permit. Other measures are being taken to facilitate the free movement of capital across the region. The problem, however, is that many of these changes are so minor that they will have no substantial impact on the CSME. Furthermore, our governments' refusal to discuss many of the more important elements of the CSME with their citizens mean that opposition parties can manipulate this lack of consultation, and as such capitalize on the ignorance of the population to achieve their short-sighted political ends. After all, the first goal of a political party is to gain political power, invariably and regrettably by any means necessary.

In many ways, the CSME's fate is unsure, given that so few people within the region are actively engaged in debating its merits and demerits; this is so unlike the case in Europe with the European Union. Unfortunately, we have failed to learn from the current debates across Europe, in relation to the European Union, about democracy and the need for political change. I would not be surprised if the ignorance and sectional interests of some politicians and commentators derailed the CSME process and progress in a few of our Caribbean countries before it can be seriously and sensibly assessed. Peace!

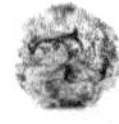

Revisiting CARICOM

(TUESDAY, JULY 01, 1997)

This week, when the CARICOM heads of government meet in Montego Bay for the 18th official time, the CARICOM single market and economy (CSME) will be high on their list of issues to be dealt with. You see, the CSME emerged out of the report of the West Indian Commission, as the main mechanism for deepening the integration thrust. Thus, the Association of Caribbean States (ACS), an institution, proposed by mechanisms to be used to widen and deepen this process.

But in spite of these official devices, there remains a great deal of disquiet about the function(ing) of CARICOM. Consequently, many of our citizens across the region still claim to know very little about CARICOM. While, at the same time, our private sectors continue to accuse the movement of not working towards the promotion of trade, and public bureaucrats also complain about the intransigence and continued nationalist orientation of sister countries in an organization designed for collective participation and regional benefit. And so, this is why in some Caribbean countries many journalists or talk show hosts are often quick to dismiss CARICOM as nothing more than a paper tiger.

But, if the truth be told, many of these people, whom one would think should know better, are extremely ignorant about the activities or work of the Caribbean Community. Now, when one speaks of CARICOM, there is a tendency to think only in terms of trade and economics; however, great emphasis is placed on the areas of functional cooperation, including such critical areas as education, agriculture, health and meteorology. So, the failings of CARICOM, and there are many, must not cloud the many successful cooperative efforts which have aimed at improving education and health. Equally, the excellent work of the Caribbean Broadcasting Union should be a constant reminder to the critics about the possibilities of the integration movement.

Perhaps, the most contentious issue in the integration movement is trade and economic cooperation. In my view, part of the problem with intra-regional trade stems from our view of development, which sees the US as the be-all and end-all of economic progress in our region. Many economists and more and more private sector individuals have also jumped on the globalization bandwagon without fully understanding what it is they are talking about. The truth is that we live in a region with a combined gross domestic product of 33 billion US dollars, most of which goes to the US to purchase many of the products we can efficiently produce for local consumption and for export to other parts of the region.

The Trinidadians have long realized this fact, and hence they remain the only CARICOM country which is trying to fully exploit the possibilities in their home market. To be sure, the Trinidadians have realized that they need to be competitive internationally, but they also recognize that international competitiveness does not come overnight, nor should this process exclude their CARICOM neighbours. The problem with many of us in CARICOM is that we want to run before we can crawl, and we want to conquer the world before we have an army. The Trinidadians have sensibly looked around in their backyard for opportunities which they have found, and they have been exploiting them with great success. It is noteworthy that, five years ago, while doing a study for CARICOM, a successful Trinidadian businessman said to me: "Let the Jamaicans go out there and conquer the world; we here want to start with our backyard first, and we'll see who will win in the long run."

Again, one of our problems in this region is that we do not carefully think through problems, fads and ideas. Too much of what we think about economic development is dictated by what I call the "business week" mentality. There is too much emphasis on what the Americans are doing and what the Japanese have done with little consideration for the context in which it was done. Furthermore, many of those who talk about CARICOM, in whatever capacity, often have very little empirical basis for their pronouncements. I hope that the CARICOM heads and secretariat staff will put measures in place to help educate our policymakers, commentators and, yes, even some of our intellectuals about CARICOM. In its widest sense, ignorance is a great threat to progress. Peace!

Whither the single market?

(TUESDAY, AUGUST 19, 1997)

Steps are now being laid by regional officials, as a result of the last Heads of Government meeting of CARICOM held in Jamaica in July of this year, to further the idea of a single market and economy. Thus, in order to keep up with the region's desire to move towards free trade and openness – which is said to characterize the global economy – various protocols are being constructed which will virtually transform the seminal Treaty of Chaguaramas. But as we look forward, the governments of Saint Lucia, the Bahamas and Suriname have opted not to sign protocol two, one of the agreements central to the realization of a single market. As such, we are forced to ask the following two questions. Are our regional governments and entrepreneurs truly committed to the idea of a single market? Will anything change within CARICOM?

Capital

Well, already some things have changed within the regional body; or have they? We have been easing capital movements across territories, and travel is also much easier. However, non-Caribbean people, mainly Americans, still find it easier to travel and move capital within the region than do Caribbean people. Some governments have made working in some CARICOM states easier, but this easy access in intra-regional employment is only applicable in respect of very few categories of workers.

Kenny Anthony, Saint Lucia's prime minister, also did not sign the protocol, because his government had just come into office, and needed to "study the protocol some more". The Bahamas, on the other hand, which has its own problems with illegal migrants from Cuba and Haiti, is not likely to join the single market in the near future. Equally, with Haiti now a new member of CARICOM, it is unlikely that there will be full freedom of movement of peoples within the region in the foreseeable future, unless of course the Haitian economy improves dramatically.

Tactical error

Thus, has CARICOM made a tactical error by allowing Haiti full membership to the regional body at this time, without first deepening the process? Or is it that the governments in the region were never fully committed to the free movement of people and human resources, and hence admitting Haiti to full membership has only served to solidify the existing status quo?

Let me make it clear, I am certainly not against Haiti becoming a full member of CARICOM. I am simply arguing that, given the internal social and economic difficulties being experienced by that country and the resultant high level of outward migration which has been occurring in that country for years, many CARICOM nations fear that their countries, rightly or wrongly, will be swamped by Haitians if full freedom of movement is allowed. Against this background, I do not see freedom of movement realistically occurring within CARICOM in the near future.

This of course makes a complete mockery of the idea of a single market and economy. For how can there be a single market and economy where labour and factors of production cannot move freely? The other issue relates to the concern expressed by Belizean and Surinamese manufacturers that they face unfair competition from Trinidad and Tobago, and Jamaica. In the same breath, they argue that in many cases there is a deliberate ploy by both countries to keep Belizean and Surinamese products out of their markets.

Business sectors

But the more worrying problem relates to the fact that both Belize and Suriname feel that their business sectors are too weak to compete within a liberalized regional market. Furthermore, Belize is trying to decide whether it should invest more in their Central American relationships rather than in those of CARICOM. For these reasons, a single market involving both Suriname and Belize seems unlikely, unless, of course, special provisions are made to accommodate their concerns.Much is being made about the foundation work being undertaken by the regional governments, and about moving towards a single market in preparation for the free trade area of the Americas by the dawn of the 21st century. However, these measures only appear set to guarantee the failure of the process. I for one do not expect the integration process to deepen or strengthen significantly in the near future; and for all intents and purposes, the single market and economy project is dead. The truth is that the single market idea now looks very much like a political ploy, designed to continue the myopic status quo of regional governance. And so, come the year 2005, we in this region will still be struggling with the same set of political and economic problems we started out with in 1968 when CARIFTA was formed. The more things change, the more they remain the same. Peace!

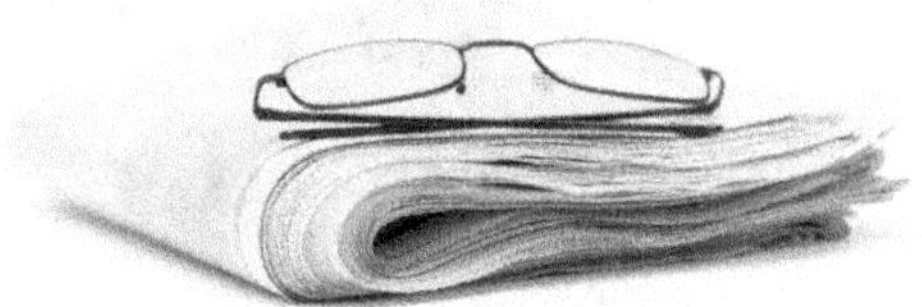

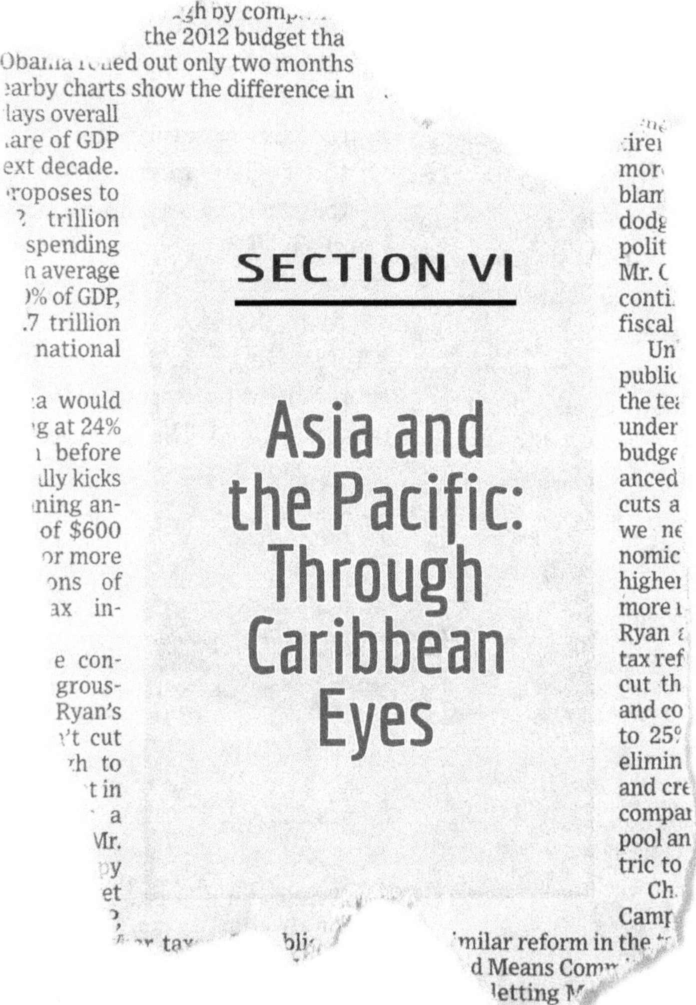

SECTION VI

Asia and the Pacific: Through Caribbean Eyes

Introduction

This section continues to explore benefits to be derived when Caribbean countries collaborate in order to take advantage of trade and other development related opportunities. A multiplicity of issues is covered within this final section. Given that the author is a Caribbean native, it seems natural that a comparison between countries of the Caribbean and countries of the Pacific region would be in order. This section, which contains only one chapter, looks at the effects of cultural diffusion and the extent to which peoples of other regions have accepted other cultures. Particular emphasis is placed on the similar usage of music as a social commentary in both the Caribbean and the Pacific region. The author emphasizes the extent to which music is used to raise consciousness and build awareness.

Added to that, the idea of a plural society is explored, with great emphasis being placed on the link between culture and capitalist development. More specifically, the chapter looks at the extent to which countries with large mixed racial populations can coexist. The author also details the impact that immigration has on indigenous groups. The collective approach to development is also emphasized in this section. The author posits that, though New Zealand and Australia are not considered Asian countries for trade purposes, they have aligned themselves with the Association of Southeast Asian Nations (ASEAN) to enhance their ability to trade.

The author also highlights the fact that, outside the North American region, Caribbean countries are seen as a single state rather than as independent nation-states. This view suggests that any political or economic ties established within the region would not affect "Brand Caribbean", since the region is known globally as a collective rather than as individual nation-states. Finally, the author could not help but explore the similarities and differences between the tourism products offered in both regions, given his interest in tourism, and due to the fact that the Pacific Islands are increasingly becoming the destination of choice for North American and European visitors, when compared with their Caribbean counterparts. A proposal for the adoption of the tourism development model used in New Zealand is documented. Trends in tourism are explored, particularly the idea of the free independent travellers (FITs). The effects of stellar customer service are also addressed.

Chapter 19 On Productivity

- Introducing the Pacific
- Paradise or paradox
- Reggae: Perceptions and sovereignty
- A hero's welcome
- Music in the Pacific
- Fiji... At last!
- The spectre of Asia
- Trinidad: A model for Fiji?
- Preparing for the future
- Changing fortunes of Asian tourism
- New approach to tourism
- Trends in tourism

Introducing the Pacific

(FRIDAY, JULY 7, 1995)

The Pacific region is one of the most interesting parts of the world. Having arrived here in New Zealand only recently, I have come to realize that even though the American influence extends to these parts – especially in sports and entertainment – the newly industrialized countries of Asia, along with Australia and Japan, are the major players in this region. Partly out of economic pragmatism, New Zealand and Australia see themselves as part of the Asian diaspora. The small poorer islands of the region are in many ways similar to us in the Caribbean. However, I believe in many ways we may be further ahead, politically and economically, than most of the South Pacific islands, partly because we have been more aggressive in the manner in which we deal with the rest of the world.

There is also a clear recognition on the part of both Australia and New Zealand of the importance of regional groupings to their future survival. Both countries have formed a common market where their citizens can travel and work freely between the two countries. Right now, there is a shortage of schoolteachers in New Zealand. The government here has intimated that it might try to attract teachers from Australia to fill the gap. Perhaps there is something in this policy that we in the Caribbean region can learn from regarding the experience of these two countries.

In this region, there is a clear recognition that the notion of going it alone economically is passé, if not foolhardy.

Prediction

While there is no ignoring the continued economic prowess of the United States, economists in this region see Asian countries as dominating the next century. And by Asia, we are not just talking about Japan and others such as Hong Kong and Taiwan, but also China and India. Economists here predict that in the next 30 years these countries will be two of the leading economic giants in the world. It is for such reasons, apart from geographical location, that both Australia and New Zealand have linked their future economic development to Asia.

One of the most interesting experiences I have had so far has to do with the apparent influence of Jamaican culture on Black peoples in this region. Bob Marley's music is very popular among many of the indigenous people of New Zealand, the Māori, and as far as Fiji, the Solomon Islands and Vanuatu in the South Pacific region. For many of the indigenous people of the Pacific, many of whom look like me but are of African descent, the music of Bob Marley, Jimmy Cliff and Peter Tosh articulates their struggles and the concerns they have as people who have been oppressed and exploited under colonialism. This identification with people of the Caribbean (and in particular Jamaica) is also reflected in the presence of Rastafari communities and symbolism, which can be observed throughout the region.

The image of Jamaica and the Caribbean is very positive among New Zealanders, Australians, and the people of the Pacific region. This image is mainly due to the influence of reggae music and our success in cricket. There is a very healthy respect for Caribbean cricket in these parts. News about the Caribbean is normally related to sports or some important international event. Selling Jamaica as a tourist destination to people in these parts is in theory fairly easy for travel agents. However, the travel costs are prohibitive given the distance between the two regions. Also, there is competition from other destinations such as Fiji and other islands of the South Pacific.

Have you ever wondered why New Zealand and Australia do so well in netball? Well, right across the two countries are large netball courts accessible to local clubs. In New Zealand, there could be as many as 15 courts in one area where teams go to play netball every weekend, even during winter. There is somewhat of an unofficial netball "academy" in the country. Perhaps there is also a lesson here for our sports administrators in the region. Peace!

Paradise or paradox

(WEDNESDAY, SEPTEMBER 6, 1995)

Countries of the South Pacific region are promoting "visit South Pacific year 1995" to boost their tourism industry. Unlike the Caribbean, South Pacific countries have a collective approach to tourism development – that is, the region as a whole is marketed, rather than any individual destination. And, although their tourist industry is not as large as ours in the Caribbean, they are biting off an increasingly larger share of the international tourist market every year.

In a recent article published in the leading South Pacific business magazine Islands Business, a spokesperson from a Brussels headquartered tourism marketing company stated that the Pacific's rivals are the Indian Ocean and the Caribbean. She also observed that with the growth of ecotourism, more European and American visitors are travelling to the South Pacific, rather than to the Caribbean. Perhaps the most critical comment made by the spokesperson was this:

> The kindness of the people is a big, big advantage. The great attraction of the Pacific Islands is definitely the people. They are so friendly, so warm, always smiling. It is a big difference compared with the Caribbean, where people are not always friendly, especially between black and white people. I think we can talk of racism in some cases. I never, never feel that in the South Pacific.

Natives

Innocent as this comment may appear, it reeks of the classic European perception of "island peoples" as smiling, happy-go-lucky natives, who are content to exist in a state of blissful ignorance. However, tear away the facade of the smiling happy-go-lucky natives of the South Pacific, and you will see that the captivating pelvic movements of the women of the Cook Islands, the gleaming lily-white smiles of the Papuans, and the enchanting sounds of Fijian choirs often camouflage a growing resentment for their former (and present) colonizers, and the paternalistic attitude of visitors from the industrialized world.

Unlike us

Much unlike us in the Caribbean, the islands of South Pacific are trapped between their often degenerated cultural past and the present forced upon them by the colonizers. As I write, there is a battle in the region over whether or not the French should test nuclear weapons on the Mururoa Atoll.

Led by Greenpeace, the opposition against nuclear testing is growing at a tremendous rate. But the French, now the world's most enthusiastic champions of the anachronistic colonialism system, are adamant that they are free to do what they please in their territory – French Polynesia. French Polynesia is an archipelago of tiny islands inhabited primarily by the indigenous peoples. Feelings are so strong that some of the leaders of the pro-independence movement in Tahiti – a French territory close to the area in which the nuclear testing is being done – have vowed to resort to violence if the testing occurs. France claims that the tests are safe; but even if that were so, they have missed the essential point. The point is that the people of that region no longer want to be patronized by a country seemingly led and administered by a megalomaniac.

But France is not the only culprit to have decimated this region; Britain, the Netherlands, Japan, and even Australia, have all been accomplices to oppression and to the subversion of justice and human rights in the region. Britain's legacy in Fiji is seen in a nation torn apart by racial conflict. Fiji is a country of about ¾ of a million people, which was colonized by the British.

Indians

As in the Caribbean, Indian indentured labourers were imported into the country to harvest sugar cane. As the years progressed, the Indian population grew exponentially, finally surpassing that of the indigenous Fijians in the latter part of the 20th century. At present, more than 50 per cent of Fiji's population is Indo-Fijian. In 1987, Colonel Sitiveni Rabuka seized power through a military coup, apparently from the Indian "dominated" Labour-National Federation Coalition Party. The Colonel's reason for staging the coup was to restore the indigenous Fijians as the true owners of the country. In other words, he sought to limit the power of the burgeoning Indian business class in the country.

Following the coup, steps were taken to ensure that indigenous Fijians retained political control over the country, through changes to the constitution. After the coup, a general election resulted in the formation of a coalition between Rabuka's party and a predominantly Indian party making him the democratically elected prime minister of the country.

Constitution

At present, the constitution is under review to redress the concerns of the Indo-Fijians who see themselves as second class citizens in their own country.

The fact remains that many indigenous Fijians continue to see racially mixed and Indo-Fijians as outsiders who must be prevented from taking away their country.

In the name of indigenization and Christian values, the 1987 coup leaders restored the old Fijian system of the Great Council of Chiefs, which was created by the British to rule the country. This move, while popular in some circles, represents the replacement of one oppressive system with yet another.

However justified some may perceive Rabuka's actions to be, one cannot help but conclude that the same Fijians who lost control of their country to the British, partly because of the prejudice of the Western European brand of Christianity, may now be guilty of similar prejudices against others. (Some Trinidadian social scientists have observed that there are many similarities between the Fiji situation and that of Trinidad and Tobago, and Guyana. If this is so, then there can be no doubt that the region is sitting on top of a potential tinderbox.)

Victims

Understandably, there are many Polynesians and Melanesians who agree with the coup in Fiji, having themselves been victims of colonization in the past, and currently experiencing an influx of Asians into the Pacific region.

Asia is the most populous region of the world, and rapid population growth coupled with oppressive political and economic conditions in some of the countries has resulted in large-scale migration of Asian people to every corner of the globe. In Aotearoa (New Zealand), some Māori fear that the Pākehā (European) state may use minorities from Asia – along the lines of the USA and pre-democratic South Africa – to deny Māori rights, particularly by making reference to a multicultural society, and by pointing to the success of the immigrants.

Not so far from Fiji is the second largest island in the world, Papua New Guinea (PNG), which is independent, and West Papua, a colony of the imperialist country of Indonesia. Papua New Guinea won its independence from Australia in 1975. However, Australia has been party to development strategies pursued by the PNG government which focus on mineral exploitation of sections of the country with little or no regard to the impact on people. So exploitative were the mining projects in one of its territories, Bougainville, that in 1988, the Bougainville Revolutionary Army (BRA) launched a guerrilla attack against the PNG government. The consequences were devastating both in terms of the loss of lives and the damage to the Papuan economy. To this day, the conflict continues amidst a growing ecological crisis within the region.

However, this conflict pales in comparison with those in the adjoining country of West Papua and the island of East Timor. Both countries were annexed by Indonesia, with the complicity of the Western powers. All of this at a time when Indonesia was at the forefront of the Third World's so-called anti-imperialist movement. In exchange for mining rights, Australia, the Netherlands, and the US in particular, have tacitly condoned the oppression of the peoples of both countries by an often cruel and racist Indonesian military. Resistance movements have been brutally dealt with by the Indonesians, and the international community has basically ignored the plight of the West Papuans, in particular – many of whom still live in simple tribal communities.

Troubled spots

Perhaps one of the most troubled spots in the South Pacific is the French dependency of New Caledonia, or Kanaky, as the indigenous people prefer to call the country. New Caledonia was seized from the Kanak people by the French, who then imported large numbers of Vietnamese labourers. The large European and Vietnamese population in the country has meant that the Melanesian (Black) people have been efficiently denied the right of self-determination.

Following numerous violent confrontations between the Kanaks and the French security forces over the past two decades, the French finally agreed to an independence referendum in 1998. However, even though the Kanak people are in support of full independence from France, they may not win the referendum because they are outnumbered by the French, the Asians, and the mixed-race people, most of whom appear to prefer a continuation of French rule, rather than a return of the country to the Kanak people.

Mythical paradise

Indeed, it is true that the South Pacific region is often perceived as the nearest thing to paradise. And for holiday makers, most of whom are privileged Europeans, Americans, New Zealanders, Australians, and increasingly East Asians, it is indeed paradise. For many of the indigenous peoples of the region, this mythical paradise constructed by the Europeans, and so ever-present on television shows and tourist brochures, has now become a quintessential paradox. Peace!

Reggae: Perceptions and sovereignty

(TUESDAY, SEPTEMBER 26, 1995)

Hamilton, New Zealand:

Having followed radio and television in this part of the world closely for the past three months, it appears to me that international reggae music is now dominated by the British, Americans and Europeans. With the exception of Inner Circle, reggae from Jamaica is rarely heard on the radio or television, even though reggae music is very popular, especially among the Māori. On the other hand, groups such as Big Mountain and UB40, and even recent reggae "converts" such as Aaron Neville can be heard daily on the radio.

Of the Jamaican artistes, Bob Marley is by far the most popular here. Bob Marley and the Wailers toured New Zealand in 1979 and left an indelible mark on the country, both in terms of popularizing reggae and spreading the ideas of Rastafari. To some people in the Pacific region, he was a prophet. Few music stores here are complete without a picture of the Bob, or Uncle Bob as some teenagers call him. Arguably, more people here wear Bob Marley T-shirts than in Jamaica.

No distinction

Many people here do not make a distinction between Jamaica and the Caribbean. To them, Jamaica and the Caribbean are one and the same. Jamaica in their eyes is the land of Bob Marley, reggae, calypso and carnival. In other words, Jamaica and the Caribbean are interchangeable.

I have had people ask me where in Jamaica do Brian Lara and Joel Garner live. Recently, a television station here advertised a show on Trinidad and Tobago and the announcer referred to Trinidad as Jamaica. This advertisement ran for days, but I recognized the mistake the first time I saw the advertisement, which ran for less than 30 seconds. Interestingly, the movie Cool Runnings was one of the longest running in this country ever.

Rastafari

There can be no doubt that what makes Jamaica special in the eyes of millions around the world are reggae music and the Rastafari religion. For oppressed people from Asia to Africa, and from the Pacific to South America, Rastafari ideas of resistance and self-determination have been of great inspiration in their struggles.

Few countries, small or large, rich or poor, can boast of having such an influence on world culture and philosophy as Jamaica. From the Navajo in the USA to the Māori in New Zealand, Rastafari ideas and lyrics, and the sounds of Bob Marley and Peter Tosh have given people a sense of identity and purpose. Undoubtedly, Rastafari and reggae have made it much easier for those in the tourism industry to promote Jamaica internationally. It is for this reason that the sharp socioeconomic cleavages which exist in our society, and which are rationalized solely on the basis of some people seizing opportunities provided by the market, cannot be justified either from an economic or moral standpoint.

Maori Congress

New Zealand is not always what it is cracked up to be. International ranking lists place New Zealand high up, in terms of criminal justice, a corruption-free government and economic quality. However, this view is not shared by the indigenous people, the Māori. A few weeks ago, I was invited to Hui, a meeting of the Māori Congress, where issues concerning sovereignty were discussed. The Māori constitute nearly 15 per cent of the population here and are increasingly vocal in their call for self-government, separate from the Pākehā or European-dominated state. Protests have grown across the country as Māori people occupy lands which belonged to them before being appropriated by the state many years go.

As the movement grows, people are becoming more outspoken, and tension is rising in some areas across the country. The police and army are routinely called in to get rid of those who have occupied land. This movement will most definitely grow in the future, and with the soon to be inaugurated Māori-led Aotearoa Party, the international community could eventually see a fast-emerging conflict which will soon reach breaking point.

As most of you might be aware, netball is a very popular sport here in New Zealand. Recently, a manager of one of their well respected netball teams told me that she and her players would like to tour, and play netball in, Jamaica sometime early next year. The team is looking for clubs who are interested in playing matches with them. If there are any netball clubs which are interested in such a tour, please write to: Mr Ted Douglas, The University of Waikato Anthropology Dept., Hamilton, New Zealand.

A hero's welcome

(TUESDAY, NOVEMBER 21, 1995)

It is 9:15 a.m., and a large crowd of people descend on the marae (meeting place) of the Māori Queen here in Aotearoa/New Zealand. My friends and I park our vehicle at the side of the traffic-congested road and enter the spectacular court of one of the tribes of northern New Zealand.

The marae is the traditional meeting place of the Māori people. There are many such places in New Zealand, but this one is special because it is the Queen's. The marae is a large open courtyard, with a number of buildings which are used to hold meetings and other festivities. The main building is usually very large with wide open spaces and decorated with some of the finest wood carvings in the world (Māori people are well known for their wood carving skills). The carvings have both spiritual and aesthetic significance.

Excitement

As we enter the marae, I sense a buzz of excitement. The now menacingly dark rain clouds fail to dampen the mood of the people. The hip-hop music adds to the festive atmosphere. Everyone is jubilant; even the contingent of policemen joke with the young people who are standing patiently. As I walk towards a seat in the beautifully decorated courtyard, there is loud flutter from above. I look up; it is the South African flag. Nelson Mandela, here in New Zealand to attend the Commonwealth Heads of Government Meeting (CHOGM), was invited to visit the marae by Māori leaders.

Undoubtedly the most popular and respected leader of the meeting, Mandela was given a hero's welcome by the people, all across the country of Aotearoa. (Renewed interest in the Commonwealth was most certainly stimulated by the presence of Mandela, along with the French nuclear testing issue and worldwide interest in political tensions in Nigeria.) Now away from the CHOGM and the hustle and bustle of Auckland – one of the world's largest cities (spatially) – Mandela was travelling to the "heartland" of New Zealand, a rural district about 50 kilometres from the city of Hamilton where I was based. Consistent with Māori hospitality and solidarity, the welcome would be special.

Preceding Mandela, who is flanked by security personnel and the usual large contingent of press people, is the guard of honour – a spectacular procession of largely Māori and Pākehā (White) children from 35 schools in the area. As Mandela, his daughter and his foreign minister enter the sacred grounds of the marae (usually cameras are not allowed on the marae), he is greeted by a performance of the haka. The haka is a traditional dance which is a form of welcome or a declaration of competition or combat. The haka is beyond verbal description; to attempt to describe it here would do an injustice to one of the unique and outstanding features of Māori-New Zealand culture. Suffice it to say, the president is visibly impressed by the performance and welcome which greet him.

As he walks into the courtyard, hundreds rise from their seats to see him; most of us have to stand on chairs, even the tall ones. In keeping with fine Māori custom, there are greetings, speeches, entertainment, and gifts – lots of them. Among the gifts are two scholarships to be awarded to two South African students to undertake tertiary studies in New Zealand each year. Mandela also hears about the famous Māori spiritual leader, Rātana, who visited South Africa in the 1920s, and later spoke of the horror of the conditions of Black South Africans. References are also made to the presence of Rātana members and descendants who now lead the Rātana church (named after its founder) whose theology is a hybrid of Māori and Christian ideas.

In response, the overwhelmed Mandela expresses his appreciation for the solidarity which Māori people showed to South Africans during the apartheid regime. He would not forget that Māori protesters battled with police many years ago to prevent the New Zealand rugby tour of South Africa. (Last month, I met with one of the leaders of that protest movement, a Māori and a former Minister of Education, who told me that those protests were some of the most violent in New Zealand's recent history.)

Euphoria

Two hours later, the function ends, and Nelson, as he is now affectionately called, wades his way through a sea of people and a battalion of security personnel. Most people simply want to touch him or shake his hand. Such is the euphoria that a schoolboy shows me his hand and says, "I shook his hand with this hand." Finally, the president disappears into the immaculate restaurant on the marae, to dine with the Māori Queen.

The marae is still buzzing with excitement, but we have to leave. The well paved New Zealand roads (I have seen only one pothole in the hundreds of kilometres of roads I have traversed) are crowded with cars, children, police and transported youth. The feelings that I experience as we drive away would help me to understand later on why Mandela would say that this event was the highlight of his visit to the "land of the long white cloud", the country of Aotearoa. Peace!

Music in the Pacific

(TUESDAY, NOVEMBER 28, 1995)

Hamilton, New Zealand:

As in other parts of the world, the influence of North American and Caribbean (mainly Jamaican) music is strong in many parts of the Pacific. From Australia to Papua New Guinea, hip-hop, rock and reggae are part of the musical diet of the peoples of this region.

In many parts of the region, indigenous music is very strong, and increasingly there is an attempt at creating hybrids, especially with rap and hip-hop, and rock, and reggae. For instance, in New Zealand there is the integration of the Polynesian drum, nose flute and singing styles with hip-hop and reggae music; and in Australia, the hauntingly beautiful sounds of the Aboriginal didgeridoo have been added to the music arsenal of Australian rock and reggae bands. This hybridization makes for some of the most exciting music I have ever heard. Without a doubt, Polynesians, Melanesians and Australian Aboriginals have some of the most beautiful voices on earth. Nowhere else in the world will one find singers with better musical harmony and melody than Polynesians.

In Aotearoa (New Zealand), some Māori people have

used the music as a form of protest against the state. In 1990, popular and controversial Māori rap-reggae group Upper Hutt Posse visited the United States as a guest of the Nation of Islam. In an interview which I conducted with the band, the leader Dean Hapeta argued that the invitation represented the highlight of their career since they, as Māori, share much in common with the struggles of Black Americans. In the eyes of Upper Hutt Posse, their music, which is a fusion of Polynesian and popular styles of the Americas, is a force for building consciousness and continuing the struggle for the rights of Māori people in Aotearoa. The aim of the Posse is not simply to transplant the artistic life from the streets of urban America to Aotearoa, but to articulate a message slanted to deal with their own reality.

The message

One band member said of their music: "We are hard core, we play revolutionary music; we talk about all of the hassles Māori people are going through".

As with the Posse, the message of other pop singers and groups, such as Moana and the Moa Hunters, is for Māori youth to learn their language, to be proud of their culture, and to resist assimilation. Moana and the Moa Hunters won the New Zealand music industry award for their song "AEIOU (Akona Te Reo)" which called on the Māori people to learn their language.

Power structure

According to Dean Hapeta of Upper Hutt Posse, Malcom X and Hōne Heke (A Māori political activist of the late 19th century) can exist side by side, because they represent the spirit of resistance against the dominant power structure. Just as American groups such as Public Enemy and Niggaz With Attitude use the cloaked language and symbolism of urban American to challenge the power structure, so do Māori performers in the Māori language. In the music of groups such as Upper Hutt Posse, Southside of Bombay and Herbs, there is often movement between the Māori language and English to get across the message and also to emphasize differences from the mainstream Pākehā (European) culture.

One of the strongest Atlantic musical influences on Māori music comes through reggae. In 1979, Bob Marley visited New Zealand and performed to a packed audience comprising both Māori and Pākehā people. Following that concert, Rastafari, which already existed in New Zealand, found new converts, most of whom were Māori and Pacific Island youth. Indeed, this was not surprising given its roots in Jamaica. Although Rasta and reggae represented anti-system movements which echoed a message of peace, they also make strong references to struggle and self-determination. The music of Marley, Jimmy Cliff, Dennis Brown and other reggae superstars is replete with references to human rights, equality, justice and identity. These messages are reflected in the music of New Zealand groups such as Herbs, Dread Beat and Blood, and Southside of Bombay. Herbs, perhaps the most popular reggae group in New Zealand, has a repertoire that includes songs such as "French Letter" which criticizes French nuclear testing in the Pacific, and "Azania (Soon Come)", a song expressing their solidarity with the struggles of Black South Africans. There is also "Rua Kenana", a song by the group Survival with celebrates the anti-colonial struggles and religious messages of the Māori prophet Rua Kenana. This ability of Māori musicians and young music lovers to identify and embrace reggae is a function of an experience which has strong parallels with many Jamaicans. According to Posse member DJ Darryl Thompson, they can identify more with the music of people like Bob Marley, Peter Tosh and Jimmy Cliff than with any number of White performers from the US and Europe.

Interestingly, dancehall music is not popular in this part of the world (except for Shabba, Shaggy and a few others). Perhaps this is due to the lack of promotion, or maybe it is because reggae is still seen as "message" music rather than simply entertainment, while dancehall is considered entertainment. However, given the vibrant culture and enormous talent in this region, especially of the indigenous people of the Pacific, it may be well worth the while of some of our musicians from the Caribbean to get in touch with the rhythm and sounds of this region. Kia Ora!

"Fiji ... At last!"

(TUESDAY, JANUARY 9, 1996)

Suva, Fiji:

As the plane touches down at the quaint Nausori Airport, one hour outside the city of Suva, I feel relieved and excited. I have finally reached that fabled land of Fiji. There are two international airports in Fiji, and I landed at the one closest to the University of the South Pacific (USP) where I would be based for the next two weeks. In typical Third World style, going through customs requires great patience – the heat and the humidity only add to the frustration. However, the Fijian officials are quite polite and friendly, and this tempers any feelings of anger. Outside the airport I take a taxi to the university where I am staying; the lush green plants, mango trees and easygoing nature of the people make me feel as though I am back in the Caribbean.

I arrived in Suva on Friday and reached USP around 4 p.m., too late to see the university officials I was scheduled to meet, or my Fijian friends whom I know from New Zealand. With no one to show me around, I got on the bus and headed downtown. We academics often talk about living in a global village by making reference to things such as the internet and air travel: however, there are two things which seem to epitomize the idea for me among developing countries – music and privately owned buses. As I entered the bus, there was reggae music, but in Fijian and Hindi. Inside the bus, there were posters of Bob Marley and Lucky Dube. However, much unlike Jamaica, service in Fiji is very efficient. The buses are generally old, but passengers are treated with a great deal of respect. Fijian roads are generally clean and well paved, and drivers navigate them with caution; this makes the trip less hazardous than in Jamaica.

The first thing I noticed about downtown Fiji is its resemblance to different Caribbean countries. There is a bit of Trinidad and Guyana with the large Indian population there; a bit of Guyana in a sea wall which circles part of the city; part of Jamaica with its high-rise buildings and the large open markets; and a bit of Barbados in the fairly orderly organization of people in stores and buses. The police do not carry guns. There is music blaring from record shops – mainly reggae and calypso, and Indian music in Hindi. Most of it, as I was soon to discover, was pirated. I have a strong feeling that very few musicians see any of the money from the sales of music in Fiji.

Since one of my main research interests in the Pacific is culture and development, I was attracted to the businesses to see how they operate. Because

Fijians are an amazingly friendly people, it was easy to talk to them, many of whom greeted me with "bula" (hello). Within an hour of my arrival in the city centre, I befriended two Fijians who volunteer to show me around the city. I explained to them that I am with the USP conducting research, which would entail getting some idea of how the commercial sector operates. I think what intrigued them most was that I told them that I was from New Zealand and Jamaica. The word Jamaica excites passion in people all over the world in a way that no other country does. I do not know how many Jamaicans know this, but reggae music and the Rastafari philosophy have created an impression of Jamaica which rivals that of some of the greatest civilizations of the world. Reggae is without a doubt the most popular music among young people in Fiji.

As I walk around the city, I am struck by two things. First, businesses are owned mainly by local Indians and Chinese, and multinational companies from Australia and New Zealand. Second, although Fijians and Indians appear to get on well with each other, they live in two completely different worlds. If ever there were a plural society, Fiji would be it. Indigenous Fijians speak Fijian while Indians speak Hindi; both speak English as a common language. Fijians do not generally intermarry with Indians. And the term Fijian is generally reserved for the indigenous people, as Indians who make up more than half of the population are still called Indians. Many Fijians still regard Indians as outsiders. Many also resent the fact that Indians have great economic power, while Indians feel that they should have a greater share of the land, of which 80 per cent is still in the communal control of Fijians.

Those who believe that there is no serious link between culture and capitalist development should visit this part of the world, for here is a treasure chest of experiences which makes that link stand out quite clearly (I shall discuss this issue at a later date). There is absolutely no doubt in my mind that Western-style economic development must be based on a set of core values, many of which are not shared by Fijians, and indeed most indigenous people of the world.

As I walk and talk with my Fijian friends who now seem to embrace me as one of their own (for in their eyes two things matter most: I am Black and from Jamaica), I drift off into a philosophical world. I ask myself why is it that people who do not place great emphasis on material possessions, people such as Fijians, should be considered intellectually inferior to those who do? Then I ask myself: is it possible for people to live outside of this modern Western ethos and survive? I will respond to my question here. Many people have tried it, but they seem to be fighting a losing battle – look at the Masi in Kenya. I think to myself: what great human tragedy has been caused by the forced adoption of these acquisitive values among people who want to exist in their own world with greater emphasis on sharing rather than on accumulation.

I am awakened from my deep philosophical pondering by a passing group of five beautiful Fijian women, elegantly clad in their traditional clothing, who eventually disappear into a yellow bus. My observant friends smile with me, and we continue on our tour. Ni sa moce! (Goodbye!)

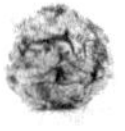

"The spectre of Asia"

(THURSDAY, MARCH 7, 1996)

Some people are nervous; others are excited; but virtually everyone is aware of the emerging economic and political clout of East and Southeast Asia. According to John Naisbitt, author of Megatrends Asia, by the next decade Asia will become the world's most influential region, politically, economically and culturally. Although I disagree with Naisbitt on the cultural issue (America will still dominate culturally well into the 21st century), there seems to be a growing consensus among social and economic forecasters everywhere on the imminent global dominance of Asia, economically and politically.

Such is the concern with Asia that, in the US, Bill Clinton has shifted much of his economic policy away from Europe to Asia; in Europe, members of the European Union (EU) are scheduled to attend a summit with members of the Association of Southeast Asian Nations (ASEAN) in Thailand so as to get onto the gravy train, as it were. Many European commentators are now arguing that Europe has spent too much time dealing with countries in Africa, Latin America, and the Caribbean, and too little with Asia. To some extent, Latin America, the Caribbean and, in particular, Africa, are now being regarded as places of declining importance to Europe. Here in the Pacific region, Australia and New Zealand are increasingly projecting themselves as Pacific-Asian nations. In Australia, the Japanese language is taught in primary schools. Chinese, Korean and other Asian languages are now part of the curriculum of universities in both New Zealand and Australia. During a recent meeting of the Association of Southeast Asian Nations, Australian prime minister, Paul Keating, described his country as an Asian nation. But not all are optimistic about the newfound fortunes of the fiery dragons from the East.

Asia has been characterized as a threat by many politicians in both Australia and New Zealand. The recent election campaign in Australia has witnessed some intriguing discussions about Australian identity and the role of Asian immigrants in the country's future. The right wing, which seemed to be gaining in the polls, was less sympathetic to the recent inflow of Asian migrants to that country. According to demographic projections, by the year 2000, Asians will comprise one out of every five citizens in the state of New South Wales in Australia. In New Zealand, the Asian debate is also heating up: recently a member of their parliament spoke to the media about unethical business practices of Asian immigrants and investors. This comment was interpreted by many as racist and xenophobic. Whether or not the comment was accurate, the swift condemnation from other politicians and members of the media was indicative of the increasing economic clout of Chinese, Korean and Japanese businesses in New Zealand.

China and the overseas Chinese are arguably the most feared and respected of the Asian players at the present moment. Overseas Chinese account for 80 per cent of all foreign investment in China the motherland. According to Naisbitt, ethnic Chinese – not Japanese – are the largest cross-border investors in Thailand, Malaysia, Indonesia, the Philippines and Vietnam. In Indonesia, four per cent of the Chinese population control 70 per cent of the economy; in Malaysia 30 per cent control over 50 per cent of the economy; in Thailand, three per cent control 60 per cent of the economy; and in the Philippines, three per cent control 70 per cent of the economy. Chinese immigrants can be found in virtually every corner of the globe. Through hard work, discipline, education and ethnic solidarity, they have managed to succeed where others have failed. Most of these immigrants have tended to concentrate on making money first, and later entering into politics.

Right across Asia, this has been the pattern. In Malaysia, Indonesia, the Philippines, and as far as Western Samoa and the USA, the economic power of overseas Chinese has translated into political clout. Unlike many other Asians, Chinese have tended to assimilate more readily into their adopted country.

In Western Samoa, for example, in order to avoid being repatriated to China, virtually all of the Chinese immigrants intermarried with the local population. In Fiji, where Indians and Fijians live apart, Chinese have intermarried with Fijians.

Perhaps the greatest area of concern of leading Western nations about Asian countries is their military intentions. Europeans have always feared Asia, especially China, for they could never understand the seemingly strange culture of this part of the world. Asian cultures and societies are perhaps the most closed and conservative in the world. Asians, in all but few cases, tend to be intolerant to outsiders. This is nowhere more evident than in China which has, until recently, protected itself from too many external influences. This lack of understanding of Asian societies, coupled with the apparent desire of the Chinese to dominate Asia (and perhaps the world), could create serious tensions within Asia, and between Asia and the West. As Asian countries become wealthier, they are investing more money in military hardware. China currently has the world's largest army; Indonesia, India and Pakistan have three of the world's largest militaries. Malaysia, Thailand, Taiwan and the Philippines are investing huge sums of money in upgrading their military hardware. Some of these countries are not reluctant to flex their military muscles. Indonesia has been especially brutal in their treatment of the indigenous people of West Papua (Irian Jaya) – a country ceded to Indonesia with the complicity of Western powers in 1969. With all the talk of genocide in Bosnia, Western countries have basically given Indonesia the permission to commit genocide in West Papua, a country which both Asians and Westerners consider to be inhabited by indigenous savages.

The Asianamania which is presently sweeping the Western world underscores the importance of economies to global relations. We in the Caribbean know less about the Asians than we do about the Americans and the Europeans. Furthermore, Asian economic and political leadership of the world will be no more sympathetic to small poor countries like ours than Europe or America. Countries like ours in the Caribbean will continue to be on the periphery of world affairs, as long as we have political and intellectual leadership which does not allow our citizens to release their creative potential. We had soon better prepare ourselves for the changing of the economic and political guards. Peace!

Trinidad – a model for Fiji?

(THURSDAY, MARCH 21, 1996)

Last month, an influential Pacific magazine, Pacific Islands Monthly, published an article which suggested that the political system in Trinidad and Tobago could be a model for Fijian society. The article entitled "The way Fiji could be" states that "historically, the other population group (Afro-Trinidadians) has controlled the prime ministership, but for the first time an Indian has the job. It went on to state that unlike in Fiji, a predominantly Afro-Trinidadian party, led by A. N. R. Robinson was able to form a successful alliance with a predominantly Indo-Trinidadian party, allowing Basdeo Panday to become prime minister. This, it was argued, is unheard of in Fiji where Fijians and Indians do not share the same political organizations. Furthermore, the article argued, the 14 per cent mixed (Afro-Indo) Trinidadian population promoted greater social cohesion than in Fiji, where marriages between Indians and ethnic Fijians are almost non-existent.

There are many in the Caribbean who would dispute the existence of the ethnic and racial cohesion in Trinidad and Tobago to which this article alludes. In fact, some observers of the Trinidadian political scene actually predict future ethnic conflict in the country unless the economic situation improves, especially for Afro-Trinidadians. However, from the perspective of some concerned with the Fijian situation, Trinidad, ethnically and politically, is a veritable paradise. Why does this article and many observers of the Fijian situation, particularly those from Western or European countries, share this view about Trinidad and Tobago?

Well, in May 1987, Colonel Sitiveni Rabuka and the Fijian military overthrew the democratically elected government of Fiji. Later that year, a second coup was staged which sought to consolidate the power of Rabuka. In the following weeks after the elections, racial tensions worsened in the country as the Taukei (indigenous) Movement warned Fijians about an imminent Indian takeover of the country. They pointed to the plight of other indigenous peoples in the region and suggested that Fijians should not be marginalized in their own country. Ostensibly, as a result of these protests, Rabuka and the military intervened, deposing the then prime minister from office. Rabuka won support from the Fijian Great Council of Chiefs (GCC).

But as a result of international pressure, he handed over the reins of government to Governor General Ratu Renaia. Then a second set of disturbances occurred, again led by the Taukei Movement, in which many Indian-owned businesses were attacked, and others destroyed. This action appears to have provided a rationale for a second coup in September 1987. Following this coup, Rabuka abolished the constitution and later declared Fiji a republic. Ratu Penaia became president, and Ratu Mara became interim prime minister.

In 1990, a new constitution was promulgated which in effect guaranteed Fijians political control over the country. Of the 70 seats in the House of Representatives, Fijians were allocated 37, Indians 27, general electors or voters received five, and Rotuma Islanders (Fijians of mainly Polynesian ancestry) one. The new Senate also consists of 34 seats, 24 of which are reserved for Fijians, nine for other races, and one for Rotuma Islanders. Furthermore, the posts of prime minister, president, heads of the army, and public service officials are basically reserved for indigenous Fijians.

Local and international criticism of the new constitution did not prevent it from being adopted by the Fijian government. It was under this new constitution that the 1992 elections were held. In 1992, Rabuka's party, the Soqosoqo Ni Vakavulewa Ni Taukei (SVT) or the Fijian Political Party, won 30 of the 37 seats guaranteed to Fijians, and he became prime minister. The SVT is a party which has the backing of the Fijian traditional elite, the Bose Levu Vakaturaga (Great Council of Chiefs). However, because he was not guaranteed support from all of the elected members in his party, Rabuka combined with the Indian-dominated Fiji Labour Party (FLP), the General Voters Party, two independents and the sole Rotuma representative to form a government and ensure his position as prime minister. In return, Rabuka promised to review land tenure and the constitution. In 1994, Rabuka was reelected by a larger margin. On this occasion, he opted for the support of the General Voters Party instead of seeking an alliance with the Indians.

Almost a decade after the coup and a general election which was won by Rabuka, there is still a great deal of uncertainty about the future of the country. Although Fijian and Indo-Fijians relate to each other well in the public sphere, distrust of Indians by Fijians and Fijians by Indians continues to fester. Following the coup and the adoption of the new constitution, Fiji was expelled from the Commonwealth and has received much international criticism for subverting the democratic process. Additionally, there has been the outward migration of a number of skilled Fiji Indians from the country and a reduction in the value of the Fijian dollar.

However, behind the apparent undemocratic nature of Fijian society lies a problem which few critics of the regime have attempted to address: the increasing marginalization of indigenous Fijians from the economic centre of the society. One of the reasons for the popularity of the Rabuka regime among many Fijians has to do with the perception that their existence is being threatened, demographically and economically, by the Indians. While this fear has been exploited by the Fijian political leadership, it is facile to dismiss this perception. Most indigenous Fijians seem to have two concerns. First, they contend that they have suddenly become a minority group in a country which their ancestors have occupied for many thousands of years. Second, they argue that they have little economic control in their country. On the other hand, many Fijians state quite categorically that they do not object to having Indians as fellow citizens, as Indians have contributed much to the country.

It would seem that the attempt to compare Trinidad and Tobago with Fiji is somewhat dangerous, since the history of the two countries is, in many ways, very different. The status of indigenous Fijians is not necessarily comparable to that of Afro-Trinidadians. As reflected in the article to which I earlier referred, Western intellectuals, commentators and politicians have a tendency to use Western-style democratic government as a panacea for some very complex social, cultural and political problems faced by developing nations. In the case of Fiji, any democratic government which does not seriously address the concerns of indigenous Fijians – while dealing with those of Indians – will continue to be threatened by large-scale social upheaval. Ni sa moce!

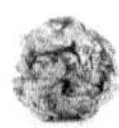

Preparing for the future

(TUESDAY, MAY 07, 1996)

"Modernity is not consumerism, or big cars, or lots of television sets. It is being an integral part of the world of your time, rather than its fool or slave."

– Edward Said (Palestinian writer)

For those following the Israeli-Palestinian peace agreement, there is no escaping the cogent arguments made against it by the noted Palestinian thinker Edward Said. A long-time activist in the struggle, Said has repeatedly warned Palestinian leadership about negotiating with Israel without preparation. That would be akin to a small country negotiating with the IMF without necessary economic data or brokering a deal with a transnational corporation without understanding the operation of the firm or the market – experiences which we here in the Caribbean are all too familiar with. Said argues that part of the reason for the weakness of the Palestinians (and Arabs) in their struggle against Israel is the leadership's inability to comprehend, beyond the superficial, what is happening in the world at large. In his book *Peace and Its Discontents* (1996), he says of the Arab world:

> The reasons we are so obsessed with and strangely dependent on the West... is that we have remained so contained within the West, and are consequently so ignorant of other worlds... To change this pattern a new courage and spirit of intellectual adventure is required... Being completely focused on yourself means that you are far more likely to fall prey to a stranger, more secure and dominating culture... Why not study and deal with others the way we are studied by them?

Said continues:

> I find it unimaginable, for instance, that Jordan, the PLO and Egypt ... have made peace with Israel at the same time as there isn't a single specialized institute or university department in any of these countries whose main object of study is Israel. Israel of course has several important institutions and departments that are full of experts on each Arab country.

Reason

Herein lies part of the reason for Israel's dominance in a region which is predominantly Arab. Perhaps there is also a lesson here for us in the CARICOM region if we want to pull our countries out from the economic rubble caused by consecutive decades of short-sighted policies.

Said's views on the weakness of Arab diplomacy are based on an acute understanding of what happens in the powerful Western countries, where political leaders invest in understanding the culture, politics and economies of countries they wish to contain or dominate. In the early days of colonialism, the British sent out anthropologists to study the cultures of countries they wished to colonize or control. In the end, the British often had such insight into the functioning of these societies that they were able to manipulate the chiefs and kings into submission. Occasionally, the British (and other European colonizers) came to understand the mood of their colonies better than the local elite.

Our political leaders seem not to have learned from these experiences, save of course where it benefits them personally. Furthermore, while some of our commentators and government officials bemoan the lack of focus on local issues by our university, across the world, universities and similar institutions are becoming more global in outlook. Without an understanding of the wider world, it is very difficult to exist in it without becoming a servant or slave, but what is the value, in real terms, of a more cosmopolitan world view? Let us look at a New Zealand experience.

Although tourism is not the most important industry here in New Zealand, more tourists visit this country yearly than they do Jamaica. Tourists who visit New Zealand come primarily from Asia, Europe and the USA. Part of the success of the tourism sector here has to do with a deliberate policy by officials of studying tourist markets and linking tourism development with other sectors such as construction, transportation and education. For instance, while the main mode of transportation here is the motor car, the railway is still busy, not only with local commuters, but also tourists. Rail stops are constructed to make travelling convenient to local people and tourists; consequently, many different types of tourism are promoted, from skiing and tramping to bike riding and sightseeing. The fruits of the industry are therefore spread to a large proportion of the population. This is economic democracy. The tourism industry in New Zealand is not confined to a few rich hoteliers, as is the case in Jamaica and throughout the Caribbean. Consequently, it is not as vulnerable to the idiosyncrasies of one or two rich mavericks.

Competitive product

To maintain a competitive tourism product, studies are taught at universities and at many of the polytechnic institutions. Universities and polytechnics supply tourism planners with information on the industry as a matter of routine – something virtually unheard of in Jamaica where tourism planners either tend to make policy based on anecdotal evidence or on information provided by an overseas consultant.

There are seven universities and numerous polytechnics and community colleges in this country of only 3.5 million people. Compare this with three universities which serve over five million people in the Caribbean. These universities attract a large number of overseas students mainly from Asia. As Asian nations become wealthier, their governments are investing more in education. Asian youth are encouraged to travel to learn about other cultures – the world they will one day conquer. Initial Southeast Asian prosperity was the result of the exploitation of cheap labour, especially female labour; but as the economies matured and the service sectors expanded, education became more widespread.

Demand

As good students of Asian societies for many years, New Zealand and Australia anticipated this demand for education and have started to capitalize on a growing market for education, particularly for those people who wish to learn the global lingua franca, English. Both Australia and New Zealand invest large sums of money in studying social, cultural and economic trends in Asia. By understanding the demands of the markets and cultures, they are able to compete with the USA and Europe for the Asian student dollar. But education in New Zealand also means that students from these countries get to promote New Zealand when they return home.

The consequence is a twofold benefit – more tourists and students. But there is a third benefit: it is that both of these countries are better suited to enter and compete in the booming East Asian market than those which are outside of this process. It is no wonder that both Australian and New Zealand universities have been advertising positions for scholars in Asian culture, politics and economics. Politicians here know that, if one is going to compete successfully, then one must be ahead of one's competition.

Less than one year here in this part of the world has made me even more aware of how interconnected we all are in this world. Jamaica and the Caribbean are fairly well known in these parts: imagine if we could capitalize on this knowledge through trade or tourism. Imagine if we understood the cataclysmic transformations which are occurring in Asia at this moment, the immense wealth that these countries have, and the possibilities for economic engagement with them. Imagine if we could capitalize on the demand for training in English in Latin America as the New Zealanders are with Asia. If we in CARICOM hope to do business with the rest of the world, competitively, then we have to understand it. Perhaps we have spent too much time trying to cope with the Americans and British while closing our eyes to the rest of the world. Why should our destinies be tied up with the Americans? After all, the overwhelming majority of people in the world live in Asia, Africa and the Pacific.

Following the trend set by the USA and Europe, emerging Asian nations are spending large sums of money, not only educating engineers and technicians, but also producing experts on the societies they wish to conduct business with. This is not esoteric, rather it is an investment in the future. There is an age-old adage which goes: the first stage in overcoming a foe is understanding how he thinks. Yet we in the Caribbean don't even know who our foe is. Kia ora!

Changing fortunes of Asian tourism

(TUESDAY, JUNE 04, 1996)

Although tourism is a greater earner of foreign exchange for Jamaica than New Zealand, New Zealand's government seems more committed to the planned development of the industry than Jamaica's. Over the past eight years, tourism expenditures have kept close pace with receipts in New Zealand. Between 1987 and 1991, New Zealand witnessed a sizeable increase in tourism receipts; during the same year, expenditure on the industry rose just as dramatically. Most of this seemed to have gone into the development of infrastructure, promotion, and long-term development of the industry.

Our various governments, on the other hand, have invested comparatively little in the development of the industry in recent times. In fact, during the 1980s and early 1990s, while receipts from tourism increased, real expenditure declined. In other words, serious investment in the tourism sector has not been part of Jamaican government policy for many years. The provision of roads, sewage plants, planned residential areas, and other forms of infrastructure have not been a feature of government (or private sector) planning, in spite of the windfall gains from tourism. As with manufacturing and the other productive sectors, successive government policy over the past decade, in relation to tourism, has been chaotic and timid.

Notwithstanding the centrality of tourism to foreign exchange generation, we should be mindful of the fact that this industry can be fickle. Here in New Zealand, last year, well over one million visitors came to the country, contributing over $3 billion US dollars to the economy. However, this year the industry is experiencing a downturn. The fall-off is greatest in the American market. Tour operators here say that one reason for the decline in American visitors is that Americans are tightening their belts because of the economic policies of the Republican-controlled Congress. Tourism analysts also explain that Germans were taking shorter holidays, and the tourism market has now become fiercely competitive.

A significant proportion of visitors to New Zealand are now coming from Asia, especially South Korea, Japan and Taiwan. However, there is competition from South Africa (interestingly, a country with one of the world's highest violent crime rates) which is offering competitive packages, including low airfares and cheaper accommodation rates. Many Asian tourists are now flocking to South Africa instead of New Zealand or Australia. Say the analysts here, beautiful scenery and the good life are simply not enough to attract tourists anymore; it is now a wide open market.

In general, Asian tourists to New Zealand tend to spend more than their European or American counterparts. During the first six months of 1995, of the tourists who visited New Zealand, South Koreans spent the most on a daily basis, averaging NZ$459, followed by Japanese tourists with NZ$390, then Americans with NZ$265, Germans, NZ$136, Australians, NZ$156, and the British who spent NZ$93. The low figures for Britain and Australia are understandable, since many New Zealanders have family ties with people from Britain and Australia.

But not all are happy with the growth in the Asian market. The expansion of the Asian market has also resulted in an increasingly Asian-controlled tourism sector. For example, Korean and Japanese-owned-and-operated shops have sprung up across New Zealand to cater to Korean and Japanese tourists. At the moment, there is controversy over unethical business practices of Korean business people who have virtually shut many other New Zealanders out of the Korean market. How this happens is that Korean-owned shops pay other Korean-owned tour operators a commission to bring the visitors to their shops. This means that non-Korean-owned shops are hardly ever patronized by many Korean visitors. The result is that while the Korean and other Asian businesses expand, the non-Asian businesses suffer. Even though this type of business is illegal in New Zealand, few non-Asian shop owners are likely to take action for fear of reprisals from tour operators.

While tourism is an important earner of foreign exchange, the experiences of countries across the world should teach us that we in the region should not put all our eggs in the sea-sand-sun basket. Furthermore, long-term planning, and a less provincial analytical approach to the industry (especially in relation to explaining changes in visitor arrivals) would serve us well if we are to understand and optimize our returns. Lest we forget, we are talking about one of the world's oldest and largest industries, where we in the Caribbean are still a few pebbles on a long, wide beach. Kia Ora!

New approach to tourism

(SATURDAY, JUNE 15, 1996)

Since the days of Thomas Cook – the man regarded as the creator of modern-day tourism – the tourism industry has changed from being the preserve of the rich, and sometimes famous, to being accessible to anyone who can save enough money to take a break from the monotony of everyday life. Nowhere is this phenomenon more evident than in industrialized countries like New Zealand. Tourism is now the largest industry in the world and is dominated by the wealthy countries.

In an attempt to get a better understanding of the tourism sector here (apart from getting a break from work), I decided to take a six-day tour to the South Island of Aotearoa (New Zealand), Land of the Long White Cloud.

Now, the South Island is about twelve times the size of Jamaica and its geography dominated by numerous majestic hills and mountains. Visitors to New Zealand, after visiting the South Island, often agree that it is difficult to find another place on earth with as much variation, grandeur, mystery and seemingly untamed plant life. The scenery defies literary description: majestic glaciers, snow-capped mountains, vast grass savannahs, deserts, seal colonies, ostrich farms, penguin and whale watching seas, magnificent rivers and waterfalls, rugged coastlines, sandy beaches, crystal clear sea water; it is all there.

What is the most amazing about all of this is not so much the great variety of attractions to see, but the accessibility of these attractions by air, sea and land. As I have stated in previous articles, New Zealand's tourism product is developed with the local population, overseas tourists, and the environment in mind. Successive governments have made the development of basic infrastructure, such as public transportation and roads, a key plank of the tourism line of march. The railway provides an important public service and is a major attraction to tourists who wish to see the country for a modest fee. Furthermore, the widespread presence of public conveniences, rest areas, scenic lookouts, public parks and other facilities serves both the local inhabitants of the country and overseas visitors alike. This common sense approach to development has meant that small entrepreneurs can get a share of the fast-growing tourism market. Unlike in the Caribbean, especially Jamaica, tourism in New Zealand is not the industry of the business don or fat moguls.

Historically, we in the Caribbean have tended to view tourists as a well-off people from Europe or North America, who come for the sea and sand. Interestingly, this type of tourism contributes only a small fraction of the global tourism market.

Most tourists are average citizens who save over a period of time so that they can get away from home for a while. It would appear that the majority of them travel around the world to experience different cultures, visit historical sites and experience the splendour of nature. Every year, hundreds of thousands of Asians travel to New Zealand to see the unique Māori culture, and experience the country's mind-boggling plants and marine life. Because of its emphasis on a clean and green society, large numbers of middle-class youth from Europe and America flock to Aotearoa in droves, annually.

While there will always be a market for sea-sand-sun

tourism, tourism planners should recognize that it is short-sighted to continue such a course. To be sure, there are white sand beaches and blue coral seas all over the globe. If the beaches of the Caribbean were to disappear tomorrow, global tourism would not be affected. Furthermore, the mogul-entrepreneur approach to the industry continues to concentrate wealth in the hands of a few and create enclaves of pockets of luxury, and of dungeons of poverty. It seems rather silly to me to invest millions of dollars in crime prevention strategies in tourist areas in Jamaica, when the source of criminal activity in the country resides in the perpetual economic and social dislocation in the country as whole. What we require in Jamaica, and in the Caribbean, is a more holistic approach to tourism, where the goals of the industry are tied to the larger goals of social and economic progress of the country. The development of manufacturing, education, housing, transportation and healthcare are all intimately related. Why is it so easy for a small relatively new country like New Zealand to comprehend this point, yet so difficult for us? What do they have that we do not? Sometimes I really wonder. Kia Ora!

Trends in tourism

(FRIDAY, JUNE 28, 1996)

Tourism operators in the Pacific are becoming more aware of what tourism analysts in New Zealand call the "free independent travellers" (FITs). While not an entirely new phenomenon, FITs now constitute a significant part of the tourism market in New Zealand and Australia. According to analysts, this is the fastest growing section of the tourism market in the world.

FITs range from young backpackers to older people who are more interested in an experience rather than leisure and relaxation. Unlike the traditional tourists who come on prepaid packages, the FIT market vacations tend to be independent, self-directed, self-selected and not-on-the-shelf. Because they usually spend small amounts of money in a larger number of places it is often difficult to estimate the financial contribution of these tourists to the local economy. However, analysts here have no doubts about their centrality to the tourism sector: according to their estimates, FITs have had a noticeable impact on the economy.

FITs are often interested in what is called ecotourism: for example, rock and mountain climbing, forest trekking, bird watching, and so on. Still, others are thrill seekers who prefer to go rafting in dangerous rapids, or go parasailing and hang-gliding, to name a few of the activities. One of the attractive features of this type of tourism, especially for poorer countries, is that there is no need for investment in massive hotels and other unfriendly edifices which separate visitors from the larger society and economy. Yet another one is that small investors can have a share in the industry, resulting in a more even distribution of the tourist dollar across the society.

Just a caveat, for this type of tourism to work, a few things are necessary: proper physical infrastructure, such as roads and transportation services; and reliable public utilities, such as hospitals, paramedic units, water, electricity and telephones. Of importance also is the need for an effective police force and a relatively crime-free environment. In the case of Jamaica, the implications are clear: there would be a need for the government to take the job of governing seriously, as investment in the public sphere would have to be a key component of government policy.

While New Zealand and Australia are witnessing an upsurge in FITs, Pacific Islands tourism is seducing foreign investors. A report by the Fiji-based Islands Business magazine states that investors from around the world, especially Asia, are clamouring to purchase properties in the region. According to the report, prospective investors are mostly interested in resorts which have a good swimming beach, about 20 rooms, and local architectural styles. Interestingly, they are not interested in concrete motel-style resorts.

At the moment, there seem to be two types of investors operating in the Pacific region. Many North Americans, Australians, New Zealanders, and Europeans seem to have an interest in small properties. Asians (viz. Singaporeans, Hong Kong natives, Chinese and Taiwanese) have a weakness for large properties, bought cheap at a fraction of replacement cost. Additionally, they are only interested in linking with international hotel chains or creating their own brands.

The economic transformation in Asia has meant a slow global shift in trade and tourism away from the Atlantic region (the Americas and Europe) to the Pacific. The Pacific region has the fastest growing economies in the world, and potentially the world's most dominant trading blocks. The island states in that region have much more of the sea-sand-sun type of tourism than we in the Caribbean can ever hope to offer. After all, Oceania has the largest group of island states in the world. Perhaps it is time for us in the Caribbean to revise our economic positioning globally, and follow closely the developments in the Pacific region. Kia Ora (Māori goodbye). Moce mada (Fijian goodbye).

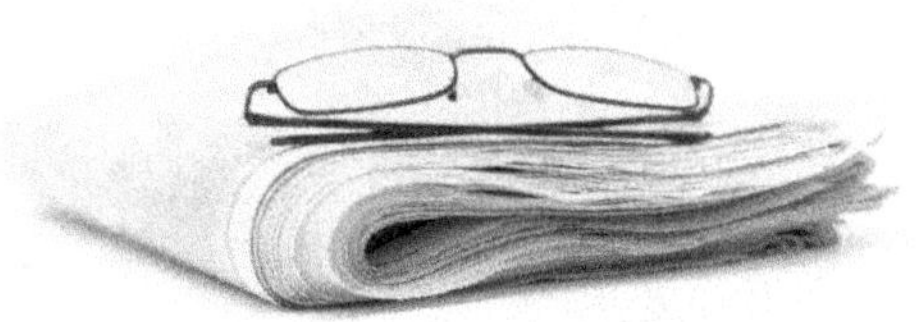

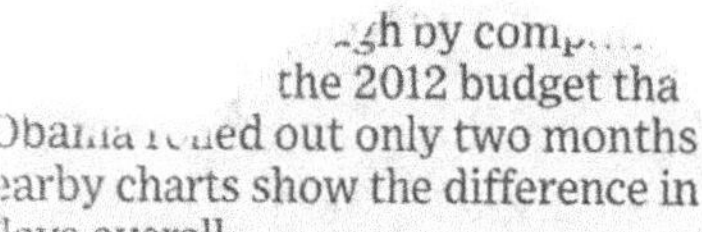

POSTSCRIPT

Writing Styles Explored

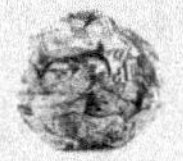

David Eric King (Retd)
Faculty of Arts & Education
UWI, Mona

Writing Styles Explored

This section is designed to provide students with some basic writing techniques

- Expository writing
- Descriptive writing
- Narrative writing

Introduction

In putting together any form of written piece, an author usually determines the techniques to be utilized as well as the audience for whom he or she is writing. Writing can at times be monotonous; however, with practice and the use of the best techniques, an author can produce a brilliant work of art. There are four techniques that a writer can employ to inform readers, spark their interest and hold their attention. These techniques are expository writing, descriptive writing, narrative and persuasive writing. This section looks at three of the four techniques with a view to share with readers steps to be taken, as well as ideas which can make a particular writing style unique. Examples are used to cement in the reader's mind the factors which distinguish one style from another.

Expository writing

Expository writing is one of the most commonly used writing forms. The word expository comes from the root word expose which has a Latin origin. Expose means to uncover or to reveal. Expository writings are factual and present an objective point of view on a topic. Expository writings are designed to answer specific questions; however, before answering the questions, the writer must state a clear position in the form of a thesis statement, then provide supporting details to either prove or clarify the idea. Details are arranged in such a way that a reader sees that there is validity in the thesis. This type of writing not only appeals to understanding, but also to reasoning. Expository writings also function to inform and to explain, educate and illuminate, and not titillate. The following structural devices are often utilized when putting together an expository piece:

1. *Classification:*

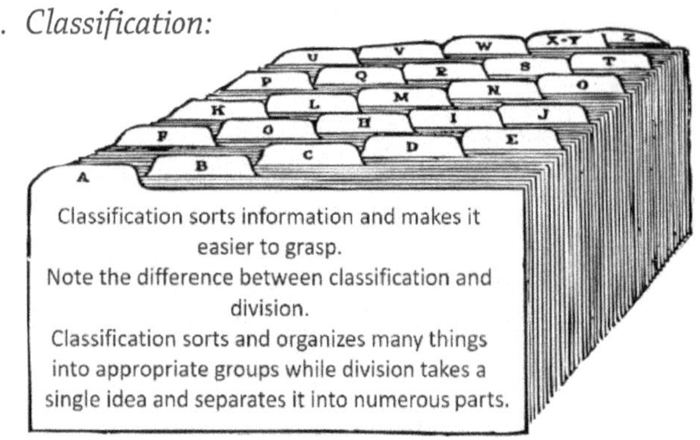

This type of writing breaks down a broad topic and categorizes its elements according to logical or relevant groupings.

   a. When doing a classification:
      i. Select one principle of classification and stick to it;
      ii. Make the purpose of your division clear to your audience;
      iii. Note whether items can switch categories;
      iv. Account for all the parts in the classification.
   b. Avoid the following pitfalls:
      i. Having too few or too many categories;
      ii. Having underdeveloped categories;
      iii. Having confusing categories or misinforming readers (Wyrick, 2020).

2. *Analysis:* this involves dividing the subject into various parts so that it can be easily understood.
3. *Definition:* this involves translating a word or an idea to help readers understand the concept. This generally starts by introducing a concept, followed by its attributes.
4. *Comparison and contrast:* this type of writing looks at similarity and difference, as well as the benefits and disbenefits of a matter.
5. *Illustration:* this clarifies a thesis by moving from a general idea to more specific ideas, using examples to bring across the ideas.
6. *Cause and effect:* this type of writing looks at the root of an event and the resultant impact or consequence of such an event taking place. In this technique, a writer often examines an event in relation to other events that precede or follow. In identifying a cause, a writer often seeks to answer the question of why a particular event occurred, whilst in identifying the effect, the writer seeks to answer the question of what happened (Abu-Ayyash, Najjar, Reiken, & Yakzan, 2015; Simmons-McDonald, Fields, & Roberts, 2012).

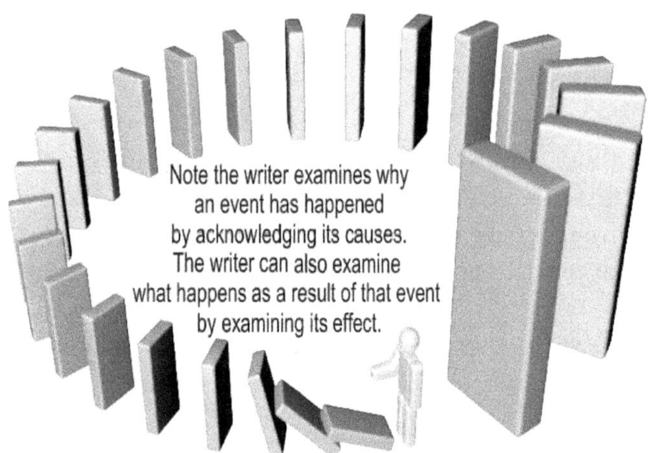

For your consideration

When wring a cause and effect essay, remember that factors such as equipment, personnel, materials and procedures may be directly related to the identified impact. Be sure to note that what is labelled as an effect has clearly and directly resulted from what has been labelled as a cause (Abu-Ayyash, Najjar, Reiken, & Yakzan, 2015).

7. *Analogy:* a comparison between one thing and another, typically for the purpose of explanation or clarification.

Finally, Simmons-McDonald, Fields, & Roberts (2012) note that expository writings can take either of two forms: technical/scientific, or an artistic form.

Analyzing an expository piece

Despite the much vaunted success of the recent attempts made by the Ministry of Education to expand educational opportunities, illiteracy remains one of the most serious problems which we face in this country.

> “ A 1994 National Literacy Survey, coordinated by sociologist, Dr Louis Sterling, showed only 57 per cent of the population to be functionally literate, 18 per cent as literate, and 3 per cent as having basic literacy skills; 21 per cent classified as absolutely illiterate. ”

The author uses **illustration** to clarify the thesis statement used in the first sentence.

> “ The report defines functional literacy as “the ability of a person to engage in all those activities in which literacy is required for effective functioning in his/her community and also for enabling him/her to continue to use reading, writing and calculation for his/her own and the community’s development”. A person classified as literate has “the ability to read and write a short, simple statement, with understanding, on his or her everyday life”. ”

In the first sentence, the author **defines** the term “functional literacy”. He then moves on to explain who a literate person is.

> “ Basic literacy refers to having nominal literacy skills, below the literate level. The report also found that a significantly larger number of women than men were literate, and illiteracy among the rural population was around 30 per cent. What is even more shocking is the fact that about six per cent of those who attended (though not necessarily completed) the most prestigious high schools in the country were judged to be absolutely illiterate. Indeed, these figures do not compare favourably with our CARICOM neighbours who, with the exception of Haiti, all have illiteracy rates well under ten per cent of the population. ”

The author uses **comparison and contrast** in a number of ways in this section. First, he does a gender comparison (females/males), then an explicit comparison of the literacy rate in Jamaica as opposed to other CARICOM countries.

Compromise

> “ One of the problems with such high rates of illiteracy is that productivity levels and quality of work are seriously compromised, since workers find it difficult to follow written instructions required for problem solving. ”

In this section, it is clear that illiteracy affects productivity. In terms of **cause and effect** illiteracy is the cause and productivity level is the effect. **Note that the cause generally comes before the effect.**

“ In a world where technology is so integral to everyday life, being able to read and write has become central to survival.

1. Mundane things, such as connecting a VCR to a television or replacing a new car part, requires an understanding of the English language, since we often need to follow instruction manuals.
2. Our country is plagued with mechanics who are unable to read or write, and who have to rely on either intuition or experience, or both, to repair vehicles.
3. We are often forced to employ masons and carpenters who are unable to follow architectural designs; and frequently we are transported by bus and taxi drivers who cannot read road signs. ”

Once again, the author uses **illustration** to clarify the points made in the thesis statement. In the first sentence, the author clarifies using a general statement; he later uses three more specific illustrations to make the ideas clearer.

Is it any wonder why there are so many road accidents, or why constructing a building is often a traumatic experience?

Although controversial, education research has shown that there is a relationship between literacy and the ability to think logically. Generally, less literate groups are said to have greater problems with logical thinking. Therefore, these groups exhibit more aggressive or violent behaviour, especially in urban settings. Social science research also shows that societies with better living standards and higher productivity levels tend to have higher literacy levels – except in cases where unfree or exploited labour is used. One caveat: researchers are not here claiming that illiteracy is a cause, but rather they argue that there is a significant and interesting correlation between literacy and a society's productivity and standard of living.

Unfortunately, my daily experience tells me that the problem of illiteracy is much worse than what the statistics show, and there is little indication that this problem will improve in the immediate future. If we are serious about development, then we ought not to make the education of our people a partisan matter. Before we can do anything about the problem, policymakers first have to acknowledge that a significant level of illiteracy exists throughout the society, and that it is a critical problem which requires urgent attention. Peace!

Descriptive writing

Desciptive writings often express how the writer perceives an event through the five senses. Descriptive writings include biographies, travel and nature wrtings, journals and poetry. These types of writings tend to give sensuous details about places, people events, etc. Some writers recommend that in order to provide adequate description, one has to move spatially over the subject, idea or event in question. While taking that spatial approach, one has to ask oneself the question what is it like? Or what is he or she or they like?

Any good descriptive writing piece should reflect the following:

1. Descriptive writings should be formatted in chronological order.
2. Descriptive writings utilize three main parts of speech: nouns, adjectives and strong action verbs.

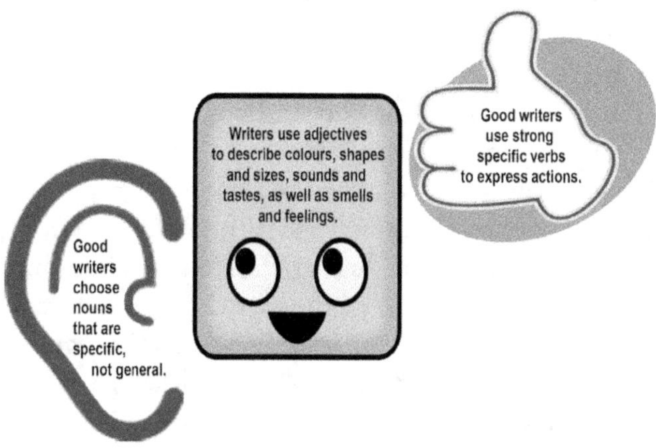

3. Descriptive writings provide a great deal of sensory details. All the senses can be utilized to create an impression.
   a) When writing about a real person, be sure to include:
      i) Details of their life;
      ii) Details of their history;
      iii) Details of their background.
   b) When writing about a fictional character, be sure to include details about:
      i) What this sort of person would say;
      ii) What this person would do;
      iii) How this person would think.
   c) When writing about a place, consider providing details about the event time and place.

Be careful!
Do not
over describe.

4. Descriptive writings embraces the use of figures of speech mainly similes, metaphors and analogies.

An analysis: "A hero's welcome"

> “ It is 9:15 a.m., and a large crowd of people descend on the marae (meeting place) of the Māori Queen here in Aotearoa/New Zealand. ”

Here the author gives a clear description of the time the event is taking place as well as details about the crowd size.

My friends and I park our vehicle at the side of the traffic-congested road and enter the spectacular court of one of the tribes of northern New Zealand. The *marae* is the traditional meeting place of the Māori people. There are many such places in New Zealand, but this one is special because it is the Queen's.

> “ The marae is a large open courtyard, with a number of buildings which are used to hold meetings and other festivities. ”

Clearly one can visualize the size of the courtyard, where the meeting is about to be held.

The main building is usually very large with wide open spaces and decorated with some of the finest wood carvings in the world (Māori people are well known for their wood carving skills). The carvings have both spiritual and aesthetic significance.

Excitement

❝ As we enter the marae, I sense a `buzz of excitement. ❞

> The author's reference to a buzz of excitement tells that there is a lot of chatter in the courtyard. One can imagine several groups of people talking at once.

❝ The now menacingly dark rain clouds fail to dampen the mood of the people. ❞

> The author's description of the clouds suggest that rain could fall at any time.

The hip-hop music adds to the festive atmosphere. Everyone is jubilant; even the contingent of policemen joke with the young people who are standing patiently.

❝ As I walk towards a seat in the beautifully decorated courtyard, there is loud flutter from above. I look up; it is the South African flag. ❞

> Based on the authors use of the word flutter to describe the sound the flag makes one can infer that the celebrations took place on a windy day.

Nelson Mandela, here in New Zealand to attend the Commonwealth Heads of Government Meeting (CHOGM), was invited to visit the *marae* by Māori leaders.

Undoubtedly the most popular and respected leader of the meeting, Mandela was given a hero's welcome by the people, all across the country of Aotearoa. (Renewed interest in the Commonwealth was most certainly stimulated by the presence of Mandela, along with the French nuclear testing issue and world-wide interest in political tensions in Nigeria.) Now, away from the CHOGM and the hustle and bustle of Auckland – one of the world's largest cities (spatially) – Mandela was travelling to the "heartland" of New Zealand, a rural district about 50 kilometres from the city of Hamilton where I was based. Consistent with Māori hospitality and solidarity, the welcome would be special.

Preceding Mandela, who is flanked by security personnel and the usual large contingent of press people, is the guard of honour – a spectacular procession of largely Māori and Pākehā (White) children from 35 schools in the area. As Mandela, his daughter and his foreign minister enter the sacred grounds of the *marae* (usually cameras are not allowed on the *marae*), he is greeted by a performance of the haka. The haka is a traditional dance which is a form of welcome or a declaration of competition or combat. The haka is beyond verbal description; to attempt to describe it here would do an injustice to one of the unique and outstanding features of Māori-New Zealand culture. Suffice it to say, the president is visibly impressed by the performance and welcome which greet him.

As he walks into the courtyard, hundreds rise from their seats to see him; most of us have to stand on chairs, even the tall ones. In keeping with fine Māori custom, there are greetings, speeches, entertainment, and gifts – lots of them. Among the gifts are two scholarships to be awarded to two South African students to undertake tertiary studies in New Zealand each year. Mandela also hears about the famous Māori spiritual leader, Rātana, who visited South Africa in the 1920s, and later spoke of the horror of the conditions of Black South Africans. References are also made to the presence of Rātana members and descendants who now lead the Rātana church (named after its founder) whose theology is a hybrid of Māori and Christian ideas.

In response, the overwhelmed Mandela expresses his appreciation for the solidarity which Māori people showed to South Africans during the apartheid regime. He would not forget that Māori protesters battled with police many years ago to prevent the New Zealand rugby tour of South Africa. (Last month, I met with one of the leaders of that protest movement, a Māori and a former Minister of Education, who told me those protests were some of the most violent in New Zealand's recent history)

Euphoria

Two hours later, the function ends, and Nelson, as he is now affectionately called, wades his way through a sea of people and a battalion of security personnel. Most people simply want to touch him or shake his hand. Such is the euphoria that a schoolboy shows me his hand and says, "I shook his hand with this hand." Finally, the president disappears into the immaculate restaurant on the *marae*, to dine with the Māori Queen.

The marae is still buzzing with excitement, but we have to leave. The well paved New Zealand roads (I have seen only one pothole in the hundreds of kilometres of roads I have traversed) are crowded with cars, children, police and transported youath. The feelings that I experience as we drive away would help me to understand later on why Mandela said this was the highlight of his visit to the "land of the long white cloud", the country of Aotearoa. Peace!

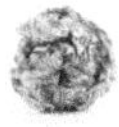

Narrative writing

Narrative essays are often about the personal experiences of a writer, presented to readers in a story form (Rollins, 2009). Narrations relate events in time by presenting details of it in a temporal sequence. Narrations can either be done using the flashback tehnique or be presented in a chronological order.

What does narrative writing contain?

1. **Exposition**: this involves introducing readers to key components of a story
2. The **rising action** is the earliest part of the story where the conflict in the story originates. At this point in the story, one meets the main characters and finds out what the problem is. Here it seems as though everything is building up to that moment. The tension comes from this part of narrative writing.
3. The **climax** involves some pivotal events in a story. The conflict in the story reaches boiling point.
4. **Falling action**: this occurs when the plot moves towards its conclusion, in other words, when the tension in the story subsides and the story approaches its end (Walch Publishing, 2005).

5. **Resolution** occurs when the events in the story reach some point of closure (Ruday, 2016).

In the article "Fiji ... At last!", the author shares his experience in Fiji in a chronological order. Though the flashback technique could have been used, the author opted to give a step-by-step review of his experience.

Fiji ... At last!

" *Suva, Fiji:* As the plane touches down at the quaint Nausori Airport, one hour outside the city of Suva, I feel relieved and excited. I have finally reached that fabled land of Fiji. There are two international airports in Fiji, and I landed at the one closest to the University of the South Pacific (USP) where I would be based for the next two weeks. In typical Third World style, going through customs requires great patience – the heat and the humidity only add to the frustration. However, the Fijian officials are quite polite and friendly, and this tempers any feelings of anger. Outside the airport I take a taxi to the university where I am staying; the lush green plants, mango trees and easygoing nature of the people make me feel as though I am back in the Caribbean. "

In this section, the author gives a detailed **introduction** of his experience upon landing in Fiji. He paints a picture of the setting of the community.

" I arrived in Suva on Friday and reached USP around 4 p.m., too late to see the university officials I was scheduled to meet, or my Fijian friends whom I know from New Zealand. With no one to show me around, I got on the bus and headed downtown. We academics often talk about living in a global village by making reference to things such as the internet and air travel; however, there are two things which seem to epitomize the idea for me among developing countries – music and privately owned buses. As I entered the bus, there was reggae music, but in Fijian and Hindi. Inside the bus there were posters of Bob Marley and Lucky Dube. However, much unlike Jamaica, service in Fiji is very efficient. The buses are generally old, but passengers are treated with a great deal of respect. Fijian roads are generally clean and well paved, and drivers navigate them with caution; this makes the trip less hazardous than in Jamaica. "

Here, **suspense** is being created; for example, the author detailed that he missed his 4 p.m. appointment with university officials. He explained how he spent his afternoon finding an alternate plan. He started off with a bus ride, which automatically created a level of suspense among readers who are curious to see how the main character would handle himself in an entirely new country. One can easily identify that a conflict is brewing since the author missed his appointment. The conflict here is between man and himself. The music he hears whilst walking the streets of Fiji confuses hm. He hints at hearing sounds that he is most familiar with in the Caribbean.

" The first thing I noticed about downtown Fiji is its resemblance to different Caribbean countries. There is a bit of Trinidad and Guyana with the large Indian population there; a bit of Guyana in a sea wall which circles part of the city; part of Jamaica with its high-rise buildings and the large open markets; and a bit of Barbados in the orderly organization of people in stores and buses. The police do not carry guns. There is music blaring from record shops – mainly reggae and calypso, and Indian music in Hindi. Most of it, as I was soon to discover, was pirated. I have a strong feeling that very few musicians see any of the money from the sales of music in Fiji. Since one of my main research interests in the Pacific is culture and development, I was attracted to the businesses to see how they operate. Because Fijians are an amazingly friendly people, it was easy to talk to them, many of whom greeted me with "bula" (hello). Within an hour of my arrival in the city centre, I befriended two Fijians who volunteer to show me around the city. I explained to them that I am with the USP conducting research, which would entail getting some idea of how the commercial sector operates. I think what intrigued them most was that I told them that I was from New Zealand and Jamaica. The word Jamaica excites passion in people all over the world in a way that no other country does. I do not know how many Jamaicans know this, but reggae music and the Rastafari philosophy have created an impression of Jamaica which rivals that of some of the greatest civilizations of the world. Reggae is without a doubt the most popular music among young people in Fiji. ❞

Here, the narrative is at its **climax**. One can see that the author is still confused about where he is; he thinks he is physically in Fiji but culturally in the Caribbean. He explores the similarity between respective Caribbean countries and Fiji. Still, he remains dissatisfied with the fact that he missed his appointment, but he seizes the opportunity to befriend two Fijian's who gave him a tour.

❝ As I walk around the city, I am struck by two things. First, businesses are owned mainly by local Indians and Chinese, and multinational companies from Australia and New Zealand. Second, although Fijians and Indians appear to get on well with each other, they live in two completely different worlds. If ever there were a plural society, Fiji would be it. Indigenous Fijians speak Fijian while Indians speak Hindi; both speak English as a common language. Fijians do not generally inter-marry with Indians. And the term Fijian is generally reserved for the indigenous people, as Indians who make up more than half of the population are still called Indians. Many Fijians still regard Indians as outsiders. Many also resent the fact that Indians have great economic power, while Indians feel that they should have a greater share of the land, of which 80 per cent is still in the communal control of Fijians. ❞

The **climax** continues here as the author looks at the composition of the business class as well as the interpersonal relations between the different ethnic groups.

❝ Those who believe that there is no serious link between culture and capitalist development should visit this part of the world, for here is a treasure chest of experiences which makes that link stand out quite clearly (I shall discuss this issue at a later date). There is absolutely no doubt in my mind that Western-style economic development must be based on a set of core values, many of which are not shared by Fijians, and indeed most indigenous people of the world. ❞

Here, we have the author moving towards a **conclusion**. Many call this the **falling action**. Clearly, one can see that the conflict that the author had is decreasing.

" As I walk and talk with my Fijian friends who now seem to embrace me as one of their own (for in their eyes two things matter most: I am Black and from Jamaica), I drift off into a philosophical world. I ask myself why is it that people who do not place great emphasis on material possessions, people such as Fijians, should be considered intellectually inferior to those who do? Then I ask myself: is it possible for people to live outside of this modern Western ethos and survive? I will respond to my question here. Many people have tried it, but they seem to be fighting a losing battle – look at the Maasai in Kenya. I think to myself: what great human tragedy has been caused by the forced adoption of these acquisitive values among people who want to exist in their own world with greater emphasis on sharing rather than on accumulation.

I am awakened from my deep philosophical pondering by a passing group of five beautiful Fijian women, elegantly clad in their traditional clothing, who eventually disappear into a yellow bus. My observant friends smile with me, and we continue on our tour. *Ni sa moce!* (Goodbye!) "

In these final paragraphs, it is clear that the author has reached a **resolution**.

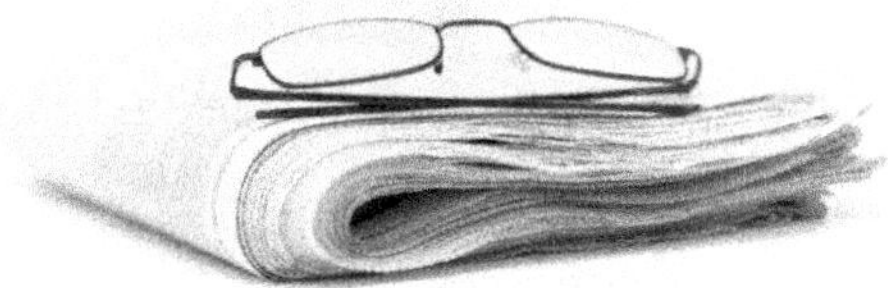

Glossary

Aotearoa is the Māori name for New Zealand.

Demokratizatsiya was a popular slogan used by the Soviet Communist Party to call for the infusion of democratic elements into the monolithic process of the time.

Didgeridoo, an Aboriginal wind instrument. *Gran Krutu* is the term used to describe a type of great meeting held by the indigenous Maroons of Suriname.

Megalomaniac: someone having a strong irritable desire for power.

Most-Favoured-Nation (MFN) is a clause or an agreement that suggests equality. In other words, countries should not discriminate between their trading partners; for example, a country which grants another country a special favour (a lower customs duty rate for one of their products) should do the same for all other WTO members.

Mururoa Atoll is the site over which the 41st nuclear test was carried out by the French military. This nuclear testing took place on 17 July 1974.

The *Shiprider Agreement* is a bilateral arrangement between respective countries of the Caribbean and their US counterparts. This agreement allows either party to intercept and curtail illicit maritime drug trafficking.

Soqosoqo Ni Vakavulewa Ni Taukei is also known as the Fijian Political Party.

Works Cited

Abu-Ayyash, A., Najjar, A., Reiken, E., & Yakzan, J. (2015). *Beyond level three: Grammar and composition*. Beirut, Lebanon: World Heritage Publishers.

Caiden, N. & Wildavsky, A. (1990). *Planning and budgeting in poor countries*. New Brunswick, NJ: Transaction Publ.

Hutchinson, E. (n.d.). *Descriptive writing*. Saddleback Educational Publishing.

Lieberson, S. (1980). *A piece of the pie: Blacks and white immigrants since 1880*. Berkeley: University of California Press.

Naisbitt, J. (1996). *Megatrends Asia: The eight Asian megatrends that are reshaping our world*. New York: Nicholas Brealey.

Simmons-McDonald, H., Fields, L., & Roberts, P. (2012). *Writing in English: A course book for Caribbean students*. Kingston, Jamaica: Ian Randle Publishers.

The International Bank for Reconstruction and Development / World bank. (1997). *World development report, 1997: The state in a changing world*. New York: Oxford University Press. Retrieved from https://www.worldbank.org

Weston, S. C. (1998). Toward a better understanding of the positive/normative distinction in economics. In C.K. Wilber (Ed.), *Economics, ethics and public policy*. Rowman and Littlefield.

World Development Report 1997. (1997). *The state in a changing world*. New York: Oxford University. Press.

INDEX

Figures are indicated by "f" following the page number.

Index

Index

www.ingramcontent.com/pod-product-compliance
Lightning Source LLC
LaVergne TN
LVHW061219100826
845148LV00004B/804

* 9 7 8 1 6 6 6 7 6 4 7 7 2 *